Sexual and Gender-Based Violence in International Law

Bharat H. Desai · Moumita Mandal

Sexual and Gender-Based Violence in International Law

Making International Institutions Work

Foreword by Peter Maurer

Springer

Bharat H. Desai
Centre for International Legal Studies
School of International Studies
Jawaharlal Nehru University
New Delhi, India

Moumita Mandal
Post-doctoral Fellow
Jawaharlal Nehru Chair
Centre for International Legal Studies
School of International Studies
Jawaharlal Nehru University
New Delhi, India

ISBN 978-981-19-0896-5 ISBN 978-981-19-0894-1 (eBook)
https://doi.org/10.1007/978-981-19-0894-1

This Springer imprint is published by the registered company Springer Nature Singapore Pte Ltd.
The registered company address is: 152 Beach Road, #21-01/04 Gateway East, Singapore 189721, Singapore

For

All the Victims-Survivors of
Sexual and Gender-Based Violence

Foreword

Sexual and gender-based violence (SGBV) is a heinously prevalent scourge, too common in all societies. It is also exacerbated by conflict, as well as other humanitarian crises and the climate emergency.

Its causes and drivers—gender inequality, abuse of power, social inequality, and impunity—manifest differently depending on the context, meaning that responses must also be tailored to contexts. This publication *Sexual and Gender-Based Violence in International Law: Making International Institutions Work* makes a timely, analytical, and thought-provoking scholarly ideational contribution. It seeks to understand SGBV, contributing factors such as culture and traditions underpinning this violence, the role of international institutions, and the ways in which it can be addressed. It applauds contemporary efforts made to address the impacts of SGBV on survivors, to provide the services needed for recovery, and to address discrimination. It warns that, without sustained commitment and action, gains can quickly be lost.

This kind of tailored and contextual analysis is critical if we are to make progress to globally eliminate SGBV. Addressing SGBV and its root causes sadly remains a crucial element of fostering inclusive and resilient societies in which all are protected and can enjoy their rights in equity. Domestic law and policy change are required as part of this picture—too often, domestic frameworks do not reflect international legal obligations—and these laws and policies should be robust, resourced, and implemented.

From the standpoint of the International Committee of the Red Cross (ICRC), efforts to prevent and address SGBV in armed conflict and other situations of violence, including in places of detention, are an institutional priority. This is because SGBV violates international humanitarian law (IHL) and international human rights law (IHRL) and generates immense humanitarian need and suffering. SGBV, including sexual violence (SV) in conflict, is life-threatening. Its survivors—who are disproportionately female as SGBV is a manifestation of unequal gender norms, but who can also be men, boys, and sexual and gender minorities—often have long-term and complex needs. They need access to health care, including mental health and psychosocial support, and economic and livelihood supports including control over land and resources.

Based on these needs, ICRC delegations work to support community resilience in times of crises. Our work to protect civilians includes engagement and services to support survivors of sexual violence—women, girls, men, boys, and sexual and gender minorities. ICRC also engages with weapon bearers and authorities on the prohibition of sexual violence (whether strategic or opportunistic) as a violation of IHL and the harm it generates for individuals, families, and communities.

Through our work, ICRC is confronted with the daily reality that despite the efforts of women's groups, international organisations, and government authorities to prevent SGBV, collectively we have much to do to attain its prevention and eradication. As this publication observes, SGBV has historically been rife; and while there is much debate about the cultural factors and dynamics that drive it, it is clear that much more concerted engagement of international institutions on addressing SGBV from all angles, including adequate placement of survivors at the centre of response and of efforts to address power dynamics, is where future endeavours must concentrate. This publication contributes to the wide field of research demonstrating that SGBV is not inevitable. And indeed, if it is predictable, it is preventable.

Peter Maurer
President
International Committee of the Red Cross
Geneva, Switzerland

Preface

Sexual and gender-based violence (SGBV) prevails since time immemorial. SGBV is still a taboo, spoken in whispers and suffered in silence. It takes place during peacetime, conflicts, and post-conflict situations. Though SGBV is perpetrated against men, women, and people of the LGBT community, this study has sought to focus on women and girls as main victims-survivors. SGBV against women and girls is a manifestation of historically unequal power relations between male and female genders rooted in patriarchal systems, stereotyped gender-based norms, and harmful cultural practices (HCPs). In fact, different cultural and social norms support different types of violence. It is one of the crucial social mechanisms by which women and girls are sought to be subjugated to a position subordinate to men. As a corollary, the control over female sexuality remains central to the social, cultural, and State-driven global normative systems. There are many prominent instances of cultural practices that are harmful to women and girls.

The United Nations data shows that more than 200 million girls and women are understood to have been subjected to female genital mutilation (FGM). In 2021 alone, 4.16 million girls around the world are at risk of undergoing FGM. This work has considered culture within the framework of equality. As such the international legal framework for protection for women and girls against SGBV also addresses the organic interlinkages between HCPs and SGBV. In the wake of two year long Covid-19 pandemic during 2020–2022 and the climatic changes, there has been an exacerbation of SGBV against women and girls. This presents a new global regulatory challenge for international law, international institutions, and the scholars.

There is a growing awareness, concern, scholarly works, and multiagency coordinated roles. It indicates a healthy trend in addressing the challenge of SGBV. Ironically, the existing corpus of international law is not adequate in specifically addressing SGBV against women and girls. As explained in a chapter on legal challenges, there is an unequivocal need to a global *lex specialis* on SGBV and an urgent need for bridging the 'normative gap' in the field. The absence of specific legally binding instrument has pushed the international humanitarian institutions such as International Committee of the Red Cross (ICRC), UN Women, UN Office of the High Commissioner for Human Rights, and the UN Human Rights Council and others to push for alternative non-binding instruments to address SGBV against women and girls. These instruments carry good normative value. However, they are not taken seriously by most of the States since they construe them as 'soft' and guiding principles.

International institutions (IIs) have been playing a pivotal role in organizing to provide legal and institutional protection to women and girls against SGBV. It is vital in the prevention and elimination of SGBV as a threat and reality against sizeable part of the global population. Most of such international institutions work under the umbrella of the United Nations (UN) as it has become catalytic symbol of multilateralism. The International Committee of the Red Cross, as the global humanitarian sentinel, also has a unique role in addressing the challenge of SGBV. As explained in the foreword of Peter Maurer, President of the ICRC, as the costodian of the 1949 Geneva Conventions, has sought to give priority attention to SGBV by regarding it as a "heinously prevalent scourge" that prevails in all the societies around the world.

Notwithstanding the stated objectives of all the legally binding agreements, soft instruments, and concerted actions of international institutions, women continue to suffer the ordeal of SGBV primarily because of their gender and sex. SGBV is cheap, easily available tool especially in armed conflicts to harm the women and girls as it hurts the targeted communities most. Ironically, SGBV remains globally prevalent with destructive consequences for women and girls due to their unequal and precarious status in most of the societies, its use as a weapon of war, and the perpetrators mostly going scot-free. In view of this sense of impunity and as international law is struggling to address the SGBV challenge, an important ideational question needs to be grappled with. How can we de-fang, de-stigmatize, and de-legitimize SGBV? This crucial question presents a big international law scholarly challenge for the future to eliminate the scourge of SGBV. This work has earnestly sought to sow some modest seeds in the scholarly realm to visualize a process for the beginning of the inevitable end of SGBV in the coming decades of the twenty-first century. Its outcome lies in the womb of the future. Only *Time* will provide an answer.

New Delhi, India
16 April 2022

Bharat H. Desai
Moumita Mandal

Contents

About the Authors

Bharat H. Desai is Professor of International Law and Jawaharlal Nehru Chair in International Environmental Law at the Centre for International Legal Studies in School of International Studies of Jawaharlal Nehru University in New Delhi. He serves as Editor-in-Chief of the *Yearbook of International Environmental Law* (Oxford: OUP) as well as *Environmental Policy & Law* (Amsterdam: IOS Press). He has formerly served as the Governing Board Member of IUCN Academy of Environmental Law (USA) as well as Vice-Chairman of Foundation for Development of International Law in Asia (The Netherlands). Some of his significant books include (i) *International Environmental Law: Collected Essays* (2022; forthcoming) (ii) *Taking International Law Seriously: Scholarly Musings* (2022; forthcoming) (iii) *Our Earth Matters: Pathways to a Better Common Environmental Future*, Editor (IOS Press, 2021) (iv) *International Environmental Governance: Towards UNEPO* (Brill Nijhoff, 2014) (v) *Multilateral Environmental Agreements: Legal Status of the Secretariats* (Cambridge University Press, 2013 and 2010) (vi) *Institutionalizing International Environmental Law* (Transnational Publishers, 2004). Professor Desai has been a member of the official Indian delegations of Indian Ministries of Environment & Forests as well as External Affairs, to various intergovernmental negotiations. He has also been consulted by Asian Development Bank (Manila), World Conservation Union (Gland) and International Council for Integrated Mountain Development (Kathmandu).

Moumita Mandal is a Ph.D in International Law and serves as a Post-doctoral Fellow with Jawaharlal Nehru Chair, at School of International Studies of Jawaharlal Nehru University in New Delhi. Dr.Mandal has contributed significant scholarly works in journals of international repute such as: *Environmental Policy and Law* (2021); *Indian Journal of International Law* (2020); *Journal of the National Human Rights Commission* (2020); *Yearbook of International Environmental Law* (2019) and *Economic and Political Weekly* (2018); Dr. Mandal is engaged in teaching and research in the field of International Law and has delivered talks at International Law symposiums on cutting-edge issues of global concern including sexual and gender-based violence (SGBV).

List of Tables

Chapter 1
Introduction

Sexual and gender-based violence (SGBV) prevails since time immemorial. SGBV is still a taboo and spoken in whispers or suffered in silence. It takes place during peacetime, conflicts, and post-conflict situations. In fact, gender becomes a turf in most of the patriarchal societies. It came to the fore graphically during the years 2020-2022 of the Covid-19 pandemic wherein cases of SGBV escalated. In a graphic reality of the day, as countries imposed Covid-19 restrictions including prolonged lockdowns, "for many around the world, lockdown meant being locked with their abuser".[1]

Since SGBV has crossed the boundaries of the States, it has become an important challenge in the field of international law. In view of this, both domestic law and international law need to play a crucial role in the prevention and ultimate elimination of SGBV.[2]

SGBV is gender-neutral: men, women, and transgender people become the victims.[3] However, studies have shown that most of the sufferers are women, girls, and children.[4] SGBV against women and girls is one of the most prevalent forms of

---

[1] ICRC (2020), "2020: A year in pictures"; available at: https://www.icrc.org/en/document/2020-year-pictures (accessed on 29 September 2021). See also, ICRC (2020), "A conflict without borders continues to play out in Sahel"; available at: https://www.icrc.org/en/document/conflict-without-borders-continues-play-out-sahel (accessed on 04 April 2021); Fried, Susana T. (2003), "Violence against Women," *Health and Human Rights*, 6(2): 88–111.

[2] Ulrich, Jennifer L. (2000), "Confronting Gender-Based Violence with International Instruments: Is a Solution to the Pandemic within Reach?" *Indiana Journal of Global Legal Studies*, 7(2): 629–654. See also, Janis, M. W. (1984) "Individuals as Subjects of International Law," *Cornell International Law Journal*: 17(1): 61–78; available at: http://scholarship.law.cornell.edu/cilj/vol17/iss1/2 (accessed on 04 April 2021).

[3] Lewis, Dustin A (2009), "Unorganized Victims: Sexual Violence against Men in Conflict Settings under International Law," *Wisconsin International Law Journal*, 27(1): 1–49.

[4] Campbell, Kristen (2007), "The Gender of Transnational Justice: Law, Sexual Violence and the International Criminal Tribunal for the Former Yugoslavia," *International Journal of Transnational Justice*, 1(3): 411–432; see also, the lexical meaning of woman is "An adult human female;" available

B. H. Desai and M. Mandal, *Sexual and Gender-Based Violence in International Law*,
https://doi.org/10.1007/978-981-19-0894-1_1

human rights violations all over the world. It does not know social, economic, political, and geographical boundaries. It is estimated that one in every three women experiences physical or sexual violence in her lifetime. Ironically, it remains enveloped by a culture of silence.[5] It has become so pervasive that 2019 report of the World Bank has graphically underscored that SGBV or gender-based violence (GBV) is a global pandemic since:

> 35% of women worldwide have experienced either physical and/or sexual intimate partner violence or non-partner sexual violence. Globally, 7% of women have been sexually assaulted by someone other than a partner. Globally, as many as 38% of murders of women are committed by an intimate partner. 200 million women have experienced female genital mutilation/cutting.[6]

The issue is not only alarming and devastating for the survivors and their families but also entails huge social and economic costs. It has been estimated that in some countries, the cost of SGBV is staggering and accounts for up to 3.7% of the GDP. It is more than double what most of the States spend on education.[7] According to UN Women, the global cost of violence against women has been estimated at approximately USD 1.5 trillion. In the aftermath of 2020-2022 Covid-19 pandemic, the figure is expected to have risen due to exacerbation in violence against women. It shows gravity of this simmering global challenge of our times.

Challenge of SGBV

The term 'SGBV' refers to any harmful act perpetrated against the will of a person, which is based on gender differences. It also includes an act that inflicts physical and psychological or sexual harm, sufferings, threat of doing such acts or any other deprivation of liberty in private or public places. It is a serious threat as well as a violation of the women's basic human right to life and bodily integrity.[8]

---

at: https://www.lexico.com/definition/woman (accessed on 04 April 2021); and 'girl' means, "A female child;" available at: https://www.lexico.com/definition/girl (accessed on 04 April 2021). Though there is no legal definition of 'woman' and 'girl' but for this study 'woman' means female, trans-female of any age and 'girl' means female child below the age of maturity. The age of maturity differ country to country based on culture, religion etc. though all the women include girls but all the girls may not always be treated as women. The Beijing Platform of Action has used some specific terminologies to specify elimination of discrimination against the girl child, e.g., minimum legal age; adolescent etc. See also, UN (1995), "The Report of the Fourth World Conference on Women (Beijing)"; available at: http://hrlibrary.umn.edu/svaw/law/un/undocs.htm (accessed on 04 April 2021).

[5] UNFPA (2016), "Gender-based violence"; available at: http://www.unfpa.org/gender-based-violence (accessed on 19 September 2021).

[6] The World Bank (2019), "Gender-Based Violence"; available at: https://www.worldbank.org/en/topic/socialsustainability/brief/violence-against-women-and-girls (accessed on 18 October 2020).

[7] Ibid.

[8] Desai, Bharat H. et al. (2018), "Quest for Women's Right to Bodily Integrity: Reflections on Recent Judicial Inroads in India", *Economic & Political Weekly*, vol.53, no.51, 29

Though SGBV is perpetrated against men, women, and people of the LGBTI community, this study has sought to focus on women and girls (the study has used the word 'women' for both) as most of the victims are women. SGBV against women can emanate from individual action as well as that of a sovereign State.[9] Women who are victims of SGBV can be the direct subject matter of international law. For example, all women in general; (civilian, combatants, or prisoners of war),[10] and women with special status such as refugees or asylum seekers, returnees, internally displaced women,[11] stateless women,[12] and other categories of women and girls come under this protective umbrella.

SGBV against women is a manifestation of historically unequal power relations between genders that are founded upon different gender-based norms and cultural practices. In fact, "different cultural and social norms support different types of violence".[13] It is one of the crucial social mechanisms by which women are sought to be subjugated to a position subordinate to men. As a corollary, the control over female sexuality is central to the social, cultural, and State normative systems. This is especially so since:

> Sexuality is a central aspect of being human throughout life and encompasses sex, gender identities and roles, sexual orientation, eroticism, pleasure, intimacy, and reproduction. Sexuality is experienced and expressed in thoughts, fantasies, desires, beliefs, attitudes, values, behaviors, practices, roles and relationships. Though, generally, women are sexually active during adolescence, they reach their peak orgasmic frequency in their 30s, and have a constant

December 2018; available at: https://www.epw.in/engage/article/quest-womens-right-bodily-integrity-judicial-inroads (accessed on 01 February 2021). Also see, OHCHR (2009), *15 Years of The United Nations Special Rapporteur on Violence Against Women (1994–2009): A Critical Review*; available at: https://www.ohchr.org/Documents/Issues/Women/15YearReviewofVAWMandate.pdf (accessed on 21 November 2020).

[9] Ulrich, Jennifer L. (2000), n.2.

[10] International Commission of Jurists (2016), "Women's Access to Justice for Gender-Based Violence: A Practitioner's Guide;" available at: http://www.icj.org/wp-content/uploads/2016/03/Universal-Womens-accesss-to-justice-Publications-Practitioners-Guide-Series-2016-ENG.pdf (accessed on 19 January 2021).

[11] UNHCR (2003), "Sexual and Gender-Based Violence against Refugees, Returnees and Internally Displaced Persons: Guidelines for Prevention and Response"; available at: https://www.unicef.org/emerg/files/gl_sgbv03.pdf (accessed on 19 January 2021).

[12] Edwards, Alice. (2009), "Displacement, Statelessness, and Questions of Gender Equality and the Convention on the Elimination of All Forms of Discrimination against Women;" available at: http://www2.ohchr.org/english/bodies/cedaw/docs/UNHCR_CEDAW_Background_Paper.pdf (accessed on 19 January 2021).

[13] WHO (2009), "Changing social and cultural norms that support violence" (briefings on violence prevention: the evidence), WHO: Geneva, p. 4. The briefing paper has documented evidence on cultural and social gender-based norms that encourage SGBV against women such as: (i) female children valued less in the society than men; (ii) harmful traditional practices; (iii) man has right to assert power over women; (iv) women's freedom should be restricted; (v) sexual violence is shameful for the victims etc.;" available at: https://www.who.int/violence_injury_prevention/violence/norms.pdf (accessed on 19 January 2021).

level of sexual capacity up to the age of 55 with little evidence that aging affects it in later life.[14]

In view of this, different types of SGBV exist in the society, e.g. within the family, within the community, and within the ambit of affairs of the States or resulting from political violence (e.g. SGBV in war, conflicts, etc.). In this context, cultural practices often justify violence against women within the family and the community.[15]

Role of Culture in SGBV

Culture or tradition plays an important role in shaping the thoughts and behaviour of men and women. It has another significant part that restricts the exercise of the basic rights of women.[16] It has been found that challenge comes from the cultural 'relativist'[17] assertion that rejects the universality of human rights, especially equality of women and the cultural approach which is inherently 'misogynist.'[18] Sometimes, culture becomes an obstacle to the realization of the women's rights to equal enjoyment of their basic human rights. It is now a growing international concern. The use of discourses of cultural relativism to challenge the universal legitimacy and

---

[14] Rao, T.S. Satyanarana, Kumar, A., and Nagaraj, M. (2015), "Female sexuality," *Indian J Psychiatry*, 57(Suppl 2): S296-S302; available at: https://www.ncbi.nlm.nih.gov/pmc/articles/PMC4539874/ (accessed on 19 January 2021). Also see Baumeister, Roy F and J.M. Twenge (2002), "Cultural suppression of female sexuality," *Review of General Psychology*, 6(2); 166–203. It states that "Control over female sexuality is one of the intention or interest of patriarchy, because it is used to prevent from realizing full potential of female. It is the accepted cultural and societal norm that only men have the right over sexuality and control over women." Some scholars have argued that the reason behind suppression of female sexuality is stabilization of property right; desire to pass on one's property to legitimate heirs; psychology of men to treat women as property; jealous desire to prevent their mates to have sex with other men; etc. so, men control power and maintain powerful position by this way. Women and girls are subjected to different forms of SGBV, i.e. honour killing, child marriage, female genital mutilation, etc. as consequences of the cultural or societal norm to control female sexuality. For detailed analysis of female sexuality, see, Andersen, Barbara L and J. M Cyranowski (1995), "Women's Sexuality: Behaviors, Responses, and Individual Differences," *J Consult Clin Psychol*, 63(6): 891–906; "General approaches, assessment strategies, and models of female sexuality are organized within the conceptual domains of sexual behaviors, sexual responses (desire, excitement, orgasm, and resolution), and individual differences, including general and sex-specific personality models;" available at: https://www.ncbi.nlm.nih.gov/pmc/articles/PMC2707786/ (accessed on 19 January 2021).

[15] OHCHR (2009), n.8.

[16] UN, *General Recommendation No. 21 (13th Session, 1994) of the CEDAW*; available at: http://www.un.org/womenwatch/daw/cedaw/recommendations/recomm.htm#recom21 (accessed on 19 January 2021).

[17] It further explains: "Cultural relativists believe that culture is the sole source of a moral right or rule. So, the rights, practices, values etc. are determined by culture only. It keeps separate a particular culture from outsider or foreign culture. Hence, culture is used as a defence against external criticism or to justify some cultural practices"; see, Donnelly, Jack (1984), "Cultural Relativism and Universal Human Rights," *Human Rights Quarterly*, 6(4): 400–419.

[18] OHCHR (2009), n.8.

applicability of human rights norms is a serious concern. Thus, there is a growing international concern that harmful traditional practices are the root causes of discrimination and violence against women. Both scientific and social studies have shown that value or culture-based discrimination is systematic and universal.[19]

There are many prominent instances of cultural practices that are harmful to women. For example, more than 200 million girls and women are understood to have been subjected to female genital mutilation (FGM) in African, Asian, and Middle East countries.[20] According to UN Women, in 2021 alone some 4.16 million women and girls were at risk of FGM. This pernicious practice continues unabated in the name of 'essential' cultural or religious traditions. Similarly, the inherent preference for a son leads to female feticide and infanticide in different Asian countries.[21] Early marriage or forced marriages take place on a large-scale in many of the Asian and African countries.

Apart from above, there are practices known as *Devadasi*, *Deuki,* or *Devaki* in countries such as India and Nepal. This comprises offering of girls to temples for providing all kinds of services, including forced prostitution.[22] In Ethiopia, the traditional practice allows kidnapping and raping of girls for forced marriages. *Trokosi* is a traditional practice in Nigeria, Ghana, and Benin whereby young girls are given to fetish shrines to serve under threat as domestic and sexual slaves. There are many countries where grotesque practice still persists in making forcibly raping of girls in the name of providing justice.[23]

Prevalence of other well-known harmful societal practices include dowry, honour killing, buying and selling women for marriage; offering girls for dispute resolution, etc. As a result, SGBV against women is often sought to be justified under these so-called cultural norms. Here, culture is used as a tool against women. It, in turn, subjects them to institutionalized forms of SGBV. It is also used as a defence to encourage the culture of impunity. Thus, cultural garb becomes a notorious a tool and a practice in cases of SGBV against women.[24]

In general, it is the girls and women who become victims of SGBV in the name of traditional or cultural practices. Still, there are some specific groups of women and girls who easily fall prey to harmful traditional practices. These women belong to minority groups, indigenous women, refugee women, migrant women living in

---

[19] United Nations (2006), "The impact of harmful traditional practices on the girl child", UN Doc. EGM/DVGC/2006/EP.4; available at: http://www.un.org/womenwatch/daw/egm/elim-disc-viol-girlchild/ExpertPapers/EP.4%20%20%20Raswork.pdf (accessed on 19 January 2021).

[20] WHO (2018), World Health Organization, "Female Genital Mutilation;" available at: http://www.who.int/news-room/fact-sheets/detail/female-genital-mutilation (accessed on 21 September 2021).

[21] UN (2006), n.19.

[22] WHO (2009), n.13.

[23] Shamsie, Kamila (2002), "The power of Pakistan's progressive press: Child abuse in Belgium 'shocks the nation'-so why is gang rape in Pakistan 'a cultural issue?" *The Guardian,* Pakistan, 6 September 2002; available at: https://www.theguardian.com/world/2002/sep/06/gender.uk1 (accessed on 21 November 2018).

[24] Ajayi, Victoria (2012), "Violence Against Women: The Ethics of Incorporating the Cultural Defense in Leg al;" *The Georgetown Journal of Legal Ethics Narrative,* 25:401.

rural or remote communities, destitute women, women in institutions or detention, female children, women with disabilities, women in conflict zones, women who are the victims of natural disasters or climate change etc.[25] The primary actors involve in the harmful SGBV practices against women are: family, community, and States. The State comes into the picture when it supports hegemonic interpretations of religion to debunk cultural relativism and support certain inherently violent and discriminatory cultures towards women.[26]

In view of this, the role and response of international law become relevant to address the cultural factors that impinge upon women's basic rights. It comprises the protection of the basic human rights of women. It has led to the adoption of the term 'harmful practices' instead of 'harmful traditional practices'. It calls for "State participation in validating alternative and non-hegemonic interpretations of culture by women and encouraging cultural negotiation." Thus, engagement of international law can be regarded as a continuous process[27] in addressing the challenge of SGBV.

The 1979 Convention on the Elimination of All Forms of Discrimination against Women (CEDAW) is prominent among relevant international legal instruments. Many of the cultural practices that involve pain, suffering, and violation of physical or bodily integrity of women come under the non-permissible threshold of customary international law. These practices invite strict penal actions and maximum security regardless of ratification of the CEDAW or any of the other international human rights treaties.

This work has considered culture within the framework of equality. The international legal framework for protection for women against SGBV also addresses the organic interlinkages between culture and violence against women. The primary roots of the universal patriarchal culture lie in gender inequality rather than in cultural expressions of people in diverse societal structures. In fact, the Committee against Torture has taken a view that it is the responsibility of the State to prevent and protect the victims of SGBV. This is especially so in cases of harmful practices such as FGM. However, the Convention against Torture and Other Inhuman or Degrading Treatment or Punishment only refers to the crime of rape without addressing other forms of SGBV. In fact, the 2014 Report of the Special Rapporteur has explicitly mentioned this as follows:

> While it may be argued that the Convention against Torture can serve as a tool for addressing violence against women, the Committee has so far only defined rape as torture, without explicitly addressing other forms of violence against women.[28]

---

[25] UN (1993), "The Declaration on the Elimination of Violence against Women," UN Doc. A/RES/48/104, 23 February 1994; available at: https://undocs.org/en/A/RES/48/104 (accessed on 19 January 2021).

[26] Ajayi, Victoria (2012), n.24.

[27] OHCHR (2009), n.8.

[28] Human Rights Council (2014), *Report of the Special Rapporteur on violence against women, its causes and consequences* (Rashida Manjoo); available at: http://undocs.org/en/A/HRC/26/38 (accessed on 19 January 2021); UN Doc. A/HRC/26/38, paragraph 24. Similarly, another report of the Economic and Social Council (ECOSOC) explains it thus: "Since it was clear that rape or other forms of sexual assault against women held in detention were a particularly ignominious violation

It is also a fact that women victims, for a variety of reasons, seldom seek help and assistance though they have the right to get justice and protection. Therefore, it is the duty of the State as well as the international community to protect their rights and provide justice by punishing the perpetrators amidst negative cultural stereotypes. It, in turn, calls for the people to view cultural traditions with new perspective that ensures centrality of the dignity of women.

Eliminating SGBV: Role of International Institutions

At the global level, many of the international institutions (IIs) play a pivotal role in organizing to provide legal and institutional protection to women against SGBV. It is vital in the prevention and elimination of SGBV as a threat and reality against sizeable part of the global population. Most of such international institutions work under the umbrella of the United Nations (UN) as it has become catalytic symbol of multilateralism.[29]

Some of the recent UN initiatives include the 2008 campaign of the Secretary-General Ban Ki-moon's on *UNiTE to End Violence against Women.* It aimed at preventing and eliminating SGBV around the world. *UNiTE* calls for work jointly with all the actors apart from the UN. It has considered SGBV against women as a global pandemic.[30] Apart from it, funding remains one of the crucial criteria for

---

of the dignity and right to physical integrity of the human being, they accordingly constituted an act of torture"; Commission on Human Rights, Forty-eight session, Summary Record 21st Meeting, UN Doc. E/CN.4/1992/SR.21 21 February 1992, paragraph 35; available at: https://digitallibrary.un.org/record/138396?ln=en http://hr-travaux.law.virginia.edu/document/cped/ecn41992sr21/nid-2460 (accessed on 17 January 2021). Also see Economic and Social Council (1995), "Report of the Special Rapporteur, Mr. Nigel S. Rodley, submitted pursuant to Commission on Human Rights resolution 1992/32, paragraph 16. It states, "Methods of torture involving sexual abuse may be characterized as essentially gender-based"; https://digitallibrary.un.org/record/226391?ln=en#record-files-collapse-header. Professor Kooijmans, in an oral introduction to his 1992 report to the Commission on Human Rights, noted that "[s]ince it was clear that rape or other forms of sexual assault against women in detention were a particularly ignominious violation of the inherent dignity and the right to physical integrity of the human being, they accordingly constituted an act of torture"; UN Doc.E/CN.4/1992/SR.21, para. 35; available at: http://hrlibrary.umn.edu/commission/thematic51/34.htm (accessed on 12 January 2021). The International Criminal Tribunal for Rwanda (ICTR) has also observed that: "Like torture, rape is used for such purposes as intimidation, degradation, humiliation, discrimination, punishment, control or destruction of a person. Like torture, rape is a violation of personal dignity, and rape in fact constitutes torture when inflicted by or at the instigation of or with the consent or acquiescence of a public official or other person acting in an official capacity", *Akeyasu Case, (The Prosecutor vs. Jean-Paul Akayesu)*, 02 September 1998; ICTR-96-4-T, paragraph 597; available at: http://unictr.irmct.org/sites/unictr.org/files/case-documents/ictr-96-4/trial-judgements/en/980902.pdf (accessed on 17 January 2021).

[29] Desai, Bharat H (2020), "UN has been at the forefront of multilateralism", The Tribune, 02 October 2020; available at: https://www.tribuneindia.com/news/comment/un-has-been-at-frontline-of-multilateralism-149629 (accessed on 28 December 2020).

[30] UN Women, "UNiTE to End Violence against Women"; available at: https://www.unwomen.org/en/what-we-do/ending-violence-against-women/take-action/unite (accessed on 5 December 2020).

the movement to put an end to SGBV. Here also, the UN plays the leading role as it has released twenty-five million USD for women-led projects in the battle against SGBV, especially for humanitarian purposes.[31] It comprises the current challenges and the SGBV issues and encourages all the sectors, including the private sector, to commit to ending SGBV. For example, it addresses the *shadow pandemic* where the issue of violence against women during pandemic has come to the before the world.[32]

As observed by Phumzile Mlambo-Ngcuka, the UN Women's Executive Director:

> Rape isn't an isolated brief act. It damages flesh and reverberates in memory...The end of the horrendous act would mean eliminating a significant 'weapon of war' from the arsenal of conflict.[33]

The UN Secretary-general's call to *UNiTE* by 2030 to *End Violence against Women* campaign encompassed marked sixteen days of activism during 25 November to 10 December 2020 under the global theme *Orange the World: Fund, Respond, Prevent, Collect.* It indicated that SGBV against women is the most pervasive breach of human rights. The campaign has sought to build on existing international law and policy to unite and work together to end SGBV.[34]

In 2020, the UN turned 75 years old. The United Nations Academic Impact (UNAI) hosted the *75 for UN75: 75 min of Conversations* that included a series of online dialogues with students, researchers, educators, and academics around the globe to discuss the global issues and challenges. The UNAI hosted a webinar on the theme'75 min of Conversation: Rethinking Gender' as part of the global issue on 19 June 2020 with the collaboration of UN Women and the global academic community.

---

[31] UN Women (2020), "United Nations releases USD 25 million for women-led projects battling gender-based violence"; Press Release of 25 November 2020; available at: https://www.unwomen.org/en/news/stories/2020/11/press-release-un-releases-funds-for-women-led-projects-battling-gender-based-violence (accessed on 5 December 2020). Also see, UN Central Emergency Response Fund (2020), "United Nations Releases $25 Million For Women-Led Projects Battling Gender-Based Violence", Press Release of 25 November 2020; available at: https://reliefweb.int/sites/reliefweb.int/files/resources/UN%20RELEASES%20%2425%20MILLION%20FOR%20WOMEN-LED%20PROJECTS%20BATTLING%20GENDER-BASED%20VIOLENCE.pdf (accessed on 5 December 2020).

[32] UN Women (2020), "As impact of COVID-19 intensifies, UN Women calls for concrete actions to respond to the concurrent shadow pandemic"; Press Release, 25 November 2020; available at: https://www.unwomen.org/en/news/stories/2020/11/press-release-16-days-of-activism-against-gender-based-violence; UN (2020), "The Shadow Pandemic"; available at: https://www.un.org/en/observances/ending-violence-against-women-day (accessed on 11 March 2021).

[33] UN News (2019), "A staggering one-in-three women, experience physical, sexual abuse", 25 November 2019; available at: https://news.un.org/en/story/2019/11/1052041 (accessed on 5 December 2020).

[34] UN (2020), "The Shadow Pandemic"; available at: https://www.un.org/en/observances/ending-violence-against-women-day; UN Women (2020), "Orange the World: Fund, Respond, Prevent, Collect!", United Nations Secretary-General's Campaign UNiTE by 2030 to End Violence against Women, 16 Days of Activism against Gender Based Violence 25th November–10 December 2020, Concept Note for engagement"; available at: https://www.unwomen.org/-/media/headquarters/attachments/sections/what%20we%20do/evaw/unite%20campaign_2020_concept%20note_final.pdf?la=en&vs=2808 (accessed on 11 March 2021).

The International Day for the Elimination of Sexual Violence in Conflict is celebrated on 19 June each year. This day is also marked as the opening of the first World Conference on the Status of Women (Mexico City, 1975) that ushered a new era of action by addressing gender equality and global efforts to promote the advancement of women.

Thus, 19 June 2020, provided appropriate occasion to examine the impact of COVID-19 on the progress made for the women's human rights since the Beijing Conference 25 years ago. Mlambo-Mgcuka, Executive Director of the UN Women, stressed on the need to ensure equal access to technology for women and girls. She pointed out that COVID-19 has widened the existing gender gap in accessing technology. The importance of research and contributions of academia were duly highlighted.[35]

In 2020, the UN celebrated the anniversary of different crucial change-making international instruments. For example, the UN Women's 'Generation Equity' campaign aims to accelerate gender equity actions and mark the 25th anniversary of the Beijing Declaration and Platform for Action to insist on global mobilization regarding human rights of all women and girls. The UN Women has also taken the initiative to celebrate the 20th anniversary of UN Security Council resolution 1325 (2000) on 'women, peace and security'; the 5th anniversary of the Sustainable Development Goals 2030. In 2019, the UN SC adopted important resolutions 2467 (2019) and 2493 (2019) under the agenda of 'women, peace and security' that focus on elimination of SGBV during armed conflicts.[36]

Apart from the UN, there are civil society organizations, judicial institutions, and other governmental, non-governmental and intergovernmental organizations are working to end the SGBV. For example, the International Committee of the Red Cross (ICRC)[37] works to end SGBV against women in conflicts as well as Amnesty International[38] and the Human Rights Watch[39] address SGBV from the human rights perspective. There are judicial institutions that are also working to address SGBV against women.[40]

---

[35] Desai (2020), n.29. Also see, UN, Academic Impact (2020), "75 for UN75: A Conversation on Rethinking Gender", 30 June 2020; available at: https://academicimpact.un.org/content/75-un75-conversation-rethinking-gender; UN (2020), "Women and Girls – Closing the Gender Gap"; available at: un75_gender.pdf (accessed on 11 March 2021).

[36] UN Women (2019), "About Generation Equality"; available at: https://www.unwomen.org/en/digitallibrary/publications/2019/05/generation-equality; (accessed on 11 March 2021).

[37] ICRC (2019), "Stepping up our efforts to end sexual and gender-based violence"; available at: https://www.icrc.org/en/event/stepping-our-efforts-end-sexual-and-gender-based-violence (accessed on 7 December 2020).

[38] Amnesty International, "Gender Based Violence"; available at: https://amnesty.org.in/projects/gender-based-violence/ (accessed on 7 December 2020).

[39] HRW (2020), "Human Rights Watch Submission to the UN Special Rapporteur on Violence Against Women"; available at: https://www.hrw.org/news/2020/05/22/human-rights-watch-submis sion-un-special-rapporteur-violence-against-women (accessed on 7 December 2020).

[40] ICC (2014), "Policy Paper on Sexual and Gender-Based Crimes"; available at: https://www.icc-cpi.int/iccdocs/otp/otp-policy-paper-on-sexual-and-gender-based-crimes--june-2014.pdf (accessed on 7 December 2020).

Though IIs are continually working to address SGBV, still lack of uniformity among these institutions results in slowing down the law and policymaking processes to end SGBV. In view of this, the study has sought to identify the gaps in the concerted responses as well as challenges faced by the IIs and their contributions to policy-making, legal, and enforcement mechanisms. After looking at the role and contributions of the IIs to put an end to SGBV, this work calls for duly institutionalizing a concerted effective international legal framework for providing protection especially to women and ultimately eliminate SGBV from the face of the Earth.

Facing the Challenge of SGBV

Now SGBV is no longer a myth. It is a graphic reality of the modern-day world. Notwithstanding aims of all the legal instruments and international institutions, women continue to suffer the ordeal of SGBV merely because of their gender and sex. It appears from reports of the international institutions and works of scholars that SGBV affects the survivors, society, and States. It impacts negatively or creates an extra burden on the economy of the States that face economic losses as a result of and spending money on addressing the SGBV challenge.

SGBV presents a barrier for the individual, community, and States' progress and development. Hence, it necessitates effective responses that squarely address the issue as well as adoption of specific international legal instruments that would send a strong message on 'zero tolerance' for SGBV as it cannot accepted, justified, or condoned under any circumstances. This work seeks to make a modest effort to understand, analyse, and craft a futuristic pathway for the prevention, delegitimization, and final elimination of SGBV as a scourge that afflicts the humankind especially girls and women on the planet earth.

Chapter 2
Sexual and Gender-Based Violence: A Global Concern

Introduction

Sexual and gender-based violence (SGBV) has become a global concern because of the seriousness of the issue and its perpetual consequences.[1] After a lot of scholarly works, concerns and campaigns by various stakeholders, the issue has come up on the global platform. In fact, reports of different international conferences[2]; international institutions such as the United Nations High Commissioner for Refugees (UNHCR), the UN Office of the High Commissioner for Human Rights (OHCHR)[3]; international non-governmental organizations (INGOs) and other actors, there is a greater scrutiny and calls for action by the respective governments.

In fact, reports of different international human rights and humanitarian actors have shown that women and girls are at high risk of SGBV during times of both peace and conflicts. SGBV is a violation of human rights as it denies the right to live with dignity[4] as well as become a simmering humanitarian concern . SGBV has been also

[1] UNHCR (2016), "SGBV Prevention and Response;" available at: http://www.unhcr.org/583577ed4 (accessed on 20 December 2020).

[2] ICRC (2016), International Committee of Red Cross, International Committee of the Red Cross, "32nd International Conference of the Red Cross and Red Crescent;" available at: https://www.icrc.org/en/document/outcomes-32nd-international-conference-red-cross-and-red-crescent (accessed on 28 November 2020).

[3] UNHCR (2016), n. 1.

[4] UNHCR (2003), "Sexual and Gender-Based Violence against Refugees, Returnees and Internally Displaced Persons: Guidelines for Prevention and Response;" available at: http://www.unhcr.org/sexual-and-gender-based-violence.html (accessed on 29 March 2021).

B. H. Desai and M. Mandal, *Sexual and Gender-Based Violence in International Law*,
https://doi.org/10.1007/978-981-19-0894-1_2

seen to be perpetrated and exacerbated in the wake of other emergencies like natural disasters, climate change and even pandemics such as COVID-19 (2020-2022).[5]

Though the fight against climate change has become a struggle to protect our environment, for many of the women, it is also a direct cause of different forms of SGBV.[6] During emergencies, especially disasters due to climate change, women are at high risk of SGBV because of crisis in the family and society; and sudden breakdown of family and community structures due to forced displacement.[7] As a result, among others, they face physical, sexual, psychological denials of resources or necessary services. Thus, it can be said that SGBV is perpetrated during peace, conflicts, post-conflicts or any other emergencies. Though it is an old crisis, now it has got heightened attention due to awareness about fundamental human rights, international humanitarian concerns and access to information through new technologies.[8]

The recent development of information and communication technology (ICT) is providing a way to prevent and respond to SGBV. In a meeting organized for the World Bank Group's 'Law, justice and Development' week, discussion took place on the risks and opportunities of growing technology concerning SGBV. On the one hand, the technology can facilitate and improve access to justice. It can also create a new risk since the perpetrators can use technology as a tool for SGBV. So, new forms of violence are coming to the fore that includes cyber violence, online SGBV

---

[5] ICRC (2020), "2020: A year in pictures"; available at: https://www.icrc.org/en/document/2020-year-pictures; 2020—A year in review through our lens | ICRC(accessed on 31 March 2022); ICRC (2020), *A conflict without borders continues to play out in Sahel*; available at: https://www.icrc.org/en/document/conflict-without-borders-continues-play-out-sahel (accessed on 31 March 2022) See also, Fried, Susana T. (2003), "Violence against Women," *Health and Human Rights*, 6(2): 88–111.

[6] Itzá Castañeda Camey, et al. (2020), *Gender-based violence and environment linkages: The violence of inequality*, Gland: IUCN; available at: https://portals.iucn.org/library/sites/library/files/documents/2020-002-En.pdf (accessed on 18 February 2021); UNDP(2020), "Why climate change fuels violence against women"; available at: https://www.undp.org/content/undp/en/home/blog/2020/why-climate-change-fuels-violence-against-women.html (accessed on 18 February 2021); UNHCR (2020) "Gender, Displacement and Climate Change"; available at: https://www.unhcr.org/5f21565b4.pdf (accessed on 18 February 2021); UN Women, "Climate Change, Disasters and Gender-Based Violence in the Pacific;" available at: https://www.uncclearn.org/sites/default/files/inventory/unwomen701.pdf (accessed on 18 February 2021).

[7] UNHCR (2003), n.4.

[8] For this see, generally, Buckley-Zistel, Susanne and Zolkos, Magdalena (2012), *Introduction: Gender in Transitional Justice*. Gender in Transitional Justice, Palgrave, 2012; available at: https://ssrn.com/abstract=2267777 (accessed on 18 February 2021).

Amanda, H. B. et al. (2016), *Ending Sexual and Gender-Based Violence in War and Peace Recommendations for the Next U.S. Administration: Peace Brief,* United States Institute of peace; available at: https://www.usip.org/publications/2016/09/ending-sexual-and-gender-based-violence-war-and-peace (accessed on 28 November 2020).

or ‘technology-facilitated gender-based violence”.[9] Thus, SGBV appears to have assumed the form of a global pandemic wherein all (men, women and LGBTI) face SGBV both in the real world and the digital world.[10] This necessitates identification of the problems, and find solution-based mechanisms for the simmering challenge.

This chapter contains four sections. The first section deals with some key concepts and meanings used in the study. Second section deals with the history of SGBV and the debate on and around it. It has explained how and why the concept of SGBV emerged and its historical background. The third section addresses different stages of SGBV experienced by women. Another sub-part has identified victims or survivors who face different forms of SGBV. The fourth section explains the causes and consequences of SGBV against women. It shows some practical instances of SGBV against women.

Some Key Concepts

In order to provide better understanding and explain broad contours of this study, some essential terms will be construed as per the explanations provided hereunder:

Sex

The definition of sex and gender is controversial. Biologists, sociologists, cultural anthropologists have tried to define ‘sex’. Still, the concept is not clear.[11] In lexical terms ‘sex’ means, “Either of the two main categories (male and female) into which humans and most other living things are divided on the basis of their reproductive functions”.[12] Similarly, sex means, “The state of being either male or female”.[13] In fact, most of the biologists, especially biological anthropologists, use word ‘sex’ to show gender status. The biological sex of a child primarily determines whether the child belongs to the male or female gender and now the third one—transgender. Sex refers to the biological characteristics at the time of birth. Thus, it is determined on the

---

[9] Hammond, Alicia, et al. (2019), “The good, the bad and the intersection of gender-based violence and technology,” World Bank Blog, 4 December 2019; available at: https://blogs.worldbank.org/voices/good-bad-and-intersection-gender-based-violence-and-technology (accessed on 11 December 2020).

[10] Ibid.

[11] Worthman, Carol M (1995), “Hormones, Sex, and Gender”, *Annual Review of Anthropology*, 24: 593–617.

[12] English Oxford living dictionaries, “Sex;” available at: https://en.oxforddictionaries.com/definition/sex (accessed on 28 November 2020).

[13] Cambridge Dictionary, “Sex;” available at: https://dictionary.cambridge.org/dictionary/english/sex (accessed on 28 November 2020).

basis of the reproductive functions of a human being.[14] According to the literature of sociology and anthropology, 'sex' is biological and emanates from birth. It pertains to biological distinction between the hitherto recognised two different sexes (male and female). It is needed to include the third (trans) sex also. Though social scientists argued that sex differentiation is based on biology, yet the influence of socialization and culture cannot be ignored.[15] As a result of this, the conventional definition of 'sex' excluded the existence of the third sex that transcends between male and female categories.

Gender

The term gender denotes, "The state of being male and female, which is typically concerning social and cultural differences rather than biological one".[16] It refers to the socially constructed characteristics between men and women as well as norms, roles, and the relationship between groups of men and women. It varies from society to society and can be changed.[17] The societal roles, responsibilities, reactions, power relations among the members of any society or culture, privileges, opportunities etc. are explicitly generated by it. Human beings learn how to behave within the society. This learned behavior is known as 'gender identity.' Ironically, in societal structures, practices and even scholarly works, hitherto, any gender identity beyond men and women was not covered. Thus, reality of existence of trans-gender was effectively ignored and obliterated. The perception of gender is influenced by different social factors such as history, tradition, religion, and social norms.[18] For instance, even Article 7(3) of the Rome Statute (1998) of the International Criminal Court (ICC) provides that 'gender' means only two sexes'male' and 'female' within the context of the society.[19] Thus traditional meaning of gender has excluded third gender or trans-gender people. However, this is now gradually changing as the human understanding widens. It may, in future, comprise other sexual orientations.

---

[14] UNHCR (2003), n. 4.

[15] Marini, Margaret Mooney (1990), "Sex and Gender: What Do We Know?" *Sociological Forum*, 5(1): 95–120.

[16] Oxfords Dictionaries, "Definition of gender in English;" available at: https://en.oxforddictionaries.com/definition/gender (accessed on 11 December 2020).

[17] World Health Organization, Gender, equity and human rights; available at: http://www.who.int/gender-equity-rights/understanding/gender-definition/en/ (accessed on 11 December 2020).

[18] UNHCR (2016), n. 1.

[19] UN (1998), *Rome Statute of the International Criminal Court*; available at: http://legal.un.org/icc/statute/99_corr/cstatute.htm (accessed on 11 December 2020).

Violence

The lexical meaning of violence is "behaviour involving physical force intended to hurt, damage or kill someone or something".[20]Article 1[21] of the UN General Assembly Declaration on the Elimination of Violence against Women (1993) defined violence against women as gender-based violence. Article 2 of the Declaration includes different forms of sexual and gender-based violence against women.[22]

In the *World Report on Violence and Helath* (2002), the WHO has defined 'violence' as:

> (T)he intentional use of physical force or power, threatened or actual, against oneself, another person, against a group or community, that either result in or has a high likelihood of resulting in injury, death, psychological harm, maldevelopment or deprivation.[23]

This definition gives a general idea of 'violence' that includes physical, psychological and sexual abuse, suicide and other self-abusive acts; deprivation or neglect against both men and women. It has used the terminology 'power' to denote physical force.[24]

---

[20] Oxford Dictionary, "Violence;" available at: https://en.oxforddictionaries.com/definition/violence (accessed on 11 December 2020).

[21] Article 1 of the UN GA Declaration on the Elimination of Violence against Women (1993), states, "For the purposes of this Declaration, the term "violence against women" means any act of gender-based violence that results in, or is likely to result in, physical, sexual or psychological harm or suffering to women, including threats of such acts, coercion or arbitrary deprivation of liberty, whether occurring in public or in private life;" available at: https://www.un.org/documents/ga/res/48/a48r104.htm (accessed on 11 December 2020).

[22] Ibid. Article 2 provides, "Violence against women shall be understood to encompass, but not be limited to, the following:

(a) Physical, sexual and psychological violence occurring in the family, including battering, sexual abuse of female children in the household, dowry-related violence, marital rape, female genital mutilation and other traditional practices harmful to women, non-spousal violence and violence related to exploitation;

(b) Physical, sexual and psychological violence occurring within the general community, including rape, sexual abuse, sexual harassment and intimidation at work, in educational institutions and elsewhere, trafficking in women and forced prostitution;

(c) Physical, sexual and psychological violence perpetrated or condoned by the State, wherever it occurs".

[23] WHO, "Violence Prevention alliance, Definition and typology of violence"; available at: http://www.who.int/violenceprevention/approach/definition/en/ (accessed on 11 December 2020).

[24] WHO (2002), "the World Report on Violence and Health," explaines: "The typology proposed here divides violence into three broad categories according to characteristics of those committing the violent act:—self-directed violence;—interpersonal violence;—collective violence;" available at: https://www.who.int/violence_injury_prevention/violence/world_report/en/introduction.pdf (accessed on 11 December 2020).

Sexual Violence

Sexual violence is referred to as the violence of sexual nature that is based on the biological sex of the individual. It is committed to establish power and control over the victim. It is a component and form of gender-based violence.[25] WHO's 2002 *World Report on Violence and Health* (Chap. 6) has defined 'sexual violence' as:

> Any sexual act, attempt to obtain a sexual act, unwanted sexual comments or advances, or acts to traffic, or otherwise directed, against a person's sexuality using coercion, by any person regardless of their relationship to the victim, in any setting, including but not limited to home and workplace.[26]

There are different forms of sexual violence e.g. rape, systematic rape (especially during the conflict), unwanted sexual advantage or sexual harassment, sexual abuse, forced marriage or cohabitation, denial in using contraception, adopting measures for protection against sexually transmitted diseases, forced abortion, violent act against the bodily integrity of women (female genital mutilation, an obligatory inspection of virginity etc.), forced prostitution for trafficking or sexual exploitation. There is no internationally accepted definition of trafficking for sexual exploitation. It encompasses only the movement of women for sex work. Victims of sexual violence include male, female and LGBTI.[27]

Gender-Based Violence

There is no particular definition of 'gender-based violence.' In most of the cases, 'gender-based violence' (GBV) and 'violence against women' (VAW) have been used interchangeably.[28] Gender-based violence is the form of violence which is committed against any particular individual or group of individuals because of their gender.

---

[25] Chatterji, Angana (2016), "Gendered and Sexual Violence in and beyond South Asia," *Indian Journal of Women and Social Change,* 1(1) 19–40.

[26] WHO (2002), "Sexual Violence" in *World Report on Violence and Health,* Chap. 6, p. 49; available at: http://www.who.int/violence_injury_prevention/violence/global_campaign/en/chap6.pdf (accessed on 11 December 2020); WHO (2002), n 24. See also, WHO (2014), *Global status report on violence prevention,* Geneva: WHO; available at: https://www.who.int/publications/i/item/978 9241564793 (accessed on 18 February 2021).

[27] Ibid.

[28] Cruz, Adrienne and Klinger, Sabine (2011), "Gender-based violence in the world of work: Overview and selected annotated bibliography", *Working paper 3/2011,* International Labor Office; available at: http://www.ilo.org/wcmsp5/groups/public/---dgreports/---gender/documents/publication/wcms_155763.pdf (accessed on 11 December 2020). Also see *the UN Declaration on the Elimination of Violence against Women.* Article 1 of the Declaration provides: "For the purposes of this Declaration, the term "violence against women" means any act of gender-based violence that results in, or is likely to result in, physical, sexual or psychological harm or suffering to women, including threats of such acts, coercion or arbitrary deprivation of liberty, whether occurring in public or in private life. Article 2: Violence against women shall be understood to encompass, but not be limited to, the following: (a) Physical, sexual and psychological violence occurring in

Gender-based violence includes sexual violence, physical violence, emotional and psychological violence, harmful traditional practices, socio-economic violence[29]; domestic violence; trafficking; forced or early marriage; coercion or threat to do such violence or any other form of violence which deprives the liberty and human rights of any individual.[30] It also includes both sexual and non-sexual violence.[31]

---

the family, including battering, sexual abuse of female children in the household, dowry-related violence, marital rape, female genital mutilation and other traditional practices harmful to women, non-spousal violence and violence related to exploitation;(b) Physical, sexual and psychological violence occurring within the general community, including rape, sexual abuse, sexual harassment and intimidation at work, in educational institutions and elsewhere, trafficking in women and forced prostitution; (c) Physical, sexual and psychological violence perpetrated or condoned by the State, wherever it occurs"; see UNGA Reso. (1993), 48/104, UN Doc. A/RES/48/104; available at: http://www.un.org/documents/ga/res/48/a48r104.htm (accessed on 11 December 2020); Hammond, Alicia, et al. (2019), n.9. Also see, *General Recommendation 19 of the Committee of CEDAW, 1992*, "6. The Convention in article 1 defines discrimination against women. The definition of discrimination includes gender-based violence, that is, violence that is directed against a woman because she is a woman or that affects women disproportionately. It includes acts that inflict physical, mental or sexual harm or suffering, threats of such acts, coercion and other deprivations of liberty. Gender-based violence may breach specific provisions of the Convention, regardless of whether those provisions expressly mention violence.

7. Gender-based violence, which impairs or nullifies the enjoyment by women of human rights and fundamental freedoms under general international law or under human rights conventions, is discrimination within the meaning of article 1 of the Convention. These rights and freedoms include:

(a) The right to life;

(b) The right not to be subject to torture or to cruel, inhuman or degrading treatment or punishment;

(c) The right to equal protection according to humanitarian norms in time of international or internal armed conflict;

(d) The right to liberty and security of person;

(e) The right to equal protection under the law;

(f) The right to equality in the family;

(g) The right to the highest standard attainable of physical and mental health;

(h) The right to just and favourable conditions of work;" available at: http://www.un.org/womenwatch/daw/cedaw/recommendations/recomm.htm (accessed on 11 December 2020); see, *Beijing Declaration and Platform for Action, 1995,* para 113 explains: "The term "violence against women" means any act of gender-based violence that results in, or is likely to result in, physical, sexual or psychological harm or suffering to women, including threats of such acts, coercion or arbitrary deprivation of liberty, whether occurring in public or private life;" available at: https://www.un.org/en/events/pastevents/pdfs/Beijing_Declaration_and_Platform_for_Action.pdf (accessed on 20 December 2020).

[29] Ibid.

[30] OHCHR (2014), "Sexual and Gender Based Violence in the Context of Transnational Justice;" available at: http://www.ohchr.org/Documents/Issues/Women/WRGS/OnePagers/Sexual_and_gender- based_violence.pdf (accessed on 11 December 2020).

[31] International Criminal Court (2014), "Policy Paper on Sexual and Gender-Based Crimes;" available at: https://www.icc-cpi.int/iccdocs/otp/OTP-Policy-Paper-on-Sexual-and-Gender-Based-Crimes--June-2014.pdf (accessed on 11 December 2020).

Sexual and Gender-Based Violence

There is no international legal instrument that defines 'sexual and gender-based violence' (SGBV). The term is constantly being used by the UN High Commissioner for Refugee (UNHCR),[32] the Office of UN High Commissioner for Human Rights (OHCHR),[33] the UN Security Council,[34] the Committee on the Elimination of All Forms of Discrimination against Women (CEDAW Committee),[35] Beijing Declaration and Platform for Action[36] the UN Women,[37] the International Committee of Red Cross (ICRC),[38] as well as in the scholarly writings.[39]

In this context, the UNHCR has defined SGBV as:

> Sexual and gender-based violence (SGBV) refers to any act that is perpetrated against a person's will and is based on gender norms and unequal power relationships. It encompasses threats of violence and coercion. It can be physical, emotional, psychological, or sexual in

---

[32] UNHCR, "Sexual and gender-based violence (SGBV) prevention and response;" available at: https://emergency.unhcr.org/entry/60283/sexual-and-gender-based-violence-sgbv-prevention-and-response (accessed on 11 December 2020).

[33] OHCHR (2017), Office of the High Commissioner of Human Rights, "Conflict-related Sexual and Gender Based Violence;" available at: http://www.ohchr.org/Documents/Countries/CF/Mapping2003-2015/Factsheet4-EN.pdf (accessed on 11 December 2020).

[34] UN SC Resolution 1960 (2010), para 15: "Encourages Member States to deploy greater numbers of female military and police personnel to United Nations peacekeeping operations, and to provide all military and police personnel with adequate training on sexual and gender-based violence, inter alia, to carry out their responsibilities"; available at: http://www.peacewomen.org/sites/default/files/sc_resolution_1960.pdf (accessed on 11 December 2020).

[35] *General Recommendation No. 30* on women in conflict prevention, conflict and post-conflict situations, para 23: "Under the Convention, States parties' obligations to prevent, investigate and punish trafficking and sexual and gender-based violence are reinforced by international criminal law,...", 38. The Committee recommends that States parties: (c) Ensure women's and girls' access to justice; adopt gender-sensitive investigative procedures to address sexual and gender-based violence; available at: http://www.ohchr.org/documents/hrbodies/cedaw/gcomments/cedaw.c.cg.30.pdf (accessed on 11 December 2020).

[36] UN (1995), *Beijing Declaration and Platform for Action, Fourth World Conference on Women*, 15 September 1995, A/CONF.177/20 (1995) and A/CONF.177/20/Add.1 (1995). In fact, para 100 of the Declaration states: "Sexual and gender-based violence, including physical and psychological abuse, trafficking in women and girls, and other forms of abuse and sexual exploitation place girls and women at high risk of physical and mental trauma, disease and unwanted pregnancy. Such situations often deter women from using health and other services;" available at: http://hrlibrary.umn.edu/instree/e5dplw.htm#one (accessed on 11 December 2020).

[37] UN Women (2015), *A Framework to Underpin Action to Prevent Violence against Women;* available at: prevention_framework_unwomen_nov2015.pdf (accessed on 18 February 2021).

[38] ICRC (2016), "Q&A: sexual violence in armed conflict;" available at: https://www.icrc.org/en/document/sexual-violence-armed-conflict-questions-and-answers (accessed on 11 December 2020).

[39] Holmes, Georgina (2014), *Women and War in Rwanda: Gender, Media and the Representation of Genocide,* New York: I.B.Tauris.

> nature, and can take the form of a denial of resources or access to services. It inflicts harm on women, girls, men, and boys.[40]

Thus, the term refers to any harmful act that is perpetrated against one person's will, and based on, hitherto, socially ascribed (gender) differences between males and females. It includes acts that inflict physical, mental, or sexual harm or suffering, threats of such acts, coercion and other deprivations of liberty, whether occurring in public or in private life.[41]

According to the OHCHR, SGBV means:

> Sexual violence is a form of gender-based violence and encompasses any sexual act, attempt to obtain a sexual act, unwanted sexual comments or advances, or acts to traffic, or otherwise directed against a person's sexuality using coercion, by any person regardless of their relationship to the victim, in any setting. Sexual violence takes multiple forms and includes rape, sexual abuse, forced pregnancy, forced sterilization, forced abortion, forced prostitution, trafficking, sexual enslavement, forced circumcision, castration, and forced nudity.[42]
>
> Gender-based violence is considered to be any harmful act directed against individuals or groups of individuals on the basis of their gender. It may include sexual violence, domestic violence, trafficking, forced/ early marriage and harmful traditional practices.[43]

There are many other international documents, and reports, of different institutional actors wherein SGBV has been defined.[44] For instance, SGBV has been defined by the ICRC as follows:

---

[40] UNHCR (2011), "Sexual and Gender Based Violence;" available at:http://www.unhcr.org/sexual-and-gender-based-violence.html (accessed on 11 December 2020).

[41] UNHCR (2011), "Action against Sexual and Gender-Based Violence: An Updated Strategy", "Although the terms gender-based violence (GBV) and sexual and gender-based violence (SGBV) are often used interchangeably, UNHCR consciously uses the latter to emphasise the urgency of protection interventions that address the criminal character and disruptive consequences of sexual violence for victims/survivors and their families;" available at: http://www.unhcr.org/4e1d5aba9.pdf (accessed on 11 December 2020).

[42] OHCHR (2014), "Sexual and gender-based violence in the context of transitional justice;" available at: http://ohchr.org/Documents/Issues/Women/WRGS/OnePagers/Sexual_and_gender-based_violence.pdf (accessed on 11 December 2020).

[43] Ibid.

[44] Barrett, Helen and Marshall, Julie (2017), *Understanding Sexual and Gender- Based Violence against Refugees with a Communication Disability and challenges to accessing appropriate support*, Manchester Metropolitan University. It states (page 7): "The term SGBV describes any harmful behavior that is imposed on a person because of their gender. It primarily relates to abuse against women and girls, but can include harmful acts against men and boys. There are many types of SGBV that include physical, sexual and psychological violence or withholding of rights. This includes control of finances and food and exposure to threats or coercion. It can be experienced as part of an intimate relationship or committed by an external known or unknown perpetrator"; available at: http://www2.mmu.ac.uk/media/mmuacuk/content/documents/hpsc/research/understanding-SGBV-in-refugees-with-a-communication-disability-literature-review.pdf (accessed on 11 December 2020). Also see, Swiss Agency for Development and Cooperation (2016), *Operational concept: Sexual and Gender-based Violence (SGBV) 2017–2020*, Swiss Humanitarian Aid Department (2016). It states (page 2) that: "SGBV is an umbrella term for any harmful act perpetrated against a person's will that is based on socially ascribed (gender) differences between males

(i) *Sexual violence*: Acts of a sexual nature committed against any person by force, threat of force or coercion. Coercion can be caused by circumstances such as fear of violence, duress, detention, psychological oppression or abuse of power. The force, threat of force or coercion can also be directed against another person. Sexual violence also comprises acts of a sexual nature committed by taking advantage of a coercive environment or a person's incapacity to give genuine consent. It furthermore includes acts of a sexual nature a person is caused to engage in by force, threat of force or coercion, against that person or another person, or by taking advantage of a coercive environment or the person's incapacity to give genuine consent. Sexual violence encompasses acts such as rape, sexual slavery, enforced prostitution, forced pregnancy or enforced sterilization. NB: For sexual violence as defined above to fall under the scope of application of international humanitarian law, it needs to take place in the context of and be associated with an armed conflict.

(ii) *Gender-based violence*: An umbrella term for any harmful act that results in, or is likely to result in, physical, sexual or psychological harm or suffering to a woman, man, girl or boy on the basis of their gender. Gender-based violence is a result of gender inequality and abuse of power. Gender-based violence includes but is not limited to sexual violence, domestic violence, trafficking, forced or early marriage, forced prostitution and sexual exploitation and abuse.[45]

Similarly, the UN Development Fund for Women (UNIFEM) has provided an explanation of SGBV on the basis of its baseline survey in Rwanda.[46]

---

and females3. It includes rape, sexual assault, intimate partner/domestic violence, sexual exploitation (including through trafficking), sexual slavery, forced prostitution, harmful traditional practices (female-genital mutilation, honor killings, early and forced marriage) and negative coping mechanisms (transactional sex, early and forced marriage). While women and girls are primarily affected by SGBV, men and boys, LGBTI are also victims;" available at: https://www.eda.admin.ch/dam/countries/countries-content/jordan/en/Operational-concept-SGBV_English.pdf (accessed on 11 December 2020).

[45] These definitions were arrived at after the ICRC's consultations with National Societies and the other components of the Movement during 2014–2015. It was worked out by the coordination group on sexual and gender-based violence (SGBV), ICRC (2015), *Sexual and gender-based violence: joint action on prevention and response:* Background report, pp. 1–2 at footnote 1; 32nd International Conference of the Red Cross and Red Crescent, Geneva, Switzerland, 8–10 December 2015; Doc.32IC/15/19.3; available at: http://rcrcconference.org/app//uploads/2015/04/32IC-Background-report-on-Sexual-and-gender-based-violence_EN.pdf (accessed on 19 February 2021).

[46] UNIFEM (2008), "Baseline survey on Sexual and Gender-Based Violence in Rwanda" states, "Operational definition of sexual gender-based violence: In brief, sexual gender-based violence may be defined as violent behaviour that is linked to sex, whose compelling forces are related to family, economic, social, and cultural precedents that encourage unequal power relationships between men and women, conferring an attitude of superiority and domination on the perpetrator and an attitude of subordination on the victim;" available at: http://www.refworld.org/pdfid/4bcc18ad2.pdf (accessed on 11 December 2020).

Usage of Different Nomenclatures

Different nomenclatures are also used to denote SGBV, such as 'sexual and other forms of gender-based violence',[47] 'sexual and gender-based crimes',[48] 'rape and other sexual violence',[49] 'sexual violence', 'gender-based violence', 'gender-based abuses', 'sexual offences and gender violence',[50] 'sexual harassment', 'conflict-related sexual violence', 'sexual violence and wartime rape',[51] 'sexual slavery',[52] 'conflict related sexual violence',[53] 'gender-targeted violence',[54] 'rape and sexual violence'[55] and 'mass rapes and genocide'.[56]

Therefore, it can be said that the term 'sexual and gender-based violence' (SGBV) is broader than only 'sexual violence or only 'gender-based violence.' The term SGBV includes all forms of 'sexual violence' as well as 'gender-based violence' at the same time. Thus, violence could be of the nature of 'sexual' and 'gender-based'. Though all the above nomenclatures are different, their differentiation lies only in

---

47 UN Office for the Coordination for the Humanitarian Affairs (2020), *End Gender Based Violence in Humanitarian Crisis*; Virtual Zoom Event on UN Web TV, 28 September 2020; available at: https://www.unocha.org/end-gender-based-violence-humanitarian-crises (accessed on 19 February 2021).

48 ICC (2014), *ICC Policy paper on sexual and gender-based crimes*; available at: https://www.icc-cpi.int/iccdocs/otp/otp-policy-paper-on-sexual-and-gender-based-crimes--june-2014.pdf (accessed on 11 December 2020).

49 Amnesty International (2015), *Sexual and gender-based violence in the Pacific*; available at: https://www.amnesty.org.nz/sexual-and-gender-based-violence-pacific (accessed on 11 December 2020).

50 Human Rights Watch (2008), "Zambia: Curbing Sexual and Gender-Based Violence;" available at: https://www.hrw.org/news/2008/12/16/zambia-curbing-sexual-and-gender-based-violence (accessed on 11 December 2020).

51 Amnesty International (2012), *Global campaign targets rape in conflict zones*; available at: https://www.amnesty.org/en/latest/news/2012/11/global-campaign-targets-rape-conflict-zones/ (accessed on 19 February 2021).

52 Caeymaex, Olivia (2014), United Nations University, *How to Stop Sexual Slavery in Conflict Zones*; available at: http://unu.edu/publications/articles/how-to-stop-sexual-slavery-in-conflict-zones.html (accessed on 11 December 2020).

53 Germano, Rebecca (2018), *Conflict-Related Sexual Violence: The Darker Side of the History and the Untold History of Conflicts under International Human Rights Law*, University of Cyprus; available at: https://repository.gchumanrights.org/bitstream/handle/20.500.11825/852/Germano.pdf?isAllowed=y&sequence=1 (accessed on 19 February 2021).

54 Manjoo and McRaith (2011), "Gender-Based Violence and Justice in Conflict and Post-Conflict Areas," *Cornell International Law Journal*, 44: 11.

55 Roca, Inés Weinberg de. (2010), "Persecuting Gender Based and Sexual Crimes against Women: The Role of the International Courts and Criminal Tribunals," in Eboe-Osuji Chile (eds.) *In Protecting Humanity: in International Law and Policy in Honour of Navanethem Pillay*, Boston: Martinus Nijhoff.

56 Prins, Gladys (2017), *Mass Rape and Genocide: International Lawand the Increased Need for Deterrence Regarding War Crimes Committed During Civil Conflict*. Master's thesis, Harvard Extension School; available at: http://nrs.harvard.edu/urn-3:HUL.InstRepos:33826641 (accessed on 19 February 2021).

theory and they fall under the rubric of SGBV. A perusal of different studies shows that international actors are now using the term SGBV since it shows the gravity and seriousness of the issue. SGBV is gender-neutral. Different organizations or actors use different terms mentioned above synonymously to address the issue of SGBV against women.[57] Hence, for the purposes of this study, a common rubric SGBV against women and girls is used. It comprises terms such as sexual violence (SV), gender-based violence (GBV), and violence against women (VAW) that are used interchangeably.[58]

The concept of violence, in general, includes all forms of violence. The term gender-based violence is used specifically to show that it is different from the common sense of violence. It denotes violence against an individual or any group of individuals who are targeted because of their gender. Though sexual violence is more specific and exclusively sexual, it is also a form of gender-based violence. Gender-based violence may or may not be sexual but sexual violence is always a form of gender-based violence. Violence against women is named as gender-based violence or sexual violence, etc. Several international actors have called SGBV as gender neutral and treat it as a serious cause of concern.[59] Though GBV and SV against women are used interchangeably, yet many scholars treat SV as a form of GBV.[60] This study has used the term SGBV to denote all forms of GBV with due emphasis upon SV against girls and women.

Sexual and Gender-Based Crime

Sexual and gender-based crimes (SGBC) are forms of SGBV that are treated as a crime. Though all forms of SGBV are not treated as crime explicitly, only some forms of SGBV are denoted as a crime under international criminal law. For example, Article 7 and 8 of the 1998, Rome Statute of International Criminal Court (ICC) has listed some forms of SGBV such as genocide and crime against humanity. Most of the literature, especially the policy papers of the ICC, have used the terminology 'gender-based crime' (GBC) as a gender-neutral terminology. It includes both sexual and non-sexual forms of GBV. Sexual crimes such as rape, enforced prostitution, and other forms of sexual violence are specifically mentioned in the Rome Statute. The important criterion for 'sexual crime' is that the act should be sexual either by direct physical contact or non-physical contact, e.g., forced nudity.[61]

---

[57] UNHCR (2016), n. 1.

[58] UNHCR (2003), n. 4.

[59] UNHCR (2016), n. 1.

[60] Kamau, Evelyn (2011), "Domestic Adjudication of Sexual and Gender-Based Violence in Armed Conflict: Considerations for Prosecutors and Judges," *Afr. J. Legal Stud,* 4:85.

[61] ICC (2014), "Policy Paper on Sexual and Gender-Based Crimes" (June 2014) states, "Sexual crimes ' that fall under the subject-matter jurisdiction of the ICC are listed under articles 7(1)(g), 8(2)(b)(xxii), and 8(2)(e)(vi) of the Statute, and described in the Elements of Crimes (Elements);"

It has also been argued that the term 'gender' and 'sex' have different meanings. In many of the cases, we conflate 'gender,' 'sex,' and 'women.' It is felt that 'gender-based' crimes are the forms of crimes where individuals are targeted because of their socially constructed gender norms (hitherto maleness and femaleness). Though in practice, GBC includes both sexual and non-sexual violence, but some crimes are mostly inflicted because of the biological sex of the victims, e.g., forced pregnancy and perpetrated against women only. Thus, some specific acts of SGBV are perpetrated against women only because of their sex or gender.

In view of the above, sexual violence (SV), gender-based violence (GBV) and sexual and gender-based violence (SGBV) against women are used inter-changeably. As such the only use of 'gender-based' or 'sexual' crimes or violence is not enough. SGBC is also serving all the purposes of gender analysis especially since it is a crime based on gender norms and inequalities in a particular society. It can be said that the discourse on SGBV or crimes against women is influenced by the gender-based norms and inequalities that prevail at a particular time in a society.

Gender-based norms and inequalities are graphic reality that varies from society to society. Therefore, it helps to provide broader meaning to SGBV in dealing with the perpetrators who are part of a particular society. There are primarily two sets of people in defining gender: (i) socially constructed 'gender' that remains fluid in nature as well as based on time and location. (ii) defining gender on the basis of sex only that excludes any consideration of sexual orientation. Therefore, it seems, consequential physical and mental harm, societal stigma, etc. associated with SV need to be treated as SGBC because these can target against any group to destroy it.[62]

Technology-Facilitated Gender-Based Violence

With the development of information and communication technology (ICT) the terminology 'technology-facilitated SGBV' 'gender-based violence online' (GBVO) are becoming familiar terms. There is a growing concern about cyber security and special circumstances that prevails in the digital world. The World Bank, the UN Office on Drugs and Crime; different human rights institutions like International Centre for Research on Women (ICRW) and some scholars have shown concern regarding technology facilitated (TF) SGBV. It means:

---

available at: https://www.icc-cpi.int/iccdocs/otp/OTP-Policy-Paper-on-Sexual-and-Gender-Based-Crimes--June-2014.pdf (accessed on 11 December 2020).

62 Oosterveld, Valerie (2018), "The ICC Policy Paper on Sexual and Gender-Based Crimes: A Crucial Step for International Criminal Law," *William & Mary Journal of Women and the Law*, 24(3); available at: https://scholarship.law.wm.edu/cgi/viewcontent.cgi?article=1476&context=wmjowl (accessed on 28 March 2021).

the use of information and communication technology (ICT) to facilitate or extend sexual and gender-based harms to victims, including technology enabled sexual assault, image-based sexual abuse, cyber stalking and criminal harassment, online sexual harassment, and gender-based harassment and hate speech.[63]

Similarly, according to ICRW, technology facilitated SGBV means:

Technology facilitated GBV is action by one or more people that harms others based on their sexual or gender identity or by enforcing harmful gender norms. This action is carried out using the internet and/or mobile technology and includes stalking, bullying, sexual harassment, defamation, hate speech and exploitation.[64]

In 2018, the Special Rapporteur on Violence against Women, sought to define online violence and explain its causes and consequences against women and girls from a human rights perspective, as:

The definition of online violence against women therefore extends to any act of gender-based violence against women that is committed, assisted or aggravated in part or fully by the use of ICT, such as mobile phones and smartphones, the internet, social media platforms or email, against a woman because she is a woman, or affects women disproportionately.[65]

In most of the cases, women, girls and LGBTI people are subjected to online or technology facilitated SGBV. In fact, women and girls from some special groups are disproportionately affected such as disable women, women from ethnic, racial, economic status, and specific religious groups. It severely impacts on the mental health of the survivors. The survivors suffer emotional distress, loss of status, low productivity and generates suicidal tendencies.

Culture

According to lexical meaning, 'culture' means the "way of life, especially the general customs and beliefs, of a particular group of people at a particular time".[66] According

---

63 UNODC (2020), "Gender-based interpersonal cybercrime"; available at: https://www.unodc.org/e4j/en/cybercrime/module-12/key-issues/gender-based-interpersonal-cybercrime.html (accessed on 28 March 2021), see also, Hammond, Alicia, et al. (2019), n. 9.

64 ICRW (2018), "Technology-Facilitated Gender-Based Violence: What is it, and how do We Measure it?"; available at: https://www.icrw.org/wp-content/uploads/2018/07/ICRW_TFGBVMarketing_Brief_v8-Web.pdf (accessed on 28 March 2021).

65 Human Rights Council (2018), "Report of the Special Rapporteur on violence against women, its causes and consequences on online violence against women and girls from a human rights perspective", UN Doc. A/HRC/38/47, 18 June 2018; available at: https://digitallibrary.un.org/record/1641160 (accessed on 28 March 2021). Similarly, in a poll carried out by Amnesty International (2017), it was revealed that approximately one-fourth of the 4,000 women surveyed in the United States, United Kingdom, Denmark, Sweden, Spain, Italy, and Poland experienced some form of online abuse (e.g., cyber harassment) at least once; see UNDOC (2020), n.63.

66 Cambridge Dictionary, "culture;" available at: https://dictionary.cambridge.org/dictionary/english/culture (accessed on 11 December 2020).

to the Committee of the Economic, Social and Cultural Rights (ECOSOC), "Culture is a broad, inclusive concept encompassing all manifestations of human existence".[67] There is no absolute legal definition of culture. As a result, legal scholars and the judges end up using the anthropological and sociological meaning of culture.[68] In 1874, an anthropologist E.B. Tyler defined 'culture' as: "That complex whole which includes knowledge, belief, art, morals, custom, and any other capabilities and habits that acquired by man as member of society".[69] In a way, the term 'culture' is commonly used to denote a society or community where most of the people live and think indifferently. A group of people or community with the same culture forms society and carry a collective identity.

The concept of culture is not only confined within the boundary of any national legal system, but it has become part of the international discourse. Thus, culture varies from national to the international system on the basis of criteria such as: (i) Ethnic and religious differences; (ii) The diversity of institutional culture, i.e., family, community, workplace, church to State; and (iii) International or global culture. It includes the *culture of universality* of human rights. In this context, the States practices and the existing cultures within the legal systems of the States have contributed in shaping the notion of global culture. There is an institutionalized 'culture of patriarchy' that forms a major obstacle, undermines the rights of women and girls and promotes all kinds of SGBV.

Ironically, it is the patriarchal culture that traumatises women from cradle-to-grave and remains antithetical to the very culture of human rights itself. Thus, 'culture' may have different meaning, on the basis of facts and circumstances. However, for the purpose of this study, 'culture' has been used to denote all the 'cultures' in the world equally. As such the study encompasses universal patriarchal culture or culture that undermines the concept of universal human rights especially the human rights of women.[70]

---

[67] ECOSOC (2009), *General Comments 21 of the Committee of ECOSOC*, UN Doc. E/C.12/GC/21, 21 December 2009; "In the Committee's view, culture is a broad, inclusive concept encompassing all manifestations of human existence. The expression "cultural life" is an explicit reference to culture as a living process, historical, dynamic and evolving, with a past, a present and a future…The Committee considers that culture, for the purpose of implementing article 15 (1) (a), encompasses, inter alia, ways of life, language, oral and written literature, music and song, non-verbal communication, religion or belief systems, rites and ceremonies, sport and games, methods of production or technology, natural and man-made environments, food, clothing and shelter and the arts, customs and traditions through which individuals, groups of individuals and communities express their humanity and the meaning they give to their existence, and build their world view representing their encounter with the external forces affecting their lives. Culture shapes and mirrors the values of well-being and the economic, social and political life of individuals, groups of individuals and communities" (paragraphs 11 and 13); available at: https://undocs.org/en/E/C.12/GC/21 (accessed on 24 March 2021).

[68] Niezen, Ronald (2003), "Culture and the Judiciary: The Meaning of the Culture Concept as a Source of Aboriginal Rights in Canada," *Canadian Journal of Law and Society*, 18 (1): 1–26.

[69] Gusfield, Joseph (2006), "Culture", *Contexts*, 5 (1): 43–44.

[70] Raday, Frances (2003), "Culture, Religion, and Gender," *International Journal of Constitutional law,* 1(4): 663–715.

Tradition, Custom and Customary Law

The lexical meaning of tradition is, "a belief, custom or way of doing something that has existed for a long time among a particular group of people; a set of these beliefs or customs".[71] Similarly, 'custom' connotes: "A traditional and widely accepted way of behaving or doing something that is specific to a particular society, place, or time".[72] In that sense customary law comprises a set of customs, practices, and beliefs that are accepted as obligatory rules of conduct by indigenous people and local communities. As a corollary, customary law would refer to "group of customs that are recognized and shared collectively by a community, people, and tribe, ethnic or religious group".[73]

Article 38(1) (b) of the Statute of the International Court of Justice (ICJ) also recognizes customary international law (CIL)[74] that consists of actual States practices and *opinio juris sive necessitatis*. CIL plays a crucial role in giving effect to the principles of State responsibility, interpretation of treaties and development of specialized branches of international law such as International Human Rights Law (IHRL) and International Humanitarian Law (IHL).[75] In fact, custom forms one of the primary sources of both international law and national law.

Religion and Religious Practices

There are various meanings of religion on the basis of different cultures.[76] The lexical meaning of religion is the "belief in and worship of superhuman controlling power, especially a personal God or gods".[77] There are scholars who have analysed the meaning of 'religion.' Harold Koenig, et al. have observed:

> Religion involves beliefs, practices, and rituals related to *transcendent*...Religion is a multi-dimensional construct that includes beliefs, behaviours, rituals, and ceremonies that may

---

[71] Oxford Lerner's Dictionaries, "Tradition;" available at: https://www.oxfordlearnersdictionaries.com/definition/english/tradition (accessed on 11 December 2020).

[72] Oxford Lerner's Dictionaries, "Custom;" available at: https://en.oxforddictionaries.com/definition/custom(accessed on 11 December 2020).

[73] WIPO, "Customary Law and Traditional Knowledge;" available at: http://www.wipo.int/edocs/pubdocs/en/wipo_pub_tk_7.pdf (accessed on 11 December 2020).

[74] Article 38(1) (b) of the Statute of the International Court of Justice 1945 states, "International custom, as evidence of a general practice accepted as law;" available at: http://legal.un.org/avl/pdf/ha/sicj/icj_statute_e.pdf (accessed on 11 December 2020).

[75] Chimni (2018), "Customary International Law: A Third World Perspective," *The American Journal of International Law*, 112(1): 5.

[76] Raday, Frances (2003), n. 70.

[77] Oxford Learner Dictionaries, "Religion;" available at: https://en.oxforddictionaries.com/definition/religion (accessed on 11 December 2020).

held or practices in private or public settings, but are in some way derived from established traditions that developed over time within community.[78]

The right to religion is a human right as laid down in Article 18 of the Universal Declaration of Human Rights.[79] Still, the question relating to 'essential religious practice' remains a debatable issue.[80] Though there are different religions, this study has treated all the religions as monotheistic in terms of the rights of women and denoted as a cultural institution. It has focused on the religious practices that promote patriarchal religion and encourage SGBV against women.[81]

Harmful Cultural Practices

There is no specific definition of 'harmful cultural practices' or 'harmful practices' in international law. Also, different terminologies are used to address the issues. There are a few regional instruments that defined harmful cultural practices. The international instrument that has clarified 'harmful practices' includes the Committee on the Elimination of Discrimination against Women and the Committee on the Rights of the Child, in their joint general recommendation no. 31 (2014) has explained the criteria for 'harmful practices', as:

> Harmful practices and behaviours that are grounded on discrimination on the basis of sex, gender, age, and other grounds as well as multiple and or intersecting forms of discrimination that often involve violence and cause physical and or psychological harm or suffering. The harm that these practices cause to the victims suppress the immediate physical and mental consequences and often has the purpose or effect of impairing the recognition, enjoyment, and exercise of the human rights and fundamental freedoms of women and children. There is also a negative impact on their dignity, physical, psychosocial and moral integrity and development, participation, health, educational, economic and social status.[82]

---

[78] Harold Koenig, et al. (2012), "Handbook of Religion and Health", New York: Oxford University Press, cited in Koening, Harold (2012), *ISRN Psychiatry*, 2012: 278,730; available at: https://www.ncbi.nlm.nih.gov/pmc/articles/PMC3671693/ (accessed on 15 December 2020).

[79] Article 18 states: "Everyone has the right to freedom of thought, conscience and religion; this right includes freedom to change his religion or belief, and freedom, either alone or in community with others and in public or private, to manifest his religion or belief in teaching, practice, worship and observance"; see, UN, The Universal Declaration of Human Rights, 1948; available at: https://www.un.org/en/universal-declaration-human-rights/ (accessed on 15 December 2020).

[80] Kantaru Rajeevaru v. Indian Young Lawyers Association Thr. Its General Secretary and Ors, The Supreme Court of India Civil Original Jurisdiction Review Petition (Civil) No. 3358/2018 In Writ Petition (Civil) No. 373/2006; available at: https://www.sci.gov.in/pdf/JUD_6.pdf (accessed on 24 March 2021).

[81] Raday, Frances (2003), n. 70.

[82] UN, CEDAW (2014), "Joint general recommendation No. 31 of the Committee on the Elimination of Discrimination against Women/general comment No. 18 of the Committee on the Rights of the Child on harmful practices"; UN Doc. CEDAW/C/GC/31-CRC/C/GC/18, 14 November 2014 (Paragraph 15: V. Criteria for determining harmful practices); available at: https://undocs.org/CEDAW/C/GC/31/CRC/C/GC/18 (accessed on 28 March 2021). Also see, Article 5 on "Elimination of Harmful Practices" of the Protocol to The African Charter on Human and Peoples' Rights

Similarly, Article 21 of the African Charter on the Rights and Welfare of the Child (1990) provides:

> Protection against Harmful Social and Cultural Practices: 1. State Parties to present Charter shall take all appropriate measures to eliminate harmful social and cultural practices affecting the welfare, dignity, normal growth and development of the child and in particular; (a) those customs and practices prejudicial to the health or life of the child; and (b) those customs and practices discriminatory to the child on the grounds of sex or other status...[83]

Harmful cultural practices (HCP) or harmful traditional practices (HTP) have been mostly addressed by the UN for many years. It includes female genital mutilation (FGM), early or child marriage, son preference, dowry price, 'honour' crimes etc.[84] There is variance as regards use of terminology. Still, all different terms such as 'harmful practices', 'cultural practices,'[85] 'harmful traditional practices,'[86] 'customary practices,' 'harmful cultural practices',[87] 'religious practices' etc. have been used interchangeably by the human rights actors. In essence, they all refer to the inerently discriminatory practices against women and girls. In view this, the study has also used all these terms inter-changeably.[88]

Victims or Survivors

'Victim' or 'survivor' is the person who has been subjected to SGBV. The term 'victim' is used in the field of law to address the victims of sexual violence during

on the Rights of Women in Africa; available at: https://www.ohchr.org/Documents/Issues/Women/WG/ProtocolontheRightsofWomen.pdf (accessed on 28 March 2021).

[83] UN (1990), *The African Charter on the Rights and Welfare of the Child, 1990;* available at: https://www.un.org/en/africa/osaa/pdf/au/afr_charter_rights_welfare_child_africa_1990.pdf (accessed on 11 December 2020).

[84] UN (2009), Division for the Advancement of Women United Nations Economic Commission for Africa Addis Ababa, *Harmful Traditional Practices Against Women And Legislation*; UN DOC. EGM/GPLHP/2009/EP.07, 11 May 2009; available at: https://www.un.org/womenwatch/daw/egm/vaw_legislation_2009/Expert%20Paper%20EGMGPLHP%20_Morissanda%20Kouyate_.pdf (accessed on 24 March 2021).

[85] UNMIL (2015), *An assessment of human rights issues emanating from harmful traditional practices in Liberia*; available at: https://unmil.unmissions.org/sites/default/files/harmful_traditional_practices_final_-_18_dec._2015.pdf (accessed on 28 March 2021).

[86] UN (2009), n. 84.

[87] UNMIL (2015), n. 85.

[88] Longman, Chia, et al. (2015) *Interrogating Harmful Cultural Practices: Gender, Culture and Coercion*, UK: Ashgate Publishing. Also see, OHCHR (1995), *Fact Sheet No. 23, Harmful Traditional Practices Affecting the Health of Women and Children*, August 1995, No. 23, available at: https://www.refworld.org/docid/479477410.html (accessed 28 March 2021); UN (2010), "15 years of The United Nations Special Rapporteur on Violence against Women, Its Causes and Consequences (1994–2009)"; available at: https://www.ohchr.org/_layouts/15/WopiFrame.aspx?sourcedoc=/Documents/Issues/Women/15YearReviewofVAWMandate.pdf&action=default&DefaultItemOpen=1 (accessed on 28 March 2021).

conflicts or displacement.[89] The UN GAR 60/147 (2005) on the victims of gross violations of IHRL and serious violations of IHL defines:

> victims are persons, who individually or collectively suffered harm…includes the immediate family or dependents of the direct victim and persons who have suffered harm in intervening to assist victims in distress or to prevent victimization.[90]

Rule 85 of the Rules of Procedure and Evidence of the Rome Statute, 1998 also defines it as: "Victims means natural persons who have suffered harm…include organizations or institutions that have sustained direct harm…".[91]

In 1985, the UN General Assembly adopted a *Declaration of Basic Principles of Justice for Victims of Crime and Abuse of Power* that defines 'victim of crime' as "a person who has directly suffered and also includes the immediate family and dependents of the direct victim and persons who have suffered harm in intervening to assist victims in distress or to prevent victimization".[92] There are some national laws like the Indian Criminal Procedure Code, 1973, Section 2 (wa) that defines the

---

[89] UNHCR (2003), n.4; see also, UNHCR (2016), n. 1.

[90] UN (2005), *Basic Principles and Guidelines on the Right to a Remedy and Reparation for Victims of Gross Violations of International Human Rights Law and Serious Violations of International Humanitarian Law*; UNGA Res. A/RES/60/147 of 16 December 2005; Paragraph V.8 of the resolution explicitly defines 'victims' as: "For purposes of the present document, victims are persons who individually or collectively suffered harm, including physical or mental injury, emotional suffering, economic loss or substantial impairment of their fundamental rights, through acts or omissions that constitute gross violations of international human rights law, or serious violations of international humanitarian law. Where appropriate, and in accordance with domestic law, the term "victim" also includes the immediate family or dependents of the direct victim and persons who have suffered harm in intervening to assist victims in distress or to prevent victimization"; available at: https://undocs.org/A/RES/60/147 (accessed on 24 March 2021).

[91] ICC (2005), *Rules of Procedure and Evidence*; Rule 85 provides definition of victims for the purposes of the Statute and the Rules of Procedure and Evidence as: (a) "Victims" means natural persons who have suffered harm as a result of the commission of any crime within the jurisdiction of the Court; (b) Victims may include organizations or institutions that have sustained direct harm to any of their property which is dedicated to religion, education, art or science or charitable purposes, and to their historic monuments, hospitals and other places and objects for humanitarian purposes"; available at: https://www.icc-cpi.int/iccdocs/pids/legal-texts/rulesprocedureevidenceeng.pdf (accessed on 24 March 2021). Also see, the UN Committee against Torture (2012), General Comment No. 3, UN Doc. CAT/C/GC/3, 13 December 2012; available at: https://www.refworld.org/docid/5437cc274.html (accessed on 24 March 2021); UNODC (2015), *Doha Declaration*; available at: https://www.unodc.org/res/ji/import/international_standards/doha_declaration/doha_declaration.pdf (accessed on 24 March 2021).

[92] UN (1985), *Declaration of Basic Principles of Justice for Victims of Crime and Abuse of Power*, the General Assembly resolution 40/34 of 29 November 1985. It defines *Victims of crime* (A) as: "1. "Victims" means persons who, individually or collectively, have suffered harm, including physical or mental injury, emotional suffering, economic loss or substantial impairment of their fundamental rights, through acts or omissions that are in violation of criminal laws operative within Member States, including those laws proscribing criminal abuse of power. 2. A person may be considered a victim, under this Declaration, regardless of whether the perpetrator is identified, apprehended, prosecuted or convicted and regardless of the familial relationship between the perpetrator and the victim. The term "victim" also includes, where appropriate, the immediate family or dependants of the direct victim and persons who have suffered harm in intervening to assist victims in distress or to prevent victimization. 3. The provisions contained herein shall be applicable to all, without distinction of

term victim as: "Victim means a person who has suffered any loss or injury caused by reason of the act or omission for which the accused person has been charged and the expression 'victim' includes his or her guardian or legal heir".[93] Also, how far secondary victimization (occurs through the attitude of the institutions or individuals towards the victims) regarding SGBV would be recognized or accepted remains a question.[94] Still, there is no uniform definition of 'victim'. It is a debateable issue whether and how far the dependents of the victims or survivors are also treated as victims or survivors as the issue is not only devastating for the survivors but also their families, communities and States.[95]

The Committee against Torture provides in the general comment no. 3 (2012) that in some cases the term survivors is preferred for the people who have suffered harm. However, 'victim' is mostly preferred since it is a legal term.[96] Some institutions such as the UNHCR have preferred the term 'survivor' because it is more preferred one in psychological or social disciplines as it implies resilience.[97] Thus, both the terminologies (victims and survivors) have been used inter-changeably in this study.

Perpetrators

The perpetrator is an individual or group of individuals, or an institution or group of institutions that directly supports, condones or inflicts SGBV. Perpetrators include an intimate partner, family members, close relatives or friends, influential community members holding the power of authority, security forces or soldiers including the peacekeepers, State or non-state actors, humanitarian workers, a person known or

---

any kind, such as race, colour, sex, age, language, religion, nationality, political or other opinion, cultural beliefs or practices, property, birth or family status, ethnic or social origin, and disability". It also describes victims of abuse of power (B.18) as: "Victims" means persons who, individually or collectively, have suffered harm, including physical or mental injury, emotional suffering, economic loss or substantial impairment of their fundamental rights, through acts or omissions that do not yet constitute violations of national criminal laws but of internationally recognized norms relating to human rights"; available at: https://www.un.org/en/genocideprevention/documents/atrocity-crimes/Doc.29_declaration%20victims%20crime%20and%20abuse%20of%20power.pdf (accessed on 24 March 2021).

[93] *The Code of Criminal Procedure*, 1973; available at: https://www.indiacode.nic.in/bitstream/123456789/1611/1/AAAA1974______02.pdf (accessed on 18 December 2020).

[94] UN (1999), *Handbook for Justice for Victims*, "Secondary victimization refers to the victimization that occurs not as a direct result of the criminal act but through the response of institutions and individuals to the victim", p. 9; available at: https://www.unodc.org/pdf/criminal_justice/UNODC_Handbook_on_Justice_for_victims.pdf (accessed on 24 March 2021).

[95] Hammond, Alicia, et al. (2019), n. 9.

[96] Committee against Torture (2012), General Comment No. 3 (2012) explains that "The term "survivors" may, in some cases, be preferred by persons who have suffered harm. The Committee uses the legal term "victims" without prejudice to other terms which may be preferable in specific contexts", n. 91.

[97] UNHCR (2016), n. 1; UNHCR (2003), n. 4.

unknown to the survivors. Perpetrators may be men or women, e.g., women forcing a child to marry or engaged in forced trafficking, etc.[98]

This term has been commonly used in the international legal instruments like the 1998, Rome Statute of the ICC. SGBV is largely rooted in an individual attitude that influences violence within the family, community, and the State.[99] It can occur both in private or public sphere.[100] In most of the cases, the perpetrators are known to the victims or persons authorized or assigned to protect the victims. It impacts negatively or creates an extra burden on the economy of States that faces economic losses in spending money on tackling the situation.[101]

Actors

Actors are individuals, group of individuals, institutions, agencies, or different organizations that are involved in preventing or responding to SGBV. Part of the actors may be local people, refugees, employees or volunteers of UN agencies, NGOs, INGOs, host government institutions, donors or any member of the international community, human rights defenders and so on.[102]

International Legal Protection

There is no legal definition of the phrase 'international legal protection.' There are many international institutions and scholars who have tried to explain the term. In this respect the Inter-Agency Standing Committee's (IASC) Gender Handbook states:

> Protection encompasses all activities aimed at obtaining full respect for the rights of the individual in accordance with the letter and the spirit of the relevant bodies of law (human rights, humanitarian and refugee law), without discrimination of kind.[103]

---

[98] ICC (1998), *the Rome Statute of the International Criminal Court*; available at: https://www.icc-cpi.int/resource-library/documents/rs-eng.pdf (accessed on 18 December 2020).

[99] UNHCR, "Sexual and Gender-based Violence;" available at: http://www.unhcr.org/sexual-and-gender-based-violence.html (accessed on 11 December 2020).

[100] UNHCR (2016), n. 1.

[101] Keygnaert, Ines, et al. (2014), "Sexual and gender-based violence in the European asylum and reception sector: a perpetuum mobile?" *European Journal of Public Health*, 1–7.

[102] UNHCR (2003), see n. 4.

[103] IASC (2006), *Gender Handbook in Humanitarian Action*, see International Legal Framework for Protection at p. 15; available at: https://interagencystandingcommittee.org/system/files/legacy_files/women_girls_boys_men_different_needs_equal_opportunities_iasc_gender_handbook_for_humanitarian_action_english_language_.pdf (accessed on 24 March 2021).

This study has used the term 'international legal protection' to denote that the rights of women and girls against SGBV are protected by international law or international legal mechanism.[104] For example, the Convention on the Elimination of All Forms of Discrimination against Women (CEDAW) provides international legal protection against any forms of discrimination against women.[105]

The term 'protection' is regarded as an "act of protecting or the state of being protected, or, the act of keeping someone or something safe from injury, damage, or loss or the state of being protected in this way".[106] It includes responsive action, remedial action and environment building. The first and foremost responsibility for international legal protection lies on the States. In this study, it is not intended to use the general meaning to examine international legal protection against SGBV. It does not seek to show that women are weak and vulnerable group of people without any right who need protection and assistance. Instead, it has been considered that as human beings, women do have rights under international law.

Therefore, women have the right to get legal protection. Here, the correlative duty to provide protection is the 'legal responsibility' rooted in international law. In most of the cases, the legal responsibility to protect the rights of the women against SGBV lies on the States or other international actors who have a responsibility under a specific international legal instrument.[107]

The need for international legal framework for protection becomes clear with reference to Hohfeld's theory of jural relationship.[108] According to this theory, the jural correlative of a right is a duty. As such if someone has a legal right, there would be someone who shall have a legal duty towards the holder of the legal right. In the specific context of SGBV, international law provides legal protection to the women by providing them legal rights and imposing commensurate legal duty on States or other actors.[109]

Historical Discourse

Violence against women is addressed in art, literature, and personal accounts of travellers and others in different regions of the world. Unfortunately, it does not find much reference in the history books. Now, people are concerned about violence

---

[104] Ibid.

[105] UN (1997), *Convention on the Elimination of All Forms of Discrimination against Women*; available at: https://www.ohchr.org/Documents/ProfessionalInterest/cedaw.pdf (accessed on 24 March 2021).

[106] Cambridge Dictionary, "Protection;" available at: https://dictionary.cambridge.org/dictionary/english/protection (accessed on 25 March 2021).

[107] IASC (2006), n. 103.

[108] Lazarev, Nikolai (2005), "Hohfeld's Analysis of Rights: An Essential Approach to a Conceptual and Practical Understanding of the nature of Rights", 9 *Murdoch University Electronic Journal of Law;* available at: http://classic.austlii.edu.au/au/journals/MurUEJL/2005/9.html#t7 (accessed on 28 March 2021).

[109] Ibid.

against women since it has been transformed into a global issue.[110] Hence, SGBV has emerged as one of the *common concerns* of our times.

Earliest accounts of 'sexual violence' have been found during the armed conflicts.[111] Ancient history especially of the ancient Greeks, Roman, Persian, Macedonia, show instances of sexual violence against women during the warfare. It was common place to see battering and sexual assaults on women both during peacetimes as well as armed conflicts resulting even in mass rapes and exploitation of the captive women by the victorious armed groups. Women were, generally, protected as civilians and most of the texts entailed protection for them. The ancient laws and customs of warfare (as reflected in *Vedas, the Ramayana, the Mahabharata, Agni Purana, Manu-Smriti, and writings of Kautilya,* etc.) inexplicably do not find mention about the existence of SGBV against women *per se*. There are, however, glaring examples of peacetime SGBV against women in the abduction of Princess Sita (later the Queen of Ayodhya) from the forest by the Lankan King Ravana and the extremely inhuman dictate in the Kaurava royal court for the dis-robing of Princess Draupadi (later the Queen of Hastinapur). Both the incidents finally contributed in the full-scale warfare against the principal perpetrators and provide finale to the epics *Ramayana* and *Mahabharata,* respectively. Hence, it shows that the women down the ages have faced the male gaze and raw treatment primarily due to their gender.

The existence of different forms of peacetime SGBV can be identified from different incidents narrated in respective literatures.[112]According to the ancient laws and customs of warfare, the civilians and civilian objects were to be protected from the adverse effect of it. Hence, women implicitly formed part of it.[113] The Roman mythology shows commission of rape against women (for instance, Sabine women in Roman mythology) as a political act. It was not an individual act against another individual. It became premeditated war plan by the Roman king Romulus.[114] The available documents of ancient Near East history have proved that rape in war was prevalent during those times as women were treated as 'spoils of war'. It, in turn, gave them legal status merely as a property.[115] In fact, during the Crusades in ancient Greece and Rome, rape was regarded as a common 'spoil of war.'[116]

---

[110] Chapman, Jane Roberts (1990), "Violence against Women as a Violation of Human Rights", *Social Justice, Criminality, Imprisonment & Women's Rights in the 1990s,* 17(2): 40.

[111] Heineman, Elizabeth D (2011), *Sexual Violence in Conflict Zones: From the Ancient World to the Era of Human Rights*, USA: University of Pennsylvania Press.

[112] Mani, V.S. (2001), "International humanitarian law: an Indo-Asian perspective, International Review of the Red Cross;" available at: https://www.icrc.org/eng/resources/documents/article/other/57jqzm.htm (accessed on 11 December 2020).

[113] Ibid.

[114] Pipe, Kennedy Caroline and Stanley (2001), "Rape in War: Lessons of the Balkan Conflicts in the 1990s," in Ken Booth (eds.), *The Kosovo Tragedy: The Human Rights Dimensions*, London: Frank Cass.

[115] Ibid.

[116] Nebesar Darren Anne (1998), "Gender-Based Violence as a Weapon", *U. C. Davis J. Int'l L. & Pol'y,* 4(2): 147.

Similarly, available evidence of the Medieval period (AD 711–1600) shows senseless attacks on civilians. Women and children were always affected by the normal outcome of the war.[117] During the sixteenth century, as seen in the writings of Hugo Grotius, women were protected as normal civilians.[118] In a vivid reflection of the prevailing notions about womenfolk, Francisco de Vitoria, sixteenth century commentator on political ethics, argued that "Rape in war is necessary for the conduct of war and act as a spur to the courage of the troops".[119] Towards the end of the long colonial era (1498–1945),[120] the humankind witnessed two World Wars during 1914–1918 and 1939–1945. These two great wars, regarded as a 'scourge' for the humankind in the preamble to the 1945 UN Charter, witnessed gross violations of all the established laws and customs of warfare.[121]

During the civil war era in the United States, the rape of slave women was rampant. In 1937, during Japanese occupation of the Chinese city of Nanking, an estimated 20,000 women were raped, sexually tortured, and murdered. This horrific incident has come to be known as "Rape of Nanking".[122] During World War II, the 'horror of war' came to the fore with the incidents of 'comfort women' or '*jugun ianfu.*' Still, in the wake of the post-war international criminal trials (especially Nurenburg and Tokyo), none of the perpetrators were punished for rape and sexual slavery.[123]

N. Basher, a historian, has opined that "Rape in war is absent in the study of war because it is too risky, too political and a subject to be dealt with comfortably by the present-day male historian".[124] Most of the time rape is not treated as a core issue to understand the subject of war. Rape against women in war is absent in the writings of many historians.[125] Many wars have witnessed horrific rapes of women, yet they are addressed by different terminologies such as 'war of gain,' 'war of fear,' 'war of doctrine' etc. Historically, rape in war has been presented merely as an inescapable by-product of war.[126]

Since 1945, the issue of 'violence against women' became one of the important parts of women's rights activism in the United Nations. It is the result of interaction between women's advocacy groups around the world and the UN system's work concerning the rights of women. Initially, some particular forms of violence against

---

[117] Pipe, Kennedy Caroline and P. Stanley (2001), n. 114.

[118] Ibid.

[119] Nebesar Darren Anne (1998), n. 116.

[120] Mani, V. S. (2001), n. 112.

[121] Ibid.

[122] Nebesar Darren Anne (1998), n. 116.

[123] Argibay, Carmen M. (2003), "Sexual Slavery and the Comfort Women of World War II," *Berkeley Journal of International Law,* 22(2): 375.

[124] Nebesar Darren Anne (1998), n. 116.

[125] Ibid.

[126] Ibid.

women, e.g., trafficking for forced prostitution; etc. was addressed in the UN.[127] This initial phase saw the focus on the civil and political rights of women. It was only in the 1960s that the UN started addressing sex-based discrimination against women in public and private spheres.[128]

Until the 1970s, the issue remained confined to violence against women in the family or domestic violence. It attained serious attention in the wake of the United Nations Decade for Women (1976–1985).[129] In the 1980s, the understanding about violence against women grew and the international community understood the link between gender and violence. The notion of violence against women shifted from violence in the family to community or public places. It was the realization that 'gender' plays a crucial role in the suppression of women and hence it encourages violence against them. The UN and civil society groups have played a crucial role in addressing the pernicious practices such as trafficking in women, sexual harassment at workplace, gender related exploitation and prostitution.

The campaigning for 'gender-based violence' (GBV) as 'violence against women' (VAW) started around this time. It came to be reflected in the crystallization of some of the international treaties and recommendations of the treaty bodies.[130] Earlier, violence against women was treated as a violation of the women' rights. In 1993, the UN World Conference on Human Rights (Vienna) declared that violation of women's rights is a violation of their human rights.[131] As a result, 'sexual violence,' 'gender-based violence', and 'violence against women' have come to be used interchangeably by the international institutional actors.[132]

In this context, SGBV has drawn attention in some specific contexts. Firstly, in the humanitarian context, it has significantly taken shape since the 1990s. Earliest initiatives of different humanitarian programmes took the form of addressing sexual violence against women in the conflict zones. It was primarily based on the refugee settings. SGBV includes much more than rape and sexual assault. It can also occur

---

[127] UN (2006), "Ending violence against women: from words to action", Study of the Secretary-General;" available at: http://www.un.org/womenwatch/daw/vaw/publications/English%20Study.pdf (accessed on 11 December 2020).

[128] UN OHCHR (2009), "15 years of The United Nations Special Rapporteur on Violence against Women, Its Causes and Consequences (1994–2009);" available at: https://www.unwomen.org/en/docs/2009/1/15-years-of-the-un-special-rapporteur-on-violence-against-women; https://www.ohchr.org/Documents/Issues/Women/15YearReviewofVAWMandate.pdf (accessed on 25 March 2021).

[129] UN (2006), n. 127.

[130] UN (2020), "Ending Violence against Women"; available at: https://www.unwomen.org/en/what-we-do/ending-violence-against-women (accessed on 28 March 2021). Also see, "The United Nations Work on Violence against Women;" available at: https://www.un.org/womenwatch/daw/news/unwvaw.html (accessed on 28 March 2021).

[131] Pickup et al. (2001), *Ending Violence against Women: A Challenge for Development and Humanitarian Work*, UK: Oxfam.

[132] FAO, "Gender-Based Violence and Livelihood Interventions: Focus on populations of humanitarian concern in the context of HIV;" available at: http://www.fao.org/fileadmin/templates/dimitra/pdf/guidance_note_gbv_livelihoods.pdf (accessed on 28 March 2021).

anywhere and at any time. It has proved lethal as a weapon of war. In 1996, in collaboration with the UNHCR, the International Rescue Committee (IRC) introduced a project titled, 'Sexual and Gender-based Violence (SGBV) Program' in refugee camps in Tanzania.[133]

The IRC program included the term gender-based violence (GBV) to differentiate between sexual violence and GBV. It sought to distinguish between common violence and GBV. It addressed non-sexual GBV, e.g., domestic violence, harmful traditional practices, etc. In 1993, the UN Declaration on the Elimination of Violence against Women has used the term GBV as synonymous of violence against women (VAW). Thus, slowly and steadily, GBV has become commonly used terminology by international institutional actors to address the deep rooted global challenge of violence and discrimination against women and girls. On the other side, the international community started addressing violence against women and girls (VAWG) in conflict zones by using the common terminology of 'SGBV'.[134] 'SGBV' was officially used for the first time by the UNHCR. In 2011, strategy document of the UNHCR clarified the reason for usage of SGBV as a generic term.[135] Cumulatively, the term SGBV shows the seriousness, urgency and disruptive consequences of sexual violence for the victims, survivors and their families.[136]

In the early 2000s, the Reproductive Health Response in Conflict (RHRC) Consortium started advocating that the humanitarian partners use the term GBV (gender-based violence) instead of SGBV to clarify that sexual violence is a component of GBV. In 2005, the Inter-Agency Standing Committee (IASC) officially adopted the term GBV in the *IASC Guidelines on Gender-Based Violence Intervention in Humanitarian Settings*. It also provides a definition of GBV that is commonly referred to in the humanitarian settings.[137] The IASC guidelines underscore that women and girls are the primary victims of GBV. But men and boys can also be the victims of GBV. The scope of the definition of GBV given by IASC is wider than the UNGA Declaration on the Elimination of Violence against Women (DEVAW).[138] The DEVAW uses GBV as synonymous of violence against women and girls. This notion has changed after the IASC guidelines. Some organizations use the term VAWG to avoid the confusion associated with the border interpretation of GBV.[139] Still, challenges remain as regards translating the terminology of GBV in the local context.[140]

---

133 UN Women (2013), "Terminology and definitions"; available at: https://www.endvawnow.org/en/articles/1474-terminology-and-definitions.html (accessed on 28 March 2021).

134 Ibid.

135 UNHCR (2011), n. 40.

136 Ibid.

137 UN Women (2012), "Terminology and definitions;" available at: http://www.endvawnow.org/en/articles/1474-terminology-and-definitions.html (accessed on 11 December 2020).

138 Ibid.

139 The World Bank (2017), "Violence against Women and Girls;" available at: http://www.worldbank.org/en/topic/socialdevelopment/brief/violence-against-women-and-girls (accessed on 11 December 2020).

140 UN Women (2012), "Terminology and definitions;" available at: http://www.endvawnow.org/en/articles/1474-terminology-and-definitions.html (accessed on 10 January 2021).

SGBV has been addressed by the different actors, organizations, governments, NGOs, civil society groups. They refer to GBV as subsuming 'sexual violence'. In this context, the UNFPA opined that "it was a policy to avoid the isolation of the two as separate or suggestively unrelated issues".[141] In fact, studies have shown that SGBV against women occurs in almost every society even during peacetime. However, it becomes more virulent during the armed conflicts wherein it is used as a tactic or weapon of war.[142]

The principal agencies and institutional actors that have taken initiatives in addressing SGBV against women include the Security Council (resolution 1325), the United Nations Population Fund (UNFPA), the UNHCR,[143] the International Committee of Red Cross (ICRC), the INGOs (Human Rights Watch, Amnesty International, etc.), the United Nations Relief and Work Agency for Palestine Refugees (UNRWA), the United Nations Children's Fund(UNICEF), the World Food Programme (WFP), the United Nations Development Programme(UNDP)[144] and the Office of the UN Secretary-General.[145] Slowly, numerous guidelines,[146] documents,

---

141 Faculty of Law, University of Oslo (2017), "Translating feminist norms and strategies through sexual and gender-based violence programming in Somalia An explorative approach to understanding norm internalization;" available at: https://www.duo.uio.no/bitstream/handle/10852/57334/8031_HUMR-5200.pdf?sequence=7 (accessed on 11 December 2020).

142 Ibid.

143 UNHCR (2003), n. 4.

144 UNDP (2013), "Guidelines on SGBV Case Management A Reference Handbook for the FSU;" available at: https://www.sl.undp.org/content/dam/sierraleone/docs/focusareadocs/undp_sle_SGBVCaseManagementGuidelines.pdf (accessed on 29 March 2021). Also see, UNDP (2013), "Annual Report Team of Experts Rule of Law/Sexual Violence in Conflict;" available at: http://www.undp.org/content/dam/undp/library/crisis%20prevention/undp_cpr_gender_toe%20svc%202013%20ar.pdf (accessed on 29 March 2021).

145 For instance, the then UN Secretary-General Kofi emphatically observed that "Underscoring the vital importance of Africa's women for economic development, fighting HIV/AIDS and achieving peace…lambasted the use of sexual and gender-based violence as a weapon of war in the continent's conflicts"; see UN News (2004), "Annan blasts use of gender-based violence as weapon in Africa's wars"; 7 July 2004; available at: http://www.un.org/apps/news/story.asp?NewsID=11262#.WnxCl1SWbIU (accessed on 29 March 2021).

146 IASC (2015), "Guidelines for Integrating Gender-Based Violence Interventions in Humanitarian Action: Reducing risk, promoting resilience and aiding recovery;" available at: https://gbvguidelines.org/wp/wp-content/uploads/2015/09/2015-IASC-Gender-based-Violence-Guidelines_lo-res.pdf (accessed on 29 March 2021).

domestic policies,[147] reports, training package,[148] etc. that seek to address SGBV have taken shape. It shows as to how sensitive and serious the issue has become.[149]

The invocation of the term SGBC has taken the discourse further in treating SGBV as a crime. Though SGBV is not treated as a crime explicitly, some forms of SGBV are denoted as a crime under international criminal law. For example, Article 7 and 8 of the 1998 Rome Statute of ICC have listed some forms of SGBV as crime against humanity and war crimes. In most of the literature, especially the policy papers of the ICC, the phrase 'gender-based crime' has been used as a gender-neutral term. It includes both sexual and non-sexual forms of GBV. 'Sexual crime,' e.g., rape, enforced prostitution, and other forms of sexual violence, etc. are specifically mentioned in the Statute as a form of GBV. The important criterion for 'sexual crime' is that the act in question should be sexual either by direct physical contact or non-physical contact, e.g., forced nudity.[150]

Some scholars have argued that the term 'gender' and 'sex' have different meanings. In many of the cases, we conflate 'gender,' 'sex,' and 'women.' It is argued that 'gender-based' crimes are the forms of crimes where individuals are targeted because of their socially constructed gender norms (maleness and femaleness). 'Gender-based crimes' comprise both sexual and non-sexual violence.[151] The biological sex of the victims mostly inflacted some crimes such as the forced pregnancy. It, in turn, also amounts to a gender-based crime perpetrated against women only. Thus, some forms of sexual and gender-based violence are only perpetrated against women because of their sex or gender. So, 'sexual violence', 'gender-based violence' and SGBV are used interchangeably. It may create inequalities between male and female victims. So, the use of the terms 'gender-based' or 'sexual' crimes or violence alone are not enough.[152]

---

[147] Consortium of Humanitarian Agencies (2017), "The Policy Framework and National Plan of Action (NPoA) to address Sexual and Gender–based Violence in Sri Lanka 2016–2020"; available at: https://humanitariansrilanka.org/2017/08/06/the-policy-framework-and-national-plan-of-actionnpoa-to-address-sexual-and-gender-based-violence-sgbv-in-sri-lanka-2016-2020-presented-at-the-second-discussion-forums-on-gender/ (accessed on 29 March 2021).

[148] UNHCR (2016), see n. 1.

[149] For instance, see Swiss Agency for Development and Cooperation SDC Humanitarian Aid Department (2016), "Operational concept Sexual and Gender-based Violence (SGBV) 2017–2020"; available at: https://www.eda.admin.ch/dam/countries/countries-content/jordan/en/Operational-concept-SGBV_English.pdf (accessed on 29 March 2021).

[150] An ICC policy paper states: "Sexual crimes ' that fall under the subject-matter jurisdiction of the ICC are listed under articles 7(1)(g), 8(2)(b)(xxii), and 8(2)(e)(vi) of the Statute, and described in the Elements of Crimes ('Elements')"; see ICC (2014), "Policy Paper on Sexual and Gender-Based Crimes June 2014"; available at: https://www.icc-cpi.int/iccdocs/otp/OTP-Policy-Paper-on-Sexual-and-Gender-Based-Crimes--June-2014.pdf (accessed on 29 March 2021).

[151] Oosterveld, Valerie (2018), "The ICC Policy Paper on Sexual and Gender-Based Crimes: A Crucial Step for International Criminal Law", *William & Mary Journal of Women and the Law,* 24(3): 443–457; available at: https://scholarship.law.wm.edu/cgi/viewcontent.cgi?article=1476&context=wmjowl (24 March 2021).

[152] Ibid.

In a way, the term SGBC serves all the purposes of gender analysis. It is a crime based on gender norms and reflects inequalities prevailing in a particular society. It can be said that SGBV/SGBC against women is influenced by the gender-based norms and inequalities in any particular society. Gender-based norms and inequalities vary from society to society. It helps to provide broader meaning to SGBV. While dealing with the perpetrators in a particular society, there is a difference between two sets of people in defining gender. One group says that 'gender' is based on a socially constructed and fluid nature that is based on time and location. Another group of people want a definition of gender that is followed by sex only or sexual role that excludes "consideration of sexual orientation as gender consideration".[153] It is claimed that physical and mental harm, societal stigma, etc. associated with sexual violence should also be treated as SGBC because these can be used against any targeted group to destroy the group.

Different Stages, Victims, and Forms

Women and girls are subjected to SGBV in different stages of their life within the family and outside the family. There are different stages of SGBV based on the place of occurrence such as family, community, etc. Women also experience different forms of SGBV during their lifetime. It needs to address the key issue of survivors or victims of SGBV.

One in three women experience physical or sexual violence at some point in their lives**.** Moreover, two in three victims of intimate partner violence or family related homicide are women.[154] Special Rapporteurs on violence against women (causes and consequences) and the Secretary-General report on all forms of violence against women have identified the stages of violence against women. These stages can be explained as follows:

Stages of Violence

A. **Violence within family**: These include different kinds of violence such as domestic violence; marital rape; battering; forced prostitution by the family; different forms of non-spousal violence; sex-selective abortion and infanticide; traditional or culturally harmful practices, e.g., FGM, dowry-related violence.[155] The studies have proved that violence by intimate partner remains

[153] Ibid.

[154] UN (2020), *The World's Women: Trends and Statistics*; available at: https://worlds-women-2020-data-undesa.hub.arcgis.com/ (accessed on 29 March 2021).

[155] Pickup et al. (2001), n. 131.

one of the most common forms of violence in the family that is globally experienced by the women.[156]

B. **Violence in the community:** Rape, assault, sexual harassment, violence within institutions, forced trafficking, forced prostitution,[157] widespread harmful traditional practices (such as female genital mutilation) and child marriage comes within the violence perpetrated by or within the community settings.[158]

C. **Violence perpetrated or condoned by State**: These include custodial violence, gender-based violence during armed conflicts or emergencies.[159] The State commits violence against women through the acts or omission of its agents or through public policy that leads to SGBV against women.[160]

Victims

Refugees, asylum seekers, undocumented migrants, individuals of low socio-economic status, impoverished people, people living in detention,[161] women in conflict-affected areas.[162] Adolescent women who are engaged in commercial sex[163]; older person, a person with disabilities[164]; orphan and vulnerable children especially girls, widows[165]; undocumented immigrant women,[166] migrant workers,[167]

---

156 UN (2020), n. 130.

157 Pickup et al. (2001), n. 131.

158 Ibid.

159 Ibid.

160 UN (2020), n. 130.

161 Keygnaert et al. (2014), "Sexual and gender-based violence in the European asylum and reception sector: a perpetuum mobile?" *European Journal of Public Health*, 25 (1): 90–6.

162 Colin, Sollitt (2016), "The Least Condemned Crime: Sexual and Gender Based Violence against Migrants and Asylum Seekers on the Move in the Horn of Africa;" available at: http://regionalmms.org/index.php/research-publications/feature-articles/item/52-the-least-condemned-crime-sexual-gender-based-violence (accessed on 11 December 2020).

163 Zhang et al. (2016), "Prevalence and correlates of sexual and gender-based violence against Chinese adolescent women who are involved in commercial sex: a cross-sectional study", *BMJ Open*; 6:e01340; available at: http://dx.doi.org/10.1136/bmjopen-2016-013409 (accessed on 11 December 2020).

164 UNHCR (2015), United Nations High Commissioner for Refugees, "Sexual and Gender-Based Violence Prevention and Response In Refugee Situations in the Middle East And North Africa;" available at: http://www.refworld.org/pdfid/568f9a014.pdf (accessed on 11 December 2020).

165 FAO, "Guidance Note: Gender-Based Violence and Livelihood"; available at: http://www.fao.org/fileadmin/templates/dimitra/pdf/guidance_note_gbv_livelihoods.pdf (accessed on 18 January 2021).

166 Goldscheid, Julie (2011), "Gender Violence and Work in the United States and South Africa: The Parallel Processes of Legal and Cultural Change," *Am. U. J. Gender Soc. Pol'y & L*, 19:921.

167 UN (2020), n. 130.

and international female students,[168] children especially female children are the victims of SGBV. Girls face violence during peace, conflict and post-conflict situations. Girl soldiers are often raped, sexually abused, sexually enslaved, and treated as 'bush wives' by their commanders and fellow soldiers. It seems, their recruitement often ends up in satiating the sexual needs of their male counterparts.

In many of the cases, girls are abducted by the armed forces and subjected to different forms of SGBV.[169] There are some groups of children that are a direct target of SGBV. In conflicts zones such as Congo (Bunia town), Haiti and East Timor, most of the abandoned children were born due to rape committed by the UN soldiers and the other UN employees. These children are left and ostracized because of mixed blood and born outside the traditional wedlock.[170]

Different Forms

There are different forms of SGBV such as domestic violence, forced and early marriage, sexual violence, abuse and exploitation faced by refugee women.[171] In fact definition of victim also changes in accordance with the level of sufferings. According to the definition of the UNHCR, there are five types of SGBV (see Table 2.1): physical, psychological, sexual, socio-economic violence, and cultural practices.[172] So, SGBV can be physical, psychological or emotional through denial of resources or access to services.[173] These forms of SGBV are not absolute.

168 Forbes-Mewett, H. and MacCulloch, J. (2015), "International Students and Gender-Based Violence against Women" Sage Publication; available at: https://journals.sagepub.com/doi/abs/10.1177/1077801215602344?journalCode=vawa (accessed on 11 December 2020).

169 Grey, Rosemary (2014), "Sexual Violence Against Child Soldiers: The Limits and Potential Of International Criminal Law"; *International Feminist Journal of Politics*, 16 (4): 601–621.

170 Ndulo, Muna (2009), "The United Nations Responses to The Sexual Abuse And Exploitation Of Women And Girls By Peacekeepers During Peacekeeping Missions", *Berkeley Journal of International Law,* 27(1): 127; available at: https://scholarship.law.cornell.edu/cgi/viewcontent.cgi?article=1058&context=facpub (accesses on 29 March 2021).

171 UNHCR (2016), n. 1.

172 Ibid.

173 Ibid.

Table 2.1 Different forms of SGBV practice around the World

Physical	Honour killing, physical assault (beating, biting, burning, kicking), slavery, infanticide, foeticide, femicide, forceful confinement, different forms of physical punishment for denying cultural norms, female genital mutilation, torture, etc.[174]
Sexual	Rape, marital rape, rape with objects (guns, branches, sticks, broken bottles, etc.),[175] child sexual abuse, sexual abuse through internet or online, genital mutilation, sexual harassment, sexual exploitation in private or public, forced trafficking, commercial sexual exploitation, sexual violence based on sexual orientation.[176] SGBV as a weapon of war, forced nudity, forced abortions, gang rape and forced sterilization.[177]
Emotional or physiological	Verbal abuse, forced confinement, forced marriage, child marriage, social exclusion based on sexual orientation, humiliation or manipulation.[178]
Denial of access to resources or services	Denial of right to education to girls and women, deprivation of the right to property, denial of full nutrition or food, denial of the right to nationality.[179]
Harmful traditional practices[180]	Some forms of violence, e.g.,forced confinement or female genital mutilation; physical, emotional and sexual violence. Some do not come directly under the forms of SGBV, but it may cause SGBV, e.g., child marriage, denial of food, etc.[181] Forced marriage and early marriages, infanticide, neglect towards girl's child, denial of education to women and girls.[182]
Socioeconomic violence	Exclusion, denial of economic, social benefits and opportunities. Limited access to employment opportunities, denial of access or control over land and natural resources, denial of access to get services, social benefits, or any other obstacles or discriminations from exercising and enjoying fundamental human rights.[183]

Causes and Consequences

The causes of SGBV are not confined to a particularly defined boundary. The causes are multifaceted depending on the political, socio-economic, cultural, geographical,

---

[174] Ibid.

[175] Isaksson, Charlotte (2014), "Fighting for Gender Equality: Why Security Sector Actors Must Combat Sexual and Gender-Based Violence," *The Fletcher Forum of World Affairs*, 38 (2): 49.

[176] UNHCR (2016), n. 1.

[177] UN OHCHR, "Violence against Women;" available at: https://www.ohchr.org/Documents/Issues/Women/WRGS/SexualHealth/INFO_VAW_WEB.pdf (accessed on 29 March 2021).

[178] UNHCR (2016), n. 1.

[179] Ibid.

[180] UNHCR (2003), n. 4.

[181] UNHCR (2016), n. 1.

[182] UNHCR (2011), n. 40.

[183] Ibid.

and social position of a country or region.[184] There is a strong causal relationship between SGBV and all the above factors. In many of the situations, the above status of women is ignored. As a result, SGBV against women is either covered up or gets ignored. These societal and individual attitudes towards women deny even acknowledgement of existence of SGBV. It, in turn, allows violence to continue from generation to generation.[185] The environmental factor is also recognized as one of the causes of SGBV. SGBV has a perpetual effect on women and the family as well as society, and the States. There are causes and consequences of SGBV against women in the family, community or society and the States.

Causes

A. **Status and role of the women**

The reports of the Special Rapporteurs of the UN on the 'causes and consequences of violence against women' underscore that the status of women in the society shows the level and the forms of violence faced by them in a particular society. Thus women's social, cultural, economic and legal status has a direct causal relationship with violence against them.[186] The reports have shown that women have been globally experiencing persistent neglect, discrimination and all types of violence. Sometimes the governments deny reformation of unequal laws that affect the existing social and cultural status of women. This also contributes to institutionalized forms (structures and processes) of violence against women.

Women experience different forms of violence in the name of cultural and social norms. In many of the societies, women are defined solely by their reproductive function, virginity, as a property and honour of the family. Thus, violence against women takes forms of harm against bodily integrity, physical and mental health. It is often reflected in the struggles such as resisting virginity tests; rights over women's body; choices in sexual activity and right of marital choice. These are discouraged or prohibited in different cultures and societies.[187]

Forced and child marriages are common practices in the name of protecting virginity. Sometimes a woman may be forced to marry the perpetrators who

---

[184] UN Human Rights Council (2019), "Report of the Special Rapporteur on violence against women, its causes and consequences, on her mission to the Occupied Palestinian Territory/State of Palestine; Doc. A/HRC/35/30/Add.2, 14 November 2019; available at: https://www.un.org/unispal/document/report-of-the-special-rapporteur-on-violence-against-women-its-causes-and-consequences-on-her-mission-to-the-optstate-of-palestine-advance-edited-version-ahrc3530add-2/ (accessed on 29 March 2021).

[185] Ibid.

[186] UN Commission on Human Rights (2000), "Report of the Special Rapporteur on violence against women, its causes and consequences" (Ms. Radhika Coomaraswamy); submitted in accordance with Commission on Human Rights resolution 1997/44; UN Doc. E/CN.4/2000/68/Add.1, 27 January 2000; available at: https://undocs.org/E/CN.4/2000/68/Add.1 (accessed on 29 March 2021).

[187] Ibid.

committed the rape. The family or community also kill women in the name of 'honour' if she decides to marry a person not acceptable by them. She may also be forced to give a degrading test that can establish her virginity. In fact, it is often claimed that the "loss of a woman's virginity is a shame which can only be wiped out in blood". As a result, a woman is treated merely as a property of her father, brother, husband, and son during her entire life.[188]

The studies carried out in indifferent disciplines have underscored inequality between genders within the society. It is such inequality that triggers violence against women both within the family and the society.[189] The deep-rooted gender inequality especially arises from roles, rights, and opportunities for men and women.[190] The harmful cultural and societal norms that support violence against women also give push to SGBV against them.[191] There are many instances wherein sexual violence is perpetrated since women are treated as 'honour' of the family or 'property of the family.' As and when a woman breaks the said norms, severe punishment is inflicted in the name of protecting the family 'honour' or societal norms. In 2016, one such public outcry, the Pakistani Women's Human Rights Organisation protested silently outside the UNHCR, Geneva on the ground that "women of Pakistan are the victims of domestic violence and honour killing".[192]

Migration, poverty or economic standards of women also contribute to SGBV against women.[193] The economic policies of the governments that force or encourage women's economic dependence on men or others often result in violence against women. In fact low economic and social status pushes women to depend on others for providing protection and the means of survival. It is now understood that an economically independent women can easily walk out from the place of violence.[194]

It is often ignored that women play multiple roles, e.g., producers, home managers, mothers, community organizers. Moreover, women do contribute, directly and indirectly, to the economy of a country. A woman takes care of her children and manages household activities that ensure the sustenance of society and create an environment of productive workplace. In fact, direct involvement of women in production

---

188 Ibid, paragraphs, 5,6,7.

189 UN (2020), n. 130.

190 UN Women (2020), "In Focus: 16 Days of Activism against Gender-based Violence"; available at: https://www.unwomen.org/en/news/in-focus/end-violence-against-women (accessed on 30 March 2021).

191 UN Women (2015), *A framework to underpin action to prevent violence against women*; available at: https://www.unwomen.org/-/media/headquarters/attachments/sections/library/publications/2015/prevention_framework_unwomen_nov2015.pdf?la=en&vs=5223 (accessed on 30 March 2021).

192 India Today (2016), "Pakistani Women Protest Outside the UNHRC Against Gender-based Violence;" Geneva, 22 September 2016; available at: https://www.indiatoday.in/pti-feed/story/pakistani-women-protest-outside-the-unhrc-against-691381-2016-09-22 (accessed on 30 March 2021).

193 Coomaraswamy (2003), "59th Session of the Commission of Human Rights: Integration of Human Rights of Women and the Gender Perspective Violation Against Women (Item 12 (a); April 2003);" available at: https://gbvguidelines.org/wp/wp-content/uploads/2015/09/2015-IASC-Gender-based-Violence-Guidelines_lo-res.pdf (accessed on 30 March 2021).

194 Ibid.

is undermined because of lack of market evaluation of her work. For example, there is a notion that cooking of food and child care etc., are not regarded as having an economic value. As compared to situation in the developed countries, the economic plight of women in most of the developing countries remains dismal.

It has been contended that "women do two-thirds of all unpaid work. While men do two-thirds of all paid work".[195] In fact low economic position of women has a far-reaching consequence for their socio-legal status in a particular society. Often women with low economic status are oppressed by partner, family, society and even the States. They face different forms of SGBV in their lifetime such as female infanticide, crimes against widows, dowry deaths, malnutrition of girls etc.[196]

The low economic and social status also has different impact on the legal status of women. It has seen that sometimes women having low economic and social status are undermined by the law and policies made by the governments. It includes unequal ownership rights, deprivation from property rights and rights of inheritance. For instance, in Nigeria, 90% land and property is owned by the men. As a result, house owners often deny giving accommodation to single woman or mother. In such a situation, women become homeless and, in turn, become vulnerable to SGBV. In South Africa, women need husband's 'signature to get credit from public banks. So, women constantly face control on their needs, sustenance and survival as they are dominated by the male members of the family, the community and the State. As a result, women become susceptible to different forms of SGBV because of their inherently weak societal status.[197]

In a way, gender is always ignored even as it remains embedded in the society and the legal theory. It is taken for granted that the primary role of women in society and family is to fulfill the needs of men. Thus, violence against women remains unabated as the family and the society tend to regard them as inferior and hence suppress their voices.[198]

Even in the labour market, there is a gender discrimination. Women employees often become victims of SGBV. Women share their experiences about oppression economically, socially, politically by the family, society, and the State. Sometimes, they are identified as a vulnerable or oppressed group of the society that needs special care and protection.[199] Sex and gender are often used as a tool for disempowerment of women.[200]

On the other hand, status of women in a conflict-affected society depends on the facts and circumstances of a conflict. Women become victims of SGBV because of their vulnerable roles and situation in the conflict zones. SGBV in a post-conflict society is the consequence of severity of the conflict. Therefore, the discourse mainly

---

195 UN Human Rights Council (2019), n. 184.

196 Ibid.

197 Ibid, paragraphs, 13–18.

198 Conaghan, Joanne. (2000), "Reassessing the Feminist Theoretical Project in Law," *Journal of Law and Society*, 27 (3): 351–385.

199 Ibid.

200 Ibid.

remains focussed on the status and role of the women during conflict, and the post-conflict situation. Earlier it was claimed that violence against women, especially SGBV, did not come under the purview of the customary international law of warfare. SGBV in conflict zones was regarded as a collateral damage of war or an inevitable consequence of war. However, the notion has now changed with the setting up of several international criminal courts and tribunals such as for former Yugoslavia (ICTY), Rwanda (ICTR), and the International Criminal Court (ICC).[201]

SGBV against women especially rape, sexual slavery, other forms of sexual as well as gender-based violence, etc. are used as a 'weapon of war' during conflicts.[202] Similarly, SGBV was used as a 'weapon of war' to destroy a particular ethnic group during the conflicts in former Yugoslavia and Rwanda.[203] There are many other instances wherein the status of women is premised upon 'honour' of the opponent group. They are treated as the members and 'honour' of the enemy groups. Women as individual human beings have very limited status or role during the conflicts.

In view of this, rape, forced pregnancy or forced miscarriages are often part of a war strategy of the armed groups. Forced miscarriages and forced pregnancy are used as a weapon to destroy a group, race, nationality or civilization.[204] After occupying any territory, the victorious party treats women as 'spoils of war.' Rape is often resorted to by the victorious party[205] and used as a tactic to take revenge against the opponent group.[206]

The perpetrators think about 'women' as weak and honour of the society. As a corollary, it is regarded as the duty or responsibility of any group or society to protect their honour by protecting women. If they fail to do that, it would be an ignominy for them. It is estimated that, during the 1990s, between 20,000 and 50,000 women were raped during the conflict in Bosnia; in Sierra Leone, between 50,000 and 64,000 internally displaced women suffered sexual assault by the combatants; in the Democratic Republic of Congo, around 350 rapes were reported on a monthly basis; in Haiti, 50% of young women were raped or sexually assaulted in violent areas.[207] Apart from these reported statistics, many remain unreported as women suffer in silence and societies suffer from shame in admitting such mass rapes.[208]

---

[201] Manjoo and McRaith, (2011), n. 54.

[202] Ibid.

[203] Coomaraswamy (1994), "Preliminary report submitted by the Special Rapporteur on violence against women, its causes and consequences, in accordance with Commission on Human Rights resolution 1994/45;" available at: http://hrlibrary.umn.edu/commission/thematic51/42.htm (accessed on 11 December 2020).

[204] Manjoo and McRaith, (2011), n. 54.

[205] Ibid.

[206] UN (2009), UN (2009), "To End Violence Against Women and Girls Is Now", Remarks of the UN Deputy Secretary-General Asha-Rose Migiro to the Women's International Forum, New York, 20 February 2009; DSG/SM/440 WOM/1711, 23 February 2009; available at: https://www.un.org/press/en/2009/dsgsm440.doc.htm (accessed on 30 March 2021).

[207] Ibid.

[208] Ibid.

The incident of 'sex slaves' during conflicts is 'akin to slavery' in international law.[209] For example, during WW- II, Japan's military forced women from Korea and other occupied Asian countries to work as 'military sex slaves.'[210] During the war, civilian women and girls were abducted by the combatants or military for doing domestic work as well as to fulfill their sexual needs.[211]

There are many instances of participation of women in hostilities. Hence, when caught, they are treated as prisoners of war (POWs). There is very less discussion about these combatant women. In her 2009 address, the UN Deputy Secretary-General, Asha-Rose Migiro, observed at the Women's International Forum that:

> The experience of women and girls in armed conflict is linked to their status in the society. If a culture of violence and discrimination against women and girls before the conflict, it will be exacerbated during the conflict. More ever, women are not only in jeopardy during periods of fighting; they are just as likely to be assaulted when there is clam, by armies, rebels, criminal gangs or even the police.[212]

It shows that even the combatant women as POWs become victims of SGBV in conflict zones.[213] Thus, it can be argued that violence against women and girls are not the sole outcome of war; rather it is the extension of the institutionalized pattern and strcture of violence against women during peacetime.[214]

B. **Patriarchy and unequal power relations**

Studies have established that patriarchy and unequal power relations between men and women are also the reason for SGBV against women. The feminist scholars' writings; the reports of the UN Special Rapporteurs and the UN Declaration on Violence against Women (1993) have specifically mentioned that patriarchy is one of the main causes of SGBV against women.[215] In this context, it has been observed that:

> Though patriarchy is hierarchical and men of different classes, races or ethnic groups have different places in the patriarchy, they are united in their shared relationship of dominance over their women. And despite their unequal resources, they are dependent on each other to maintain that domination.[216]

---

209 Coomaraswamy (1996), "Report on the mission to the Democratic People's Republic of Korea, the Republic of Korea and Japan on the issue of military sexual slavery in wartime;" available at: http://hrlibrary.umn.edu/commission/country52/53-add1.htm (accessed on 11 December 2020).

210 Ibid.

211 Manjoo and McRaith, (2011), n. 54.

212 UN (2009), n. 206.

213 Krill, Françoise (1985), *International Review of the Red Cross*, No. 249 (1985); available at: https://www.icrc.org/en/doc/resources/documents/article/other/57jmfj.htm (accessed on 30 March 2021).

214 Manjoo and McRaith, (2011), n. 54.

215 Charlesworth, Hilary, et. al. (1991), "Feminist Approaches to International Law", *The American Journal of International Law*, 85 (4): 613–645.

216 Ibid.

Unequal power relation between men and women set by gender norms remain the key factor in perpetuating SGBV against women.[217] A person with less power has less choice and is always abused by the powerful people in the family, community, and the State.[218] Different factors contribute to the power imbalances in the society, e.g., poverty or economic reason, cultural factors, displacement, conflict or war, religion etc.[219] The forms of violence vary on the basis of facts, circumstances and subject. Women are targeted during peace or war as an individual, members of ethnic groups, and specific sex or gender, etc.[220]

It has been argued that SGBV against women or gender-based violence against women or violence against women could differ from other forms of violence on the basis of unequal patriarchal power relations. Thus, it can be said that SGBV against women occurs to uphold such unequal patriarchal power relation between the genders. In this process, the patriarchal structures get support from cultural practices, societal values, institutions, and the existing laws.[221] This has been corroborated in the preamble to the 1993 Declaration on the Elimination of Violence against Women.[222]

The 2014 reports of the UN Special Rapporteur on 'causes and consequences of violence against women' also acknowledged that the role of patriarchy and unequal power relations between men and women resulting in discrimination and SGBV against women.[223] The history also shows that the resolution of the International Congress of Women, 1915 (Hague)[224] gave a broader picture of the relationship between war and women or gender. It underscored as to how patriarchy remains one of the entrenched reasons for warfare and how women become the victims of SGBV in the conflict zones.[225]

---

[217] UNHCR (2016), n. 1.

[218] Ibid.

[219] Ibid.

[220] Isaksson, Charlotte (2014), n. 175.

[221] Ertürk, Yakın (2009), "Towards a Post-Patriarchal Gender Order: Confronting the universality and the particularity of violence against women", *Sociologisk Forskning, årgång* 46, nr 4.

[222] UN (1993), *Declaration on the Elimination of Violence against Women*; General Assembly resolution 48/104 of 20 December 1993. It states: "Recognizing that violence against women is a manifestation of historically unequal power relations between men and women, which have led to domination over and discrimination against women by men and to the prevention of the full advancement of women, and that violence against women is one of the crucial social mechanisms by which women are forced into a subordinate position compared with men;" available at: https://www.un.org/en/genocideprevention/documents/atrocity-crimes/Doc.21_declaration%20elimination%20vaw.pdf (accessed on 30 March 2021).

[223] UN GA (2014), Human Rights Council, "Report of the Special Rapporteur (Rashida Manjoo) on violence against women, its causes and consequences"; UN Doc. A/HRC/26/38, 28 May 2014; available at: https://undocs.org/en/A/HRC/26/38 (accessed on 30 March 2021).

[224] The International Congress of Women (1915), the Hague (28 April to 1 May 1915); available at: https://www.history.com/this-day-in-history/international-congress-of-women-adopts-resolutions (accessed on 30 March 2021).

[225] Ibid.

Some studies have shown that it is not only the men who bear the responsibility of SGBV against women. Women also to some extent play crucial roles in perpetuating the environment of violence against women. This takes place through their active collaboration with the perpetrators or non-cooperation with the survivors or victims of SGBV. This situation is facilitated by the entrenched patriarchy.[226] The negative patriarchic effects encourage the mutual violent relationship among women in comparision with men.[227]

As already seen, the control over women's sexuality is one of the patriarchical tools to continue violence against women. They often manipulate social, political, religious, cultural and economic mechanisms to justify violation of women's human rights. In a patriarchal society, women are regarded as inferior and personal property (chattel) of the male members.[228] The honour of the family and the male member is tailored to a female virtue. So, even if a woman informs or shares her experiences of sexual violence, she faces the consequences such as ostricisation due to perceived fears of loss of family dignity and honour.[229]

C. **Political factors**

The power inequality and gender-role in the family, community, and State encourage SGBV. There are many cases wherein the sexual violence against women is an act of political violence or politically motivated. Rape is recognized as genocide, crime against humanity and war crime under the Rome Statute. It does not always need the presence of war or conflicts for sexual violence. Generally, political violence means "any form of organized violence carried out by the political actors that includes governments, rebel groups, insurgents, or terrorist organizations".[230]

The question remains as to: why sexual violence or other forms of SGBV are used politically? There is a need to find a causal relation between SGBV and the political intent. Both the causal analysis of SGBV and critical feminist analysis of gender-based violence can yield answers to this simmering question. It seems structural gender-based discrimination and gender oppression in the society provides the main causes of SGBV. It, in turn, gives an opportunity to the political organizations to use SGBV as a tool for political gain. So, mass SGBV, collective rape, mass sexual violence is the result of deeply embedded societal gender discrimination that is used as a weapon to generate political violence. Gender inequality, militarization, conflict or emergencies or civil wars, ethnic cleavages, economic crisis, lack of education,

---

226 Gull Tarar and Pull (2014), "Patriarchy, Gender Violence and Poverty amongst Pakistani Women: A Social Work Inquiry", *International Journal of Social Work and Human Services Practice Horizon Research Publishing,* 2 (2): 56–63.

227 Suzanne et al., (2008), "A Review of Research on Women's Use of Violence with Male Intimate Partners", *Violence Vict*, 23(3): 301–314; available at: https://www.ncbi.nlm.nih.gov/pmc/articles/PMC2968709/pdf/nihms244725.pdf (accessed on 30 March 2021).

228 Gull Tarar and Pull (2014), n. 226.

229 Hadi, Abdul (2014), "Patriarchy and Gender-Based Violence in Pakistan", *European Journal of Social Sciences Education and Research*, 4(4): 297.

230 Davies Sara E, Jacqui True (2015), "Reframing conflict-related sexual and gender-based violence: Bringing gender analysis back in"' *Security Dialogue 46(6).* 46(6):495–512.

poverty, culture or harmful cultural practices, the culture of impunity add deadly cumulative ammunition to the use of SGBV as a politically violent tool against the opponent political groups.[231]

Many scholarly studies[232] have sought to make people aware of the impacts of war especially on women. This includes seminal works such as the 1915, International Congress of Women's resolution,[233] writings of Rosa Luxemburg (*the Crisis in German Social-Democracy: the 'Junius'Pamphlet*),[234] Freud's essay on 'the International Congress of Women' etc.[235] The world experienced SGBV against women during WW-II as well as in the post-UN Charter conflicts such as the former Yugoslavia, Rwanda, Afghanistan, Libya etc. It has seen that armed conflicts in these countries gave a major fillip to SGBV.[236]

The International Congress of Women met in The Hague (28 April to 01 May 1915) for an immediate end of war and establishment of peace.[237] The Congress adopted a resolution at its Business Session.[238] It was pointed out that 'gender' was one of the reasons for warfare and it protested against the violence in war. The Congress opposed that women were the victims of war and all the horrible wrongs of war.[239] It was claimed that "foreign policy shall be subject to democratic control with equal representation of men and women".[240] Furthermore, it observed that the "combined influence of the women of all countries is one of the strongest forces

---

[231] Ibid.

[232] For instance, see Wright, Quincy (1944), *A Study of War*, Chicago: University of Chicago.

[233] Suzanne et al. (2008), n. 227.

[234] "Rosa Luxemburg (1915), "On Capitalism, Imperialism and War", (2015), *London Review of International Law,* 3 (2): 253. Also see, Rosa Luxemburg (1916), "The Junius Pamphlet the Crisis of German Social Democracy (1915);" available at: https://www.marxists.org/archive/luxemburg/1915/junius/ (accessed on 30 March 2021).

[235] Chimni (2015), "Peace Through Law: lessons from 1914," *London Review of International Law*, 3 (2):245–265.

[236] Ibid.

[237] International Congress of Women (1915), *Report of the International Congress of Women*; available at: https://ia800306.us.archive.org/15/items/internatcongrewom00interich/internatcongrewom00interich_bw.pdf (accessed on 30 March 2021).

[238] Ibid.

[239] Ibid, ICW Resolution 2 provided: "Women's Sufferings in War: This International Congress of Women opposes the assumption that women can be protected under the conditions of modern warfare. It protests vehemently against the odious wrongs of which women are the victims in time of war, and especially against the horrible violation of women which attends all war"; see International Congress of Women (1915).

[240] Ibid, ICW Resolution 8 provided: "Democratic Control of Foreign Policy: Since war is commonly brought about not by the mass of the people, who do not desire it, but by groups representing particular interests, this International Congress of Women urges that Foreign Politics shall be subject to Democratic Control; and declares that it can only recognise as democratic a system which includes the equal representation of men and women"; see International Congress of Women (1915).

for the prevention of war". As a result, they demanded "for equal political rights of women with men,"[241,242]

D. **Socio-economic factors**

There are special socio-economic factors such as migration, poverty and others that also contribute to SGBV against women.[243] Women are generally considered to be vulnerable or oppressed group in the society that needs special care, attention and protection.[244] Many of the conflicts trigger an economic and social crisis. In the absence of any male member, it becomes a compulsion for women to carry out many tasks to look after the family and the dependants. The opponent groups often abduct women at the time of collecting fire woods, fetching water or they become victims of exposure to a landmine.[245] Impunity for the perpetrators and the societal tradition of silence on issues of women's honour contribute to SGBV in conflict zones.[246]

SGBV is also connected with another type of war that has emerged recently. It can be described as 'war against nature.' There is a nexus between SGBV and illicit extraction of natural resources. Forced displacements result in an economic loss for both the individual and the nation. That results in the migration and refugee problems. For instance, rape has been used against the civilian population in the Democratic Republic of Congo (DRC) as a punishment for preventing illegal poaching as well rampant mineral and wild-life trafficking by the armed groups. It shows the nexus between SGBV and illicit use of natural resources and susceptibility of women living in those areas.[247] Similarly, during and after the disasters, families face an economic crisis as a result of displacement or loss of assets. Children especially girls and women often are compelled to earn money through sexual works for sharing

---

[241] Ibid, ICW Resolution 9 stated: "The Enfranchisement of Women in: Since the combined influence of the women of all countries is one of the strongest forces for the prevention of war, and since women can only have full responsibility and effective influence when they have equal political rights with men, this International Congress of Women demands their political enfranchisement"; see International Congress of Women (1915). and also the need "of equal civil and political rights in national and international politics".

[242] Ibid, ICW Resolution 15 provided: "Women in National and International Politics: This International Congress of Women declares it to be essential, both nationally and internationally to put into practice the principle that women should share all civil and political rights and responsibilities on these terms as men".

[243] Coomaraswamy (2003), "Integration of Human Rights of Women and the Gender Perspective Violation Against Women", 59th Session of the Commission of Human Rights (Item 12 (a), April 2003);" available at: http://www.peacewomen.org/sites/default/files/un_stmtradhikavaw_apr2003_0.pdf (accessed on 03 April 2021).

[244] Conaghan, Joanne. (2000), "Reassessing the Feminist Theoretical Project in Law," *Journal of Law and Society*, 27 (3): 351–385; available at: https://onlinelibrary.wiley.com/doi/abs/10.1111/1467-6478.00159 (accessed on 03 April 2021).

[245] UN (2009), Deputy Secretary General, "The Whispering must end; There must be an Outcry. Enough is enough. The Time to End Violence against Women and Girls is Now;" available at: http://www.un.org/press/en/2009/dsgsm440.doc.htm (accessed on 11 December 2020).

[246] Coomaraswamy (1994), n. 203.

[247] UN Women (2002), "Women, Peace and Security;" available at: https://www.un.org/ruleoflaw/files/womenpeaceandsecurity.pdf (accessed on 02 April 2021).

economic burdens with other family members. It pushes them to become victims of SGBV alongside their family.[248]

There have been many cases wherein women face sexual violence and other forms of gender-based violence in the wake of extraction of natural resources. For example, in the Peace River region of north-eastern British Columbia, the difference between incomes of locals and highly paid male employees results in violence against women. Similarly, in North Dakota (Bakken oil fields) highly paid oil workers living in camps with limited spending opportunities are often engaged in rape, murders, trafficking, assault and, so on. In DRC, sexual violence against women was widespread in the wake of the conflict over natural resources. The institutions or actors or transnational resource corporations engaged were mostly from the Global North. The growing number of these companies encouraged SGBV against the local women of the Global South.[249]

Some Canadian mining companies operating in Latin America have been accused of rape, gang-rape, abduction and other forms of violence against women. For example, Talisman Energy Ltd. was charged with grave violation of human rights by the Sudanese government forces and government-sponsored militia between 1998 and 2003. These forces displaced the local people around the oil fields that resulted in conflict in South Sudan. Women became victims of SGBV resorted to by the government militias during armed conflicts. In many other cases women have faced SGBV because of economic reasons. However, in most of the cases the perpetrators went scot-free as the cases were dismissed in the courts of law. Porgera gold mine project in Papua New Guinea, local women were subjected to physical and sexual abuse and rapes. In Guatemala in the works of *Coal v Hud Bay Minerals Inc*, local community women faced SGBV by the military personnel. In fact SGBV was used as an instrument to evict the community forcefully so as to exploit the resources.[250]

SGBV perpetrated, in the wake of transnational resource extortion, is the result of institutionalized gender inequality and subordination of women in the society. Thus, SGBV against women is not confined within the family, community, and States. Ironically, it is embedded in the global power structure and corporate stranglehold over natural resources in many of the developing countries. The issue has not yet come on the global radar screen even as the transnational financial institutions continue to avoid and do not take challenge of prevalence of SGBV against women seriosuly.[251]

---

248 UN Women (2015), "Climate Change, and Disasters and Gender-Based Violence in the Pacific;" available at: https://www.uncclearn.org/wp-content/uploads/library/unwomen701.pdf (accessed on 03 April 2021).

249 Simons, Penelope (2017), "Unsustainable International Law: Transnational Resource Extraction and Violence against Women", *Transnat'l L. & Contemp. Probs*, 26:415. Also see Goitam, Hanibal (2017), "Canadian Courts Are Taking a Step toward Corporate Liability of Multinationals for Wrongdoings Abroad"; available at: https://blogs.loc.gov/law/2017/11/canadian-courts-are-taking-a-step-toward-corporate-liability-of-multinationals-for-wrongdoings-abroad/ (accessed on 03 April 2021).

250 Simons, Penelope (2017), n. 249.

251 Ibid.

As seen, the socio-economic vulnerability of women in a particular society or among the refugees or the displaced people is one of the major contributory factors of SGBV. Socio-economic vulnerability contributes to poverty, early marriages or child marriages; child labour; sexual exploitation in the sex market; forced work in unhealthy and dangerous settings. These provide a fertile ground for SGBV against women at any time.[252]

It appears that lack of legal norms and the absence of penal laws alone cannot explain why SGBV is perpetrated against women and girls. Is SGBV constructed and sought to be legitimized within a societal context? It is necessary to understand parts of the problems to provide an effective remedy for SGBV.[253] The study of the relationship between GBV, HIV, and livelihoods explains that gender inequality, an unequal power relations, limited access and control over land and other natural resources; lack of education, health services; food insecurity; and civil war cumulatively exacerbate various forms of SGBV.[254] In such circumstances, women and girls easily become the cannon fodder to satiate the greed of multiple actors.

A WHO study has found that educated and economically independent women suffer less violence in the family, community, and State. Social and economic inequality in the form of lack of opportunity to access personal property, land, wages and credits, household resources, productive resources etc. reduce the chances of economic and social independence of woman. The study has shown that though men and women both live in poverty, women face SGBV as an additional burden arising from the socio-economic factors.[255]

E. **Culture**

Cultural factors often discourage reporting on SGBV cases. The culture of stigmatization, shame, and silence on SGBV against women gives further fillip to it. In a 2014 assessment, after the tropical cyclone in Tonga found that stigma about SGBV extended beyond the family to the village level. As a result, it discouraged the survivors to report their cases.[256] Moreover, studies have shown that the percentage of SGBV is more in a society wherein SGBV is a taboo, women are treated as inferior to men, gender-based discrimination is normal phenomenon, and people prefer

[252] UNHCR (2015), "Sexual and Gender-Based Violence Prevention and Response in Refugee Situations in the Middle East and North Africa;" available at: https://www.refworld.org/pdfid/568f9a014.pdf (accessed on 03 April 2021).

[253] Davies Sara E, Jacqui True (2015), n. 230.

[254] UNHCR (2011), n. 41.

[255] WHO (2021), "Violence against Women"; available at: https://www.who.int/news-room/fact-sheets/detail/violence-against-women (accessed on 30 March 2021).

[256] UN Women (2014), "Climate Change, Disasters and Gender-Based Violence in the Pacific;" available at: https://www.uncclearn.org/wp-content/uploads/library/unwomen701.pdf (accessed on 30 March 2021).

to remain silent about violence against women and girls.[257] Thus, SGBV remains deeply rooted in history, societal values and culture.[258]

The environment of a society or community can be influenced by culturally accepted notions that encourage SGBV with impunity. For example, FGM and other harmful forms of SGBV practices reflects upon the cultural gender stereotypes in different communities.[259] As a result, domestic and sexual violence against women are sought to be sanctified and made to appear 'normal'. In turn, it can only embolden the perpetrators to commit it with impunity.[260]

F. **Environmental factors**

Evidence shows that SGBV increases during and after disasters. As the people become more vulnerable, it encourages all sorts of gender-based crimes such as SGBV against women. Impacts of many disasters result in women at a greater risk of SGBV due to societal gender inequalities and power imbalances.[261] In fact disasters exacerbate pre-existing rates of SGBV. For example, after tsunami in 2007 in the Solomon Islands, women and girls faced SGBV in the camps while fetching water, bathing, collecting fire word, foods, etc.[262]

G. **Discriminatory Law, Policy and Institutional Framework**

It has been seen that gender-discriminatory or gender-insensitive policies, laws and institutional structures contribute to unequal power relations in a society. Thus, lack of legal redressal mechanisms and legal protection lead to various forms of gender-based and sexual violence. As women feel powerless and insecure, chances of impunity only grow.

If the legal institutions, community leaders or States fail to hold the perpetrators accountable for the SGBV, a sense of impunity encourages the other perpetrators to resort to carry out more such crimes. It causes subordination and powerlessness of the survivors as well as strengthens the perception that SGBV against women is acceptable and inevitable.[263] For example, it is very difficult to measure domestic violence in South Africa because the police statistics have not recognized 'domestic violence' as a crime that need to be registered separately. As a result, it is reported that a woman is killed by the intimate partner every six hours and one in four women are physically abused during their lifetimes in South Africa.[264]

---

[257] Davies Sara E, Jacqui True (2015), n. 230.

[258] Chatterji, Angana (2016), "Gendered and Sexual Violence in and beyond South Asia", *ANTYAJAA: Indian Journal of Women and Social Change* 1(1): 19–40; available at: https://journals.sagepub.com/doi/abs/10.1177/2455632716646278?journalCode=jwsa (accessed on 03 April 2021).

[259] Luping, Dianne (2009), "Investigation and Prosecution of Sexual and Gender-Based Crimes before the International Criminal Court", *Journal of Gender, Social Policy & The Law*, 17: (2) 431.

[260] Goldscheid, Julie (2011), n. 166.

[261] UN Women (2014), n. 256.

[262] Ibid.

[263] Ibid.

[264] Goldscheid, Julie (2011), n. 166..

H. **Pandemic, development of technology**

With the development of information and communication technology (ICT), SGBV against women has taken another lethal form. The years 2020-2022 brought in COVID-19 pandemic that has caused an unprecedented socio-economic stress, restricted movements and social isolations that confined people within their houses. It made women more vulnerable and heightened SGBV as the perpetrators had easy access to the victims. Available UN data[265] shows that SGBV against women both in the real and virtual world has sharply grown. SGBV is now manifested in different technology driven forms such as online or cyber violence.

According to the UN Women report, in the US, two out of ten women and girls (aged 18 to 29) were subjected to online sexual violence. Moreover, women and girls from specific groups such as human rights defenders, indigenous women, transgender women, and women from the ethnic minority; women with disability are subjected to technology-facilitated (TF) gender-based violence (GBV). Thus, during 2020-2022 period, the ICT facilitated SGBV has taken a virulent form under the shadow of the COVID-19 pandemic.

I. **Non-recognition**

As already seen earlier, SGBV works as a violent act against any gender. It has also been accepted that it is a violent, aggressive, and hostile act. It seeks to degrade, humiliate, terrorize and control over the victims, the family and the community. Behind all this, presence of *actus reus* and *mens rea* lurks and comes within the ambit of a serious crime. In the changing societal dynamics, SGBV needs to be taken seriously as an egregious crime. This is especially so since recognition of SGBV within the legal framework remains rare.[266] In view of such reluctance, confusion and lack of acceptance of SGBV as separate crime can only pave the way for impunity.[267]

Consequences

SGBV affects human development that curbs the right to life with human dignity. The consequence of SGBV against women results in forced displacement and breakdown of family and community structure.[268] Some of the specific consequences could be identified as follows:

---

[265] UN Women (2020), "Online and ICT facilitated violence against women and girls during COVID-19;" available at: https://www.unwomen.org/-/media/headquarters/attachments/sections/library/publications/2020/brief-online-and-ict-facilitated-violence-against-women-and-girls-during-covid-19-en.pdf?la=en&vs=2519 (accessed on 03 April 2021). See also, ICRW (2018), n. 64.

[266] Isaksson, Charlotte (2014), n. 175.

[267] Luping, Dianne (2009), "Investigation and Prosecution of Sexual and Gender-Based Crimes before the International Criminal Court", *Journal of Gender, Social Policy & The Law*, 17:(2) 431.

[268] UN OHCHR (2019), "Women's human rights and gender-related concerns in situations of conflict and instability"; available at: https://www.ohchr.org/EN/Issues/Women/WRGS/Pages/PeaceAndSecurity.aspx (accessed on 03 April 2021).

A. **Individual level**

Sometimes the victims of SGBV are forced to marry the perpetrators or family members of the perpetrators in countries such as Mali, the Central African Republic, Somalia, South Sudan, and Yemen,etc. It pushes the victims into more vulnerable situations and provides immunity to the perpetrators. In turn, the message on 'acceptability' of SGBV spreads within the society. That encourages post-conflict violence including rape and sexual slavery[269] as well as unwanted pregnancy by the victims of wartime rape. Sometimes, victims of SGBV face critical health problems during an abortion. Lack of proper health services create more critical situations for them. Pregnant women face miscarriages because of SGBV.[270] Children born out of rape, face life long social, economic and individual stigma and other complexities. They are forced to live in extreme poverty and ignored by their relatives. They face psychological and socio-economic problems.[271] Society shows grave indifference towards plight of these children.[272]

In many cases rape, the victims were divorced by their husbands. For instance, 25% of rape victims in Liberia are divorced by their husbands.[273] Since, post-conflict justice mechanism and reparation mechanism are generally male-centric, they tend to overlook needs of the female victims.

B. **Effect on health**

SGBV victims do face a lot of health problems such as sexually transmitted diseases, e.g., HIV/AIDS, infections in reproductive organs as well as other health problems like trauma, shock, memory loss, sexual dysfunction, anxiety, suicidal tendencies etc.[274] Most of the survivors lack access to mechanisms for sexual and reproductive health. In fact, adolescent girls suffer more due to sexually transmitted infections, unwanted pregnancy, and unsafe abortion.[275] Female sex workers have been recognized as one of the key groups that experiences SGBV, lack of contraceptives heighten risks of HIV and sexually transmitted infections. Violence in conflicts

---

[269] UN (2013), *Sexual violence in conflict: Report of the Secretary-General*; Doc. A/67/792–S/2013/149, 14 March 2013; available at: https://www.un.org/sexualviolenceinconflict/wp-content/uploads/report/sexual-violence-in-conflict-report-of-the-secretary-general/SG-Report-2013.pdf (accessed on 03 April 2021).

[270] UNIFEM (2002), *Women, War and Peace: The Independent Experts' Assessment on the Impact of Armed Conflict on Women and Women's Role in Peace-Building* (by Elisabeth Rehn and Ellen Johnson Sirleaf); available at: https://unfpa.org/sites/default/files/pub-pdf/3F71081FF391653DC1256C69003170E9-unicef-WomenWarPeace.pdf (accessed on 03 April 2021).

[271] Ibid.

[272] World Health Organization (2005), *Sexual and Gender Based Violence in Democratic Republic of Congo*; available at: https://www.who.int/hac/crises/cod/sgbv/sgbv_brochure.pdf?ua=1 (accessed on 03 April 2021).

[273] Manjoo and McRaith, (2011), n. 54.

[274] Ibid.

[275] Zhang et al. (2016), "Prevalence and correlates of sexual and gender-based violence against Chinese adolescent women who are involved in commercial sex: a cross-sectional study", *BMJ Open*; available at: https://bmjopen.bmj.com/content/bmjopen/6/12/e013409.full.pdf (accessed on 03 April 2021).

prevents them from accessing health-related information and services. Due to cultural taboo regarding premarital sex and pregnancy also deprive the survivors from getting proper health services.[276]

In disaster affected areas, survivors of SGBV suffer from stress, trauma, and lack of support system to cope up with brutality. For example, in 2012 after tropical cyclones in Fiji, men forced their wives to have sex amidst overcrowding and without privacy in the relief camps. The children born out of SGBV or orphan children affected by disease face SGBV; for example, in sub-Saharan Africa, orphan children are sexually exploited.[277] Social stigma and gender discrimination lead to trauma, sense of powerlessness. It reduces the capacity to participate in any productive activities, social and community activities.[278]

C. Threats to safety and security

Different studies have confirmed that the victims or survivors and the families of rape and other forms of SGBV face social stigma, dishonour and shame. Sometimes the survivors are ostracised and become outcast by the family or the community. In some cases, husbands demand divorce and it results in beatings, mutilation or sexual assault by the family members. Thus the victims suffer double victimization, first by from the perpetrator of crime and then by the family or the community due to deeply entrenched patriarchal mindsets.[279]

SGBV is one of the most serious threats to the safety and security of those affected by conflict or displacement. The displaced women, refugees or sexual minorities become most vulnerable to SGBV.[280] In this context, William Hague, former British Foreign Secretary graphically observed that SGBV has become "a weapon of war that is a substitute of the gun". It has been invoked with lethal effect to humiliate

---

[276] Ibid.

[277] Itzá Castañeda Camey et al. (2020), "Gender-based violence and environment linkages: The violence of inequality", Gland: IUCN; available at: https://portals.iucn.org/library/sites/library/files/documents/2020-002-En.pdf (accessed on 03 April 2021).

[278] FAO (2017), "Gender-Based Violence affects food security and nutrition"; available at: http://www.fao.org/fao-stories/article/en/c/1069792/ (accessed on 03 April 2021). See, UN Women (2012), "Terminology and definitions"; available at: https://www.endvawnow.org/en/articles/1474-terminology-and-definitions.html (accessed on 03 April 2021). The General Assembly resolution 143/2007 stated: "Recognizing the serious immediate and long-term implications for health, including sexual and reproductive health, as well as an increased vulnerability to HIV/AIDS, and the negative impact on psychological, social and economic development that violence against women represents for individuals, families, communities and States"; UN Doc. A/RES/61/143; available at: UN Doc. A/RES/61/143; available at: https://undocs.org/A/RES/61/143 (accessed on 03 April 2021).

[279] Simons, Penelope (2017), n. 249.

[280] UNHCR (2013), "Access to Justice for victims of sexual and gender-based violence Access to justice for victims of sexual and gender-based crimes is crucial to protect and assist survivors, and to prevent its recurrence"; Statement delivered by Simone Schwartz-Delgado, Senior Liaison Officer (Human Rights), CEDAW Half-Day General Discussion on Access to Justice, 18 February 2013; available at: https://www2.ohchr.org/english/bodies/cedaw/docs/Wrapup/UNHCR.pdf (accessed on 03 April 2021).

and destroy an ethnic, religious or opponent group. It has been regarded as a threat to international peace and security and even NATO forces needed to intervene.[281]

D. **Economic and social development**

Thus, gender-based violence is a violation of fundamental human rights. It is an obstacle in the social and economic development of the communities and States.[282] It has been estimated that in some countries SGBV can cost up to 3.7% of their GDP. It is tantamount to double the amount spent on education[283] in some states. It affects women and girls more since SGBV has huge negative impacts on them. For instance, girls are forced to leave their studies; forced to undergo early marriages; forced to engage in commercial sex for food, money, and livelihoods. SGBV causes low productivity and a shortage of workforce in the markets and overall deleterious effect on the economy of a country.

Victims or survivors often avoid interacting with community and society due to illness, emotional or psychological consequences and social stigma. In some societies, free health and counselling service provided to the survivors (especially HIV affected) of SGBV is considered a violation of societal norms. Cumulatively, the consequences could comprise adverse effect on social and economic development; recurrence of SGBV; social disturbances; breakdown in law and order; growth in crimes and an economic crisis that may trigger a civil war or a conflict.[284]

In different occasions, it has seen that SGBV remain unreported because of multiple reasons such as fear of social stigmatization, the threat of secondary victimization by the perpetrators, lack of witness protection, the risk of reprisal, lack of faith in law enforcing authority, etc.[285] Victims are treated as unmarriageable because society believes that the woman victim has lost her virginity and the loss of family honour.[286] It also leads to growth in refugees and internally displaced persons,[287] cases of human trafficking and prostitution[288] and the women victims are deprived of their legitimate opportunities in the society.[289]

As per UN Women's estimate of 736 million women (almost one in three) subjected to SGBV, the global cost prior to 2020 COVID-19 pandemic was placed

---

281 Isaksson, Charlotte (2014), n. 175.

282 FAO, "Gender-Based Violence and Livelihood Interventions: Focus on populations of humanitarian concern in the context of HIV;" available at: http://www.fao.org/fileadmin/templates/dimitra/pdf/guidance_note_gbv_livelihoods.pdf (accessed on 03 April 2021). Moreover, the General Assembly resolution 143/2007 states: "Recognizing further that violence against women impedes the social and economic development of communities and States, as well as the achievement of the internationally agreed development goals, including the Millennium Development Goals;" see, UN Women (2012), n. 278.

283 Hammond, Alicia, et al. (2019), n. 9.

284 Ibid.

285 Coomaraswamy, R. (1994), n. 203.

286 Lindsey (2001), "Women Facing War: ICRC study on the impact of armed conflict on women;" available at: https://www.icrc.org/en/doc/assets/files/other/icrc_002_0798_women_facing_war.pdf (accessed on 03 April 2021).

287 Manjoo and McRaith (2011), n. 54.

288 Ibid.

289 UN (2020), n. 130. Also see UNIFEM (2002), n. 270.

at approximately USD 1.5 trillion.[290] Earlier estimates of enormous cost in the US (Dollar 5.8 billion), the UK (Pound 23 billion) and Canada (Dollar 1 billion)[291] shows the sheer enormity of the challenge and cost of SGBV in different countries. It remains daunting task for a researcher to avail the data even as international institutions struggle hard to assess situation in individual countries. It calls for concerted multi-agency global mechanism to take stock of the harm caused by SGBV globally, sensitize the governments and provide concrete measures to remedy the situation. In turn, it necessitates a balanced scholarly analysis and ideas in prevention, delegitimization and elimination of SGBV as a global scourge in the twenty-first century.

In the aftermath of COVID-19 pandemic (2020-2022), international institutions have expressed grave concern as regards exacerbation of SGBV. Women have become more vulnerable during the prolonged lockdowns in 90 countries wherein some 4 billion people were confined to homes in close proximity to the perpetrators. The exacerbation of violence during 2020-2022, is expected to have given push to this staggering cost of SGBV. The societal cost, generally, would comprise health services for the victims and their children; costs for the post-conflict justice mechanism and the cost to bring the powerful perpetrators to justice. The indirect costs include loss of employment both by the victims and the perpetrators as well as reduction of productivity in the employment (Table 2.2).[292]

---

[290] UN Women (2020), *Violence against women and girls: the shadow pandemic, Statement by Phumzile Mlambo-Ngcuka, Executive Director of UN Women;* available at: https://www.unwomen.org/en/news/stories/2020/4/statement-ed-phumzile-violence-against-women-during-pandemic (accessed on 03 April 2021).

[291] For these estimated figures see, generally, UN Secretary General (2008), "UNiTE to End Violence Against Women"; available at: http://www.peacewomen.org/sites/default/files/vaw_factsheet_undpi_feb2008_0.pdf; UN Vienna (2009), "Violence Against Women"; available at: http://unis.unvienna.org/pdf/factsheets/UNiTE_TheSituation_en.pdf; The World Bank (2019), "Gender-based Violence"; available at: https://www.worldbank.org/en/topic/socialsustainability/brief/violence-against-women-and-girls; UN Women (2020), "Violence Against Women and Girls: The Shadow Pandemic"; available at: https://www.unwomen.org/en/news/stories/2020/4/statement-ed-phumzile-violence-against-women-during-pandemic (all accessed on 03 April 2021).

[292] WHO (2021), "Violence against Women," available at: https://www.who.int/news-room/fact-sheets/detail/violence-against-women (accessed on 03 February 2021); WHO (2021), "Violence Against Women: Prevalence Estimates, 2018"; available at: https://cdn.who.int/media/docs/default-source/documents/violence-prevention/vaw_report_web_09032021_oleksandr.pdf?sfvrsn=a82ef89c_5&download=true (accessed on 03 April 2021); WHO (2020), *RESPECT women: Preventing violence against women: A framework for policymaker*; https://www.who.int/publications/i/item/WHO-RHR-18.19 (accessed on 03 April 2021).

Table 2.2 Different types of SGBV against women around the World

No	Country	Year	Victims/survivors	Perpetrators	Types of SGBV
1	Egypt[293]	Peacetime and conflict, 2015–2016[294]	Refugee and asylum seekers during conflict and peacetime faced SGBV (Syrian refugees in Egypt). In Egypt, 1.7 million women suffered sexual harassment, 3.7% faced violence in the workplace, 16,000 girls harassed in educational institutions[295]	Individuals, stakeholders, employers etc.	Domestic violence, sexual harassment at public places, harmful traditional practices, e.g., child marriages, FGM[296]

(continued)

[293] UNHCR (2017), ""Art Therapy to Prevent and Respond to SGBV – Egypt" (Chap. 6) in *Gender Equality Promising Practices: Syrian Refugees in the Middle East and North Africa*. Geneva: UNHCR; available at: https://www.refworld.org/pdfid/5a38dd264.pdf (accessed on 03 April 2021).

[294] Ibid.

[295] Ibid.

[296] Ibid.

Table 2.2 (continued)

No	Country	Year	Victims/survivors	Perpetrators	Types of SGBV
2	Africa[297]	Peacekeeping operations, 2000-2015; [Taking Boko Haram Joint Task Force, Burundi Central African Republic, Chad (EUFOR, Comoros (political intervention, and Cote d'Ivoire Ebola Epidemic Guinea, Guinea-Bissau (political & int. peace building) Kenya (AU Panel) Liberia, Libya (NATO intervention and UN mission) Madagascar (AU & SADC political missions) Mali Sierra Leone Somalia South Sudan Sudan Abyei and "Two Areas Darfur (AMIS and Western Sahara Zimbabwe (political mission)]	Civilians during conflicts and peace; man, women, boy, girls	Armed forces of the peacekeepers	Sexual violence; sexual humiliation,;rape of women, girls, men and boys; rape with object; mass rape; forced incest sexual relation; slavery; forced marriage; forced pregnancy; forced sterelization; torture; mutilation; indiscriminate killing; child soldiers; forced concription; enforced disappearance; hostage taking etc.
3	Fiji[298]	Cyclone, 2012;	Women and girls	Family members	Forced sexual intercourse with wives; forced sexual work
4	Solomon Islands[299]	Floods, 2014 and Tsunami, i2007	Homeless women and girls	Male members of family and the community	73% of women in the Solomon Islands believe that it is acceptable for a man to beat his wife; unwanted sexual contact; SGBV including rape

(continued)

[297] World Peace Foundation (2016), *Protection of Civilians from Sexual and Gender-Based Violence: Insights for African Union Peace Missions* (by Dyan Mazurana, andd Dallin Van Leuven); available at: https://sites.tufts.edu/wpf/files/2017/07/9.-Protection-from-SGBV-Mazuranaf.pdf (accessed on 11 December 2020).

[298] UN Women (2014), n. 256.

[299] Ibid.

Table 2.2 (continued)

No	Country	Year	Victims/survivors	Perpetrators	Types of SGBV
5	Kiribati[300]	During peace, natural disasters and after disasters	Women and girls within and outside the family	Husband, intimate partner and non-partner male member of the society	68% of women in Kiribati have experienced physical and sexual violence by a husband or intimate partner, women also face sexual violence by non-partner, child sexual abuse, etc
6	Tanna Tafe Province in Vanuatu[301]	Tropical cyclones, 2018	Women and girls of different ages	Family members	30% The increase in new domestic violence cases reported by the Tanna Women's Counseling Centre
7	Tonga[302]	Tropical cyclone, 2014	Women and girls	Family and community	Stigma around SGBV
8	Asia- Pacific, Latin America[303]	During peace, conflicts or emergency like natural disasters	Women and girls	Within family, outside family, non-sate actors or by States' militia	Adolescent girls 15–19 years face SGBV, SGBV faced by the adolescent women engaged in commercial sex work
9	Syria, Iraq, Yemen and Libya	During peace and conflicts	Thousands of women, girls, men, and boys affected	Family, community, terror groups, non-state actors, state military forces	Forced and early marriage, sexual violence, including sexual abuse and exploitation and domestic violence

(continued)

300 Ibid.

301 Ibid.

302 Ibid.

303 Goldscheid, Julie (2011), n. 166.

Table 2.2 (continued)

No	Country	Year	Victims/survivors	Perpetrators	Types of SGBV
10	Uganda[304]	Emergency, 2015-2016	Women and girls especially refugee women	Partner and non-partner	Sexual exploitation by aid workers is a reality in emergency settings. All facets of women's health (including physical, sexual and reproductive, mental, and behaviorial) are impacted by SGBV sometimes for the long-term and in a chronic manner.
11	Japan	During the Second World War 1939–1945[305]	East Asian women especially Korean women and girls (known as 'comfort women')	Imperial army of Japan[306]	Sexual slavery by building 'comfort stations.'
12	Bangladesh [307]	During liberation war in 1971[308]	Estimated 200,000 women were raped	Pakistani soldiers	Torture, rape, other inhumane acts[309]

(continued)

[304] Population Council (2016), "Effectiveness of A Community-Based SGBV Prevention Model In Emergency Settings in Uganda: Testing The 'Zero Tolerance Village Alliance' Intervention;" available at: https://www.popcouncil.org/uploads/pdfs/2016RH_SGBVPreventionUgandaZTVA.pdf (accessed on 03 April 2021).

[305] Coomaraswamy (1996), "Report on the mission to the Democratic People's Republic of Korea, the Republic of Korea and Japan on the issue of military sexual slavery in wartime;" E/CN.4/1996/53/Add.1, 4 January 1996; available at: http://hrlibrary.umn.edu/commission/country52/53-add1.htm (accessed on 11 December 2020).

[306] "Announcement by Foreign Ministers of Japan and the Republic of Korea at the Joint Press Occasion December 28, 2015;" available at: https://www.mofa.go.jp/a_o/na/kr/page4e_000364.html (accessed on 03 April 2021).

[307] Coomaraswamy (1996), n. 305.

[308] Ibid.

[309] International Crimes Tribunal-1 (2015), *ICT-BD [ICT-1] Case No.02 OF 2015*; available at: https://www.ict-bd.org/ict1/Judgment%202016/ICT-BD%20Case%202%202015.pdf (accessed on 03 April 2021).

Table 2.2 (continued)

No	Country	Year	Victims/survivors	Perpetrators	Types of SGBV
13	Former Yugoslavia	Armed conflict, 1991–2001 conflict[310]	Against various ethnic group of Croatia, Bosnia, Herzegovina, Serbia, Kosovo and former Yugoslav Republic of Macedonia	Head of the State and senior officials	Rape, enslavement, torture and sexually abused[311]
14	Rwanda	Conflict between the Rwandan Patriotic Front and the Rwandan Government in 1994[312]	Against Tutsi civilians (estimated 150,000–250,000 women were raped)[313]	Hutu (High ranking military officers, government officials, politician, businessmen, etc.)	Rape and other forms of SGBV
15	Liberia	Civil Conflict in Liberia[314] (1989–2003)[315]	400,000 women were raped. Nearly 50% of the victims among the 658 rape survivors were children of the age of 5–12 years[316]	Attackers were known to the victims	Rape, sexual violence

(continued)

[310] UN ICTY, *About the ICTY*; available at: https://www.icty.org/en/about (accessed on 03 April 2021).

[311] UN ICTY, *Enforcement of Sentence*; available at: https://www.icty.org/en/cases/enforcement-of-sentences (accessed on 03 April 2021).

[312] UN ICTR, *The ICTR in Brief*; available at: https://unictr.irmct.org/en/tribunal (accessed on 03 April 2021).

[313] UN IRMCT, *The Genocide*; available at: https://unictr.irmct.org/en/genocide (accessed on 11 December 2020).

[314] UN OCHA (2019), "Gender-based violence: A closer look at the numbers", 21 May 2019; available at: https://www.unocha.org/story/gender-based-violence-closer-look-numbers (accessed on 02 February 2021).

[315] UN (2014), *Outreach Program on the 1994 Genocide Against the Tutsi in Rwanda and the United Nations;* available at: https://www.un.org/en/preventgenocide/rwanda/ (accessed on 03 April 2021).

[316] Ibid. Also see, UNOCHA (2019), n. 314.

Table 2.2 (continued)

No	Country	Year	Victims/survivors	Perpetrators	Types of SGBV
16	Sierra Leone	Civil war, 1991–2002[317]	60,000 Women and girls of Sierra Leone suffered	Government forces and their allies	The extraordinary levels of rape, sexual violence, and other gross human rights violations[318]
17	Democratic Republic of Congo	Armed conflicts[319]	Thousands women and girls raped. 40,000 survivors of SGBV[320]	UN officials or peace keeping forces;[321] Government armed group in conflict[322]	Rape, mutilation, gang rape, unwanted pregnancy, sexual slavery, forced marriages, etc[323]

(continued)

[317] Ibid.

[318] UN, *The Special Court for Sierra Leone rests—for good*; available at: https://www.un.org/africarenewal/magazine/april-2014/special-court-sierra-leone-rests-%E2%80%93-good (accessed on 03 April 2021).

[319] UN (2014), n. 315. Also see, UNOCHA (2019), n. 314.

[320] WHO, *Sexual and Gender Based Violence in Democratic Republic of Congo*; available at: https://www.who.int/hac/crises/cod/sgbv/sgbv_brochure.pdf?ua=1 (accessed on 03 April 2020).

[321] UN (2014), n. 315. See also, UNOCHA (2019), n. 314.

[322] UN (2020), *Democratic Republic of the Congo*; available at: https://www.un.org/sexualviolenceinconflict/countries/democratic-republic-of-the-congo/ (accessed on 03 April 2021).

[323] UNU (2012), *Sexual violence in the Democratic Republic of the Congo*; available at: https://unu.edu/publications/articles/sexual-violence-in-the-democratic-republic-of-the-congo.html.
(accessed on 03 April 2021).

Table 2.2 (continued)

No	Country	Year	Victims/survivors	Perpetrators	Types of SGBV
18	Kosovo	Armed conflict, 1998–1999[324]	10–45 thousand women were victims[325]	Serbs against ethnic Albanians[326]	Rape, gang rape and other form of sexual violence[327]
19	Myanmar	In 1992, 2017[328]	Women of the Rohingya community	Government troops	Rape and other forms of sexual violence.
20	Mali	Armed conflict,[329] 2012–2013	Women and girls	Armed forces	Conflict-related sexual violence, rape, sexual violence, etc
21	Somalia	Armed conflict, 2014[330]	2891 incidents were reported, maximum victims from minority groups	Armed militants allied with the Government; the clan militias	Rape, sexual assault, forced marriage.[331]
22	South Sudan	Armed conflicts, 2013[332]	200 case of abduction, 167 conflicts related to sexual violence; maximum victims women and girls of other nationality	Sudan People's Liberation Army, Dinka youth and armed cattle keepers, members of South Sudan's National Police Service, Lord's Resistance Army, etc	Rape, gang rape, sexual slavery, abduction, castration, forced nudity, forced abortion, forced pregnancy

(continued)

324 UN Women (2016), *Path to justice for survivors of Kosovo's sexual violence*; available at: https://eca.unwomen.org/en/news/stories/2016/08/q-and-a-with-siobhan-hobbs (accessed on 03 April 2021).

325 Kosovo Women's Network (2017), *Women's Rights are Human Rights*; available at: https://womensnetwork.org/wp-content/uploads/2018/10/20180326143802724.pdf (accessed on 03 April 2021).

326 UNHCR (2002), *The Kosovo Women's Initiative*; available at: https://www.unhcr.org/3db019784.pdf (accessed on 03 April 2021).

327 HRW, *Gender Based Violence against Kosovar Albanian Women*; available at: https://www.hrw.org/reports/2000/fry/Kosov003-02.htm (accessed on 03 April 2021).

328 Coomaraswamy, R. (1994), see n. 203. See also, HRW (2017), "All of My Body Was Pain" "Sexual Violence against Rohingya Women and Girls in Burma", Summary, 16 November 2017; available at: https://www.hrw.org/report/2017/11/16/all-mybody-was-pain/sexual-violence-against-rohingya-women-and-girls-burma (accessed on 31 March 2022).

329 UN (2020), "Sexual Violence in Conflict" (Mali); available at: https://www.un.org/sexualviolenceinconflict/countries/mali/ (accessed on 04 April 2021).

330 UN (2020), "Sexual Violence in Conflict" (Somalia); available at: https://www.un.org/sexualviolenceinconflict/countries/somalia/ (accessed on 04 April 2021).

331 Human Rights Watch (2014), "Here Rape is Normal: A Five Point Plan to Curtail Sexual Violence in Somalia"; available at: https://www.hrw.org/report/2014/02/13/here-rape-normal/five-point-plan-curtail-sexual-violence-somalia (accessed on 04 April 2021).

332 UN (2020), "Sexual Violence in Conflict" (South Sudan); available at: https://www.un.org/sexualviolenceinconflict/countries/south-sudan/ (accessed on 04 April 2021).

Table 2.2 (continued)

No	Country	Year	Victims/survivors	Perpetrators	Types of SGBV
23	Sudan	Armed conflict, 2013[333]	147 reported victims in 2014 were women and girls 4–70 years	Armed men from Arab tribes	Rape, sexual violence
24	The Syrian Arab Republic	Armed conflicts[334]	Women and girls	By pro-government forces	Abduction, exclave, forced marriage, rape, sexual violence, commercialization of sex within the camp
25	Central African Republic[335]	Armed conflicts	Armed herders	2527 cases reported	Rape perpetrated to terrorize the civilians
26	Columbia	Internal armed conflict[336]	7353 victims are registered during 1985–2014	Paramilitary leaders (Mancuso and others)	Abduction, sexual slavery, forced sterilization, forced abortion, prostitution, sexual assault
27	Nepal	Civil war, 1996–2006[337]	Women and girls of Nepal	Government forces	Rape, sexual assault, sexual harassment,

(continued)

333 UN (2020), "Sexual Violence in Conflict" (Sudan, Darfur); available at: https://www.un.org/sexualviolenceinconflict/countries/sudan-darfur/ (accessed on 04 April 2021).

334 UN (2020), "Sexual Violence in Conflict" (Syrian Arab Republic); available at: https://www.un.org/sexualviolenceinconflict/countries/syrian-arab-republic/ (accessed on 04 April 2021).

335 UN, "Sexual Violence in Conflict" (Central African Republic); available at: https://www.un.org/sexualviolenceinconflict/countries/central-african-republic/ (accessed on 04 April 2021).

336 UN, "Sexual Violence in Conflict" (Colombia); available at: https://www.un.org/sexualviolenceinconflict/countries/colombia/ (accessed on 04 April 2021).

337 Human Rights Watch (2014), "Silenced and Forgotten Survivors of Nepal's Conflict-Era Sexual Violence;" available at: https://www.hrw.org/sites/default/files/reports/nepal0914_ForUpload_0.pdf (accessed on 04 April 2021).

Table 2.2 (continued)

No	Country	Year	Victims/survivors	Perpetrators	Types of SGBV
28	India	Riots, 1992[338]	Women and girls	Government forces, anti-social elements	Rape, gang rape, sexual assault
29	Darfur	Armed conflict, 2005-2006[339]	200 women experienced sexual violence in a single five-week period. 500 raped survivors got medical care	Military, militia, police, rebels, criminal gangs, etc	Rape and sexual violence
30	Cote d'Ivoire	Conflict, 2014[340]	325 rape cases (against 2–17 years) girls	Police, ex-combatants	Rape, gang rape and sexual abuse
31	Nigeria	Armed insugency by Boko Haram 2009[341]	276 schoolgirls abducted, girls and women are the sufferers	Nigerian security forces, allied forces, Boko Haram	Abduction, forced marriages, rape, sexual abuse, forced labour, physical and psychotically abuse, forced conversion
32	Sri Lanka	Armed conflict (26 years) between LTTE and Government)[342]	Women and girls	Police, army, LTTE	Rape, sexual abuse, other forms of sexual violence
33	El Salvador, Guatemala, Honduras, Northern Triangle countries[343]	Armed conflict, 2017	Women, girls, and LGBTI persons	Family members, gangs, and drug traffickers most frequently perpetrate SGBV; violence by police and other authorities	High levels of homicide forced disappearances and kidnappings in these countries

[338] Population Council (2016), n. 304.

[339] HRW (2008), "Sexual Violence in Darfur in 2007–2008," available at: https://www.hrw.org/reports/2008/darfur0408/5.htm (accessed on 04 April 2021).

[340] UN (2020), "Sexual Violence in Conflict" (Cote d'lvoire); available at: https://www.un.org/sexualviolenceinconflict/countries/cote-divoire/ (accessed on 04 April 2021).

[341] HRW (2014), "Those Terrible Weeks in Their Camp: Boko Haram Violence against Women and Girls in Northeast Nigeria"; available at: https://www.hrw.org/report/2014/10/27/those-terrible-weeks-their-camp/boko-haram-violence-against-women-and-girls (accessed on 04 April 2021).

[342] HRW (2013), "We Will Teach You a Lesson: Sexual Violence against Tamils by Sri Lankan Security Forces"; available at: https://www.hrw.org/report/2013/02/26/we-will-teach-you-lesson/sexual-violence-against-tamils-sri-lankan-security-forces (accessed on 04 April 2021).

[343] Latin America Working Group (2017), "Sexual and Gender Based Violence (SGBV) & Migration Fact Sheet"; available at: https://supportkind.org/wp-content/uploads/2017/06/SGBV-and-migration-fact-sheet-June-2017.pdf (accessed on 04 April 2021).

Conclusion

In view of the above discussion, it can be surmised that SGBV is gender neutral. However, most of the victims remain girls and women. Hence, this chapter and rest of the chapters in this study have commonly used the terminologies described herein to understand and address the challenge of SGBV against women. SGBV is no longer a myth as seen from the facts and data arising from different UN reports and processes as well as works of other international institutions. Different forms of SGBV are multidimensional. With the passage of time and situation, the usage of terminology has also changed. Some of the causes and consequences of SGBV have been examined. Still, many others remain to be identified. The consequences are perpetual, and sufferings are immeasurable.

Victimization is not only confined to a particular individual or time; rather it affects the present and future of an individual, family, community, and the States. It has emerged as one of the significant threats to international peace and security. With pre-2020 COVID-19 pandemic estimated cost of dollars 1.5 trillion, SGBV remains one of the biggest challenges for the humankind. As a scourge, SGBV against women has emerged as a heinous crime. The culture of silence, tendency to hide the incidents, 'normalization' of sexual violence against girls and women in societies and a sense of 'impunity' for the perpetrators remain some of the key barriers to a concerted global action,. It calls for an effective role for the relevant international institutions as well as sharper working of appropriate international legal mechanisms to provide a robust protective shield for girls and women against SGBV.

Chapter 3
International Legal Protection Against SGBV

Introduction

As discussed in the previous chapter, girls and women are the main victims of sexual and gender-based violence (SGBV) during peace, conflicts, and post-conflicts situations.[1] Ironically, the SGBV against women is considered as a normal phenomenon and denied by the family, society, and the States. Hence, it is a crucial challenge to end SGBV against women.[2]

SGBV has been taken seriously after the 1990s though sexual violence against women has grown in conflict zones.[3] The existing international law shows that there is no specific international legal instrument to address SGBV directly. Some international legal instruments, however, contain provisions that implicitly address the issues such as discrimination against women, torture, forced prostitution, and crime against humanity, war crimes. Still, they do not deal with all forms of SGBV.[4]

---

[1] Mani, V. S. (2001), "International humanitarian law: an Indo-Asian perspective," *International Review of the Red Cross*; available at: https://www.icrc.org/en/doc/resources/documents/article/other/57jqzm.htm (accessed on 04 April 2021).

[2] True, Jacqui (2016), "Working Paper Ending violence against women in Asia: International norm diffusion and global opportunity structures for policy change", *UNRISD Working Paper, No. 2016-5*; available at: https://www.unrisd.org/80256B3C005BCCF9/httpNetITFramePDF?ReadForm&parentunid=0AE05C2AE73E998DC1257FD10051838E&parentdoctype=paper&netitpath=80256B3C005BCCF9/(httpAuxPages)/0AE05C2AE73E998DC1257FD10051838E/$file/True.pdf (accessed on 04 April 2021).

[3] Kritz, Brian A. (2010), "Brian A. Kritz, International Legal Protection for Women and Female Children: Rwanda - A Case Study," *Suffolk Transnational Law Review*, 33(1): 1–35; see also, Mannix, Bridget (2014–2015), "A Quest for Justice: Investigating Sexual and Gender Based Violence at the International Criminal Court," *James Cook U. L. Rev*, 21: 7.

[4] Gaggioli, Gloria (2014), "Sexual violence in armed conflicts: A violation of international humanitarian law and human rights law," *International Review of the Red Cross*, 96 (894): 503–538; available at: https://www.cambridge.org/core/journals/international-review-of-the-red-cross/article/sexual-violence-in-armed-conflicts-a-violation-of-international-humanitarian-law-and-human-rights-law/F14982FBF972DE4A86D8399695154FD5 (accessed on 04 April 2021).

B. H. Desai and M. Mandal, *Sexual and Gender-Based Violence in International Law*,
https://doi.org/10.1007/978-981-19-0894-1_3

There are two types of laws: one is *lex generalis* that is applicable during times of both peace and conflicts; another is the *lex specialis* that is applicable only to a specific subject or situation. *Lex generalis* and *lex specialis* include both hard and soft international legal instruments. However, it is the soft law instruments that primarily mater in the field. It is no wonder that the development of international law in the fields of human rights and humanitarian law has taken place on the bedrock of *soft* instrumentality. They constitute a large corpus of resolutions of the political organs of the UN especially the General Assembly and the Security Council, practices of the subsidiary bodies such as the Human Rights Council and Office of the High Commissioner for Human Rights as well as guidelines of the International Committee of the Red Cross (ICRC).

In this context, this chapter has been divided into four parts. First part explains the sources of international law. Second part discusses the historical development of international law as regards SGBV against women. Third part analyses international legal protection for women against SGBV. Last part explains the gaps within the existing legal framework and the way forward.

Sources of International Law

While discussing international legal protection relating to SGBV against women, it is pertinent to explain the sources of international law. The most accepted sources are mentioned in the Statute of the International Court of Justice (ICJ), 1945. According to Article 38(1)[5] of the Statute of ICJ, the primary sources of international law are international convention or treaties (general or particular), international customs, the general principle of law recognized by nations, judicial decisions, and the teachings of the highly qualified publicists of the various nations as the subsidiary sources.[6]

Treaties are the international legal instruments (known as agreements, conventions, protocols etc.) between States or between States and international organizations. According to the 1969 Vienna Convention on the Law of the Treaties (VCLT) and under the customary international law (CIL), States are bound by the treaties to which they are the parties (i.e. *pacta sunt servnda*). VCLT is an example of the codification process and contains substantial amount of CIL. When a particular treaty or a provision of the treaty contains principles of CIL, it binds the States irrespective of being parties to the treaty in question.[7]

---

[5] Article 38(1) (a) of *Statute of the ICJ* provides: "The Court, whose function is to decide in accordance with international law such disputes as are submitted to it, shall apply: a. international conventions, whether general or particular, establishing rules expressly recognized by the contesting states; b. international custom, as evidence of a general practice accepted as law; c. the general principles of law recognized by civilized nations; d. subject to the provisions of Article 59, judicial decisions and the teachings of the most highly qualified publicists of the various nations, as subsidiary means for the determination of rules of law. 2. This provision shall not prejudice the power of the Court to decide a case *ex aequo et bono*, if the parties agree thereto;" available at: https://www.icj-cij.org/en/statute (accessed on 10 April 2021).

[6] Ibid.

[7] Ibid.

Custom is the oldest source of international law. It is binding on all the States irrespective of being a party to any treaty. A customary norm crystallizes by virtue of actual State practice and *opinion juris*. ICJ has opined in the *North Sea Continental Shelf* that even a short-term States practice with *opinion juris* can become a rule of new CIL.[8]

The general principle of law recognized by civilized nations is the third primary source of international law. The ICJ and other international courts and tribunals (ICTs) sometimes do use this source of international law. For instance, in the *Barcelona Traction* case, ICJ adopted the legal personality of the corporations as a widely accepted postulate of the national legal system. Similarly, widely accepted principles, like *res judicata*, emanating from the national legal systems are accepted as a source of international law.[9]

Judicial decisions are treated as secondary or subsidiary sources of international law. According to Article 59 of the Statute of ICJ,[10] the decisions of the ICJ are binding only on the parties to the dispute and applicable only in that dispute. As a result, the concept of judicial precedent, generally, does not prevail. Still, the decisions of the ICJ or other judicial bodies are respected and followed by the ICTs. The Statute of the ICJ does not distinguish between the decisions of ICTs as they provide an authoritative interpretation of international law. The decisions of national courts do contribute to the State practice that forms an essential element for the CIL.[11]

Similarly, the writings of 'most highly qualified publicists of the various nations' are regarded as a subsidiary means for the determination of rules of law. There are a few examples wherein scholarly works have been cited as subsidiary sources of international law such as the *Calvo* (Carlos) doctrine (on two concepts of non-intervention and absolute equality of foreigners with nationals)[12] and the *Hull* (Cordell) Doctrine (prompt, effective, and adequate compensation).[13]

Article 38(1) of the Statute of ICJ does not mention all the sources of international law. For example, the resolutions of the UN (especially the General Assembly and the Security Council) do not find a mention.[14] These resolutions have an important role in

---

[8] Ibid.

[9] Crawford, James R. (2012), *Brownlie's Principles of Public International Law* (8th Edition), UK: Oxford University Press.

[10] ICJ Statute, n.5; Article 59 of the Statute: "The decision of the Court has no binding force except between the parties and in respect of that particular case".

[11] Greenwood, Christopher (2008), "Sources of International Law: An Introduction"; available at: https://legal.un.org/avl/pdf/ls/greenwood_outline.pdf (accessed on 10 April 2021).

[12] Ibid. Also see, Shan, Wenhua (2007), "From North-South Divide to Private-Public Debate: Revival of the Calvo Doctrine and the Changing Landscape in International Investment Law", *Nw. J. Int'l L. & Bus.* 27(3): 631, 632; available at: https://scholarlycommons.law.northwestern.edu/cgi/viewcontent.cgi?article=1658&context=njilb&httpsredir=1&referer= (accessed on 10 April 2021).

[13] Dawson, Frank G. and Weston, B.H. (1962), "Prompt, Adequate and Effective": A Universal Standard of Compensation?", *Fordhman L. Rev.* 30: 727; available at: https://ir.lawnet.fordham.edu/cgi/viewcontent.cgi?article=1730&context=flr (accessed on 10 April 2021).

[14] Ibid.

the international law-making process. A resolution makes a contribution to the development of international law by wide acceptance[15] of the States. The reports of the International Law Commission (ILC) on issues such as the Articles on the Responsibility of States for Wrongful Acts, 2001[16] (taken note of *vide* GA Res. 56/83 of 12 December 2001) contribute in the development of international law. Similarly, the Security Council resolutions (such as 1325 of 31 October 2000 on the impact of armed conflict on women and girls) have different features depending upon the authority invoked. For instance, the resolutions are adopted under Chapter VII (enforcement), as compared to Chapter VI, have a binding effect on all the members of the UN (Article 25).[17]

In the *Lockerbie case*,[18] the ICJ observed that a decision taken under Article 103[19] of the UN Charter will prevail over all other international obligations. Moreover, as per ruling of the Tribunal in the *Tadic* case (ICTY), the UNSC does not create a new rule but imposes obligations on some specific issues as it is not a legislature.[20] The subsidiary sources of international law are known as soft law that include the resolutions of GA and SC and the 'work-in-progress' reports of ILC. Notwithstanding issues regarding effectiveness of soft law instruments, the subsidiary sources of international law play crucial role in stregthening the corpus of international law arising from customs and treaties. The thin dividing line between hard and soft law often gets blurred if the sovereign States take an internatioal instrument (hard or soft) seriously. The Universal Declaration of Human Rights (adopted *vide* the GA Res. 217 A of 10 December 1948) is the best example of it.

Current State of International Law

In this backdrop, since there is no specific international legal instrument dealing with SGBV, relevant provisions of the laws relating to warfare, protection of human rights and individual criminal responsibility for the international crimes are sought

[15] For a detailed discussion on why nations observe law see, generally, Louis Henkin (1968), *How Nations Behave: Law and Foreign Policy*, Pall Mall, London, Chapter IV at p. 45.

[16] Wolfrum, Rüdiger (2011), "Customary international law", *Max Planck Encyclopedia of International Law*, Oxford: OUP; available at: https://www.academia.edu/38007948/EPIL_Sources_of_International_Law_pdf (accessed on 10 April 2021).

[17] United Nations (1945), *Charter of United Nations;* Article 25 provides: "The Members of the United Nations agree to Accept and carry out the decisions of the Security Council in accordance with the present Charter;" available at: https://treaties.un.org/doc/Publication/CTC/uncharter.pdf (accessed on 10 April 2021).

[18] *Lockerbie (Libyan Arab Jamahiriya v. United States of America)*, (1998), ICJ; available at: https://www.icj-cij.org/en/case/88 (accessed on 10 April 2021).

[19] UN (1945), n.17. Article 103 of *UN Charter* provides: "In the event of a conflict between the obligations of the Members of the United Nations under the present Charter and their obligations under any other international agreement, their obligations under the present Charter shall prevail".

[20] Wolfrum (2011), n.16.

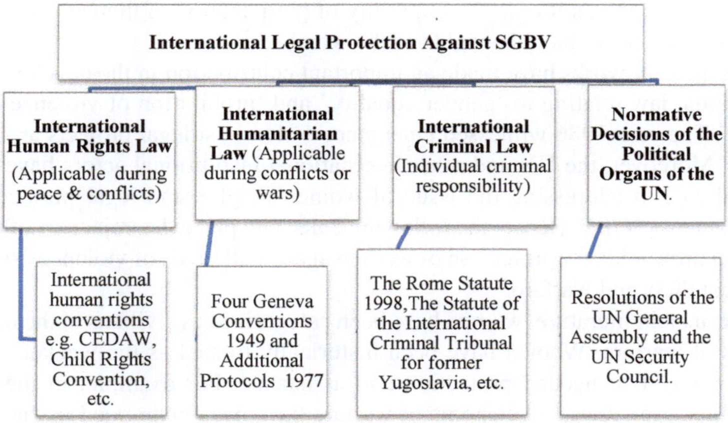

Fig. 3.1 International Legal Protection to Women Against SGBV

to be applied to SGBV. These international legal mechanisms protect individuals affected by the armed conflicts, victims of violation of human rights during peace and conflict as well as victims of international crimes. Therefore, relevant international legal mechanisms pertaining to SGBV include international human rights law, international humanitarian law (also known as the law of war or the Geneva Law), international criminal law, and other normative instruments adopted especially under the auspices of the UN. Cumulatively, this corpus covers all the sources of international law. Thus, in the absence of specific international legal instrument, these scattered international law provisions can be applied to provide international legal protection to women against SGBV (Fig. 3.1).[21]

Historical Developments

The development of the legal protection relating to 'violence against women,' 'gender-based violence' or SGBV began especially after advent of the 1945 Charter of the United Nations (UN). The UN Charter provides for women's human rights. The concept of 'promoting equality and non-discrimination throughout the world'; 'fundamental human rights'[22]; 'encouragement and promotion of human rights and

[21] UN (2002), "Women, Peace and Security: Study submitted by the Secretary-General pursuant to Security Council resolution 1325 (2000)"; available at: https://www.un.org/ruleoflaw/files/womenpeaceandsecurity.pdf (accessed on 10 April 2021).

[22] *Preamble to the UN Charter states*: "to reaffirm faith in fundamental human rights, in the dignity and worth of the human person, in the equal rights of men and women and of nations large and small"; see UN (1945), n.17.

fundamental freedoms for all'[23]; 'eligibility of participation of men and women'[24]; and 'gender equality' include 'rights of the women.'[25]

The scholarly works have made an important contribution in the development of international law relating to 'gender equality,' and 'prohibition of violence against women.' The year 1986 witnessed emergence of feminist legal projects around the world.[26] Moreover, the UN and other international institutional actors have played a pivotal role in addressing the issue of women's rights and legal protection for women against SGBV. Hence, the following enlist and place the trajectory of various historical thresholds for protection of women against all kinds of violence especially during conflicts and warfare.

In the ancient literature, women have been categorized as civilians in the laws and customs of warfare. Women have been historically treated as the weaker sections of the society that needed protection and assistance. For example, in the Indian subcontinent, the laws and customs of warfare have been elaborated in the ancient texts such as the *Vedas, the Ramayana, the Mahabharata, the Agni Purana, the Manu-Smriti*, and in the writings of *Kautilya.* During the ancient period, warfare was often categorized as *Dharma Yuddha* (righteous war) and *Adharma Yuddha* (unrighteous war). Therefore, the primary focus of these legal thresholds included: (i) means and methods of war (ii) use of weapons of war, (iii) treatment of persons wounded or taken as prisoners, and (iv) the treatment of civilians including women.[27] Hence, these ancient Indian laws protected women primarily as civilians.[28]

During the mediaeval period, it was the duty of the rulers to protect civilians from the effects of war.[29] The *Viqayet* text (written around 1280 A.D.) contained laws of war. However, its focus was on the protection of women, children, old and sick people.[30] During the sixteenth and seventeenth century, most of the States were colonized. The international law as it is known today has originated primarily from the needs, thinking, and value systems of the European colonial powers. It is contended

[23] Ibid; Article 1(3) "To achieve international co-operation in solving international problems of an economic, social, cultural, or humanitarian character, and in promoting and encouraging respect for human rights and for fundamental freedoms for all without distinction as to race, sex, language, or religion…".

[24] Ibid; Article 8: "The United Nations shall place no restrictions on the eligibility of men and women to participate in any capacity and under conditions of equality in-its principal and subsidiary organs.".

[25] Defeisq, Elizabeth F. (2011), "The United Nations and Women – A Critique", *Wm. & Mary J. Women & L.* 17: 395.

[26] 1986 was a significant year for the feminist project in law, both in Australia and elsewhere, see, Graycar, Regina (1986), "Yes, Virginia There Is Feminist Legal Literature", *Australian Journal of Law and Society, 3: 105.*

[27] Mani (2001), n.1.

[28] Ibid.

[29] Ibid.

[30] Meurant, Jacques. (1987), "Inter Arma Caritas: Evolution and Nature of International Humanitarian Law," *Journal of Peace Research,* 24 (3): 237–249; https://journals.sagepub.com/doi/10.1177/002234338702400304#articleCitationDownloadContainer (accessed on 11 April 2021).

that most of the women's rights movements begun in the European countries, and moorings of modern international law have been Eurocentric.[31]

Thus, available literature shows that the women's rights movements begun in the Global North (Europe and America), because most of the other territories or countries (in Latin America, Africa and Asia) were colonized at that time.[32] The law relating to the rights of the women started with the *Declaration of Sentiments and Resolutions: Women's Rights Convention*, held at Seneca Falls, 19–20 July 1848. It is necessary to discuss the history to see how the movement started.[33]

In 1833, an issue of Robert Owen's socialist journal titled, the *Crisis* (*New Women's Feminist Declaration*), addressed a strong feminist appeal in front of the public. It raised the demand for political and economic justice, liberty, and equality for women and equal rights in the marriage laws. In the *Call to Women*, French socialists and feminists affirmed justice for all women of the world. They claimed the movement for the women's right as a global cause. As a result, many people especially women from America, Britain, and France started supporting the theories of Charlse Fourier, Robert Owen, Claude Henri de Rouvroy, and Count Saint-Simon that challenged all aspects of the contemporary *status quo*. They argued that "society could not be effectively recognized without the active support of the female half of humanity".[34] It was altogether a joint movement for the rights of the women.

It led to gradual acceptance of women in Europe as full human beings. Christine de Pizan and Mary Astell were the first 'feminists' who rejected religious and social traditions that spoke about female inferiority. The writings of the scholars on the history of the movements for the women rights show the involvement of women of a very few countries such as the UK, the USA, France, and Germany. The movement for the women's rights, however, began and remained confined within the domestic legal systems. It was during the period of 1840–1853 that women's rights movement became internationalized through the adoption of various international legal instruments.[35]

For instance, the World Anti-Slavery Convention was adopted in 1840. It was one of the memorable conventions, because the actual women's rights movement took birth during this period. However, women were prohibited from participating as speakers and voters even at the Anti-Slavery Convention. This convention did not

---

[31] Maynard, Douglas H. (1960), "The World's Anti-Slavery Convention of 1840," *The Mississippi Valley Historical Review*, 47 (3): 452–471; available at: https://academic.oup.com/jah/article-abstract/47/3/452/682866?redirectedFrom=fulltext (accessed on 11 April 2021).

[32] Hewitt, Nancy A. (2001), "Origin Stories: Remapping First Wave Feminism", *Proceedings of the Third Annual Gilder Lehrman Center International Conference at Yale University Sisterhood and Slavery: Transatlantic Antislavery and Women's Rights*, Yale University New Haven, Connecticut; available at: https://glc.yale.edu/sites/default/files/files/hewitt.pdf (accessed on 11 April 2021).

[33] Batlan, Felice (2017), "Politics and Mythology in the Early Women's Rights Movement", *Tulsa L. Rev.* 52: 405; available at: https://digitalcommons.law.utulsa.edu/cgi/viewcontent.cgi?referer=&httpsredir=1&article=3059&context=tlr (accessed on 11 April 2021).

[34] Anderson, Bonnie. S. (2000), *Joyous Greetings: The First International Women's Movement*, 1830–1860, London: Oxford University Press.

[35] Ibid.

address women's rights, but the denial of women's participation in this convention gave an impetus and encouraged the future women's rights movements.[36]

It led to the movement for the rights of women's suffrage at the 1848 Women's Rights Convention.[37] The organizers were Cady Stanton and Lucretia Mott. This convention was mainly a collective initiative to address the legal, social, and economic disadvantages of women, especially married women. They drafted proposals that included a preamble and twelve resolutions. It demanded the right to equality[38] (on all sides, e.g. marital, educational, moral, economic, and religious) and the right to suffrage for women.[39] It came to be known as the *Declaration of Sentiments* (1848).[40] The declaration did not directly speak about the 'violence against women.' However, it addressed specific issues such as, the subordination of women within the family and society by the patriarchal mentality and corrupted customs.[41] The phrases 'Law of God' or 'natural law' were used to justify the rights of the women. Though the 1848 Declaration did not use strict legal language in the text, still it explained the plight of women prevailing at that time.[42]

Similarly, in 1853, American feminists organized two women's rights conventions. One was in New York City and another one was in Cleveland (Ohio). They

---

[36] Jansson, Bruce S. (2014), *The Reluctant Welfare State: Engaging History to Advance Social Work Practice in Contemporary Society (8th eds.), USA*, Change Learning.

[37] Maynard, Douglas H (1960), "The World's Anti-Slavery Convention of 1840," *the Mississippi Valley Historical Review*, 47 (3): 452–471.

[38] Woman's Rights Convention (1848), *The Declaration of Sentiments (19 July 1848)*, Report of the Convention, Seneca Falls, Rochester, N.Y; available at: https://www.nps.gov/wori/learn/historyculture/report-of-the-womans-rights-convention.htm (accessed on 11 April 2021). *The Declaration of Sentiments (19 July 1848)* of the Women's Rights Convention: "*Resolved*, That all laws which prevent woman from occupying such a station in society as her conscience shall dictate, or which place her in a position inferior to that of man, are contrary to the great precept of nature, and therefore of no force or authority. *Resolved*, That woman is man's equal—was intended to be so by the Creator, and the highest good of the race demands that she should be recognized as such. *Resolved*, That the women of this country ought to be enlightened in regard to the laws under which they -live, that they may no longer publish their degradation, by declaring themselves satisfied with their present position, nor their ignorance, by asserting that they have all the rights they want. *Resolved*, that the equality of human rights results necessarily from the fact of the identity of the race in capabilities and responsibilities".

[39] Ibid, *the Declaration of Sentiments (1848)*, "*Resolved*, That it is the duty of the women of this country to secure to themselves their sacred right to the elective franchise."

[40] Oxford University Press (1988), "The Women's Rights Convention at Seneca Falls: A Lesson Plan", *OAH Magazine of History, Special Double Issue on Women's History and History of the 1970s*, 3(3/4): 53–56.

[41] "*Resolved*, that woman has too long rested satisfied in the circumscribed limits which corrupt customs and a perverted application of the Scriptures have marked out for her, and that it is time she should move in the enlarged sphere which her great Creator has assigned her", see *The Declaration of Sentiments (1848)*, n.38.

[42] Ibid. For instance, it: "*Resolved*, That such laws as conflict, in any way, with the true and substantial happiness of woman, are contrary to the great precept of nature, and of no validity; for this is "superior in obligation to any other." *Resolved*, that all laws which prevent woman from occupying such a station in society as her conscience shall dictate, or which place her in a position inferior to that of man, are contrary to the great precept of nature, and therefore of no force or authority.".

drew participation of both black and white women who spoke on equal terms in these conventions. The New York Convention strengthened the international ties especially with Britain and other countries of Europe. The main focus of these conventions was the equal rights of women in the fields of politics, law, employment, public life, and morality.[43]

In the same vein, the *Lieber Code* of 1863 became the first codified form modern international humanitarian law. Some provisions of this Code covered treatment of women during the warfare. For example, Articles 19, 22, 31–47 contained the general provisions for the protection of the inhabitants including women.[44] Article 19 of the *Lieber Code* provided that "Women and children should be removed before bombardment"[45] Article 22 provided, "Unarmed citizens should be spared in person, property, and honour."[46] Article 44 prohibited rape of inhabitants of the occupied country.[47] Article 46 mentioned the protection of 'family honour' and the lives of persons.[48] Article 47 of the Code provided for punishment to the American soldiers for committing rape during war.[49] The above provisions of the Code protected women as inhabitants or civilians. There were only three Articles (Articles 44, 46 and 47) that provided specific attention for prohibition of wartime rape and punishment for it. Ironically, these provisions also showed charity-based approach towards women by use of terms such as family honour.

---

[43] Batlan (2017), n.33.

[44] Levie, Howard S. (2000), "History of the law of war on land", International Review of the Red Cross, No. 838; available at: https://www.icrc.org/en/doc/resources/documents/article/other/57jqhg.htm (accessed on 11 April 2021).

[45] Lieber Code (1863), Article 19 provides: "Commanders, whenever admissible, inform the enemy of their intention to bombard a place, so that the noncombatants, and especially the women and children, may be removed before the bombardment commences. But it is no infraction of the common law of war to omit thus to inform the enemy. Surprise may be a necessity;" available at: https://ihl-databases.icrc.org/applic/ihl/ihl.nsf/ART/110-20019?OpenDocument (accessed on 11 April 2021).

[46] Ibid. Art. 22 provides: "Nevertheless, as civilization has advanced during the last centuries, so has likewise steadily advanced, especially in war on land, the distinction between the private individual belonging to a hostile country and the hostile country itself, with its men in arms. The principle has been more and more acknowledged that the unarmed citizen is to be spared in person, property, and honor as much as the exigencies of war will admit.".

[47] Ibid. Art. 44 provides: "All wanton violence committed against persons in the invaded country, all destruction of property not commanded by the authorized officer, all robbery, all pillage or sacking, even after taking a place by main force, all rape, wounding, maiming, or killing of such inhabitants, are prohibited under the penalty of death, or such other severe punishment as may seem adequate for the gravity of the offense. A soldier, officer or private, in the act of committing such violence, and disobeying a superior ordering him to abstain from it, may be lawfully killed on the spot by such superior.".

[48] Ibid. Art. 46 provides: "Family honour and rights, the lives of persons, and private property, as well as religious convictions and practice, must be respected. Private property cannot be confiscated.".

[49] Ibid. Art. 47 provides: "Crimes punishable by all penal codes, such as arson, murder, maiming, assaults, highway robbery, theft, burglary, fraud, forgery, and rape, if committed by an American soldier in a hostile country against its inhabitants, are not only punishable as at home, but in all cases in which death is not inflicted, the severe punishment shall be preferred.".

In 1904, the International Agreement for the Suppression of International 'White Slave Traffic'[50] was adopted in Paris. It was amended by the Protocol signed at Lake Success, New York, 4 May 1949. The objective of the agreement was to provide effective protection to the women and girls of full age or underage who suffered abuse or compulsion by criminal traffic or "White Slave Traffic."[51] It sought cooperation of the States to provide protection as regards "the procuring of women or girls for immoral purposes abroad."[52] The main focus was on women and girls who were the "victims" of trafficking, or used as "prostitutes;"[53] women and girls who lived "immoral life," etc.[54] The contracting States agreed to assist with the collaboration of the State of origin to send the trafficked women back to their country of origin.[55]

The *Lieber* Code influenced further codification of laws of war and adoption of similar regulation by the non-member States. It led to a project for an international convention on the laws of war. It was presented before the Brussels Conference in 1874. It encouraged adoption of the Hague Conventions 1899 and 1907 on laws of war on land.[56] In comparison to earlier conferences, a larger number of sovereign States participated (44 out of 47 States and 256 delegates[57]) in the Second Hague Conference that took place during 15 June to 18 October 1907.[58]

---

[50] *International Agreement for the Suppression of International 'White Slave Traffic'*, Paris, 1904; available at: https://treaties.un.org/doc/Treaties/1920/09/19200907%2006-00%20AM/Ch_VII_8p.pdf. For the text of 10 other international conventions on "Traffic in Persons"; available at: see https://treaties.un.org/pages/CTCTreaties.aspx?id=7&subid=A&clang=_en (accessed on 11 April 2021).

[51] Ibid, preamble states: "…being desirous of securing to women of full age who have suffered abuse or compulsion, as also to women and girls under age, effective protection against the criminal traffic known as the 'White Slave Traffic'.".

[52] Ibid.,Article 1 provides: "the procuring of women or girls for immoral purposes abroad.".

[53] Ibid, Article 3 provides: "The Governments undertake, when the case arises, and within legal limits, to have the declarations taken of women or girls of foreign nationality who are prostitutes.".

[54] Ibid, Article 2 provides: "Each of the Governments undertakes to have a watch kept, especially in railway stations, ports of embarkation, and en route, for persons in charge of women and girls destined for an immoral life. With this object instructions shall be given to the officials, and all other qualified persons, to obtain, within legal limits, all information likely to lead to the detection of criminal traffic…". Also see, Dubler, Ariela R. (2006), "Immoral Purposes: Marriage and the Genus of Illicit Sex," *Yale Law Journal*, 115(4): 756; available at: https://www.yalelawjournal.org/pdf/338_d2p5wpm5.pdf (11 April 2021).

[55] Ibid, Article 3 states: "The Governments also undertake, within legal limits, and as far as possible, to send back to their country of origin those women and girls who desire it, or who may be claimed by persons exercising authority over them.".

[56] *Instructions for the Government of Armies of the United States in the Field (Lieber Code)*, 24 April 1863; available at: https://ihl-databases.icrc.org/ihl/INTRO/110 (accessed on 11 April 2021).

[57] Tryon, James L. (1911), "The Hague Conferences," *The Yale Law Journal*, 20 (6): 470–485; available at: https://digitalcommons.law.yale.edu/cgi/viewcontent.cgi?article=2171&context=ylj (11 April 2021).

[58] ICRC (2010), "Development of modern international humanitarian law;" available at: https://www.icrc.org/en/doc/who-we-are/history/since-1945/history-ihl/overview-development-modern-international-humanitarian-law.htm (accessed on 11 April 2021). Also see, Desai, Bharat. H.

In 1907 (eight years after the first Hague Peace Conference of 1899), the Hague Convention was adopted for further development of the international humanitarian law.[59] The 1907 Convention replaced the 1899 Convention on 'laws and customs of war on land' and its annexes.[60] This convention imposed responsibility to both States and individuals for violation of 'laws and customs of war.'[61] The provisions of this convention have mainly focused on the limited use of means and methods of warfare.[62]The provisions of both the Conventions 1899 and 1907 on laws and customs of war have been regarded as a part of customary international law. The States are bound by provisions of these two conventions irrespective of being a party to them.[63] In fact, at the 1946 Nuremburg Trial, the Nazi war criminals were punished on the basis that "the Hague Convention of 1907 is customary international law".[64]

The main focus of the Hague Convention of 1907 was on the protection of prisoners of war. The Preamble to the Hague Convention protects inhabitants. However, it did not include women specifically.[65] Article 46[66] of the 1907 Convention denoted that the military authority must respect family honour, rights, and lives of persons of the occupied territory.[67] It has been argued that though Article 46 does not explicitly

---

(2012), "Protection of Cultural Property in Times of Armed Conflicts", *International Humanitarian Law Lecture Series Lectures,* delivered at the Centre for International Legal Studies, School of International Studies, Jawaharlal Nehru University: New Delhi, 20 March 2012 (on file with the author).

59 Ibid.

60 Article 4 of the 1907 Hague Convention provides: "The present Convention, duly ratified, shall as between the Contracting Powers, be substituted for the Convention of 29 July 1899, respecting the laws and customs of war on land. The Convention of 1899 remains in force as between the Powers which signed it, and which do not also ratify the present Convention;" available at: https://www.refworld.org/docid/4374cae64.html (accessed on 11 April 2021).

61 Ibid.

62 Meurant, Jacques. (1987), "Inter Arma Caritas: Evolution and Nature of International Humanitarian Law," *Journal of Peace Research*, 24 (3): 237–249; available at: https://journals.sagepub.com/doi/10.1177/002234338702400304 (accessed on 18 April 2021).

63 ICRC, "Convention (IV) respecting the Laws and Customs of War on Land and its annex: Regulations concerning the Laws and Customs of War on Land. The Hague, 18 October 1907"; available at: https://ihl-databases.icrc.org/ihl/intro/195 (accessed on 18 April 2021).

64 For details see, BBC, *Rules and Conventions*; available at: http://www.bbc.co.uk/ethics/war/overview/rules.shtml (accessed on 21 December 2020).

65 ICRC (2005), *Rules of International Humanitarian Law and Other Rules Relating to the Conduct of Hostilities: Collection of Treaties and Other Instruments*; available at: https://www.icrc.org/en/doc/assets/files/other/icrc_002_0467.pdf (accessed on 18 April 2021).

66 Article 46 (Annex to the 1907 Convention) provides, "Family honour and rights, the lives of persons, and private property, as well as religious convictions and practice, must be respected. Private property cannot be confiscated;" available at: https://www.loc.gov/collections/united-states-treaties-and-other-international-agreements/about-this-collection/bevans/m-ust000001-0631.pdf; https://ihl-databases.icrc.org/ihl/WebART/195-200056 (accessed on 18 April 2021).

67 ICC Women, *Treatment of Sexual Violence in International Law*; available at: http://iccwomen.org/resources/crimeschart.html (accessed on 18 April 2021).

mention rape, still this provision could be relied upon as the prohibition of rape in conflict zones.[68]

The International Convention for the Suppression of the White Slave Trade, 1910[69] provided for the protection of girls and women from trafficking. However, the forms of violence except forced trafficking did not find mention in the convention.[70] The gender issue also found reflection in the International Congress of Women (ICW) held in The Hague, the Netherlands, during 28 April–1 May 1915. Its objective was for immediate end of war and establishment of peace.[71] The Congress adopted one resolution at its Business Session.[72] It was pointed out that 'gender' was one of the reasons for war and they protested against violence in war. The Congress expressed concern about women's suffering as victims of war due to all the horrible wrongs of war.[73]

It was claimed that "foreign policy shall be subject to democratic control with equal representation of men and women."[74] It was felt that "the combined influence of the women of all countries is one of the strongest forces for the prevention of war." Therefore, it called for the "need of equal political rights of women with men"[75]

---

[68] Ibid.

[69] UNESCO (1999), *Human Rights of Women A Collection of International and Regional Normative Instruments 1979–1999*; available at: https://unesdoc.unesco.org/ark:/48223/pf0000119140 (accessed on 18 April 2021).

[70] Article 1 of the *International Convention for The Suppression of The White Slave Traffic, 1910*, provides: "Whoever, in order to gratify the passions of another person, has procured, enticed, or led away, even with her consent, a woman or girl under age, for immoral purposes, shall be punished, notwithstanding that the various acts constituting the offence may have been committed in different countries. Article 2: Whoever, in order to gratify the passions of another person, has, by fraud, or by means of violence, threats, abuse of authority, or any other method of compulsion, procured, enticed, or led away a woman or girl over age, for immoral purposes, shall also be punished, notwithstanding that the various acts constituting the offence may have been committed in different countries;" see International Convention for the Suppression of the "White Slave Traffic," May 4, 1910, as amended by Protocol Amending the International Agreement for the Suppression of the White Slave Traffic, and Amending the International Convention for the Suppression of the White Slave Traffic, May 4, 1949; entered into force June 21, 1951; 2 U.S.T. 1999, 30 U.N.T.S. 23; available at: http://hrlibrary.umn.edu/instree/whiteslavetraffic1910.html (accessed on 18 April 2021).

[71] *Report of the International Congress of Women* (2015); available at: https://ia800306.us.archive.org/15/items/internatcongrewom00interich/internatcongrewom00interich_bw.pdf; resolutions_1915.pdf (gu.se) (accessed on 18 April 2021).

[72] Ibid.

[73] Ibid, ICW Resolution I (2) provides: "This International Congress of Women opposes the assumption that women can be protected under the conditions of modern warfare. It protests vehemently against the odious wrongs of which women are the victims in time of war, and especially against the horrible violation of women which attends all war", p. 11.

[74] Ibid, ICW Resolution III (8) called for 'democratic control of foreign policy': "Since war is commonly brought about not by the mass of the people, who do not desire it, but by groups representing particular interests, this International Congress of Women urges that Foreign Politics shall be subject to Democratic Control; and declares that it can only recognise as democratic a system which includes the equal representation of men and women",p. 13.

[75] Ibid, ICW Resolution III (9) called for the 'enfranchisement of women': "Since the combined influence of the women of all countries is one of the strongest forces for the prevention of war, and

and "need of equal civil and political rights in national and international politics."[76] The Congress also called for "a permanent international conference holding regular meetings in which women should take part to deal with practical proposals for further international cooperation among the States."[77] It spoke about the necessity of active participation of women in the peace processes.[78] The Congress of Women claimed about "universal disarmament"[79] and showed sympathy and sorrow for the sufferings in war.[80]

Unfortunately, no State or international organization ever gave effect to these futuristic resolutions of the 1915 ICW. However, some scholars have claimed that the proposals of ICW were considered during the deliberations for the 1919 Peace Treaty of Versailles though the resolutions had no direct influence on it. Notwithstanding this, the resolutions can be said to have had a remarkable role in enlightening the development of the international legal system over the subsequent century.[81] The Congress encouraged the envoys to visit the head of the States with their proposals, and hence, they visited 14 countries (the Netherlands, UK, Germany, Austria, Hungary, Switzerland, Italy, the Holy See, Belgium, Denmark, Norway, Sweden, Russia, USA) where they met highest officials including the US President Woodrow Wilson.[82] As a result, it took initiative to establish a permanent international committee. Initially, the committee was called the 'International Committee

since women can only have full responsibility and effective influence when they have equal political rights with men, this International Congress of Women demands their political enfranchisement".

[76] Ibid, ICW Resolution IV (15) provides for role of 'women in national and international politics': "This International Congress of Women declares it to be essential, both nationally and internationally to put into practice the principle that women should share all civil and political rights and responsibilities on these terms as men", p. 15.

[77] Ibid, ICW Resolution IV (11.b) provides, "As a development of the constructive work of the Hague Conference, a Permanent International Conference holding regular meetings in which women should take part, to deal not with the rules of warfare but with practical proposals for further International Cooperation among the States", p. 14.

[78] Ibid, ICW Resolution VI (18) provides, "This International Congress of Women urges that representatives of the people should take part in the conference that shall frame the peace settlement after' the war, and claims that amongst them women should be included", p. 16.

[79] Ibid, ICW Resolution IV (12) spoke about 'general Disarmament': "The International Congress of Women, advocating universal disarmament and realizing that it can only be secured by international agreement, urges, as a step to this end, that all countries should, by such an international agreement, take over the. Manufacture of arms and munitions of war and should control all international traffic in the same. It sees in the private profits accruing from the great armament factories a powerful hindrance to the abolition of war", p. 14.

[80] Ibid, ICW Resolution II (3) provides for the 'peace settlement': "This International Congress of Women of Different nations, classes, creeds and parties is united in expressing sympathy with the suffering of all, whatever their nationality, who are fighting for their country or labouring under the burden of war", p. 11.

[81] Baetens, Freya (2012), "International Congress of Women (1915)" in Rudiger Wolfrum (ed.), *Max Planck Encyclopedia of Public International Law,* V: 455–459, New York: OUP; available at: http://opil.ouplaw.com/view/10.1093/law:epil/9780199231690/law-9780199231690-e2102 (accessed on 21 December 2020).

[82] Ibid.

of Women for Permanent Peace'. It was later renamed as the Women's International League for Peace and Freedom (WILPF). It is still in existence with a headquarter in Geneva as well as 'national sections' in 37 countries.[83]

Most of the States were colonized at the time of adoption of the resolutions of the 1915 ICW.[84] Thus, there were no representatives of women from the colonized countries. The resolutions of the ICW have significance even today[85] as it gave a broader picture of the relationship between war and women. The ICW's concern reflected in its resolution shows that patriarchy has been one of the reasons for war and how women become the victims of war. Therefore, patriarchy remains one of the key reasons of SGBV in the conflict zones.

The contemporary incidents of SGBV in conflict zones show the gaps in international humanitarian laws. The resolution of the ICW (1915) expressly spoke about it.[86] Though the resolutions did not mention any forms of SGBV against women per se, it can be deciphered form the language such as: "the horror of war",[87] "odious wrongs of which women are the victims," "horrible violation of women", "protection of women,"[88] "women should be granted equal political rights",[89] etc.

Anti-trafficking movement is another step towards the development of international law to stop violence against women. Radhika Coomaraswamy, UN Special Rapporteur on Violence against Women, opined that the history behind the anti-trafficking movements was the notion of 'threat to purity' or 'chastity' of women, especially the white women.[90] International Convention relating to traffic in women and children 1921,[91] also dealt with trafficking in women and children. The language underscored that women and children remain the weaker sections in the society who

[83] Ibid.

[84] ICW (1915), n.71.

[85] Chimni, B.S. (2015), "Peace through Law: lessons from 1914," *London Review of International Law*, 3 (2): 245–265.

[86] Ibid.

[87] ICW Resolution I (1) explicitly protested "against the madness and the horror of war, involving as it does a reckless sacrifice of human life and the destruction of so much that humanity has laboured through centuries to build up"; n.71.

[88] Ibid, ICW Resolution I (2) stated: "This International Congress of Women opposes the assumption that women can be protected under the conditions of modern warfare. It protests vehemently against the odious wrongs of which women are the victims in time of war, and especially against the horrible violation of women which attends all war".

[89] Ibid, ICW Resolution II (3) stated, "That woman should be granted equal political rights with men" and Resolution III (9) stated, "The Enfranchisement of Women. Since the combined influence of the women of all countries is one of the strongest forces for the prevention of war, and since women can only have full responsibility and effective influence when they have equal political rights with men, this International Congress of Women demands their political enfranchisement".

[90] University of Minnesota, *Trafficking In Women, Law And Policy, The International Legal Framework*; available at: http://hrlibrary.umn.edu/svaw/trafficking/law/intl.htm (accessed on 19 April 2021).

[91] *International Convention for the Suppression of the Traffic in Women and Children 1921*; available at: https://ec.europa.eu/anti-trafficking/sites/antitrafficking/files/1921_international_convention_en_1.pdf (accessed on 19 April 2021).

need protection and assistance.[92] It is reflected in phrases such as 'protection of women and children',[93] 'undertake to make regulations,' 'administrative and legislative measures',[94] etc. International Convention for the Suppression of the Traffic in Women of Full Age, 1933 also focused on women, girls, and children.[95] The act of trafficking was denoted as 'immoral act' and 'punishable offence.'[96]

The main changes have occurred in law for the prevention of SGBV, GBV, sexual violence or violence against women, only after the establishment of the UN Charter. Hence, our discussion has sought to spot the changes in terminology or language of international law to address the issue of SGBV in the post-UN Charter period. The Charter itself has called for 'equal rights of men and women'; 'respect for human rights and fundamental freedom of all sex',[97] etc. The Universal Declaration of Human Rights 1948 explicitly has used terms that underscore the rights to women 'without distinction of sex'.[98] Still, it did not specifically focus on violence against women, gender-based violence or SGBV against women.

The Four Geneva Conventions 1949 (Additional Protocols 1977 came later) adopted by the initiative of ICRC have included references to some forms of SGBV against women, e.g. rape, etc.[99] The GA resolution 843 (IX) 1954 (Status of women in private law: customs, ancient laws, and practices affecting the human dignity of women) was one of the earliest action by the UN to introduce the concept of harmful cultural or traditional practices that is also a form of SGBV against women.[100] It has

[92] UN Women, "United Nations Treaties, Conventions and General Recommendations;" available at: https://www.endvawnow.org/en/articles/536-united-nations-treaties-conventions-and-general-recommendations.html (accessed on 19 April 2021).

[93] See n.91, Article 3 (Protection of women and children seeking employment in another country).

[94] Ibid, Article 7. It states: "The High Contracting Parties undertake in connection with immigration and emigration to adopt such administrative and legislative measures as are required to check the traffic in women and children. In particular, they undertake to make such regulations as are required for the protection of women and children travelling on emigrant ships, not only at the points of departure and arrival, but also during the journey and to arrange for the exhibition, in railway stations and in ports, of notices warning women and children of the danger of the traffic."

[95] League of Nations (1934), *The International Convention for the Suppression of the Traffic in Women of Full Age, 1933*; *League of Nations Treaty Series*, vol. 150, p. 431, available at: https://treaties.un.org/doc/Publication/UNTS/LON/Volume150/v150.pdf (accessed on 19 April 2021).

[96] Ibid. Article 1. It provides: "Whoever, in order to gratify the passions of another person, has procured, enticed or led away even with her consent, a woman or girl of full age for immoral purposes to be carried out in another country, shall be punished, notwithstanding that the various acts constituting the offence may have been committed in different countries. Attempted offences, and, within the legal limits, acts preparatory to the offences in question, shall also be punishable…".

[97] United Nations (1945), Articles 1, 13, and 55; *Charter of the United Nations;* available at: https://treaties.un.org/doc/Publication/CTC/uncharter.pdf (accessed on 19 April 2021).

[98] UN (2014), "Women's Rights Are Human Rights"; available at: https://www.ohchr.org/Documents/Events/WHRD/WomenRightsAreHR.pdf (accessed on 19 April 2021).

[99] ICRC (2010), "The Geneva Conventions of 1949 and their Additional Protocols"; available at: https://www.icrc.org/en/war-and-law/treaties-customary-law/geneva-conventions (accessed on 19 April 2021).

[100] United Nations (1954), General Assembly Resolution (1954), 843 (IX); available at: https://www.un.org/en/ga/search/view_doc.asp?symbol=A/RES/843(IX) (accessed on 19 April 2021).

specifically addressed some forms of SGBV, e.g. practice of bride price or dowry, child marriage, etc.[101]

The issue of rights and non-discrimination against women came to be addressed exclusively through the adoption of the Declaration on the Elimination of Discrimination against Women, 1967.'[102] The language of the declaration comprises phrases such as 'equal rights of men and women,'[103] 'existence of discrimination against women,'[104] (discrimination against women by denying or limiting their equality of rights with men as an) 'offence against human dignity,'[105] 'women on equal terms with men, without any discrimination' (Article 4), 'all forms of traffic in women and exploitation of prostitution of women.'[106] In fact, the declaration sought to focus specific grounds of discrimination against women on the basis of gender, legal, culture, social, political and economic. It did not address the issue of SGBV against women per se. Still, it prohibited some practices that came under the rubric of SGBV such as the prohibition of child marriage[107]; combating all forms of traffic in women and exploitation of a position of women.[108]

As a sequel to 1967 Declaration, in 1979, the Convention on Elimination of All Forms of Discrimination against Women (CEDAW) came to be adopted. It did not include any explicit language of violence against women. However, in view of the very spirit of CEDAW, it can be construed to cover violence against women. The UN Special Rapporteur on causes and consequence of violence against women, Rashida Manjoo, observed that the "States must acknowledge that violence against women is not the root problem, but that violence occurs because other forms of discrimination are allowed to flourish." Thus, inherent discriminatory practices against women in

---

[101] Ibid, paragraph 1. It states: "Urges all States...to take all appropriate measures in the countries...under their jurisdiction with a view to abolishing such customs, ancient laws and practices by ensuring complete freedom in the choice of spouse; abolishing the practice of bride price; guaranteeing the right of widows the custody of their children and their freedom as to remarriage; eliminating completely child marriage and the betrothal of young girls before the of puberty and establishing appropriate penalties where necessary...".

[102] UN General Assembly (1967), *Declaration on the Elimination of Discrimination against Women 1967*, Resolution 2263 (XXII); UN Doc. A/RES/22/2263, 07 November 1967; available at: http://www.un-documents.net/a22r2263.htm; http://www.eods.eu/library/UNGA_Declaration%20Women_1967_en.pdf (accessed on 20 April 2021).

[103] Ibid, Article 2.

[104] Ibid, Preamble, paragraph 4. It states: "Concerned that, despite the Charter of the United Nations, the Universal Declaration of Human Rights, the International Covenants on Human Rights and other instruments of the United Nations and the specialized agencies and despite the progress made in the matter of equality of rights, there continues to exist considerable discrimination against women".

[105] Ibid, Article 1.

[106] Ibid, Article 8.

[107] Ibid, Article 6(3). It states: "Child marriage and the betrothal of young girls before puberty shall be prohibited, and effective action, including legislation, shall be taken to specify a minimum age for marriage and to make the registration of marriages in an official registry compulsory.".

[108] Ibid, Article 8. It provides, "an appropriate measure, including legislation, shall be taken to combat all forms of traffic in women and exploitation of prostitution of women.".

family, society, and State is one of the primary causes of violence against women.[109] Since, the 1985 UN Women's Conference (Nairobi), women activists have actively lobbied for drawing global attention on violence against women. At the 19th General Recommendation of the Committee of CEDAW (11th session, 1992), call was given for inclusion of violence against women in the reports. It did finally concede that discrimination includes violence against women.[110] It has mentioned different forms of 'gender-based violence,' and 'sexual violence.'[111]

Then Vienna Declaration of 1993 was the landmark that declared women rights as the human rights.[112] International Criminal Tribunals and Courts especially the International Criminal Court (ICC) have a role in addressing the issue of 'gender,' and SGBV against women during conflicts.[113] The resolutions of the General Assembly and the Security Council of the UN have also contributed in recent years in addressing the issue of 'violence against women,' 'gender-based violence,' 'sexual violence' and 'sexual and gender-based violence.'[114]

Thus, the above-mentioned discussion shows the evolutionary history of SGBV against women in international law. It shows how the idea and content of international legal protection for women's human rights and against violence has crystallized over the years. It appears to be an incremental process that seeks to make a dent on the mindsets. For obvious reasons, soft normativity has been at the forefront to grapple with the challenge of SGBV. In other cases, there still exists confusion, contradictions, and ambiguities as regards use of various formulations and terminology relating to SGBV.

In view of this, it appears, legitimate to use phrases such as 'violence against women,' 'gender-based violence' and 'SGBV' synonymously. Though the scope and gravity of SGBV is much larger than all other terms, still all relevant instruments concerning 'violence against women' and 'gender-based violence' during

---

109 UN (2020), *UN Human Rights Treaties*; available at: https://www.stopvaw.org/un_treaties_on_violence_against_women (accessed on 20 April 2021).

110 Chinkin, Christine (1995), "Violence against Women: The International Legal Response", *Gender and Development*, 3 (2): 23–28.

111 UN Women (1992), *General Recommendation 19*, paragraph 1. It provides: "Gender-based violence is a form of discrimination that seriously inhibits women's ability to enjoy rights and freedoms on a basis of equality with men;" available at: https://www.un.org/womenwatch/daw/cedaw/recommendations/recomm.htm#recom19 (accessed on 20 April 2021).

112 UN OHCHR (1993), *Vienna Declaration and Programme of Action 1993*; available at: https://ohchr.org/EN/ProfessionalInterest/Pages/Vienna.aspx (accessed on 20 April 2021).

113 International Criminal Court (2014), "Policy Paper on Sexual and Gender-Based Crimes;" available at: https://www.icc-cpi.int/iccdocs/otp/otp-policy-paper-on-sexual-and-gender-based-crimes--june-2014.pdf (accessed on 20 April 2021).

114 UN Security Council (2010), Resolution 1960, S/RES/1960, 16 December 2010, paragraph 15; "Encourages Member States to deploy greater numbers of female military and police personnel to United Nations peacekeeping operations, and to provide all military and police personnel with adequate training on sexual and gender-based violence, inter alia, to carry out their responsibilities;" available at: http://www.securitycouncilreport.org/atf/cf/%7B65BFCF9B-6D27-4E9C-8CD3-CF6E4FF96FF9%7D/WPS%20SRES%201960.pdf (accessed on 20 April 2021).

peace, conflicts and post-conflict situations would be also applicable to SGBV against women.

Protection in International Law

Ironically, the existing corpus of international law is not adequate in specifically addressing SGBV against women. The existing 'normative gap' was underscored by the UN Special Rapporteur, Rashida Manjoo. The absence of specific legally binding instruments lead to relevant international institutions such as ICRC, UN Women, UN HRC, UN OHCHR, etc. to push for alternative non-binding instruments to address SGBV against women. Though these instruments carry good normative value, yet they are generally regarded as guiding principles by the States.[115]

Thus, all specific and related international legal instruments for protection of women against SGBV can be categorized mainly under three areas of international law: (A) international human rights law (IHRL) (B) international humanitarian law (IHL) and (C) international criminal law (ICL). These would also comprise, where appropriate, relevant soft and hard instruments adopted by the political organs of the UN (especially the General Assembly and the Security Council). We need to make sense of the efficacy of the existing corpus of international legal mechanisms for addressing the challenge of SGBV against women.

(A) International Human Rights Law

IHRL is applicable during peace, conflict, and post-conflict situations. It is applicable irrespective of time, place and situation. There is, however, no IHRL instrument that specifically deals with SGBV against women. Even the existing human rights treaties do not have a specific provision for SGBV. There are only a few provisions within the treaties that deal with discrimination against women, such as torture, and forced prostitution.[116]

The World Conference on Human Rights (Vienna, 1993), reviewed existing human rights machinery. The women rights activists claimed that women rights are human rights and need to be augmented by the international community. The 1993 Conference adopted the Vienna Declaration and Programme of Action. It stated: "The human rights of women and girl child are the inalienable, integral, indivisible part of universal human rights". In turn, it sought elimination of all forms of gender-based violence.[117] Subsequent World Conferences on Women, especially the 1995 Beijing

---

[115] UN OHCHR, *Asia Pacific, Gender-Based Violence Against Women And International Human Rights Law: Options For Strengthening The International Framework Discussion Paper*; available at: https://www.ohchr.org/Documents/Issues/Women/SR/Framework/2.IWRAW-AsiaPacificDiscussionPaperOptionInternationalMechnisms.pdf (accessed on 20 April 2021).

[116] Gaggioli, Gloria (2014), n.4.

[117] UN OHCHR (2014), *Women's Rights are Human Rights*; available at: https://www.ohchr.org/Documents/Events/WHRD/WomenRightsAreHR.pdf (accessed on 24 April 2021).

Conference,[118] advocated ending violence against women during times of peace and conflicts.[119]

The year 2020 marked the 25th anniversary of the adoption of the Beijing Platform for Action. For the first time, the progress on implementation of the action was reviewed in the light of Sustainable Development Goals 2030 (SDGs 2030), where focus has been on progress, gaps, and challenges related to the advancement of gender equality and women's rights. The UN (especially the UN Women) plays a crucial role in this respect. Six themes selected to examine the challenges include "freedom from violence, stigma, and stereotypes; participation, accountability, and gender-responsive institutions; and so on." The report called for changes such as women's movement, leadership and harnessing technology for gender equality. The concern for this generation and the next has been highlighted in seeking implementation of the Platform for Action.[120]

The 1993 UN Declaration on the Elimination of Violence against Women defined 'violence against women' as 'gender-based violence.'[121] As a corollary, the 2011 UN Guiding Principles on Business and Human Rights have given special attention to both gender-based violence and sexual violence in connection with control over natural resources, territory and conflict.[122] However, these instruments contain soft normativity and follow a charity-based approach. They comprise terminologies such as 'States *should* condemn,' 'women subjected to violence *should* be provided,' etc. Still, in the absence of subject-specific legal instruments, they provide general international human rights instruments to address SGBV against women.

The existing IHRL (both *Lex specialis and Lex generalis*) has addressed the issue of SGBV. Within the limits of time and space, this study has sought to identify some mainstream international human rights instruments as regards their role in addressing SGBV against women.

The 1979 Convention on the Elimination of all Forms of Discrimination against Women (CEDAW) is one of the subject-specific human rights treaties that deals with discrimination against women. It is a women-specific treaty that also contributes to mainstream gender analysis. As such it has been regarded as one of the important

---

[118] UN (1995), *The Beijing Declaration and Platform for Action 1995*; available at: https://www.un.org/womenwatch/daw/beijing/pdf/BDPfA%20E.pdf (accessed on 24 April 2021).

[119] Ibid.

[120] UN Women (2020), *Gender equality: Women's rights in review 25 years after Beijing*; available at: https://www.unwomen.org/-/media/headquarters/attachments/sections/library/publications/2020/gender-equality-womens-rights-in-review-en.pdf?la=en&vs=934 (accessed on 24 April 2021).

[121] UN (1994), *Declaration on the Elimination of Violence against Women* (1993), Article 1; UN Doc. A/RES/48/104, 20 December 1993; available at: https://undocs.org/en/A/RES/48/104 (accessed on 24 April 2021).

[122] UN OHCHR (2011), "Supporting business respect for human rights in conflict affected areas: 7... (b) Providing adequate assistance to business enterprises to assess and address the heightened risks of abuses, paying special attention to both gender-based and sexual violenc"; see, OHCHR, *UN Guiding Principle on Business and Human Rights*: Implementing the United Nations "Protect, Respect and Remedy" Framework; available at: https://www.ohchr.org/Documents/Publications/GuidingPrinciplesBusinessHR_EN.pdf (accessed on 24 April 2021).

human rights treaties that follows the rights-based approach.[123] However, CEDAW does not explicitly cover all types of rights such as the right not to be subjected to SGBV.[124] The CEDAW text also does not even include the term 'violence' or SGBV. It took a long time to accept that the gender-based violence (GBV) is a result of discrimination against women including discriminatory legislations or customary laws.[125]

The CEDAW has defined 'discrimination against women'[126] without spelling out violence against women *per se.* A 2012 commentary on CEDAW shows that'discrimination against women' is based on 'sex' that takes many forms. The generic term 'discrimination' could include the exclusion of women and limitations on their rights in various spheres as well as economic marginalization, stereotypes that limit women's opportunities, inequality between men and women, and violence against women in the family and community.[127]

The CEDAW is a women-specific international legal instrument. It was specially designed notwithstanding generic provisions for the protection of human rights in the UN Charter, 1948 UDHR, and the two 1966 Covenants (ICCPR and ICESCR) that address the rights of both men and women.[128]

Notwithstanding the above-mentioned international human rights instruments, they were not regarded as adequate to specifically meet the rights and needs of women. In 1946, the Commission on the Status of Women (CSW) was established by the Economic and Social Council (ECOSOC) as a subsidiary organ of the UN Commission on Human Rights. In 1947, the USA proposed to make it a full commission under the ECOSOC.[129] It is this Commission on the Status of Women that has contributed in the crystallization and adoption of 1979 CEDAW by the UN

---

[123] Bayefsky, Anne F. et al. (2000), "The CEDAW Convention: Its Contribution Today," *Proceedings of the Annual Meeting (American Society of International Law)*, 94: 197–203.

[124] Gaggioli, Gloria (2014), n.4.

[125] Zorn, Jean G. (2016), "Translating and Internalizing International Human Rights Law: The Courts of Melanesia Confront Gendered Violence," in Aletta Biersack, Margaret Jolly, Martha Macintyre, Eds. (2016), *Gender Violence & Human Rights: Seeking Justice in Fiji, Papua New Guinea & Vanuatu* Australia: ANU Press; available at: https://press-files.anu.edu.au/downloads/press/n2168/pdf/book.pdf (accessed on 25 April 2021).

[126] UN OHCHR (1979), *Convention on the Elimination of all forms of Discrimination against Women*; adopted by the General Assembly resolution 34/180 of 18 December 1979; available at: https://www.un.org/en/development/desa/population/migration/generalassembly/docs/globalcompact/A_RES_34_180.pdf (accessed on 25 April 2021).

[127] Freeman, Marsha A., Chinkin, Christine and Rudolf, Beate, Eds. (2012), *The UN Convention on the Elimination of All Forms of Discrimination Against Women: A Commentary*, New York: Oxford University Press.

[128] UN (1995), *Report by the Committee on the Elimination of Discrimination against Women*; UN Doc. A/CONF.177/7, 21 June 1995; available at: https://www.un.org/esa/gopher-data/conf/fwcw/off/a--7.en (accessed on 25 April 2021).

[129] Galey, Margaret E. (1979), "Promoting Nondiscrimination against Women: The UN Commission on the Status of Women", *International Studies Quarterly, Special Issue on Human Rights International Perspectives*, 23(2): 273–302; available at: https://academic.oup.com/isq/article-abstract/23/2/273/1804551?redirectedFrom=fulltext (accessed on 25 April 2021).

General Assembly. It can be considered as the International Bill of Rights for Women. Hence, it remains the primary legal instrument to address discrimination—but not violence *per se*—against women. Only in 1992, CEDAW started addressing the issue of violence against women through its general recommendations (GR).[130]

The UN Committee on Discrimination against Women has been entrusted with responsibility for implementation of CEDAW. Now, 'violence' remains one of the important items on its agenda[131] as specified by GR 12 and 19. These GRs (12 and 19) make detailed recommendations for the States parties.[132] GR12 (8th session, 1989) provided that Articles 2, 5, 11, 12, and 16 of CEDAW give responsibility to act in cases of violence against women within the family, community (e.g. work place), and the State (e.g. any other area of social life).[133] GR19 (11th session, 1992) explicitly considered GBV as a form of discrimination.[134] It has interpreted important provisions like Articles 1, 2, 3, 5, 6, 11, 12, 14, 15, and 16 of the CEDAW and has defined 'discrimination against women.'[135] It explicitly states that violation of any of the rights and freedoms listed in the GR would be treated as GBV and a breach of Article 1 of CEDAW. The general comments in the GR19 of the Committee of CEDAW have directly mentioned that 'discrimination' as an inclusive term. It states:

> The definition of discrimination includes gender-based violence, that is, violence that is directed against a woman because she is a woman or that affects women disproportionately. It includes acts that inflict physical, mental or sexual harm or suffering, threats of such acts, coercion and other deprivations of liberty. Gender-based violence may breach specific provisions of the Convention, regardless of whether those provisions expressly mention violence.[136]

It has shown that woman face violence because of gender-based discrimination between male and female. It includes physical, psychological harms, and deprivation of liberty. It is also stated that GBV can be treated as a breach of any particular provision of the convention. If there is a breach of enjoyment of fundamental freedoms, human rights, or any other right under international law as a result of GBV,

[130] Robinson, Nancy P. (2006), "Origins of the International Day for the Elimination of Violence against Women: The Caribbean Contribution," *Caribbean Studies*, 34 (2): 141–161.

[131] Chapman, Jane Roberts (1990), "Violence against Women as a Violation of Human Rights," *Social Justice, Criminality, Imprisonment & Women's Rights in the 1990s*, 17 (2)40: 54–70.

[132] UN Women (2020), "Global Norms and Standards: Ending Violence against Women;" available at: https://www.unwomen.org/en/what-we-do/ending-violence-against-women/global-norms-and-standards (accessed on 25 April 2021).

[133] UN Women, *General Recommendations*; available at: https://www.un.org/womenwatch/daw/cedaw/recommendations/ (accessed on 25 April 2021).

[134] Ibid; GR 19 states, "Gender-based violence is a form of discrimination that seriously inhibits women's ability to enjoy rights and freedoms on a basis of equality with men.".

[135] UN (1979), n.126; Article 1 of CEDAW provide*s,* "For the purposes of the present Convention, the term "discrimination against women" shall mean any distinction, exclusion or restriction made on the basis of sex which has the effect or purpose of impairing or nullifying the recognition, enjoyment or exercise by women, irrespective of their marital status, on a basis of equality of men and women, of human rights and fundamental freedoms in the political, economic, social, cultural, civil or any other field".

[136] UN Women (2020), General Comment 6 to the GR 19, n.133.

it will come under the preview of discrimination under CEDAW.[137] It also constitutes GBV if there is a violation of any of the rights and freedoms[138] listed in the general comments since it is a breach of Article 1. GBV includes violence faced within the family, community or by the public authorities or the State.[139]

Article 2[140] of CEDAW imposes responsibility on the States parties to denounce and eliminate all forms of discrimination against women. In view of provisions of CEDAW Articles 2, 5, 11, 12 and 16, the GR12 has called upon the States parties "to protect women against violence of any kind."[141] Such discrimination could be "within the family, at the work place or in any other area of social life".[142] Article 3[143] calls upon States to take all appropriate measures including legislation for the "exercise and enjoyment of human rights and fundamental freedoms on a basis of equality with men". Thus, both Articles 2 and 3 prescribe comprehensive legal obligation for the States to eliminate discrimination against women.[144]

Similarly, provisions in Articles 5 to 16 of the CEDAW lay down specific obligations for the States to eliminate discrimination against women by imposing obligations through usage of emphatic terms such as the "State parties shall…".[145] Thus,

---

[137] Ibid, GR 19; General comments state: "Gender-based violence, which impairs or nullifies the enjoyment by women of human rights and fundamental freedoms under general international law or under human rights conventions, is discrimination within the meaning of article 1 of the Convention…".

[138] Ibid, GR 19: It explains, "These rights and freedoms include: (a) The right to life; (b) The right not to be subject to torture or to cruel, inhuman or degrading treatment or punishment; (c) The right to equal protection according to humanitarian norms in time of international or internal armed conflict; (d) The right to liberty and security of person; (e) The right to equal protection under the law; (f) The right to equality in the family; (g) The right to the highest standard attainable of physical and mental health; (h) The right to just and favourable conditions of work.".

[139] Ibid.

[140] UN (1979), n.126; Article 2 of CEDAW provides: "States Parties condemn discrimination against women in all its forms, agree to pursue by all appropriate means and without delay a policy of eliminating discrimination against women and, to this end, undertake:…".

[141] UN Women (2020), GR 12, n.133. It states: "Considering that articles 2, 5, 11, 12 and 16 of the Convention require the States parties to act to protect women against violence of any kind occurring within the family, at the work place or in any other area of social life".

[142] Ibid.

[143] UN (1979), n.126; Article 3 of CEDAW provides: "States Parties shall take in all fields, in particular in the political, social, economic and cultural fields, all appropriate measures, including legislation, to ensure the full development and advancement of women, for the purpose of guaranteeing them the exercise and enjoyment of human rights and fundamental freedoms on a basis of equality with men."

[144] Ibid.

[145] Ibid; Article 5 provides: "States Parties shall take all appropriate measures: (a) To modify the social and cultural patterns of conduct of men and women, with a view to achieving the elimination of prejudices and customary and all other practices which are based on the idea of the inferiority or the superiority of either of the sexes or on stereotyped roles for men and women; (b) To ensure that family education includes a proper understanding of maternity as a social function and the recognition of the common responsibility of men and women in the upbringing and development of their children, it being understood that the interest of the children is the primordial consideration in all cases."

CEDAW enjoins upon the States parties that they *shall* eliminate SGBV including harmful traditional practices stated in Articles 2(f) and 5(a) of the CEDAW.[146]

In fact, States are assigned to take appropriate measures regarding traffic in women and exploitation by an established form of trafficking (Article 6 of the CEDAW). This is the only CEDAW provision that explicitly addresses one of the forms of SGBV against women. There are many other forms of sexual exploitation such as sex tourism, forced and organized marriages with foreign nationals from developed countries and women from developing countries being used as domestic labour. Cumulatively, these situations put women at the risk of SGBV including pervasive forms such as trafficking, prostitution, slavery and other forms of violence against women in conflict zones.[147] CEDAW (Article 11) also provides for equality in employment. According to the general comments to GR19, violence against women at the workplace infringes upon the right to equality in employment.[148]

In a major development in 2019, International Labour Organization (ILO) adopted a significant convention on the Elimination of Violence and Harassment in the World of Work. This appears to be the first global legal instrument that has defined 'violence' as follows:

> the term "gender-based violence and harassment" means violence and harassment directed at persons because of their sex or gender, or affecting persons of a particular sex or gender disproportionately, and includes sexual harassment.[149]

This ILO Convention sets global standards that calls for "zero tolerance to violence and harassment" at the workplace.[150] The adoption of such an international legal instrument sends a strong message by making the issue of SGBV visible. It only underscores that violence against women is not accepted or justified by any practice.[151]

Article 16 provides for taking appropriate measures to prohibit discrimination within the family as well as in marital relations.[152] It highlights all types of discrimination against women form a basis for violence against them within family and by the partners such as battering, rape, sexual assault etc.[153] In fact, intimate partner violence

---

[146] Ibid.

[147] Ibid; Article 6 provides: "States Parties shall take all appropriate measures, including legislation, to suppress all forms of traffic in women and exploitation of prostitution of women."

[148] Ibid.

[149] ILO (2019), *Violence and Harassment Convention, 2019*; adopted by the ILO Conference at its 108th Session, Geneva, 21 June 2019; available at: https://www.ilo.org/dyn/normlex/en/f?p=NORMLEXPUB:12100:0::NO::P12100_ILO_CODE:C190 (accessed on 25 April 2021).

[150] ILO (2019), "Eliminating Violence and Harassment in the World of Work"; Convention no.190 (2019) and Recommendation no.206 (2019); available at: https://www.ilo.org/global/topics/violence-harassment/lang--en/index.htm (accessed on 25 April 2021).

[151] Shauna Olney, What is the significance of the Violence and Harassment Convention, 2019 (No. 190) and Recommendation (No. 206)? available at: https://www.ilo.org/global/about-the-ilo/newsroom/news/WCMS_711891/lang--en/index.htm (accessed on 19 October 2020).

[152] Article 16 of the CEDAW provides, "1. States Parties shall take all appropriate measures to eliminate discrimination against women in all matters relating to marriage and family relations…".

[153] UN Women, GR 19, n.133.

is considered to be one of the most common forms of violence since one in three women globally experience such physical and sexual violence during their lifetime. Moreover, SGBV gets exacerbated during emergencies like climatic change, violent conflicts and global pandemic such as COVID-19. Since early 2020, during the pandemic, there has been an increase in intimate partner violence and other forms of violence against girls and women since access to justice mechanism became difficult during the lockdowns.[154] It raises questions as regards efficacy of the domestic systems of States to provide protection to the women and take all measures to stop invisible forms of SGBV within the families.[155]

The GR19 (1992) of the Committee of CEDAW has carved out 'gender-based violence' within the rubric of 'discrimination' that includes physical, mental, or sexual harm or threat to commit theses harms, coercion or other deprivations of liberty. It has also recognized that women living within the conflict zones face special forms of violence.[156] The CSW has sought to address issues of gender equality and advancement of women. It meets annually and brings together the Members States and representatives of civil society to examine the contemporary issues that women face.[157] There used to be lot of discussion in the CSW (e.g. in 1969, 2004) on the protection and participation of women in conflict and post-conflict situations. The CEDAW was one of the outcomes of the CSW agenda. But it did not cover women in conflict. In a refreshing initiative, the CEDAW Committee took the initiative to give highlight violence against women in the conflict zones. It led to the adoption of the GR30 (women in conflict prevention conflict and post-conflict situations).[158]

The GRs include not only GBV or VAW but also threats, coercion, and other deprivation of liberty that led to such violence. It clarifies that States are responsible for private acts of violence if they fail to prevent violence or support it.[159] There

[154] WHO (2020), *Violence Against Women and Girls: Data Collection during COVID-19*, 25 June 2020; available at: https://www.who.int/publications/i/item/violence-against-women-and-girls-data-collection-during-covid-19. Also see UN Women (2020), *Violence against Women and Girls: Data Collection during COVID 19*, 17 April 2020; available at: https://www.unwomen.org/-/media/headquarters/attachments/sections/library/publications/2020/vawg-data-collection-during-covid-19-compressed.pdf (accessed on 25 April 2021).

[155] UN OHCHR, *General Recommendation No.19: Violence against Women*, Committee on The Elimination of Discrimination Against Women, 11th session, 1992; available at: https://tbinternet.ohchr.org/Treaties/CEDAW/Shared%20Documents/1_Global/INT_CEDAW_GEC_3731_E.pdf (accessed on 25 April 2021).

[156] Manjoo, R. and C. McRaith (2011), "Gender-Based Violence and Justice in Conflict and Post Conflict Areas," *Cornell International Law Journal*, 44: 11–31.

[157] UN Women (2015), *Preventing Conflict Transforming Justice Securing the Peace: A Global Study on the Implementation of UN Security Council Resolution 1325*; available at: https://www.unwomen.org/~/media/files/un%20women/wps/highlights/unw-global-study-1325-2015.pdf (accessed on 22 December 2020).

[158] Ibid.

[159] Klugman, Jeni (2017), *Gender based violence and the law: Background Paper Governance and the Law* (for World Development Report 2017) at p. 7; available at: https://thedocs.worldbank.org/en/doc/232551485539744935-0050022017/original/WDR17BPGenderbasedviolenceandthelaw.pdf (accessed on 25 April 2021).

are several issues concerning efficacy of CDEAW to prevent GBV. The GRs of the Committee of CEDAW are not legally binding. Moreover, many of the States have prescribed reservation to some important provisions of the CEDAW. Thus, implementation and efficacy of CEDAW is based on the consent of the parties.[160]

In 2017, the CEDAW Committee marked the 25th anniversary of GR19 and further strengthened international mechanisms to address SGBV by adopting GR 35. It is stated that "The *opinion juris* and State practice suggest that the prohibition of gender-based violence against women has evolved into a principle of customary international law" and as such, binding for all the States irrespective of the party of the treaty.[161]

On 6 October 1999, the General Assembly, without a vote, adopted the Optional Protocol to the CEDAW. The uniqueness of the Protocol is the complaint mechanism it stipulates for the individual or groups. It also creates an inquiry procedure for situations of grave or systematic violations of women's rights. The Protocol entered onto force on 22 December 2000 without any reservations by the Parties.[162] There are concerns as regards effectiveness of CDEAW and GRs that are not considered legally binding.[163] Moreover, some States have filed declarations and reservations (under Article 28) to important provisions of the CEDAW. For instance, India has filed a declaration for Article 5 and 16 and reservation to Article 29[164] of CEDAW.

The 1989 Convention on the Rights of the Child (CRC) and the CEDAW Protocol (2000) lay down the basic framework of human rights for children. Article 19(1)[165]

---

[160] Ibid.

[161] UN CEDAW (2017), *General recommendation No. 35 on gender-based violence against women, updating general recommendation No. 19*; UN Doc. CEDAW/C/GC/35, 26 July 2017; available at: https://www.ohchr.org/EN/HRBodies/CEDAW/Pages/GR35.aspx (accessed on 26 April 2021).

[162] UN (1999), *Optional Protocol to the Convention on the Elimination of All Forms of Discrimination against Women*; Annex to the UNGA Resolution 54/4 of 06 October 1999; UN Doc. A/RES/54/4 15 October 1999; available at: https://documents-dds-ny.un.org/doc/UNDOC/GEN/N99/774/73/PDF/N9977473.pdf?OpenElement (accessed on 30 April 2021).

[163] Klugman, Jeni (2017), "Gender based violence and the law;" available at: https://thedocs.worldbank.org/en/doc/232551485539744935-0050022017/original/WDR17BPGenderbasedviolenceandthelaw.pdf (accessed on 30 April 2021).

[164] UN CEDAW (2006), *Declarations, reservations, objections and notifications of withdrawal of reservations relating to the Convention on the Elimination of All Forms of Discrimination against Women*, Doc. CEDAW/SP/2006/2 of 10 April 2006; see Indian declaration of 9 July 1993 at p. 14; available at: https://documents-dds-ny.un.org/doc/UNDOC/GEN/N06/309/97/PDF/N0630997.pdf?OpenElement (accessed on 30 April 2021); Freeman, Marsha A. (2009), *Discussion Paper, Reservation to CEDAW: An Analysis for UNICEF*; available at: https://searchlibrary.ohchr.org/record/10415?ln=en (accessed on 30 April 2021).

[165] UNICEF (1990), *Convention on the Rights of the Child*; adopted and opened for signature, ratification and accession by General Assembly resolution 44/25 of 20 November 1989; entered into force on 2 September 1990. Article 19 (1) provides: "States Parties shall take all appropriate legislative, administrative, social and educational measures to protect the child from all forms of physical or mental violence, injury or abuse, neglect or negligent treatment, maltreatment or exploitation, including sexual abuse, while in the care of parent(s), legal guardian(s) or any other person who has the care of the child. 2. Such protective measures should, as appropriate, include effective procedures for the establishment of social programs to provide necessary support for the child and for those who have the care of the child, as well as for other forms of prevention and

and 34[166] provide protection of children from all forms of physical, mental violence, and sexual exploitation and sexual abuse when the child is in the care of parent(s), legal guardian(s), or any other authorized person.[167] These provisions apply to the protection of both girls and boys. Article 24[168] provides for the right to health that also includes all the harmful cultural practices against girls. Hence, this article provides for the right to health and health-related services for the children.[169]

Article 35[170] provides for prevention of sale, and trafficking of children. Abduction, sale, and trafficking of children are the way to push girl children into the situations that expose them to different forms of SGBV. Article 38[171] provides for the

---

for identification, reporting, referral, investigation, treatment and follow-up of instances of child maltreatment described heretofore, and, as appropriate, for judicial involvement"; available at: https://www.unicef.org/child-rights-convention/convention-text (accessed on 30 April 2021).

166 Ibid; Article 34 provides, "States Parties undertake to protect the child from all forms of sexual exploitation and sexual abuse. For these purposes, States Parties shall in particular take all appropriate national, bilateral and multilateral measures to prevent: (a) The inducement or coercion of a child to engage in any unlawful sexual activity; (b) The exploitative use of children in prostitution or other unlawful sexual practices; (c) The exploitative use of children in pornographic performances and materials.".

167 Pinheiro, Paulo Sérgio (2006), *World report on Violence against Children*; available at: https://archive.crin.org/en/docs/UNVAC_World_Report_on_Violence_against_Children.pdf (accessed on 30 April 2021).

168 Article 24 of the CRC provides, "1. States Parties recognize the right of the child to the enjoyment of the highest attainable standard of health and to facilities for the treatment of illness and rehabilitation of health. States Parties shall strive to ensure that no child is deprived of his or her right of access to such health care services. 2. States Parties shall pursue full implementation of this right and, in particular, shall take appropriate measures: (a) To diminish infant and child mortality; (b) To ensure the provision of necessary medical assistance and health care to all children with emphasis on the development of primary health care; (c) To combat disease and malnutrition, including within the framework of primary health care, through, inter alia, the application of readily available technology and through the provision of adequate nutritious foods and clean drinking-water, taking into consideration the dangers and risks of environmental pollution; (d) To ensure appropriate pre-natal and post-natal health care for mothers; (e) To ensure that all segments of society, in particular parents and children, are informed, have access to education and are supported in the use of basic knowledge of child health and nutrition, the advantages of breastfeeding, hygiene and environmental sanitation and the prevention of accidents; (f) To develop preventive health care, guidance for parents and family planning education and services. 3. States Parties shall take all effective and appropriate measures with a view to abolishing traditional practices prejudicial to the health of children. 4. States Parties undertake to promote and encourage international co-operation with a view to achieving progressively the full realization of the right recognized in the present article. In this regard, particular account shall be taken of the needs of developing countries"; see UNICEF (1990), n.165.

169 Ibid, Article 14.

170 Ibid; Article 35 provides, "States Parties shall take all appropriate national, bilateral and multilateral measures to prevent the abduction of, the sale of or traffic in children for any purpose or in any form."

171 Ibid; Article 38 provides: "1. States Parties undertake to respect and to ensure respect for rules of international humanitarian law applicable to them in armed conflicts which are relevant to the child. 2. States Parties shall take all feasible measures to ensure that persons who have not attained the age of fifteen years do not take a direct part in hostilities. 3. States Parties shall refrain from recruiting any person who has not attained the age of fifteen years into their armed forces. In recruiting among

prohibition of forced recruitment in the armed groups for sexual exploitation.[172] The CRC is supplemented by two optional protocols that were adopted in the year 2000. One Protocol provides for the rights of the children during the armed conflicts.[173] Another one protects children from specific forms of violence.[174] It prohibits sale of children, child prostitution, and child pornography.[175]

The Convention on the Elimination of All Forms of Racial Discrimination (CERD, 1969) is another global instrument that can be applicable to SGBV against women. In a way, racial discrimination affects men and women differently. Women suffer racial discrimination to a different and higher level as it often results in violence against women. Women face double victimization both as a human and due to their female gender. Women of a particular racial group suffer heightened forms of SGBV such as trafficking, sexual slavery, organized sexual abuse, forced impregnation and rape both during peace or conflicts.[176] Women from any particular ethnic or racial group could face dual or multiple forms of discrimination on the basis of their "race, gender, religion, nationality, social class, caste, age, and other status."[177] The 1948 UDHR (Article 8) and the 1966 ICCPR (Article 2.3) prohibit racial discrimination. Article 6 of the 1965 Convention on Racial Discrimination (CERD)[178] is more

---

those persons who have attained the age of fifteen years but who have not attained the age of eighteen years, States Parties shall endeavour to give priority to those who are oldest. 4. In accordance with their obligations under international humanitarian law to protect the civilian population in armed conflicts, States Parties shall take all feasible measures to ensure protection and care of children who are affected by an armed conflict."

[172] Grey, Rosemary (2014), "Sexual Violence Against Child Soldiers: The Limits And Potential Of International Criminal Law"; *International Feminist Journal of Politics*, 16 (4): 601–621; see also, Ndulo, Muna (2009), "The United Nations Responses To The Sexual Abuse And Exploitation Of Women And Girls By Peacekeepers During Peacekeeping Missions", *Berkeley Journal of International Law*, 27(1): 127.

[173] UN-OHCHR, *Optional Protocol to the Convention on the Rights of the Child on the involvement of Children in Armed Conflict, 2000*; adopted vide UN General Assembly resolution 54/263 of 25 May 2000, Annex I; Doc. A/Res/54/263, 16 March 2001; available at: https://www.un.org/ga/search/view_doc.asp?symbol=A/RES/54/263; https://www.ohchr.org/EN/ProfessionalInterest/Pages/OPACCRC.aspx (accessed on 22 May 2021).

[174] Pinheiro, Paulo Sérgio (2006), n.167.

[175] UN (2000), *Optional Protocol to the Convention on the Rights of the Child on the Sale of Children, Child Prostitution and Child Pornography*; adopted vide UN General Assembly resolution 54/263 of 25 May 2000, Annex II; Doc. A/Res/54/263, 16 March 2001; available at: https://www.un.org/ga/search/view_doc.asp?symbol=A/RES/54/263 (accessed on 22 May 2021).

[176] UN-OHCHR (2001), *Gender Dimensions of Racial Discrimination*; available at: https://documentation.lastradainternational.org/lsidocs/362%20Gender%20Dimnsions%20of%20Racial%20Discrimination.pdf (accessed on 22 May 2021).

[177] Ibid.

[178] UN-OHCHR, *International Convention on the Elimination of All Forms of Racial Discrimination*; adopted by UNGA resolution 2106 (XX) of 21 December 1965; Article 6 provides: "States Parties shall assure to everyone within their jurisdiction effective protection and remedies, through the competent national tribunals and other State institutions, against any acts of racial discrimination which violate his human rights and fundamental freedoms contrary to this Convention, as well as the right to seek from such tribunals just and adequate reparation or satisfaction for any damage

explicit on this. Similarly, the 1979 CEDAW (Article 1.c) has defined discrimination that includes gender-based racial discrimination.[179]

Earlier racial discrimination and gender-based discrimination used to be seen in parallel. Now an interlinkage between the two has been recognized. Women face different forms of SGBV as a combined effect of racial and gender-based violence. Though the Convention on Racial Discrimination has not specifically included any provision that deals with racial discrimination leading to violence against women; yet practically women face violence due to their race and gender. In fact, the interlinkage between racial discrimination and gender has been established by the International Criminal Tribunal for Rwanda (ICTR).[180] Beijing + 5 sought to address the issue of racism and racially motivated violence against women and girls during peace and conflicts. The women have faced violence because of their being 'women of colour,' 'minority women', 'ethnic women,' 'marginalized women' 'radicalized women,' etc. Hence, it can be surmised that both CEDAW and CERD are interlinked.[181]

Similarly, Article 2 of the 2006 Convention on the Rights of Persons with Disabilities (CRPD) and its Optional Protocol[182] has defined the term discrimination on the basis of disability. Article 3(b and g) provides for non-discrimination and equality between men and women. They form the main grounds for SGBV against women. Article 6[183] deals with women with disabilities. Article 16[184] provides for freedom

---

suffered as a result of such discrimination;" available at: https://ohchr.org/EN/ProfessionalInterest/Pages/CERD.aspx (accessed on 22 May 2021).

179 Romany, Celina and Katherine Culliton (2002), "The UN World Conference Against Racism: A Race-Ethnic and Gender Perspective", *Human Rights Brief* 9 (2): 14–17.

180 UN, International Residual Mechanism for Criminal Tribunals, International Criminal Tribunal for Rwanda; available at: https://www.irmct.org/en (accessed on 24 May 2021); UN (2000), *Gender and racial discrimination: Report of the Expert Group Meeting*, 21–14 November 2000, Zagreb, Croatia; available at: https://www.un.org/womenwatch/daw/csw/genrac/report.htm (accessed on 24 May 2021).

181 Ibid.

182 UN (2006), *Convention on the Rights of the persons with Disabilities.* Article 2 provides, "Discrimination on the basis of disability" means any distinction, exclusion or restriction on the basis of disability which has the purpose or effect of impairing or nullifying the recognition, enjoyment or exercise, on an equal basis with others, of all human rights and fundamental freedoms in the political, economic, social, cultural, civil or any other field. It includes all forms of discrimination, including denial of reasonable accommodation;" available at: https://treaties.un.org/doc/Publication/CTC/Ch_IV_15.pdf; https://treaties.un.org/Pages/ViewDetails.aspx?src=TREATY&mtdsg_no=IV-15-a&chapter=4&clang=_en (accessed on 24 May 2021).

183 Ibid; Article 6 provides, "1. States Parties recognize that women and girls with disabilities are subject to multiple discrimination, and in this regard shall take measures to ensure the full and equal enjoyment by them of all human rights and fundamental freedoms. 2. States Parties shall take all appropriate measures to ensure the full development, advancement and empowerment of women, for the purpose of guaranteeing them the exercise and enjoyment of the human rights and fundamental freedoms set out in the present Convention.".

184 Ibid; Article 16 provides: "Freedom from exploitation, violence and abuse: 1. States Parties shall take all appropriate legislative, administrative, social, educational and other measures to protect persons with disabilities, both within and outside the home, from all forms of exploitation, violence and abuse, including their gender-based aspects.

from exploitation and protection from violence and abuse. Article 17[185] deals with the protection of the integrity of the person and Article 22[186] provides for privacy. Apart from these, the International Convention on the Protection of the Rights of All Migrant Workers and Members of Their Families (1990)[187]; Convention against Transnational Organized Crime (2000), and the Protocol to Prevent, Suppress and Punish Trafficking in Person, especially Women and Children (2000)[188] are other relevant international legal instruments that indirectly address the issue of SGBV against women.

The United Nations Convention on Torture (Torture Convention) is considered as a reflection of the state practice in international law. It provides for a strong

---

2. States Parties shall also take all appropriate measures to prevent all forms of exploitation, violence and abuse by ensuring, inter alia, appropriate forms of gender- and age-sensitive assistance and support for persons with disabilities and their families and caregivers, including through the provision of information and education on how to avoid, recognize and report instances of exploitation, violence and abuse. States Parties shall ensure that protection services are age-, gender- and disability-sensitive.

3. In order to prevent the occurrence of all forms of exploitation, violence and abuse, States Parties shall ensure that all facilities and programmes designed to serve persons with disabilities are effectively monitored by independent authorities.

4. States Parties shall take all appropriate measures to promote the physical, cognitive and psychological recovery, rehabilitation and social reintegration of persons with disabilities who become victims of any form of exploitation, violence or abuse, including through the provision of protection services. Such recovery and reintegration shall take place in an environment that fosters the health, welfare, self-respect, dignity and autonomy of the person and takes into account gender- and age-specific needs.

5. States Parties shall put in place effective legislation and policies, including women- and child focused legislation and policies, to ensure that instances of exploitation, violence and abuse against persons with disabilities are identified, investigated and, where appropriate, prosecuted.".

[185] Ibid; Article 17 provides: "Protecting the integrity of the person: Every person with disabilities has a right to respect for his or her physical and mental integrity on an equal basis with others.".

[186] Ibid; Article 22 provides: "Respect to privacy: 1. No person with disabilities, regardless of place of residence or living arrangements, shall be subjected to arbitrary or unlawful interference with his or her privacy, family, home or correspondence or other types of communication or to unlawful attacks on his or her honour and reputation. Persons with disabilities have the right to the protection of the law against such interference or attacks.

2. States Parties shall protect the privacy of personal, health and rehabilitation information of persons with disabilities on an equal basis with others.".

[187] UN (1990), *International Convention on the Protection of the Rights of All Migrant Workers and Members of Their Families*; adopted by General Assembly resolution 45/158 of 18 December 1990; Article 14 provides: "No migrant worker or member of his or her family shall be subjected to arbitrary or unlawful interference with his or her privacy, family, correspondence or other communications, or to unlawful attacks on his or her honour and reputation. Each migrant worker and member of his or her family shall have the right to the protection of the law against such interference or attacks"; available at: https://www.ohchr.org/EN/ProfessionalInterest/Pages/CMW.aspx (accessed on 24 May 2021).

[188] United Nations (2000), *Convention against Transnational Organized Crime and the Protocols Thereto;* adopted by the General Assembly resolution 55/25 of 15 November 2000; UNTS, vol. 2225, no. 39574, p. 129; available at: https://treaties.un.org/doc/Publication/UNTS/Volume%202225/v2225.pdf (accessed on 24 May 2021).

basis to prohibit virtually all forms of SGBV at all times. Article 1[189] of the Torture Convention has defined the meaning of torture. It has been, generally, seen that only 'rape' is considered as torture because victims suffer severe pain or suffering.[190] In 1986, even the Special Rapporteur against Torture noted that 'sexual abuse' is one of the forms of physical torture.

In many of the human rights cases that occur around the world, sexual abuse or sexual violence specially 'rape' by the security forces or during conflicts would be covered under the provisions of the Torture Convention.[191] Article 7 of the 1966 ICCPR also provides for prohibition of torture and degrading and inhuman treatment to any person. SGBV in conflict zones comes under the scope of this provision.[192] Article 5 of the 1948 UDHR[193] did explicitly prohibit torture. In its 1998 judgement in *Akeyesu* case, the ICTR (paragraph 687) opined that "rape in fact constitutes torture when it is inflicted by or at the instigation of or with the consent or acquiesces of a public official or other person acting in an official capacity."[194]

[189] UN (1984), *Convention Against Torture and Other Cruel, In Human Or Degrading Treatment Or Punishment*; adopted by the General Assembly resolution 39/46 of 10 December 1984; Article 1 provides: "For the purposes of this Convention, the term 'torture' means an act by which severe pain or suffering, whether physical or mental, is intentionally inflicted on a person for such purposes as obtaining from him or a third person information or a confession, punishing him for an act he or a third person has committed or is suspected of having committed, or intimidating or coercing him or a third person, or for any reason based on discrimination of any kind, when such pain or suffering is inflicted by or at the instigation of or with the consent or acquiescence of a public official or other person acting in an official capacity. It does not include pain or suffering arising only from, inherent in or incidental to lawful sanctions"; available at: https://treaties.un.org/doc/Publication/UNTS/Volume%201465/volume-1465-I-24841-English.pdf (accessed on 22 December 2020).

[190] Amnesty International (2011), *Rape and Sexual Violence Human Rights Law and Standards in the International Criminal Court*, London: Amnesty, p. 38; available at: https://www.amnesty.org/en/documents/ior53/001/2011/en/ (accessed on 24 May 2021).

[191] Ibid.

[192] UN (1966), *International Covenant on Civil and Political Rights* and its *Optional Protocol*; adopted by the General Assembly resolution of 21/2200A of 19 December 1966; Article 7 provides: "No one shall be Subjected to torture or to cruel, inhuman or degrading treatment or punishment. In particular, no one shall be subjected without his free consent to medical or scientific experimentation"; available at: https://treaties.un.org/doc/Publication/UNTS/Volume%20999/volume-999-I-14668-English.pdf (accessed on 24 May 2021).

[193] UN (1948), *Universal Declaration of Human Rights*; Article 5 provides: "No one shall be subjected to torture or to cruel, inhuman or degrading treatment or punishment"; available at: https://www.un.org/en/about-us/universal-declaration-of-human-rights (accessed on 24 May 2021).

[194] UN-ICTR (1998), *Akeyasu Case* (The Prosecutor vs. Jean-Paul Akayesu), 02 September 1998 ICTR-96-4-T; available at: https://unictr.irmct.org/en/cases/ictr-96-4 (accessed on 24 May 2021).

Article 8[195] and 17[196] of the ICCPR and Articles 4[197] and 12[198] of UDHR provide for prohibition of slavery, unlawful attack on honour and reputation as well as a basis for the protection of women against SGBV.

The 1993 Vienna Declaration on Human Rights also provides that:

> The human rights of women and of the girl-child are an inalienable, integral and indivisible part of universal human rights ... and the eradication of all forms of discrimination on grounds of sex are priority objectives of the international community. Gender-based violence and all forms of sexual harassment and exploitation, including those resulting from cultural prejudice and international trafficking, are incompatible with the dignity and worth of the human person, and must be eliminated.[199]

It called for the adoption of national and international mechanisms to protect children from sexual exploitation[200] and explicitly mentioned some forms of SGBV by emphasizing on the:

> importance of working towards the elimination of ... all forms of sexual harassment, exploitation and trafficking in women, the elimination of gender bias in the administration of justice and the eradication of any conflicts which may arise between the rights of women and the harmful effects of certain traditional or customary practices, cultural prejudices and religious extremism ... Violations of the human rights of women in situations of armed conflict are violations of the fundamental principles of international human rights and humanitarian law. All violations of this kind, including in particular murder, systematic rape, sexual slavery, and forced pregnancy, require a particularly effective response.[201]

Apart from it, the declaration has spoken about (in paragraphs 45–53) the rights of children and called for effective measures against child prostitution, child pornography, the sale of children, other forms of sexual abuse, harmful customary practices, etc.[202]

In the growing corpus of international instruments on the rights of women, the 1993 *Declaration on Elimination of Violence against Women*[203]defines 'violence

---

[195] ICCPR (1966), n.192; Article 8 provides "1. No one shall be held in slavery; slavery and the slave-trade in all their forms shall be prohibited. 2. No one shall be held in servitude..."

[196] Ibid; Article 17.

[197] UDHR (1948), n.193; Article 4 provides: "No one shall be held in slavery or servitude; slavery and the slave trade shall be prohibited in all their forms"; Article 5 also provides: "No one shall be subjected to torture or to cruel, inhuman or degrading treatment or punishment".

[198] Ibid; Article 12 of the UDHR provides: "No one shall be subjected to arbitrary interference with his privacy, family, home or correspondence, nor to attacks upon his honour and reputation. Everyone has the right to the protection of the law against such interference or attacks."

[199] UN OHCHR (1993), *Vienna Declaration and Programme of Action*; adopted by the World Conference on Human Rights, Vienna, 25 June 1993; available at: https://www.ohchr.org/EN/ProfessionalInterest/Pages/Vienna.aspx (accessed on 25 May 2021).

[200] Ibid; paragraph 21.

[201] Ibid, paragraph 38.

[202] Ibid, paragraphs 48, 49.

[203] UN (1993), *Declaration on the Elimination of Violence against Women*; proclaimed by the General Assembly resolution 48/104 of 20 December 1993; UN Doc. A/RES/48/104; Article 1 provides: "Concerned that some groups of women, such as women belonging to minority groups,

against women.' It has regarded 'violence against women' as 'gender-based violence.' Similarly, Article 2 has included different forms of violence against women within family, community, and States.[204] The expression of concern has been reflected in the usage of different phrases such as: 'States should condemn,' 'women subjected to violence should be provided',[205] etc. It came to be reflected in the 1995, Beijing Declaration and Platform for Action wherein VAW was considered as GBV etc. have specifically deal with violence against women. It has elaborately discussed different forms of violence against women.[206] In the same vein, the UN Guiding principles on Business and Human Rights have given special attention to both gender-based violence and sexual violence.[207]

On the basis of the above-mentioned discussion on IHRL, it can be surmised that there is no specific IHRL instrument *per se* that exclusively deals with SGBV against women. In fact, the related laws do not even mention the term 'SGBV.'[208] The gradual crystallization of the discourse on SGBV is a result of developments within international institutions especially the UN system as well as the humanitarian sentinel, the ICRC. Still, in most of the cases, the time, application and interpretation of IHRL would depend on the discretion of the presiding judges and expertise of the legal counsels as well as an analysis and interpretation provided by the scholars.[209]

Ironically, the existing 'normative gap' that was underscored by the UN Special Rapporteur Rashida Manjoo and the absence of specific legally binding instruments have given a push for an alternative mechanisms of 'soft normativity'. These non-binding international soft instruments have considerably grown in addressing SGBV. However, they work largely as guiding principles for the States.[210]

Apart from it, there appears lack of coherence in the work and approach of the international institutions, within the confines of their respective mandates in dealing with SGBV. These include the use of different terminologies that create

indigenous women, refugee women, migrant women, women living in rural or remote communities, destitute women, women in institutions or in detention, female children, women with disabilities, elderly women and women in situations of armed conflict, are especially vulnerable to violence"; available at: https://www.ohchr.org/EN/ProfessionalInterest/Pages/ViolenceAgainstWomen.aspx (accessed on 25 May 2021).

[204] Ibid.

[205] Ibid, Article 4.

[206] UN (1995), *Report of the Fourth World Conference on Women*, Beijing, 4–15 September 1995, paragraphs 112 to 123 on "violence against women"; available at: https://www.un.org/womenwatch/daw/beijing/pdf/Beijing%20full%20report%20E.pdf (accessed on 25 May 2021).

[207] UN OHCHR (2011), *Guiding Principle on Business and Human Rights*; available at: https://www.ohchr.org/Documents/Publications/GuidingPrinciplesBusinessHR_EN.pdf (accessed on 25 May 2021).

[208] (Ibid)

[209] (Ibid)

[210] UN OHCHR, "Gender-Based Violence Against Women And International Human Rights Law: Options For Strengthening The International Framework Discussion Paper" (IWRAW, Asia-Pacific); available at: https://www.ohchr.org/Documents/Issues/Women/SR/Framework/2.IWRAW-AsiaPacificDiscussionPaperOptionInternationalMechnisms.pdf (accessed on 28 May 2021).

confusion and ambiguity. Therefore, it calls for uniformity in approach, a well-calibrated process and an umbrella entity that can coordinate with all the relevant international institutions and the sovereign states.

Goal 5 of the SDG also focuses on gender equality, which includes putting an end to SGBV.[211] After the Covid 19 pandemic of 2020-2022 period, the entire world order has changed and gravity of the SGBV challenge has heightened. As a result, the effectiveness of the existing IHRL and other human rights mechanisms need to be re-evaluated.

In view of the difficulties resulting from fragmented responses and soft law instruments, it is high time that the international human rights institutions especially within the UN system need to work towards crystallization of a specific global convention on SGBV or an optional protocol to CEDAW to place the challenge of SGBV on the global agenda as a one of the 'common concerns of humankind.'[212] This could entail a strong rights-based international instrument that would include a victim-centric approach as well as a coherent process and structure for de-legitimizing the use of SGBV against women and girls. The nature of the new global convention or an optional protocol should be such that it can provide a comprehensive international legal framework to exclusively deal with SGBV during peace, conflicts, post-conflict situations, global disasters including climate change and other contingencies. It would help in bridging the crucial normative gaps in international law to prevent and finally eliminate SGBV especially against women and girls.

(B) **International Humanitarian Law**

IHL is also known as the law of the warfare and the Geneva Law. ICRC (Geneva) is the costodian of the corpus of the four 1949 Geneva Conventions and the two protocols of 1977 and one of 2005. It aims at humanizing wars since they cannot be banished altogether. It took shape much before the IHRL and even the contemporary ICL deals with individual criminal responsibility for violations of laws and customs of warfare as well as international crimes such as genocide and crimes against humanity.[213] This part discusses the contemporary IHL that directly or indirectly deals with SGBV against women. Before 1992, the main focus of IHL was on the protection of women as civilians.[214]

---

[211] UNDP, *Gender Equality*; available at: https://www.undp.org/sustainable-development-goals#gender-equality (accessed on 27 May 2021).

[212] For a comprehensive view on this, see Desai, Bharat H. et al. (2019), "Climate change as a common concern of humankind: some reflections on the international law-making process" in Jordi Jaria-Manzano, and Susana Borràs, *Research Handbook on Global Climate Constitutionalism*, Cheltamham: Edward Elgar, Chapter 10.

[213] UN OHCHR, "The Prosecution of Sexual Violence in conflict: The Importance of Human Rights as Means of Interpretation" (by Sellers, Patricia Viseur); available at: https://www.ohchr.org/Documents/Issues/Women/WRGS/Paper_Prosecution_of_Sexual_Violence.pdf; Also see UN OHCHR (2019), *Protection of victims of sexual violence: Lessons learned*; available at: https://www.ohchr.org/Documents/Issues/Women/WRGS/Paper_Prosecution_of_Sexual_Violence.pdf (accessed on 28 May 2021).

[214] UN ECOSOC (1994), *Preliminary report submitted by the Special Rapporteur on violence against women, its causes and consequences*; in accordance with Commission on Human Rights

The *Lieber Code* (1863) is considered as the first codified version of modern IHL. Some provisions of the Code covered the effect of war on women. It includes Articles 19, 22, 31–47.[215] The *Lieber Code* provides that "women and children should be removed before the bombardment",[216] "unarmed citizens should be spared in person, property, and honour",[217] explicitly prohibits "all rape"[218] and provides for "severer punishment" for "rape" if committed by an American soldier in a hostile country against its inhabitants".[219] Thus, in letter and spirit, the Code provided for protection of women in warfare though only three Articles (Articles 44, 46 and 47) specifically provide for prohibition and punishment for wartime rape.

As compared to the *Lieber Code*, the main focus of the Hague Convention of 1907 was on the protection of prisoners of war. Its Preamble underscored "the interests of humanity and the ever-progressive needs of civilization" as well as guided by the desire for "greater precision or to confining them within such limits as would mitigate their severity as far as possible".[220] Though it did not include women specifically, yet it called upon the military authority to respect "Family honour and rights, the lives of persons"[221] in the occupied territory.[222] This provision could apply to SGBV against women in conflict zones under the notion of 'family honour.'

The 1929 Geneva Convention on Prisoners of War protects the women prisoners, detained women, and combatant women. Women taking part in hostilities come under the purview of this convention. The 1929 Convention sought to address the issue under the rubric of 'person and honour' (Article 3).[223] The same formula came to be adopted in (Article 14) of the 1949 Geneva Convention (III) Relative to the

resolution 1994/45 (Ms. Radhika Coomaraswamy); UN Doc. E/CN.4/1995/42 of 22 November 1994; available at: http://hrlibrary.umn.edu/commission/thematic51/42.htm (accessed on 28 May 2021).

[215] ICRC, "History of the law of war on land"; available at: https://www.icrc.org/en/doc/resources/documents/article/other/57jqhg.htm (accessed on 28 May 2021).

[216] *The Lieber Code: Instructions for the Government of Armies of the United States in the Field*, General Order No.100; Prepared by Francies Lieber and Promulgated by Abraham Lincoln on 24 April 1863; available at: http://www.ecclesia.org/forum/library/Lieber_Code.pdf; https://avalon.law.yale.edu/19th_century/lieber.asp. Also see Baxter, R.R. (1963), "The First Modern Codification of The Law of War Francis Lieber and General Orders No. 100", *International Review of The Red Cross*, No. 25, April 1963, pp. 171–189; available at: https://www.loc.gov/rr/frd/Military_Law/pdf/RC_Apr-1963.pdf (accessed on 28 May 2021).

[217] Ibid, Article 22.

[218] Ibid, Article 44.

[219] Ibid, Article 47.

[220] *Convention Respecting the Laws and Customs of War on Land*; signed at The Hague October 18, 1907, with annex of regulations and entered into force on 26 January 1910; available at: https://www.loc.gov/collections/united-states-treaties-and-other-international-agreements/about-this-collection/bevans/m-ust000001-0631.pdf; https://avalon.law.yale.edu/20th_century/hague04.asp (accessed on 28 May 2021).

[221] Ibid, Article 46.

[222] ICC, "Treatment of Sexual Violence in International Law"; available at: http://iccwomen.org/resources/crimeschart.html (accessed on 28 May 2021).

[223] ICRC, *Convention relative to the Treatment of Prisoners of War, Geneva, 27 July 1929*; Article 3 provides: "Prisoners of war are entitled to respect for their persons and honor. Women shall be

Treatment of Prisoners of War as it provides for 'person and honour' of the prisoners of war in all circumstances.

There are several provisions that seek to protect civilian women during an armed conflict. For instance, Article 27 of the 1949 Geneva Convention (IV) Relative to the Protection of Civilian Person in Times of War provides that "Women shall be especially protected against any attack on their honour, in particular against rape, enforced prostitution, or any form of indecent assault"[224]Articles 75 [(1), (2.b)], 76 and 77 of the 1977 Additional Protocol I comprise respect for 'honour' of a person; prohibition of 'outrage of personal dignity especially humiliating and degrading treatment, enforced prostitution and any form of indecent assault' against women[225]; protection of women against rape[226]; protection of children from indecent assault.[227] The 1977 Additional Protocol II provides that 'honour' of civilians should be respected, and there should be a prohibition of outrage of personal dignity including rape, enforced prostitution and any form of indecent assault or slavery (Article 4)[228] as well as general protection of civilians (Article 13).[229] In fact, common Article 3[230] of the 1949 Geneva Conventions can be said to provide for the protection of 'personal dignity' of the women. It includes a member of the armed forces who has not taken part—*hors de combat*—in the hostilities.

There are many provisions in the *Leiber Code* (applicable only to the soldiers of the USA), the 1949 Geneva Conventions and the 1977 Additional Protocols relating to protection of women in the war zones. However, very few provisions explicitly

---

treated with all consideration due to their sex. Prisoners retain their full civil capacity;" available at: https://www.icrc.org/en/doc/resources/documents/misc/57jnws.htm (accessed on 28 May 2021).

224 "*Geneva Convention Relative to the Protection of Civilian Persons in Time of War 12 August 1949*;" available at: https://www.un.org/en/genocideprevention/documents/atrocity-crimes/Doc.33_GC-IV-EN.pdf (accessed on 28 May 2021).

225 *Protocol additional to the Geneva Conventions of 12 August 1949*, and relating to the protection of victims of international armed conflicts (Protocol I), Article 1 and 2; adopted at Geneva on 8 June 1977; *UN Treaty Series*, vol. 1125, no. 17512, 1979, p. 3; available at: https://treaties.un.org/doc/publication/UNTS/Volume%201125/v1125.pdf (accessed on 29 May 2021).

226 Ibid, Article 76.

227 Ibid, Article 77.

228 *Protocol additional to the Geneva Conventions of 12 August 1949*, and relating to the protection of victims of non-international armed conflicts (Protocol II), Article 4; adopted at Geneva on 8 June 1977; *UN Treaty Series*, vol. 1125, no. 17513, 1979, p. 609; accessed on: https://treaties.un.org/doc/publication/unts/volume%201125/volume-1125-i-17513-english.pdf (accessed on 29 May 2021).

229 Ibid, Article 13.

230 ICRC, *The Geneva Conventions and their Commentaries*; available at: https://www.icrc.org/en/war-and-law/treaties-customary-law/geneva-conventions (accessed on 31 May 2021). Article 3 *Common to the Four Geneva Conventions 1949* provides: "1) Persons taking no active part in the hostilities, including members of armed forces who have laid down their arms and those placed hors de combat by sickness, wounds, detention, or any other cause, shall in all circumstances be treated humanely, without any adverse distinction founded on race, colour, religion or faith, sex, birth or wealth, or any other similar criteria. To this end, the following acts are and shall remain prohibited at any time and in any place whatsoever with respect to the above-mentioned persons: a) violence to life and person, in particular murder of all kinds, mutilation, cruel treatment and torture; c) outrages upon personal dignity, in particular, humiliating and degrading treatment."

deal with occurrence of SGBV in the conflict zones affecting different categories of women such as prisoners of war, internee, wounded and sick women, women not taking part in hostilities; pregnant women, civilian and non-civilian mothers, and other civilian women.

Ironically, there is no clearly defined provision on SGBV against women in the above mentioned IHL instruments. The provisions that can be said to be relevant contain phrases that are vague at best: 'prohibition to violence to life of person' including 'cruel treatment,' 'outrage of personal dignity,' and 'respect their person and honour.'[231] Moreover, the use of the terms such as 'taken into consideration;' 'special privileges;' 'in accordance to' clearly reflect charity-based approaches towards women since they can evoke pity or viewed as mere museum pieces. There are only four Articles that focus elements that would constitute SGBV in the conflict zones. Article 27 of the Geneva Convention (IV), Article 75 and 76 of the Additional Protocol I and Article 4 of the Additional Protocol II (already discussed above) contain terms such as 'rape,' 'forced prostitution,' 'indecent assault' and 'outrages of personal dignity'.

It seems to be the reflection of the prevailing attitudes and status of women in societies that these four articles do not specify the term 'SGBV' and, in turn, do not cover all forms of SGBV in the conflict zones as they are known today. It is only recently that the above-mentioned violence has come to be construed as a war crime by the ICTR and the Special Court for Sierra Leon.[232] and 'rape' has been considered as a crime against humanity and genocide under the ICTY and the Rome Statute of the ICC. This has been discussed in the subsequent section.[233]

As seen, the scope of these four provisions remains limited as they are applicable only for the protection of the civilian women. The usage of the phrase 'honour of women should be protected' does reflect the crux of the problem. The Geneva Conventions and the Additional Protocols treat women by their status, and relationship rather than as individual human beings with their own independent rights.[234] The word 'women's honour' attributes certain characteristics that are sexual in nature (primitive and mediaeval) or gender-specific such as modesty, chastity, virginity, etc.[235] The term used in the provisions is 'protection' rather than 'prohibition.' As a corollary, they give a charity-based shape to the provisions that deal with women in the conflict zones. It only shows big gap as regards lack of the rights-based approach in the entire IHL scheme of things (Table 3.1).[236]

---

[231] ICRC, *Rule 93: Rape and Other forms of Sexual Violence*; available at: https://ihl-databases.icrc.org/customary-ihl/eng/docs/v1_rul_rule93 (accessed on 31 May 2021).

[232] Ibid.

[233] Ibid.

[234] Gardam, Judith and H. Charlesworth (2000), "Protection of Women in Armed Conflict," *Human Rights Quarterly*, 22 (1): 148–166.

[235] Ibid.

[236] Ibid.

Table 3.1 Treatment of SGBV under the 1949 Geneva Conventions and the 1977 Additional Protocols

No.	Provisions	Nature of SGBV	Protected persons	Liability	Use of specific words
1.	Article 44 and 47 Article of *Leiber Code* 1863	Rape, punishment for rape committed during the war by the combatants	Inhabitants of occupied territory	US soldiers	Shall
2.	Article 27 Geneva Convention Relative to the Protection of Civilian Person in Times of War 1949	Any attack on honour, rape, enforced prostitution, indecent assault	Civilian women	High contracting parties (a party to the conflict or an occupying power)	Shall
3.	Article 75.2.b and Article 76 (protection of women) of Additional Protocol I (general protection to all sex)	An attack on honour, rape, enforced prostitution, and indecent assault, outrages upon personal dignity, humiliating and degrading treatment	Women civilian population of the occupied territory	Committed by civilian or military, contracting parties	Shall
4.	Article 4(1) and (2.e) of Additional Protocol II	Respect for honour, outrage upon personal dignity, humiliating and degrading treatment, rape, enforced prostitution and any form of indecent assault	Persons not taking part in hostilities or ceased to take part in hostilities	High contracting parties	Shall
5.	Article 3, Common to the Four Geneva Conventions	(a) Violence to life and person (torture etc.) (b) Outrages upon personal dignity, in particular, humiliating and degrading treatment	Persons including a member of armed forces not taking part in the hostilities	Contacting parties	Shall

(C) International Criminal Law

There are controversies as regards the origin and development of ICL. It seems majority of the scholars have accepted that ICL has originated from the general principle of international law especially treaties, customary international law and the general principle of law recognized by the 'civilized' nations.[237] The contemporary ICL is a product of the post-World War II. The international criminal tribunals and the courts of the time have a direct contribution in the emergence of ICL.[238] There are several important components of ICL such as the laws and customs of war which protect individuals in armed conflicts, genocide, and crime against humanity (laws relating to human rights abuses by their governments) etc.[239]

After World War II, the Nuremberg (1945) and the Tokyo (1946) Tribunals were established to punish the perpetrators of war crimes. However, it was the ICTY and the ICTR can be said to have laid the foundation of contemporary ICL. In fact, the 1990s witnessed placing of the ICL on a stronger institutionalized form.[240] In a way, there is a direct connection between the emergence of ICL and the laws of armed conflict. ICL is situation-based law. The existing IHL or laws relating to international crimes resulting from armed conflicts (e.g. Genocide Convention, etc.) are part of the substantive ICL. ICL can be treated as the substantive as well as the procedural law. Under this law, perpetrators are punished for violating some provisions of IHL and any other form of international law which protects human being against international crimes.[241] ICL provides the post-conflict justice mechanism. For these, individuals have been regarded as criminally liable especially for violation of the laws and customs of war, genocide and crimes against humanity.[242]

The main objective of ICL is to provide justice to the victims of international crimes by imposing international criminal responsibility on the perpetrators (natural person).[243] According to some, SGBV against women in the conflict zones can no longer be regarded as mere 'collateral damage' in armed conflicts within or between States. International law needs to resolutely affix accountability and eliminate impunity for the perpetrators of SGBV in conflict zones. It is now widely accepted that the perpetrators must not be able to avail impunity[244] at any cost. Though there is no specific law relating to SGBV in conflict zones, still progress

---

[237] Partin, Gail (2015), "International Criminal Law;" available at: https://www.asil.org/sites/default/files/ERG_CRIM.pdf?v=1 (accessed on 06 June 2021).

[238] Anderson, Kenneth (2009), "The Rise of International Criminal Law: Intended and Unintended Consequences," *The European Journal of International Law*, 20 (2): 331–358.

[239] Cryer, Robert et al. (2010), *An Introduction to International Criminal Law and Procedure*, UK: Cambridge University Press.

[240] Anderson (2009), n.238.

[241] Ibid.

[242] Cryer et al. (2010), n.239.

[243] Anderson (2009), n.238.

[244] Ibid.

took place during 1990–2000.[245] The ICTs has brought to the fore a mechanism by interpreting the existing law[246] for its application to SGBV in conflict zones.

It came in the wake of the establishment of two ad hoc ICTs as post-conflict justice mechanisms for former Yugoslavia (ICTY) and Rwanda (ICTR) that were enunciated through the resolutions of the United Nations Security Council (UNSC) as its subsidiary organs. For the first time, these tribunals have, in some cases, punished[247] the perpetrators of SGBV in conflict zones especially in cases of 'rape' against women as a war crime and crime against humanity.[248] The precedents set by these two tribunals provided a basis for inclusion of 'gender' in the 1998 Rome Statute of the ICC that came into effect in 2000 as well as the Statute of the Special Court for Sierra Leone. It also encouraged the UNSC to adopt the path-breaking resolution 1325 (2000) on the issue. Since then the UNSC has adopted nine more resolutions (till 2493 of 29 October 2019) under the agenda item on 'women, peace and security' (Secretaty-General's WPS report 827 of 27 September 2021).[249]

On a positive side, this development has broken the long silent relating to SGBV in conflicts.[250] The concerted international legal processes have come to accept the normative value of secondary sources of international law such as the decisions of the international courts and tribunals, resolutions of the principal organs of the UN: the General Assembly and the Security Council etc. Though there is no concept of 'precedent' in international law, still the 'precedents' do play role in the formation and interpretation of international law.

(a) **Sources of International Criminal Law**

The main sources of ICL relating to SGBV in conflict zones include the treaty-based ICL. It can be said to comprise the Hague Convention on Laws and Custom of War 1907 and the Four Geneva Conventions 1949 and the two Additional Protocols 1977 (which are also known as IHL or laws and customs of war), the Genocide Convention 1948, and the Rome Statute of the ICC 1998. These treaties provide a basis for the international crimes that come under the jurisdiction of the ICTs and the ICC.[251] Though international treaties apply only to the States parties, these can impose international criminal liability on the individuals.[252]

---

[245] Halliday, Terence C. (2010), "Symposium on Systematic Sexual Violence and International Criminal Law," *Law & Social Inquiry*, 35 (4): 835–838.

[246] UN-ICTR (1998), *Akeyasu Case* (2 September 1998 ICTR-96-4-T), n.194.

[247] Ibid.

[248] Leatherman, Janie (2007), "Sexual Violence and Armed Conflict: Complex Dynamics of Re-Victimization," *International Journal of Peace Studies*, 12 (1): 53–71.

[249] Ibid.

[250] Ibid.

[251] Cryer et al. (2010), n.239.

[252] Ibid.

The PCIJ in its advisory opinion in *Jurisdiction of the Courts in Danzig Case*, 1928[253] opined that the treaty law can apply to the individual directly if there was the intention of the drafters to that effect. It does not mean that all the treaty laws can impose international criminal liability. In that sense only that particular treaty and its provisions are applicable which are intended specifically for the purpose.[254] It is necessary that the commission of an offence should be within the territory of a state party to the particular treaty or the perpetrator must come under the scope of that law.

There are some concerns as regards the application of customary international law as a form of ICL. It is argued that CIL is vague enough and un-codified and hence it cannot be sufficient to impose criminal liability.[255] Still, CIL can impose liability on any perpetrator irrespective of the fact whether his home state is a party to the treaty or not. A glaring case in this respect is the ICC Prosecutor, Fatou Bensouda, seeking authorization (November 2017) for investigation[256] into role of the US soldiers in Afghanistan notwithstanding the fact that the USA is not a party to the Rome Statute. It led to a stand-off with the USA that attacked the ICC, its judges and revoking US visa of the Prosecutor (in November 2019).

There are many instances wherein ICTs have adopted the 'general principle of law recognized by nations.' There are differences in national and international trials. It has seen that international tribunals have followed the general principles of law. It has become part of the discussion on case law.[257] The SC resolutions also have contributed as sources of international criminal law. For instance, it was the SC resolutions that brought into being the Statutes of the ICTY, the ICTR, the Special Court for Seirra Leone and the Special Tribunal for Lebanon.

(b) International Criminal Tribunals

The prosecution for SGBV especially for 'rape' has been relatively a new occurrence before the ICTs. In fact, ICTR has been in the forefront in this respect.[258] Though

---

253 Permanent Court of International Justice (1928), *Jurisdiction of the Courts of Danzig*, Advisory Opinion, 1928 P.C.I.J. (Series B) No. 15 (03 March 1928); available at: http://www.worldcourts.com/pcij/eng/decisions/1928.03.03_danzig.htm (accessed on 25 June 2021).

254 Cryer et al. (2010), n.239.

255 Ibid.

256 ICC (2017), "The Prosecutor of the International Criminal Court, Fatou Bensouda, requests judicial authorization to commence an investigation into the Situation in the Islamic Republic of Afghanistan (20 November 2007);" available at: https://www.icc-cpi.int/Pages/item.aspx?name=171120-otp-stat-afgh (accessed on 25 June 2021). Also see, Simsons, M and M. Specia, "U.S. Revokes Visa of ICC Prosecutor Pursuing Afghan War," *The New York Times*, 5 April 2019; available at: https://www.nytimes.com/2019/04/05/world/europe/us-icc-prosecutor-afghanistan.html (accessed on 25 June 2021).

257 Cryer et al. (2010), n.239.

258 Roca, Inés Weinberg de. (2010), "Persecuting Gender Based and Sexual Crimes against Women: The Role of the International Courts and Criminal Tribunals," in Eboe-Osuji Chile (eds.) *In Protecting Humanity: in International Law and Policy in Honour of Navanethem Pillay*, Boston, MA: Martinus Nijhoff.

it started with the establishment of the ICTY,[259] the issue received serious attention during the trial of *Jon Paul Akeyasu* (ICTR).[260] SGBV did not form part of the criminal charges (as a separate form of crime) in the original 1996 indictment in this case.[261]

i. *Nuremberg and Tokyo Tribunals*

Prior to the establishment of ICTY and ICTR, there were two precursor tribunals set up at Nuremberg (the International Military Tribunal at Nuremberg, 1945)[262] and Tokyo (the International Military Tribunal for the Far East, 1946).[263] Both these tribunals were established for the prosecution of the military personnel and leaders of the vanquished Axis Powers (Germany and Japan) who were charged with commission of war crimes during the World War II. The Nuremberg and the Tokyo Tribunals were established by the victorious Allied Powers[264] (that is why the trials have often been dubbed as the 'victor's justice'). Those who were prosecuted at Nuremburg and Tokyo tribunals were accused of waging of war and systematic slaughter of civilians. The tribunals recorded a significant number of evidence of large-scale sex crimes committed during the World War II. Unfortunately, due to the circumstances in which the tribunals came to be established as well as the nature of trials carried out, the issue of criminal charges for sexual and gender-based crimes just did not figure since the criminal trials could give limited treatment to these crimes in the judgements. The Tokyo Tribunal ignored the incident of systematic rape and sexual slavery (especially in the infamous 'comfort stations') carried out by the Japanese troops during the World War II.[265]

It has been widely believed that during the World War II, large numbers of women were raped by the Allied forces too. There were forced sterilizations, forced abortions, and sexual mutilations both in Europe and Asian war zones. The Nazis experimented forced sterilizations in Europe, and the sexual slavery was resorted to especially by the Japanese soldiers in Asia. These reasons must have contributed to the side lining of SGBV related crimes both by the prosecution and the tribunals (Nuremberg and Tokyo). It led to focusing only on prosecution of crimes against peace.[266]

---

[259] Askin, Kelly D. (2004), "Decade of the Development of Gender Crimes in International Courts and Tribunals: 1993 to 2003," *Human Rights Brief*, 11(3): 1–5.

[260] Ibid.

[261] Ibid.

[262] United States Holocaust Memorial Museum, "International Military Tribunal at Nuremburg;" available at: https://encyclopedia.ushmm.org/content/en/article/international-military-tribunal-at-nuremberg (accessed on 28 June 2021).

[263] Office of the Historian, "The Nuremberg Trial and the Tokyo War Crimes Trials (1945–1948);" available at: https://history.state.gov/milestones/1945-1952 (accessed on 28 June 2021).

[264] Fitzpatrick, Georgina (2014), "War Crimes Trials, 'Victor's Justice' and Australian Military Justice in the Aftermath of the Second World War", Kevin Heller and Gerry Simpson (eds.), *the Hidden Histories of War Crimes Trials,* United Kingdom: Oxford.

[265] Ibid.

[266] Ibid.

ii. *International Criminal Tribunal for Former Yugoslavia*

The ICTY came to be established almost fifty years after the end of World War II.[267] On 2 February 1993, the UNSC resolved[268] to establish the *ad hoc* ICTY. It came to be set up after the failure to control unmanageable armed conflict in the Balkans.[269] ICTY's primary mandate was to punish the perpetrators for violation, since 1991, of the IHL that took place in the former Yugoslavia. The Statute of the ICTY was attached to the Security Council resolution 827.[270] In the late 1980s and early 1990s, people witnessed a dramatic political and social change across Eastern Europe and the Soviet Union (collapse of the majority of the communist systems and renewal of nationalism). In 1992, the Socialist Federal Republic of Yugoslavia (Bosnia and Herzegovina; Croatia; Macedonia; Slovenia and Serbia including the regions of Kosovo and Vojvodina[271]) was dissolved, it violently broke up into several parts and it led to growth of militant nationalism.[272]

In the early 1990s, hostilities first broke out in Slovenia (conflict, known as the ten-day war in 1991). It soon turned into brutal conflicts in Croatia, Bosnia, and Herzegovina. The mass atrocities were committed first in Croatia and later in Bosnia-Herzegovina. It led to thousands of civilians being raped and tortured in the detention camps. Victims were the civilian of all the ethnic groups. In Bosnia and Herzegovina (during April to November 1992), an estimated more than 100,000 people killed, two million people fled from their homes and thousands of Bosnian women were raped systematically.[273] In July 1995, following the Bostonian Serb takeover of Srebrenica, around 8000 Bosnian men and boys were killed. Women were separated from men and put into overcrowded buses and transported. The lives of the women were torn apart and most were not able to recover from the trauma of SGBV.[274]

In 1992, in the municipality of Foca, the Bosnian women were separated from men and kept under detention in terrible conditions. They were subjected to systematic

---

267 Ibid.

268 The ICTY was formally established by the adoption of the UN Security Council Resolution 827, without a vote and by the general agreement of the fifteen UNSC members on 25 May 1993; see UN SC Resolution 827; UN Doc. S/RES/827 (1993); available at: https://www.icty.org/x/file/Legal%20Library/Statute/statute_827_1993_en.pdf (accessed on 11 July 2021).

269 Schabas, William A. (2006), "The UN International Criminal Tribunals: The Former Yugoslavia, Rwanda and Sierra Leone;" available at: https://www.cambridge.org/core/books/un-international-criminal-tribunals/610335DF35E3C6E70D7B149A8325CEE6 (accessed on 11 July 2021).

270 Ibid.

271 United Nations, "International Criminal Tribunal for the former Yugoslavia, What is the Former Yugoslavia?" available at: https://www.icty.org/en/about/what-former-yugoslavia (accessed on 11 July 2021).

272 Ibid.

273 Ibid.

274 Brammertz, Serge and M. Jarvis (2010), "Prosecuting Sexual Violence at the ICTR" in Chile Eboe-Osuji (2010), Ed., *Protecting Humanity: Essays in International Law and Policy in Honour of Navanethem Pillay*, Leiden: Brill Nijhoff; available at: https://brill.com/view/title/18293?language=en (accessed on 11 July 2021).

rape and other forms of sexual abuse.[275] The Yugoslavian conflict became the first major example of SGBV against women in conflict zones. Still, it was the ICTR which gave first punishment for the commission of such SGBV in the conflict zone.[276] So, it is in the fitness of things to discuss the history of the ICTR that brought to the fore SGBV cases.

iii. *International Criminal Tribunal for Rwanda*

It was for the first time in the history that an international criminal tribunal (ICTR) punished the perpetrators for committing the crime of genocide. For the first time, 'rape' was recognized as part of the crime of genocide.[277] ICTR was established by the Security Council resolution of 955 (1994)[278] under Chapter VII of the UN Charter.[279] The Tribunal was given the mandate to prosecute the perpetrators for commission of genocide, serious violations of IHL that took place in the territory of Rwanda and the neighbouring States between 1 January 1994 and 31 December 1994.[280]

The civil war in Rwanda led to systematic massacre for several weeks resulting in killing of one million people and 150,000 to 250,000 women subjected to mass rape. The majority of victims were from the minority Tutsi community and the perpetrators included the government officials, soldiers, and military personnel. They fled to the Democratic Republic of Congo (DRC) after committing genocide.[281] On 8 November 1994, the ICTR was established to punish the perpetrators. The investigation began in May 1995, the first accused was brought before the Tribunal in May 1996 and the first trial started in January 1997.[282] The Tribunal completed all the trials in December 2012[283] and closed its work on 31 December 2015. The Residual Mechanism, based at The Hague, now caters "to preserve and promote the legacy of the UN International Criminal Tribunals".[284]

---

275 Ibid.

276 UN-ICTR (1998), *Akeyasu Case* (The Prosecutor vs. Jean-Paul Akayesu), n.194.

277 UN, "The ICTR in Brief;" available at: https://unictr.irmct.org/en/tribunal (accessed on 11 July 2021).

278 UN (1994), Security Council resolution 955; UN Doc. S/RES/955 (1994), 8 November 1994; available at: https://www.irmct.org/specials/ictr-remembers/docs/res955-1994_en.pdf?q=ictr-remembers/docs/res955-1994_en.pdf (accessed on 11 July 2021).

279 Ibid.

280 UN, "Rwanda: A Brief History of the Country"; available at: https://www.un.org/en/preventgenocide/rwanda/historical-background.shtml (accessed on 11 July 2021).

281 Ibid.

282 Ibid.

283 UN, Background Information on the Justice and Reconciliation Process in Rwanda; available at: https://unictr.irmct.org/en/genocide (accessed on 11 July 2021).

284 UN, The International Residual Mechanism for Criminal Tribunals; available at: https://www.irmct.org/en (accessed on 11 July 2021).

iv. *International Criminal Court*

The Statute of the International Criminal Court (ICC)[285] is significant since it has expanded the scope of SGBV in the conflict zones. ICC is the institutional outcome and permanent court that has jurisdiction over war crimes, a crime against humanity, genocide, and the act of aggression.[286] It has jurisdiction to impose individual criminal responsibility not only the Member States but also on individuals associated with mass atrocities. It is the first treaty-based criminal court which functions outside of the UN system. The applicability of the 1998 Rome Statute of the ICC is dependent on the ratification by the States and, as on 3 April 2022, 123 States are Parties to it. The limited application of the ICC Statute remains a hindrance since some of the major powers (such as China, India, Russian Federation and the USA) are not parties to it.[287]

In the post-World War II era, for the first time, the Rome Statute has explicit authority to prosecute the perpetrators of rape, sexual slavery, forced prostitution, forced sterilization, forced pregnancy, and any other form of sexual violence of comparable gravity as war crimes and crimes against humanity.[288] The inclusion of 'gender' in the Rome Statute has been the result of long negotiations. After intense debate among States, NGOs, diplomats, etc., the term 'gender' came to be included

---

[285] United Nations (1998), *International Criminal Court*. The ICC's Statute was signed in Rome on 17 July 1998 and it entered into force on 1 July 2002 after ratification by 60 states. The treaty is also known as the 'Rome Statute'; available at: https://www.icc-cpi.int/resource-library/Documents/RS-Eng.pdf (accessed on 11 July 2021).

[286] Ibid.

[287] Lake, Milli. (2014), "Ending Impunity for Sexual and Gender-Based Crimes: The International Criminal Court and Complementarity in the Democratic Republic of Congo," *African Conflict & Peace building Review*, 4 (1): 1–32.

[288] Ibid.

in Article 7(3) under 'crime against humanity'[289] and in Article 8(2)[290] under 'war crimes'.[291]

The crime against humanity has been regarded "as part of a widespread or systematic attack directed against any civilian population, with knowledge of the attack," and war crime committed "as part of a plan or policy or as part of a large-scale commission of such crimes".[292] Some scholars have argued that mass rapes committed during the conflict can be treated as a crime of genocide because they were committed "with the intent to destroy in whole or in part national, ethical, religious and racial groups"[293] The Statute has expanded the definition of rape[294] to include non-penile penetration (e.g. insertion of objects or oral sex). It appears to be the first codified definition of 'rape' under international law (international criminal law).[295] The Statute has ruled out the possibility of defence by nominal consent of the victims of SGBV in the conflicts. Rule 70 of the ICC Statute has made it clear that a person is incapable of

---

[289] UN (1998), *The Rome Statute*, n.285. Article 7 (g) provides, "For the purpose of this Statute, "crime against humanity" means any of the following acts when committed as part of a widespread or systematic attack directed against any civilian population, with knowledge of the attack: ...(g) Rape, Sexual slavery, enforced prostitution, forced pregnancy, enforced sterilization, or any other form of sexual violence of comparable gravity". For the purpose of the Rome Statute, "the term "gender" is understood to refer to the two sexes, male and female, within the context of society. The term "gender" does not indicate any meaning different from the above".

[290] Ibid, *The Rome Statute*, Article 8 (2) (b) provides: "For the purpose of this Statute, "war crimes" means: (xxi) Committing outrages upon personal dignity, in particular humiliating and degrading treatment; (xxii) Committing rape, sexual slavery, enforced prostitution, forced pregnancy, as defined in article 7, paragraph 2 (f), enforced sterilization, or any other form of sexual violence also constituting a grave breach of the Geneva Conventions; (e) Other serious violations of the laws and customs applicable in armed conflicts not of an international character, within the established framework of international law, namely, any of the following acts: (vi) Committing rape, sexual slavery, enforced prostitution, forced pregnancy, as defined in article 7, paragraph 2 (f), enforced sterilization, and any other form of sexual violence also constituting a serious violation of article 3 common to the four Geneva Conventions".

[291] Oosterveld, Valerie. (2014), "Constructive Ambiguity and the Meaning of "Gender" for the International Criminal Court", *International Feminist Journal of Politics*, 16 (4): 563–580.

[292] Manjoo, R. and C. McRaith, (2011), n.156.

[293] Ibid.

[294] ICC (2011), *Elements of Crime*, The Hague: ICC, p. 8. An elaboration of "Crime Against humanity of rape", under Article 7 (1) (g)-1, constitutes the following *elements of crime*: "1. The perpetrator invaded the body of a person by conduct resulting in penetration, however slight, of any part of the body of the victim or of the perpetrator with a sexual organ, or of the anal or genital opening of the victim with any object or any other part of the body. 2. The invasion was committed by force, or by threat of force or coercion, such as that caused by fear of violence, duress, detention, psychological oppression or abuse of power, against such person or another person, or by taking advantage of a coercive environment, or the invasion was committed against a person incapable of giving genuine consent. 3. The conduct was committed as part of a widespread or systematic attack directed against a civilian population. 4. The perpetrator knew that the conduct was part of or intended the conduct to be part of a widespread or systematic attack directed against a civilian population;" available at: https://www.icc-cpi.int/NR/rdonlyres/336923D8-A6AD-40EC-AD7B-45BF9DE73D56/0/ElementsOfCrimesEng.pdf (accessed on 11 July 2021).

[295] Lake, Milli. (2014), n.287.

giving genuine consent if she is affected by coercive environment etc.[296] In its *Rules and Procedure of Evidence*, it has included special provision for the treatment of victims of SGBV.[297]

There are some leading cases wherein rape and sexual violence were treated as war crimes and crime against humanity, e.g. *Bemba case.*[298] In this case, the perpetrator (Bemba; a military commander) found guilty by the Trial Court and sentenced to 18 years imprisonment by the ICC on 21 March 2016 for crime against humanity (including murder and rape) and war crimes (including murder, rape, and pillaging).[299] The crimes were committed in the Central African Republic (CAR) during 2002–2003. It was a non-international armed conflict between national armed forces and rebel groups of Central African Armed Forces. Bemba had effective authority to control the troops who committed those crimes. There was a widespread and systematic attack on the civilian population especially women who became victims of SGBV in the armed conflict.[300] On 8 June 2018, however, in reversing the Trial Court ruling, the Appeal Chamber of the ICC acquitted Jean-Pierre Bemba Gombo from the charges of war crimes and crimes against humanity.[301]

Chapter 2 and the above-mentioned discussion in this chapter, have identified different forms of SGBV in conflict zones. However, the forms of SGBV listed under the Rome Statute do not cover all forms of SGBV. Hence, the scope of SGBV under the ICC Statute is very limited.[302]

v. *Hybrid Courts and Tribunals*

Hybrid Courts or Tribunals (HCTs) are the recent development in the field of the post-conflict justice mechanisms. These HCTs are unique because they have a mixed

[296] ICC (2013), *Rules of Procedure and Evidence*, The Hague: ICC, pp. 24–25. Rule 70 lays down the principles of evidence in cases of sexual violence: "In cases of sexual violence, the Court shall be guided by and, where appropriate, apply the following principles: (a) Consent cannot be inferred by reason of any words or conduct of a victim where force, threat of force, coercion or taking advantage of a coercive environment undermined the victim's ability to giving voluntary and genuine consent; (b) Consent cannot be inferred by reason of any words or conduct of a victim where the victim is incapable of giving genuine consent; (c) Consent cannot be inferred by reason of the silence of, or lack of resistance by, a victim to the alleged sexual violence; (d) Credibility, character or predisposition to sexual availability of a victim or witness cannot be inferred by reason of the sexual nature of the prior or subsequent conduct of a victim or witness cannot be inferred by reason of the sexual nature of the prior or subsequent conduct of a victim or witness;" available at: https://www.icc-cpi.int/iccdocs/PIDS/legal-texts/RulesProcedureEvidenceEng.pdf (accessed on 11 July 2021).

[297] Lake, Milli. (2014), n.287.

[298] ICC (2008), *Bemba Case* (The Prosecutor v. Jean-Pierre Bemba Gombo), 21 March 2016; ICC-01/05-01/08; available at: https://www.icc-cpi.int/car/bemba (accessed on 11 July 2021).

[299] Ibid.

[300] ICC (2010), *Bemba Case: Alleged crimes (non-exhaustive list)*; available at: https://www.icc-cpi.int/car/bemba/pages/alleged-crimes.aspx (accessed on 11 July 2021).

[301] ICC Appeals Chamber (2018), Press Release: "ICC Appeals Chamber acquits Mr Bemba from charges of war crimes and crimes against humanity", 08 July 2018; available at: https://www.icc-cpi.int/Pages/item.aspx?name=pr1390 (accessed on 11 July 2021).

[302] Gaggioli, Gloria (2014), n.4.

composition of international and domestic prosecutors, judges and defence attorneys. They have been established mainly to prosecute the perpetrators of war crimes, crimes against humanity and genocide. Some of the tribunals have completed their work, for example, East Timor, Sierra Leone, Kosovo, etc. Some are still functioning, e.g. Cambodia, Bangladesh and Lebanon, etc. The jurisprudence of the ICTY and the ICTR serves as a precedent for these HCTs. The forms of SGBV tried by these HCTs comprise rape, sexual slavery and other forms of gender violence.[303] For instance, the Special Court for Sierra Leone (SCSL) in *the Revolutionary United Front* (*RUF*) case[304] convicted the accused of SGBV in conflict with other crimes. The Tribunal treated sexual slavery and forced marriage as a crime against humanity and inhumane acts.[305]

C. Some Leading Cases Relating to SGBV

i. *Akayesu* Case, (ICTR)[306]

In this case, the main perpetrator was in charge of maintaining law and order. The other perpetrators were the subordinates (local militia and communal police). The perpetrator (*Akayesu*) was arrested in Zambia on 10 October 1995. He was presented before the Trial Chamber I of the ICTR on 30 May 1996. The charges against him included genocide, crimes against humanity (Article 2[307] and Article 3[308] of the ICTR Statute), Article 3 common to the Four Geneva Conventions 1949 (protection of victims of internal armed conflict) and Article 4 of the Additional Protocol 1977 (protection of victims of internal armed conflict).

---

303 Ibid.

304 Special Court for Seirra Leone (2004), *Prosecutor v Issa Hassan Sesay & Ors-GBAO*, 26th October 2009, SCSL-04-15-AR73 (2004) SCSL 24, 23 November 2004; available at: https://sierralii.org/sl/judgment/special-court/2004/24 (accessed on 11 July 2021).

305 Oosterveld, Valerie (2011), "The Gender Jurisprudence of the Special Court for Sierra Leone: Progress in the Revolutionary United Front Judgments," *Cornell International Law Journal*, 44: 49.

306 UN-ICTR (1998), *Akeyasu Case* (*The Prosecutor vs. Jean-Paul Akayesu*; 2 September 1998 ICTR-96-4-T), n.194.

307 UN (1994), *Statute of The International Tribunal for Rwanda* (Security Council resolution 955 of 8 November 1994), n.278. Article 2 of the *ITR Statute* provides: *Genocide*: "1. The International Tribunal for Rwanda shall have the power to prosecute persons committing genocide as defined in paragraph 2 of this Article or of committing any of the other acts enumerated in paragraph 3 of this Article. 2. Genocide means any of the following acts committed with intent to destroy, in whole or in part, a national, ethnical, racial or religious group, as such: (a) Killing members of the group; (b) Causing serious bodily or mental harm to members of the group; (c) Deliberately inflicting on the group conditions of life calculated to bring about its physical destruction in whole or in part; (d) Imposing measures intended to prevent births within the group; (e) Forcibly transferring children of the group to another group.".

308 Ibid, UN (1994), *Statute of the ITR*; Article 3 provides: *Crimes against Humanity*: "The International Tribunal for Rwanda shall have the power to prosecute persons responsible for the following crimes when committed as part of a widespread or systematic attack against any civilian population on national, political, ethnic, racial or religious grounds: (a) Murder; (b) Extermination; (c) Enslavement; (d) Deportation; (e) Imprisonment; (f) Torture; (g) Rape; (h) Persecutions on political, racial and religious grounds; (i) Other inhumane acts.".

Till the end of the first part of the trial before the Chamber I (on 24 May 1996), there were no charges of rape or other forms of sexual violence against women. The allegations of sexual violence came before the Tribunal for the first time through the testimony of the prosecution witness (a Tutsi woman). She claimed that her six-year-old daughter was raped by the men of the accused.[309] Subsequently, many other women witnesses from the prosecution side came to share their horror stories of sexual violence perpetrated during the conflict.[310] On 17 June 1997, sexual violence with other charges framed under Article 3(g) (rape as a crime against humanity), Article 3(i) (other inhumane acts as crimes against humanity) and Article 4(e) (violation of Article 3 common to the Geneva Conventions and 4.2. e. Additional Protocol II of 1977[311]) of the Statute of ICTR.[312] The charges of sexual violence against the Tutsi women were framed following the investigation done by the Tribunal. The different forms of sexual violence that occurred included rape, forced public nudity, rape in public in the presence of children and young men,[313] forced to march naked in front of public, forced piecing of wood into the sexual organ of women,[314] forced delivery or forced termination of pregnancy by rape and torture,[315] forced to walk, run, exercise naked, forced pregnancy by rape.[316]

The Tribunal did treat 'rape' as genocide. It was opined that the "Genocide Convention already has been treated as customary international law," and Rwanda was the party to the Genocide Convention since 12 February 1975.[317] The Tribunal viewed that all the elements of genocide had been proved. While interpreting, Article 2.2(d) of the Statute of ICTR, the Tribunal observed that 'rape' and 'sexual violation' came under the preview of "imposing measures intended to prevent births within the group' and that it also formed part of genocide."[318] The measures of prevention of birth within the rival groups were, "sexual mutilation, the practice of sterilization,

[309] UN-ICTR (1998), *Akeyasu Case*; 2 September 1998 ICTR-96-4-T, paragraph 416, n.194.

[310] Ibid, paragraph 416, 417, 421–434, 436–438.

[311] UN (1994), *Statute of the ITR*; n.278. Article 4 provides for *Violations of Article 3 Common to the Geneva Conventions and of Additional Protocol II*: "(e) Outrages upon personal dignity, in particular humiliating and degrading treatment, rape, enforced Prostitution and any form of indecent assault;" Article 2 of the *Statute Of The International Tribunal For Rwanda* provides "Genocide: 1. The International Tribunal for Rwanda shall have the power to prosecute persons committing genocide as defined in paragraph 2 of this Article or of committing any of the other acts enumerated in paragraph 3 of this Article. 2. Genocide means any of the following acts committed with intent to destroy, in whole or in part, a national, ethnical, racial or religious group, as such: (a) Killing members of the group; (b) Causing serious bodily or mental harm to members of the group; (c) Deliberately inflicting on the group conditions of life calculated to bring about its physical destruction in whole or in part; (d) Imposing measures intended to prevent births within the group; (e) Forcibly transferring children of the group to another group.".

[312] UN-ICTR (1998), *Akeyasu Case*, 2 September 1998 ICTR-96-4-T, n.194.

[313] Ibid, para. 423.

[314] Ibid, para. 427, 429.

[315] Ibid, para.437.

[316] Ibid.

[317] Ibid, para. 495, 496.

[318] Ibid, para. 507.

forced birth control, separation of sexes and prohibition of marriages, deliberately impregnated the women of the opponent group to deliver the child of the perpetrator (because children are known by the name of the father's group)."[319] The Tribunal strongly felt that "rape can be measured to prevent birth, and it includes physical as well as mental trauma of rape can be affected on subsequent procreation."[320]

Article 3(g) of the ICTR included 'rape' as a crime against humanity.[321] The Trial Chamber took the view that "rape is a form of aggression and cannot be captured in a mechanical description of objects or body parts."[322] It became obvious that torture and other cruel and inhumane and degrading treatments took place as State-sanctioned violence. Therefore, like torture, "rape is used for such purposes as intimidation, degradation, humiliation, discrimination, punishment, control or destruction of a person."[323] In fact, rape was also treated as a violation of personal dignity as torture.[324]

The Chamber did define 'rape.'[325] It was different from the definition applied in the national law in different States. The Tribunal included all the above-mentioned forms of sexual violence coming under the preview of rape[326] and finally decided that the perpetrator was criminally responsible.[327] The Tribunal took the view that:

> These rapes resulted in physical and psychological destruction of Tutsi women, their family, and their communities. Sexual violence was an integral part of the processes of destruction, specifically targeting Tutsi women and specifically contributing to their destruction and to the destruction of the Tutsi group as a whole.[328]

---

[319] Ibid, para.507.

[320] Ibid, para. 508.

[321] Ibid, para. 586.

[322] Ibid, para. 597.

[323] Ibid.

[324] Ibid.

[325] Ibid, para. 598. "The Chamber defines rape as a physical invasion of a sexual nature, committed on a person under circumstances which are coercive. Sexual violence which includes rape is considered to be any act of a sexual nature which is committed on a person under circumstances which are coercive. This act must be committed: (a) as part of a wide spread or systematic attack; (b) on a civilian population; (c) on certain catalogued discriminatory grounds, namely: national, ethnic, political, racial, or religious grounds"; *Akeyasu Case*, (*The Prosecutor vs. Jean-Paul Akayesu*), 2 September 1998 ICTR-96-4-T, n.194.

[326] Ibid, para. 688. "The Tribunal defines rape as a physical invasion of a sexual nature, committed on a person under circumstances which are coercive The Tribunal considers sexual violence, which includes rape, as any act of a sexual nature which is committed on a person under circumstances which are coercive. Sexual violence is not limited to physical invasion of the human body and may include acts which do not involve penetration or even physical contact.".

[327] Ibid, para. 719, 734. "In the opinion of the Chamber, Akayesu is indeed individually criminally responsible by virtue of such acts for having ordered, aided and abetted in the preparation or execution of the killings of members of the Tutsi group and in the infliction of serious bodily and mental harm on members of said group.".

[328] Ibid, para. 731.

Notwithstanding this, it was held that the respondent was not liable under Article 3 of the Common to the Geneva Conventions1949 and Article 4(2) (e) of the Additional Protocol 1977.[329]

Thus, it seems that women were subjected to rape not because they were women or for their gender but because they belonged from a particular ethnic group (Tutsi). This case made it clear that women were treated not as a different gender or different sex, but they symbolized as a symbol or identity of a specific group. SGBV against women has been treated as a *tactic or weapon of war* to destroy an ethnic group. The statements of the perpetrators (such as: "Never ask me again what a Tutsi woman tastes like;"[330] "when rats are killed you don't spare rats that are still in the form of foetus"; [331] "Now, let's see what the vagina of a Tutsi" etc.[332]) made it clear that women were ill treated as the member of the Tutsi opponent group. Women from other groups, especially Hutu, were set free on the ground that Tutsi women married to Hutu men "were left alone because these women deliver Hutu children".[333]

ii. The *Celebici Case*[334] (ICTY)

The trend of punishing the perpetrators of sexual violence started with the trial of the *Akayesu* case (ICTR). After two and half months of the *Akayesu* judgement, the ICTY gave another landmark judgement in the *Celebici* case. In this case, the focus was on sexual and gender-besed crimes committed in the Balkans. The perpetrators (Zejnil Delali, Zdravko Muci, Hazim Deli, and Esad Lando) were charged for serious violations of the IHL. The atrocities were committed in the territory of Yugoslavia since 1990. The *Calibici* case was tried in the ICTY during 10 March 1997 to 15 October 1998. All the alleged crimes were committed in the Celebici prison camp.[335] The prison camps were established during the armed conflict on behalf of the government. People were detained in the camp as a result of military operations on behalf of the government of Bosnia and Herzegovina. The perpetrators had committed the atrocities in the performance of their official duties as a member of the Bosnian forces.[336]

According to the findings of the Trial Chamber, it was an international armed conflict. The victims did not belong to the nationality of the parties to the armed

[329] Ibid. "Count 15 (Verdict) Count 15: Not guilty of Violation of Article 3 common to the Geneva Conventions and of Article 4(2)(e) of Additional Protocol II (Outrage upon personal Dignity, in particular. Count 2: Not Guilty of Complicity in Genocide Count 14: Guilty of Crime against Humanity (Other Inhumane Acts) Rape, Degrading and Humiliating Treatment and Indecent Assault).".

[330] Ibid, para. 422.

[331] Ibid, para. 427.

[332] Ibid, para. 437.

[333] Ibid, para. 429.

[334] UN ICTY (1998), *The Celebici Case* (*Prosecutor vs, Zejnil Delali, Zdravko Muci and Esad Landao*), 16 November 1998, ICTY-IT-96-21-T; available at: https://www.icty.org/x/cases/mucic/tjug/en/981116_judg_en.pdf (accessed on 11 July 2021).

[335] Ibid, para. 196.

[336] Ibid.

conflict. The victims or persecutions of the case were 'persons protected' under the 1949 Geneva Convention (IV).[337] The accused were charged for confinement of civilians in the camp unlawfully.[338] The majority of the prosecution witnesses were the eye witnesses and the victims.[339] The charges specifically included 'torture and rape' against the perpetrators.[340] The forms of sexual violence were rape, multiple rape on the same night; taking women out each night to commit rape, and so on.[341] The rape were carried out to get information about husbands (who were considered as armed rebels) and sometimes as being a woman.[342] Rapes were committed by the armed officials, the guards of the prison camp, other people who worked in the camp, inmates, etc. by creating an atmosphere of fear and powerlessness.[343]

The sexual violence including multiple rapes have been considered as 'torture' and grave breaches of the 1949 Geneva Convention (IV) and violation of the laws and custom of war.[344] According to Article 2(b)[345] and Article 3 of the Statute of ICTY, rape and sexual offices are treated as torture. Hence, all the perpetrators were held criminally liable under Article 7 of the ICTY Statute. The Trial Chamber treated sexual assault and rape as 'torture.'[346] The Chamber referred to the judgement of *Akayesu* case (ICTR) in defining 'rape' that has been defined as 'crime against humanity'[347] and compared with 'torture'.[348] The Trial Chamber concluded that

---

[337] Ibid, para. 274.

[338] Ibid, para. 559, 1125–1145.

[339] Ibid, para. 595.

[340] Ibid, para. 925 and 24.

[341] Ibid, para. 936–946.

[342] Ibid.

[343] Ibid.

[344] Ibid, para. 965 and 475.

[345] Ibid. Article 2(b), on 'Grave breaches of the Geneva Conventions of 1949', of the Statute of ICTY provides: "torture or inhuman treatment, including biological experiments." Article 3 on 'Violation of Laws and Custom of War' states: "The International Tribunal shall have the power to prosecute persons violating the laws or customs of war. Such violations shall include, but not be limited to: (a) employment of poisonous weapons or other weapons calculated to cause unnecessary suffering; (b) wanton destruction of cities, towns or villages, or devastation not justified by military necessity; (c) attack, or bombardment, by whatever means, of undefended towns, villages, dwellings, or buildings; (d) seizure of, destruction or willful damage done to institutions dedicated to religion, charity and education, The arts and sciences, historic monuments and works of art and science; (e) plunder of public or private property;" available at: https://www.icty.org/x/file/Legal%20Library/Statute/statute_sept09_en.pdf (accessed on 12 July 2021). *The Celebici Case* (*Prosecutor vs, Zejnil Delali, Zdravko Muci and Esad Landao*), 16 November 1998, ICTY-IT-96-21-T; available at: https://www.icty.org/x/cases/mucic/tjug/en/981116_judg_en.pdf (accessed on 12 July 2021).

[346] *The Celebici Case*, n.334, para. 475.

[347] Ibid, para. 478.

[348] Ibid. Paragraph 478 explains it as: "rape is a form of aggression and that the central elements of the crime of rape cannot be captured in a mechanical description of objects and body parts. The Convention against Torture and Other Cruel, Inhuman and Degrading Treatment or Punishment does not catalogue specific acts in its definition of torture, focusing rather on the conceptual framework of state sanctioned violence. This approach is more useful in international law…The Chamber defines rape as a physical invasion of a sexual nature, committed on a person under the circumstances which

"rape is a physical invasion of sexual nature, committed on a person under circumstances that are coercive;"[349] as well as "rape of any person to be a despicable act which strikes at the very core of human dignity and physical integrity."[350] The Trial Chamber looked at the decision of the international and regional judicial bodies; reports of the UN Special Rapporteur on Torture (1992), etc.[351] and termed 'rape' and 'other form of sexual assault' as 'torture.'[352]

iii. The *Furundzija Case* (ICTY)[353]

In an interesting turn of events, less than a month after the *Celebici* judgement and after three months of the judgement in the *Akayesu* case, the ICTY gave another landmark judgement in the *Furundzija* case. The judgement of this case is important since, for the first time in the history, 'rape' was explicitly recognized as 'violation of laws and custom of war' that "outrages of personal dignity including rape." The trial in the case took place during the period of 8 June 1998 to 12 November 1998.[354]

The accused, a local commander,[355] was directly charged for committing acts of torture, inhumane treatment, and outrage of personal dignity including rape.[356] According to the testimonies of the witnesses, women faced different forms of SGBV. The accused forced the civilian women to undress and threatened to put the knife inside the vagina.[357] Thus women were subjected to forced nudity, sexual assault, humiliation by forcibly attacking their person[358] as well as faced vaginal, anal and oral

are coercive. Sexual violence which includes rape is considered to be any act of a sexual nature which is committed under circumstances which are coercive.".

349 Ibid, para. 479.

350 Ibid, para. 495.

351 Ibid, para. 491. It took the view that "since it was clear that rape or other forms of sexual assault against women in detention were a particularly ignominious violation of the inherent dignity and the right to physical integrity of the human being, they accordingly constituted an act of torture.".

352 Ibid, para. 494–497. It explained thus: "In view of the above discussion, the Trial Chamber therefore finds that the elements of torture, for the purposes of applying Articles 2 and 3 of the Statute, may be enumerated as follows: (i) There must be an act or omission that causes severe pain or suffering, whether mental or physical, (ii) which is inflicted intentionally, (iii) and for such purposes as obtaining information or a confession from the victim, or a third person, punishing the victim for an act he or she or a third person has committed or is suspected of having committed, intimidating or coercing the victim or a third person, or for any reason based on discrimination of any kind, (iv) and such act or omission being committed by, or at the instigation of, or with the consent or acquiescence of, an official or other person acting in an official capacity.".

353 UN ICTY (1998), *The Furundzija Case* (*Prosecutor v. Furundzija*), 10 December 1998 ICTY-IT-95-17/1-T; available at: https://www.icty.org/x/cases/mucic/tjug/en/981116_judg_en.pdf (accessed on 12 July 2021).

354 Ibid, para. 1.

355 Ibid, para. 40, 2.

356 Ibid, para. 2.

357 Ibid.

358 Ibid, para. 45.

sexual penetration.[359] These atrocities were committed against the women only to get information about the opponent group.[360]

The Trial Chamber decided on the charges relating to rape and serious sexual violence in accordance with relvant aspects of IHL[361] (Geneva Conventions 1949 and the Additional Protocols I and II of 1977, *Lieber Code*, the Hague Convention 1907, the Nuremberg Tribunal, the Tokyo International Military Tribunal etc.); the human rights law[362] (laws relating to protection of physical integrity and torture); the Statute of ICTY[363] (Article 5: Crimes against humanity and Article 3: outrage of personal dignity); the decision of *Akeyesu*[364] (definition of rape); and other national laws.[365]

The Trial Chamber concluded that the accused was individually liable for the outrage of personal dignity including rape as a violation of laws and customs of war under Article 3 of the Statute. However, crime against humanity was not discussed in detail.[366] Finally, the perpetrator was imprisoned for eight years.[367] In 2000, the Appellate Chamber of this case upheld the decision of the Trial Chamber regarding punishment for rape and sexual assault.[368]

iv. The *Kunarac* Case[369] (ICTY)

The judgement of this case came on 22 February 2001. This case strengthened the previous case laws and further developed gender-related crimes. It was the first case where 'rape' was directly charged as a crime against humanity. Moreover, this was the first case in the history where rape and enslavement were treated as sexual slavery. Three perpetrators (Dragoljub Kunarac, Radomir Kovac, Zoran Vukovic) were charged for violation of IHL since 1992 in the territory of the former Yugoslavia. The Trial Chamber conducted the proceedings during 20 March 2000 to 22 November 2000.

The perpetrators were charged for 'rape as a crime against humanity' under Article 5(g), Article 3 of the Statute of the ICTY (laws and custom of war) and 'outrages upon personal dignity' as a violation of laws and custom of war under Article 3(1) (c) of the 1949 Geneva Conventions.[370] The accused resorted to different forms of

[359] Ibid, para. 46.

[360] Ibid, para. 70–89.

[361] Ibid.

[362] Ibid, para. 170–171.

[363] Ibid, para. 172–173.

[364] Ibid, para. 176.

[365] Ibid, para. 180.

[366] Ibid, para. 270–275.

[367] Ibid.

[368] Ibid.

[369] *The Kunarac Case* (*Prosecutorvs. Dragoljub Kunarac Radomir Kovac and Zoran Vukovic*), 22 February 2001, ICTY-IT-96-23-T & IT-96-23/1-T; available at: https://www.icty.org/x/cases/kunarac/tjug/en/kun-tj010222e.pdf (accessed on 14 July 2021).

[370] Ibid, para. 4–10.

sexual violence comprising rape, rape in full view (even in the presence of ten year old son),[371] gang rape,[372] forced pregnancy (giving birth to Serb babies)[373] and forced to do impossible sexual acts with the soldiers etc.[374]

The civilian women of opponent groups were also detained and raped.[375] Both *Akayesu* case (ICTR) and *Furundzija* case (ICTY) were cited to construe rape as an international crime[376] including sexual assault[377]; forcible stripping and made to dance naked.[378] The Trial Chamber concluded that the perpetrators were individually liable for rape as a crime against humanity as well as laws and customs of war. In fact, the outrage upon personal dignity was treated as a violation of laws and custom of war.[379]

v. The *Kvoka* case[380] (ICTY)

In this case, the perpetrators were convicted for sexual crimes as crimes against humanity.[381] The victims (women from opponent groups and ethnicity) were captured in the Omarska camp. The forms of sexual violence included rape, other forms of sexual violence, gang rape, etc.[382] The Trial Chamber cited the decisions of *Akeyesu, Furundiza* and cases to define rape.[383] The perpetrators were individually held responsible, under Article 5 of the Statue of ICTY,[384] for rape and sexual assault as a crime against humanity.[385]

Thus, it can be seen that since the World War II, there have been some 13 international criminal courts and tribunals [Nuremberg Tribunal (1945); Tokyo Tribunal (1946); International Criminal Tribunal for the Former Yugoslavia (1993); International Criminal Tribunal for Rwanda (1994); United Nations Transitional Administration in East Timor (UNTAET) (1999–2002)[386]; Special Court for Sierra Leone

---

371 Ibid.

372 Ibid, para.36.

373 Ibid, para. 322, 342.

374 Ibid, para. 348, 352.

375 Ibid, para. 574.

376 Ibid.

377 Ibid.

378 Ibid, para. 767–773.

379 Ibid, para. 883–890.

380 UN ICTY (2001), *The Kvoka case (Prosecutor vs Miroslav Kvoka Milojica Kos Mla\O Radi, Zoranzigi Dragoliub Prca)*, 2 November 2001, ICTY-IT-98-30/1-T; available at: https://www.icty.org/x/cases/kvocka/tjug/en/kvo-tj011002e.pdf (accessed on 12 July 2021).

381 Ibid.

382 Ibid, para. 98–109.

383 Ibid, para. 175–183.

384 Ibid, para. 199.

385 Ibid, para. 751–766.

386 Benzing, Markus (2005), "Midwifing a New State: The United Nations in East Timor" in A. von Bogdandy and R. Wolfrum, (Eds.), *Max Planck Yearbook of United Nations Law*, vol. 9, 2005, pp. 295–372. Also see, United Nations Transitional Administration in East Timor; available at: https://peacekeeping.un.org/en/mission/past/etimor/etimor.htm (accessed on 12 July 2021).

(2000); The Court of Bosonia and Herzegovina or the War Crime Chamber Bosonia and Herzegovina (2002)[387]; International Criminal Court (Rome Statute adopted in 1998); Extraordinary Chambers in the Courts of Cambodia (2004)[388]; Iraqi Higher Criminal Court (2005/2003)[389]; Special Tribunal for Lebanon (2006)[390]; Bangladesh International Crimes Tribunal (2008); Extraordinary African Chambers, 2013[391] have been established as a part of the transnational post-conflict justice mechanisms. Though the incidents of SGBV during war were rampant and systematic, still within the limits of time and space of this study very few leading cases have been discussed to highlight the pattern of SGBV at work and gravity of the challenge. SGBV especially rape, sexual slavery, forced prostitution and other forms of sexual violence are considered as crimes against humanity, war crimes, or genocide. Still, a cumulative scrutiny of varied cases shows that SGBV itself has not yet been considered separately as a specific crime *per se*.[392]

(D) United Nations Resolutions

Since 1945, the UN has been working on the issue of SGBV against women. It has contributed to international law-making and law enforcement processes for ending SGBV against women. The UN organs, subsidiary bodies, specialized agencies, and other institutions of the UN system have played crucial roles in these processes.

---

387 The Court of Bosonia and Herzegovina; available at: http://www.sudbih.gov.ba/ (accessed on 12 July 2021); Human Rights Watch (2006), *Looking for Justice: The War Crimes Chamber in Bosnia and Herzegovina*; available at: https://www.hrw.org/report/2006/02/07/looking-justice/war-crimes-chamber-bosnia-and-herzegovina (accessed on 12 July 2021).

388 Extraordinary Chambers in the Courts of Cambodia; available at: https://www.eccc.gov.kh/en/node/39457 (accessed on 12 July 2021).

389 Al-Waqa'I Al-Iraqiya (2005), *Iraqi High Criminal Court Law*; available at: https://ihl-databases.icrc.org/applic/ihl/ihl-nat.nsf/0/62dfa419b75d039cc12576a1005fd6c1/$FILE/IST_statute_official_english.pdf (accessed on 12 July 2021).

390 The Special Tribunal for Lebanon is the first tribunal of international character to prosecute terrorist crimes; available at: https://www.stl-tsl.org/en (accessed on 12 July 2021).

391 Extraordinary African Chambers, 2012; available at: http://www.chambresafricaines.org/index.php (accessed on 12 July 2021).

392 For instance, the Celebici Case; the Furundzija; the Kunarac; the Kvoka; Blaskic; Baralo; Bardanin; Cesis; Halilovic; Kordic and Cerkez; Krajisnik; Krnojelac; Krstic; Kupreskic and 5 others; Milutinovic and 5 others; Nikolic; Plavsic; Rajic; Sikirica and 2 others; Simic and 2 others; Stakic; Milan Simic; Tadic; Todorovic; Vasiljevic; Zelenovic; Akeyasu Case; Bagosora and 3 others; Bisengimana; Gacumbitsi; Kajelijeli; Kamuhanda; Kayishema and Ruzindana; Muhimana; Musema; Barayagwiza and Ngeze; Ndindabahizi; Niyitegeka; Ntakirutimana; Nzabirindan; Rugambarara; Rukondo; Rutaganda; Semanza; Serushago; The RUF case; Brima and 2 others; CDF; Radovan Stanković; Boban Šimšić; Zrinko Pinčić; Željko Mejakić, Momčilo Gruban and Duško Knezević; Gojko Janković; etc. Ongwen; Yekatom and Ngaïssona; Simone Gbagbo; Dominic Ongwen; Bosco Ntaganda; Mathieu Ngudjolo Chui (Acquitted); Sylvestre Mudacumura; Callixte Mbarushimana; Kony et al.; Khaled; Khaled; Kenyatta; Katanga (Trial chamber acquitted); Hussein; Harun and Kushayb; Gbagbo and Blé Goudé Case (Trial Chamber acquitted); Bemba (acquitted); Al Hassan; Al Basir Case 002/02 (NUON Chea KHIEU Samphan); 003 (Measured gold); 004 (Yim Tith); Case 004/02 (Ao An/Anon); Dujali case etc. Also see Amnesty International (2009), "'Whose Justice?' the Women of Bosnia and Herzegovina are Still Waiting"; available at: https://www.amnesty.org/en/documents/EUR63/006/2009/en/ (accessed on 14 July 2021).

There are many General Assembly (GA) and Security Council (SC) resolutions that have played a key role in addressing the issue of SGBV against women so as to give shape to international law-making process.[393] The resolutions of the GA have focused on the different forms of 'violence against women.' The resolutions of the SC, especially since 2000 (resolution 1325) have contributed in addressing the issue of SGBV during the armed conflicts under the agenda item of 'women, peace and security'.

(i) Resolutions of the UN General Assembly

Since 1993, the GA has been formally adopting different resolutions to address the issue of violence against women under various themes. These themes are:

> Intensification of efforts to eliminate all forms of violence against women; all forms of violence against women; trafficking in women and girls; violence against women migrant workers; intensifying global efforts for the elimination of female genital mutilations; rape and other forms of sexual violence; crimes committed in the name of honour; traditional or customary practices affecting the health of women and girls; domestic violence; in-depth study on all forms of violence against women; international day for the violence against women.[394]

In 1993, the GA adopted the landmark Declaration on the Elimination of All Forms of Violence against Women.[395] Through a 1999 resolution (54/134 of 17 December) of the GA, 25 November has been designated as the 'International Day for the Elimination of Violence against Women'.[396] This resolution has defined the phrase "violence against women "means" any act of gender-based violence that results in, or is likely to result in, physical, sexual or psychological harm or suffering to women, including threats of such acts, coercion or arbitrary deprivation of liberty, whether occurring in public or in private life".[397] Therefore, the study has sought to examine the resolutions of the GA, chronologically, under different sub-themes in Table 3.2.

(ii) Resolutions of the UN Security Council

After the establishment of the United Nations (1945), the Commission on the Status of Women (CSW) was created (*vide* ECOSOC resolution 11 (II) of 21 June 1946). The main aim of CSW has been "promotion of gender equality and the empowerment of women". It meets annually and brings together the Members States and representatives of civil society to discuss the contemporary issues which women

---

[393] UN Women, "Work of the General Assembly on violence against women;" available at: https://www.un.org/womenwatch/daw/vaw/v-work-ga.htm (accessed on 14 July 2021).

[394] Ibid.

[395] UN (1993), General Assembly resolution 48/104; UN Doc. A/RES/48/104 (1993), 20 December 1993; available at: http://un-documents.net/a48r104.htm (accessed on 14 July 2021).

[396] UN (1999), General Assembly resolution 54/134; UN Doc. A/RES/54/134 (1999); available at: https://digitallibrary.un.org/record/404761#record-files-collapse-header (accessed on 14 July 2021).

[397] Ibid.

Table 3.2 Expression of concern for SGBV against women in the UNGA resolutions

No.	Themes	UN GA resolutions	Objectives	Violation of the rights	Regulatory mechanisms suggested	Terminology used for SGBV
1.	Intensifying global efforts for the elimination of female genital mutilations (2012)	67/146 (2012)[398]	Discussed in Chapter 4	–	–	–
2.	Rape and other forms of sexual abuse (2007)	62/134 (2007)[399]	Eliminating rape and other forms of sexual violence in all their manifestations, including in conflict and related situations	Violence against women is an offence against the dignity and integrity of the women	Sexual violence must not be used or condoned; necessary assistance to child born out of rape; special measures to protect women form gender-based violence, rape, and sexual violence; end impunity, access to services by the victims; promote human rights education; financial support; Ratification of human rights treaties; protection of victims; etc.	Gender-based violence, rape and other forms of sexual violence unlawful
3.	Intensification of effort to eliminate all forms of violence against women (2006–2012)	61/143 (2006)[400]	Prevent and eliminate all forms of violence against women and girls	Violence against women is the unequal power relations that nullifies enjoyment of human rights and fundamental freedom; impedes social and economic development; an impediment to achieve gender equality, development and peace	All forms of violence against women need to treat as a crime; stop taking cultural defence by state; empowerment of women; prosecuting and punishment strategies, policies, health services, protection of refugee and women during armed conflicts and post-conflicts situation	Violence against women; all forms of gender-based violence by family, community and states, education, awareness, and capacity building

(continued)

398 UN (2012), General Assembly resolution/67/146; UN Doc. A/RES/67/146 (2012); available at: https://undocs.org/A/RES/67/146 (accessed on 14 July 2021).

399 UN (2007), General Assembly resolution 62/134; UN Doc. A/RES/62/134 (2007), 18 December 2007; available at: https://undocs.org/en/A/RES/62/134 (accessed on 14 July 2021).

400 UN (2006), General Assembly resolution 61/143; UN Doc. A/RES/61/143 (2006), 19 December 2006; available at: https://undocs.org/A/RES/61/143 (accessed on 14 July 2021).

Table 3.2 (continued)

No.	Themes	UN GA resolutions	Objectives	Violation of the rights	Regulatory mechanisms suggested	Terminology used for SGBV
4.	In depth study of all forms of violence against women (2003–2005)	58/185 (2003)[401]	Conduct an in-depth study to combat and eliminate all forms of violence against women	Effects on health social and economic costs	Resources, legislation, policies, programmes, etc.	Violence against women
		60/136 (2005)[402]	Same as above	Effects on health social and economic costs	Resources, legislation, policies, programmes, etc.	Violence against women
		62/133 (2007)[403]	Same as above	Effects on health social and economic costs	Resources, legislation, policies, programmes, etc.Also added: Prevent, investigate, punish, eliminate impunity and protect the victims	All forms of violence against women

(continued)

401 UN (2003), General Assembly resolution 58/185; UN Doc. A/RES/58/185 (2003), 22 December 2003; available at: https://undocs.org/en/A/RES/58/185 (accessed on 14 July 2021).

402 UN (2005), General Assembly resolution 60/136; UN Doc. A/RES/60/136 (2005), 16 December 2005; available at: https://undocs.org/en/A/RES/60/136 (accessed on 14 July 2021).

403 UN (2007), General Assembly resolution 62/133; UN Doc. UN Doc. A/RES/62/133 (2007), 18 December 2007; available at: https://undocs.org/A/RES/62/133 (accessed on 9 January 2021).

Table 3.2 (continued)

No.	Themes	UN GA resolutions	Objectives	Violation of the rights	Regulatory mechanisms suggested	Terminology used for SGBV
		63/155 (2008)[404]	Same as above	Effects on health social and economic costs. Also added: Rape as a war crime, a crime against humanity, genocide and torture Violence against women violets and impair or nullifies enjoyment of all forms of human rights and fundamental freedom	Same as above. Also added: Full representation of women and equal participation in decision-making; enactment of legislation and adoption of national action plan; campaign e.g. Unite; avoid cultural defence; respect to IHL and IHRL; exclusion of killing and maiming girls; proper training, sensitization to stop re-victimization; stop impunity and culture of tolerance; victim assistance and rehabilitation; stop media stereotype; abolition of discriminatory laws, practice and customs; systematic collection of data; finance; taking measures against harmful cultural practices	Resources, legislation, policies, programmes, etc.Also added: Violence against women (defined); killing and maiming girls prohibited under international law and sexual violence crimes
		64/137 (2009)[405]	Same as above	Same as above	Added: advocacy by UN, e.g. 'No to Violence against women'; 'Stop rape now' for conflicts	Same as above

(continued)

[404] UN (2008), General Assembly resolution 63/155; UN Doc. A/RES/63/155 (2008), 18 December 2008; available at: https://undocs.org/en/A/RES/63/155 (accessed on 14 July 2021).

[405] UN (2009), General Assembly resolution 64/137; UN Doc. A/RES/64/137 (2009), 18 December 2009; available at: https://undocs.org/en/A/RES/64/137 (accessed on 14 July 2021).

Table 3.2 (continued)

No.	Themes	UN GA resolutions	Objectives	Violation of the rights	Regulatory mechanisms suggested	Terminology used for SGBV
		65/187 (2010)[406]	Same as above	Same as above	Same as above. Also added: Treating all forms of violence against women and criminal offence	Same as above
		67/144 (2012)[407]	Same as above. Also added: Including the elimination of domestic violence	Same as above	Same as above. Also added: Full participation of women both conflict and post-conflict resolution; appropriate measures in the field of education, modify the social and cultural pattern, eliminate harmful cultural practices; gender sensitive curricula in education	Same as above. Also added: Killing and maiming women both conflicts and post-conflicts
5.	Domestic violence (2003)	58/147 (2003)[408]	Prevent and eliminate domestic violence; violets and impairs or nullifies human rights and fundamental freedoms	Unequal power relation and human rights issue; effect on sexual and reproductive health	Both men and women's participation in gender equality; economic independence; legal, economic, educational, social and other measures by the governments; awareness; legislation; denial of cultural defence	Physical, psychological. Sexual violence; domestic violence includes economic deprivation and isolation; gender-based violence; sexual violence in marriage; marital rape, sexual abuse

(continued)

406 UN (2010), General Assembly resolution 65/187; Doc. A/RES/65/187 (2010), 21 December 2010; available at: https://undocs.org/en/A/RES/65/187 (accessed on 14 July 2021).

407 UN (2012), General Assembly resolution 67/144; UN Doc. A/RES/67/144 (2012), 20 December 2012; available at: https://undocs.org/A/RES/67/144 (accessed on 14 July 2021).

408 UN (2003), General Assembly resolution 58/147; UN Doc. A/RES/58/147 (2003), 22 December 2003; available at: https://undocs.org/en/A/RES/58/147 (accessed on 9 January 2021).

Table 3.2 (continued)

No.	Themes	UN GA resolutions	Objectives	Violation of the rights	Regulatory mechanisms suggested	Terminology used for SGBV
6.	Violence against women migrant worker (2001–2011)	56/131 (2001)[409]	Grave abuses and violence against women migrant workers Protection, promotion of the rights and welfare	Vulnerable to abuse and exploitation vilation of human rights.	Joint and collaborative approaches at all levels; allocation of resources; penal and criminal sanction	Sham marriages for migration; violation of human rights of women; gender-based violence and discrimination; trafficking
		58/143 (2003)[410]	Added participation of civil society and States in combating violence against women migrant workers	Violation of rights of migrant workers and human rights	Added joint and colaborative approaches and starategies at bilateral, regional, interregional, international levels	Added link between migration and trafficking, violence against women, gender-based violence and discrimination, abuse and violence.

(continued)

[409] UN (2001), General Assembly resolution 56/131, UN Doc. A/RES/56/131, (2001), 19 December 2001; available at: https://www.un.org/en/development/desa/population/migration/generalassembly/docs/globalcompact/A_RES_56_131.pdf (accessed on 14 July 2021).

[410] UN (2003), General Assembly resolution 58/143; Un Doc. A/RES/58/143 (2003), 22 December 2003; available at: https://www.un.org/en/development/desa/population/migration/generalassembly/docs/globalcompact/A_RES_58_143.pdf (accessed on 14 July 2021).

Table 3.2 (continued)

No.	Themes	UN GA resolutions	Objectives	Violation of the rights	Regulatory mechanisms suggested	Terminology used for SGBV
		60/139 (2005)[411]	Added combating violence against women migrant workers.	Abuse and exploitation violation of human rights of women migrant workers	Gender-sensitive policies; awareness at all level	Sexual and gender-based violence (SGBV); trafficking; domestic and family violence; racist and xenophobic act; abusing labour practices.
		62/132 (2007)[412]	Protection and promotion of human rights and welfare; deter illegal migration; protect unaccompanied girls regardless of migrant status	Discrimination faced by women from developing countries, indigenous women	Comprehensive and broad-based information; gender-perspective and human rights-based legislation and policies	Gender-based violence in particular sexual violence, etc.; economic exploitation, discrimination, sexual harassment, violence and sexual abuse at work place; illegal deprivation of liberty
		64/139 (2009)[413]	Same as above	Same as above	Non-discrimination on the ground of child birth and pregnancy	Same as above

(continued)

[411] UN (2005), General Assembly resolution 60/139; UN Doc. A/RES/60/139 (2005), 16 December 2005; available at: https://www.un.org/en/development/desa/population/migration/generalassembly/docs/globalcompact/A_RES_60_139.pdf (accessed on 14 July 2021).

[412] UN (2006), General Assembly resolution 62/132; UN Doc. A/RES/62/132 (2007), 18 December 2007; available at: https://undocs.org/en/A/RES/62/132 (accessed on 14 July 2021).

[413] UN (2009), General Assembly resolution 64/139; UN Doc. A/RES/64/139 (2009), 18 December 2009; available at: https://www.un.org/en/development/desa/population/migration/generalassembly/docs/globalcompact/A_RES_64_139.pdf (accessed on 14 July 2021).

Table 3.2 (continued)

No.	Themes	UN GA resolutions	Objectives	Violation of the rights	Regulatory mechanisms suggested	Terminology used for SGBV
		66/128 (2011)[414]	Same as above	Same as above	Prompt investigation and punishment to the perpetrators	Abusive labour practice, the exploitive condition of work, contemporary form of slavery, forced labour, trafficking; gender-based violence is a forms of discrimination
7.	Trafficking in women and girls (2000–2012). Eight resolutions adopted	GA Res. 55/67, 2000, Trafficking in women and girls[415]	Eradication of trafficking of women and girl children especially in developing countries	Sexual and commercial exploitation are a contemporary form of slavery and violations of human rights	Identification of root factors; bilateral and regional cooperation; international cooperation and technical assistance; criminalize trafficking and punishment; national coordinating mechanism; allocation of resources; witness protection; victim protection	Sexual violence, sexual exploitation; gender-based crimes; child pornography through the internet. The bride and sex tourism

(continued)

414 UN (2011), General Assembly resolution 66/128; UN Doc. A/RES/66/128 (2011), 19 December 2011; available at: https://www.un.org/en/development/desa/population/migration/generalassembly/docs/globalcompact/A_RES_66_128.pdf (accessed on 14 July 2021).

415 UN (2000), General Assembly resolution 55/67; UN Doc. A/RES/55/67 (2000), 4 December 2000; available at: https://undocs.org/en/A/RES/55/67 (accessed on 14 July 2021).

Table 3.2 (continued)

No.	Themes	UN GA resolutions	Objectives	Violation of the rights	Regulatory mechanisms suggested	Terminology used for SGBV
		GA Res. 57/176 (2002), Trafficking in women and girls[416]	Impact of the globalization of trafficking in developing countries	Trafficking in women is a violation of human rights. Victims are disadvantaged and marginalized to recognize their human rights are exposed to other forms of violence	Identification of toot factors; International cooperation and technical assistance; comprehensive and multidisciplinary approach; strengthen existing legislation and punishment; adoption of anti-trafficking measures; action plans; criminalize trafficking; strengthening national coordinating mechanism; raise public awareness; allocation of resources; victim protection	Sexual exploitation, commercial sexual exploitation; child pornography and sex tourism and trafficked as a bride; force marriage, forced labour
		GA Res. 59/166 (2004), Trafficking in women and girls[417]	(Same as the previous resolutions) added: Combat and eliminate all forms of trafficking of women and girls	(Same as the previous resolutions) added: Failure in punishing the perpetrators and victims' protection is a violation of human rights and fundamental freedoms	(Same as the previous resolutions) added: States' obligation to punish and protect the victims; appointment of Special Rapporteur; identification of root factors includes; criminalization of all forms of trafficking in person; allocation of resources for legal and health assistance (e.g. HIV/AIDS); gender sensitive training	(Same as the previous resolutions) added: Discrimination based on gender; gender inequality; violence against women in particular trafficking

(continued)

416 UN (2002), General Assembly resolution 57/176; UN Doc. A/RES/57/176, (2002), 18 December 2002; available at: https://www.un.org/en/development/desa/population/migration/generalassembly/docs/globalcompact/A_RES_57_176.pdf (accessed on 14 July 2021).

417 UN (2004), General Assembly resolution 59/166; UN Doc. A/RES/59/166, (2004), 20 December 2004; available at: https://www.un.org/en/development/desa/population/migration/generalassembly/docs/globalcompact/A_RES_59_166.pdf (accessed on 14 July 2021).

Table 3.2 (continued)

No.	Themes	UN GA resolutions	Objectives	Violation of the rights	Regulatory mechanisms suggested	Terminology used for SGBV
		GA Res.61/144, (2006), Trafficking in women and girls[418]	Added fight for trafficking and protection of victims	Added trafficking against women and girls is violation of human rights	Added: Need for strong gender and age sensitive approach; victim-centric policies and programmes; protection from re-victimization; cooperation with other actors; education for both men and women on gender equality; training to those involved with emergency situation	Added: Trafficking based on gender; trafficking as a serious crime; trafficking during emergency and post-conflict situation
		GA Res. 63/156, (2008), Trafficking in women and girls[419]	Added full respect to the victims of trafficking	Added trafficking in persons violets, impairs, or nullifies the enjoyment of the human rights and fundamental freedoms.	Added punsih the perpetrators and rescue the victims. need of global efferorts and international cooperations.	Added: Gender- and age specific vulnerability; poverty and gender inequality; gender-based violation

(continued)

[418] UN (2006), General Assembly resolution 61/144, UN Doc. A/RES/61/144 (2006), 19 December 2006; available at: https://undocs.org/A/RES/61/144 (accessed on 14 July 2021).

[419] UN (2008), General Assembly resolution 63/156; UN Doc. A/RES/63/156 (2008), 18 December 2008; available at: https://undocs.org/en/A/RES/63/156 (accessed on 14 July 2021).

Table 3.2 (continued)

No.	Themes	UN GA resolutions	Objectives	Violation of the rights	Regulatory mechanisms suggested	Terminology used for SGBV
		64/293 (2010), United Nations global plan and action against trafficking in person[420]	Reaffirmed the role of UN under the Charter Identified contributing factors	Serious threat to human dignity, human rights and development trafficking as an organized crime	a global plan of action against trafficking Urgent action to prevent trafficking in person	Definition of trafficking in the global action plan
		65/190 (2010), Trafficking in women and girls[421]	Same as above	Same as above	Same as above. Also added: UN System; elimination of all demands that foster trafficking; human rights perspective strategy; special protection of young women and children	Trafficking for organ removal Sexual assault of the victims in the custody

(continued)

[420] UN (2010), General Assembly resolution 64/293; UN Doc. A/RES/64/293 (2010), 30 July 2010; available at: https://undocs.org/en/A/RES/64/293 (accessed on 14 July 2021).

[421] UN (2010), General Assembly resolution 65/190; UN Doc. A/RES/65/190 (2010), 21 December 2010; available at: https://www.un.org/en/development/desa/population/migration/generalassembly/docs/globalcompact/A_RES_65_190.pdf (accessed on 14 July 2021).

Table 3.2 (continued)

No.	Themes	UN GA resolutions	Objectives	Violation of the rights	Regulatory mechanisms suggested	Terminology used for SGBV
		67/145 (2012) Trafficking in women and girls[422]	Added reason for vulnerability to trafficking; the link between migration and trafficking	Added international trafficking in person is violation of national laws and international standards. Trafficking is violation of full enjoyment of human rights	Added Speedy disposal of cases of trafficking Joint research and study; sensitization on the special need for women and girls victims; effective legislation and prgramme and collection of adequate data.	Added sex turism, gender-based violence, child pornography, sexual exploytation of children paedophilia; sexual exploytation

(continued)

[422] UN (2012), General Assembly resolution 67/145; UN Doc. A/RES/67/145 (2012), 20 December 2012; available at: https://undocs.org/en/A/RES/67/145 (accessed on 14 July 2021).

Table 3.2 (continued)

No.	Themes	UN GA resolutions	Objectives	Violation of the rights	Regulatory mechanisms suggested	Terminology used for SGBV
8.	Crimes Committed in the name of honour (2000–2004)	Three resolutions adopted. As these are coming under the harmful cultural practices, so, discussed in Chap. 4 of this thesis[423]	–	–	–	–

(continued)

[423] Ibid, it explains it thus: "These three resolutions are: Working towards the elimination of crimes against women committed in the name of honor (A/RES/55/66 of 4 December 2000); Working towards the elimination of crimes against women committed in the name of honour (A/RES/57/179 of 18 December 2002); Working towards the elimination of crimes against women and girls committed in the name of honour (A/RES/59/165, of 20 December 2004)."

Table 3.2 (continued)

No.	Themes	UN GA resolutions	Objectives	Violation of the rights	Regulatory mechanisms suggested	Terminology used for SGBV
9.	All forms of violence against women (2000–2004). Three resolutions adopted[424]	Res. 55/68, 2000; "Elimination of all forms of violence including crimes against women"; Res. 55/68, 2000, Elimination of all forms of violence against women, including crimes identified in the outcome document of the twenty-third special session of the General Assembly, entitled "Women 2000: Gender equality development and peace for the twenty-first century."[425]	Concern for all forms of violence and crimes against women all over the world. All forms of violence against women and girls need to treat as criminal offence including violence based on discrimination	Violence against women both violets and impairs or nullifies the human rights and fundamental freedoms	Empowerment of women; legal and administrative measures by the governments; awareness and preventive measures; urges UN and the Special Rapporteurs and Secretary-General to focus on the issue	Elimination of violence against women and girls. Crimes against women
		Res. 56/181, 2002, Elimination of all forms of violence against women, including crimes identified in the outcome document of the twenty-third special session of the General Assembly, entitled "Women 2000: Gender equality development and peace for the twenty-first century."[426]	Concern for all forms of violence and crimes against women all over the world especially commercial sexual and economic exploitation. All forms of violence against women and girls need to treat as criminal offence	Violence against women both violets and impairs or nullifies the human rights and fundamental freedoms	Economic empowerment of women as a tool to eliminate violence. Special legal and comprehensive legislative measures; strategies and action plans; administrative measures; awareness; education and research, invites UN assistance especially Special Rapporteurs and Secretary-General	Elimination of violence against women and girls; crimes against women

(continued)

[424] UN Women, "Work of the General Assembly on violence against women"; available at: https://www.un.org/womenwatch/daw/vaw/v-work-ga.htm (accessed on 14 July 2021). Three resolutions are: 1. Elimination of all forms of violence, including crimes against women (A/RES/55/68 of 4 December 2000); 2. Elimination of all forms of violence against women, including crimes identified in the outcome document of the twenty-third special session of the General Assembly, entitled "Women 2000: gender equality, development and peace for the twenty-first century" (A/RES/57/181 of 18 December 2002); 3. Elimination of all forms of violence against women, including crimes identified in the outcome document of the twenty-third special session of the General Assembly entitled "Women 2000: gender equality, development and peace for the twenty-first century". (A/RES/59/167 of 20 December 2004).

[425] UN (2001), General Assembly resolution 55/68; UN Doc. A/RES/55/68 (2001), 4 December 2002; available at: http://www.worldlii.org/int/other/UNGA/2000/194.pdfb (accessed on 14 July 2021).

[426] UN (2002), General Assembly resolution 57/181; UN Doc. A/RES/57/181 (2002), 18 December 2002; available at: https://undocs.org/en/A/RES/57/181 (accessed on 14 July 2021).

Table 3.2 (continued)

No.	Themes	UN GA resolutions	Objectives	Violation of the rights	Regulatory mechanisms suggested	Terminology used for SGBV
		Res. 59/167, 2004, Elimination of all forms of violence against women, including crimes identified in the outcome document of the twenty-third special session of the General Assembly, entitled "Women 2000: Gender equality development and peace for the twenty-first century."[427]	Concern for all forms of violence and crimes against women all over the world especially commercial sexual and economic exploitation	Violence against women both violets and impairs or nullifies human rights and fundamental freedoms All forms of violence against women need to treat as criminal offence	Economic empowerment; legal and comprehensive legislative measures; strategies, action plans; legal, administrative and other measures by the governments; participation of men and boys; UN and Special Rapporteur, Secretary-General's assistance	All forms of violence against women and girls; gender-based violence
10.	54/134. International day for the elimination of violence against women, 1999[428]	Decides to designate 25 November as the International day for the elimination of violence against women[429]	Focused on special categories of women. violence against women is a crucial social mechanism for domination	Violence against women is violence of human rights	Human rights of women and children need to be protected; all forms of cooperation	Violence against women

(continued)

[427] UN Women, "Work of the General Assembly on violence against women"; available at: https://www.un.org/womenwatch/daw/vaw/v-work-ga.htm (accessed on 14 July 2021).

[428] UN (1999), General Assembly resolution 54/134; UN Doc. A/RES/54/134 (1999), 17 December 1999; available at: https://undocs.org/sp/A/RES/54/134 (accessed on 14 July 2021).

[429] Ibid, it states: "Reiterating that, according to article 1 of the Declaration on the Elimination of Violence against Women, the term "violence against women" means any act of gender-based violence…" that results in, or is likely to result in, physical, sexual or psychological harm or suffering to women, including threats of such acts, coercion or arbitrary deprivation of liberty, whether occurring in public or in private life, Decides to designate 25 November as the International Day for the Elimination of Violence against Women; 2. Invites, as appropriate, Governments, the relevant agencies, bodies, funds and programmes of the United Nations system, and other international organizations and non-governmental organizations, to organize on that day activities designed to raise public awareness of the problem of violence against women.".

Table 3.2 (continued)

No.	Themes	UN GA resolutions	Objectives	Violation of the rights	Regulatory mechanisms suggested	Terminology used for SGBV
11.	Traditional and customary practices affecting the health of women and girls (1997–2004)	GA adopted five resolutions on the issue in between 1997 and 2001[430]	Discussed in Chapter 4	–	–	–

[430] UN Women, "Work of the General Assembly on violence against women"; available at: https://www.un.org/womenwatch/daw/vaw/v-work-ga.htm (accessed on 14 July 2021). These resolutions are: Traditional or customary practices affecting the health of women and girls (A/RES/52/99 of 12 December 1997); Traditional or customary practices affecting the health of women and girls (A/RES/53/117 of 9 December 1998); Traditional or customary practices affecting the health of women and girls (A/RES/54/133 of 17 December 1999); Traditional or customary practices affecting the health of women and girls (A/RES/56/128 of 19 December 2001).

face.[431] There have been a lot of CSW's discussions (e.g. in 1969, 2004) on the protection and participation of women in conflict and post-conflict situations.[432] The 1979 CEDAW was one of the outcomes of the CSW agenda. However, as discussed earlier, CEDAW does not deal with situation of women during armed conflicts. In fact, it was the Committee of CEDAW which took the initiative to give importance to the plight of women in conflict zones. It adopted GR30 (women in conflict prevention conflict and post-conflict situations)[433] to address this issue.

The 1995 Fourth World Conference on Women (Beijing), brought together representatives of 189 Member States, around 400 NGOs and 400,000 members of women's civil societies. The theme of 'women in armed conflict' was one of the important areas discussed by the participants. It was accepted that there should be more participation of women in the resolution of conflicts as well as the protection of women who live in the zones of armed conflicts.[434] After the Beijing Platform for Action, the meeting of the CSW was held in March 2000. In an address to the meeting, the President of the UN Security Council observed:

> As the first International Women's Day of the new millennium is observed throughout the World, members of the Security Council recognize that peace is inextricably linked with equality between women and men. They affirm that the equal access and full participation of women in power structures and their full involvement in all efforts for the prevention and resolution of conflicts are essential for the maintenance and promotion of peace and security.[435]

It finally led to the adoption of the Security Council resolution (SCR) 1325 (2000) under the theme of *women, peace and security*.[436] It was considered a result of the campaign by the UN bodies and the civil society organizations. The gravity and persistence of the SGBV challenge has been duly underscored in the UN Secretary-General's 30 March 2021 report wherein he observed that "the needs of survivors of sexual violence cannot be put on pause, and neither can the response to such violence".[437] The UNSC, under the theme of 'women peace and security' (WPS), has sought to address the challenge of SGBV against women as follows:

---

[431] UN (2015), "Preventing Conflict Transforming Justice Securing the Peace;" available at: https://www.unwomen.org/~/media/files/un%20women/wps/highlights/unw-global-study-1325-2015.pdf (accessed on 14 July 2021).

[432] Ibid.

[433] Ibid.

[434] Ibid.

[435] Ibid.

[436] UN (2020), *Women, Peace and Security: Report of the Secretary General*; UN Doc. S/2020/946, 25 September 2020; available at: https://www.securitycouncilreport.org/atf/cf/%7B65BFCF9B-6D27-4E9C-8CD3-CF6E4FF96FF9%7D/s_2020_946.pdf (accessed on 14 July 2021). Also see, UN (2015), "Preventing Conflict Transforming Justice Securing the Peace;" available at: https://www.unwomen.org/~/media/files/un%20women/wps/highlights/unw-global-study-1325-2015.pdf (accessed on 14 July 2021).

[437] UN (2021), *Conflict Related Violence: Report of the Secretary General*; UN Doc. S/2021/312, 30 March 2021; available at: https://www.securitycouncilreport.org/atf/cf/%7B65BFCF9B-6D27-4E9C-8CD3-CF6E4FF96FF9%7D/s_2021_312.pdf (accessed on 14 July 2021).

i. **Russian Draft SCR (30 October 2020).** The UNSC's internal negotiation process is difficult to decipher specially in cases where consensus among the P5 (permanent members) is required. Hence, what transpired in the non-adoption of the Russian draft resolution S/2020/1054 remains unclear. The draft required to fulfil two conditions of (i) nine affirmative votes and (ii) no negative vote (veto) by a permanent member.[438] The draft resolution expressed grave concern regarding disproportionate negative impact (especially socio-economic) of the COVID-19 pandemic on women across the world especially in conflict zones, post-conflict situations or humanitarian crises. It emphasized:

> 3 ... that advancing gender equality and women's political, social, and economic empowerment is critical to the prevention of and response to sexual violence in conflict and post-conflict situations, and that the safety and empowerment of women and girls is important for their meaningful participation in peace processes, preventing conflicts and rebuilding societies, and that therefore women's protection and participation are inextricably linked and mutually-reinforcing as reflected by all previous resolutions on women, peace and security.[439]

The draft resolution has been criticized by many countries on the ground that the draft consists exclusively of previously agreed language by the UNSC and the text is not balanced because it places more emphasis on the socio-economic aspects instead of the rights-based aspects including language of human rights.

ii. **SCR 2493 (2019).**[440] It recognized that an understanding of the impact of armed conflict on women and girls, effective institutional arrangements to guarantee their protection and full participation in the peace process can significantly contribute to the maintenance and promotion of international peace and security, recognizing the opportunity presented by the number of significant anniversaries in 2020 notably the 20th anniversary of resolution 1325, the 75th anniversary of the United Nations, the 25th anniversary of the Beijing Declaration and Platform for Action. It called upon all the Member States to commit to the promotion of women and girls' empowerment in peace and security processes and to use these anniversaries to intensify their national efforts and international cooperation.

---

[438] UN (2020), Security Council Report, *Women, Peace and Security: Vote on a Draft Resolution*, 30 October 2020; available at: https://www.securitycouncilreport.org/atf/cf/%7B65BFCF9B-6D27-4E9C-8CD3-CF6E4FF96FF9%7D/s_2020_1054.pdf; https://www.securitycouncilreport.org/whatsinblue/2020/10/women-peace-and-security-vote-on-a-draft-resolution.php (accessed on 14 July 2021).

[439] UNSC, *Russian Federation: draft resolution*; UN Doc. S/2020/1054 (30 October 2020); available at: https://www.securitycouncilreport.org/atf/cf/%7B65BFCF9B-6D27-4E9C-8CD3-CF6E4FF96FF9%7D/s_2020_1054.pdf (accessed on 14 July 2021).

[440] UN (2019), Security Council resolution 2493 (2019); UN Doc. S/RES/2493 (2019), 29 October 2019; available at: https://www.securitycouncilreport.org/atf/cf/%7B65BFCF9B-6D27-4E9C-8CD3-CF6E4FF96FF9%7D/s_res_2467.pdf (accessed on 14 July 2021).

iii. **SCR 2467 (2019)**. It was adopted by 13 votes in favour with China and Russia abstained from voting. The SC adopted the resolution to call upon the belligerents worldwide to adopt concrete commitments on ending sexual violence in conflict.[441] It urged the States for "prompt investigation, prosecution and punishment of perpetrators of sexual and gender-based violence, as well as reparations for victims as appropriate." It also acknowledged the inclusion of sexual and gender-related crimes in the Rome Statute[442] as well as urged for adoption of survivor-centred approach in preventing and responding to sexual violence during conflicts and post-conflict situations.[443]

iv. **SCR 2122 (2013)**. It was adopted on 18 October 2013.[444] It sought to focus on the participation of women in conflict resolution and recovery.[445] It was concerned with prevention and prosecution for violence against women during conflict and post-conflict situations.[446] In a 2015 report, the Security Council explicitly underscored incidents of SGBV in conflicts. It explained different forms of sexual violence especially against women in conflict zones as in these terms:

> The term 'conflict- related sexual violence,' which appears throughout the present report, refers to rape, sexual slavery, forced prostitution, forced pregnancy, enforced sterilization and other forms of sexual violence of comparable gravity perpetrated against women, men, girls or boys that is linked, directly or indirectly (temporally, geographically or causally) to a conflict. This link may be evident in the profile of the perpetrator; the profile of the victim; in a climate of impunity or State collapse; in the cross-border dimensions; and/or in violations of the terms of a ceasefire agreement.[447]

While referring to the situations in 19 countries, the SC report observed that the SGBV in conflicts is a threat to international peace and security. Therefore, it recommended for punishing the perpetrators under international law and also made a reference to the cases before the International Criminal Court.[448]

---

[441] UN (2019), "Security Council Adopts Resolution Calling upon Belligerents Worldwide to Adopt Concrete Commitments on Ending Sexual Violence in Conflict"; Doc. SC/13790, 23 April 2019 available at: https://www.un.org/press/en/2019/sc13790.doc.htm (accessed on 14 July 2021).

[442] UN (2019), Security Council resolution 2467 (2019); UN Doc. S/RES/2467 (2019); 23 April 2019, paragraph 15. It acknowledged the inclusion of sexual and gender-related crimes among the most serious crimes of international concern in the Rome Statute of the International Criminal Court; available at: https://www.securitycouncilreport.org/atf/cf/%7B65BFCF9B-6D27-4E9C-8CD3-CF6E4FF96FF9%7D/s_res_2467.pdf (accessed on 14 July 2021).

[443] Ibid.

[444] UN (2013), Security Council resolution 2122 (2013); UN Doc. S/RES/2122 (2013), 18 October 2013; available at: https://undocs.org/en/S/RES/2122(2013) (accessed on 14 July 2021).

[445] Ibid.

[446] Ibid.

[447] UN (2015), *Conflict-related Sexual Violence: Report of the Secretary-General*; UN Doc. S/2015/203 (2015), 23 March 2013; available at: https://www.securitycouncilreport.org/atf/cf/%7B65BFCF9B-6D27-4E9C-8CD3-CF6E4FF96FF9%7D/s_2015_203.pdf (accessed on 14 July 2021).

[448] Ibid.

v. **SCR 1960 (2010)**. The SC adopted this resolution on 16 December 2010. It sought to carry forward and implement the *ratio* of the previous resolutions adopted by the SC in the field. The concern of this resolution was on the protection of women and children against sexual violence in conflicts.[449] It reiterated "the necessity for all States and non-State parties to the conflicts to comply fully with their obligations under applicable international law, including the prohibition on all forms of sexual violence."[450] The resolution recalled:

> the responsibilities of States to end impunity and to prosecute those responsible for genocide, crimes against humanity, war crimes, and other egregious crimes perpetrated against civilians and, in this regard, noting with concern that only limited numbers of perpetrators of sexual violence have been brought to justice, while recognizing that in conflict and in post conflict situations national justice systems may be significantly weakened.[451]

Thus, the UNSC sought to affix primary responsibility of the States to put an end to impunity as well as all forms of violence taking place especially during armed conflicts.

vi. **SCR 1888 (2009)**. In this resolution, the main focus was on the SGBV against civilian women and girls in armed conflicts. Sexual violation against women in conflicts was denoted as a threat to international peace and security.[452] It gave a mandate to the parties to the armed conflict to protect civilian women against sexual violation and requested the UN Secretary-General to appoint a representative in this regard.[453] It considered it the responsibility of the States as regards "bringing perpetrators of sexual violence in conflicts to justice" as well as for "ensuring that survivors have access to justice, are treated with dignity throughout the justice process and are protected and receive redress for their suffering".[454] The UN peacekeeping operations, as well as mandates of the UN Secretary-General, also found a mention in this resolution.[455]

vii. **SCR 1820 (2008)**. On 19 June 2008, UNSC unanimously adopted resolution 1820. In this resolution, it condemned use of sexual violence as a tactic of war.[456] This resolution mainly sought to reinforce the SCR 1325 (2000).[457]

---

449 UN (2010) Security Council resolution 1960; UN Doc. S/RES/1960 (2010); available at: http://unscr.com/files/2010/01960.pdf (accessed on 18 July 2021).

450 Ibid.

451 Ibid.

452 UN (2009), Security Council resolution 1888; UN Doc. S/RES/1888 (2009); available at: https://www.un.org/en/ga/search/view_doc.asp?symbol=S/RES/1888%20(2009) (accessed on 18 July 2021).

453 Ibid, paragraph 3 and 4.

454 Ibid, paragraph 6.

455 Ibid, paragraph 10, 16, 17, 18, 19–22, 24–27.

456 UN (1820), Security Council resolution 1888; UN Doc. S/RES/1820 (2008); available at: http://unscr.com/files/2008/01820.pdf. Also see, "Ending Sexual Violence in Conflict: United Nations Security Council Resolution 1820"; available at: http://cafi-online.org/iec/Briefing-paper-on-UNSCR1820.pdf (accessed on 18 July 2021).

457 Ibid.

Though SCR 1325 mentioned SGBV in conflict, its main focus was on ensuring the participation of women in conflict prevention and peacebuilding processes. Hence, the resolution 1820 drew a direct relationship between the widespread and systematic use of sexual violence as an instrument of conflict as well as a threat to maintenance of international peace and security.[458]

viii. **SCR 1325 (2000).**[459] It was the first resolution on theme of "women, peace, and security". It was unanimously adopted by the UNSC on 31 October 2000. It was for the first time that the SC addressed the disproportionate and unique impact of armed conflicts on women. It focused on the participation of women in conflict prevention, peacekeeping, conflict resolution, and peacebuilding processes. It also stressed on women's equal and full participation in the peace and security operation.[460] The resolution has specifically mentioned international conventions that are applicable for the protection of women and girls and children during armed conflicts. It explicitly contained the following:

> "10. Calls on all parties to armed conflict to take special measures to protect women and girls from gender-based violence, particularly rape and other forms of sexual abuse, and all other forms of violence in situations of armed conflict";
> "11. Emphasizes the responsibility of all States to put an end to impunity and prosecute those responsible for genocide, crimes against humanity, and war crimes including those relating to sexual and other violence against women and girls, and in this regard stresses the need to exclude these crimes, where feasible from amnesty provisions."[461]

This resolution has become pioneer in addressing the challenge of SGBV. It has specifically provided protection for women against gender-based violence as rape and other form of sexual abuse. It emphasized upon the responsibility of States to end impunity and punish the perpetrators for genocide, crimes against humanity and war crimes including the sexual and other form of violence against women and girls in conflicts.

After adoption of the SCR 1325, the normative framework for the protection and promotion of women's rights in conflict and post-conflict situations has dramatically expanded. This expansion has taken place both in terms of rights and obligation to impellent the resolution. The UNSC's attention, deliberations, and the consistent threshold over the past two decades (2000–2020) shows that the SGBV especially in the conflict and post-conflict situations presents a serious global challenge to the UN system, UN member states, and modern international law. Thus, the UNSC has adopted four more resolutions (1820/2008, 1888/2009, 1960/2010 and 2106/2013)

---

[458] UN (2008), Security Council resolution 2008; available at: http://unscr.com/files/2008/01820.pdf. Also see, "Security Council Resolution 1820 (2008) - Women & Sexual Violence;" available at: https://www.securitycouncilreport.org/atf/cf/%7B65BFCF9B-6D27-4E9C-8CD3-CF6E4FF96FF9%7D/CAC%20S%20RES%201820.pdf (accessed on 18 July 2021).

[459] UN (2000), Security Council resolution 1325; UN Doc. S/RES/1325 (2000); available at: https://www.un.org/ruleoflaw/files/res_1325e.pdf (accessed on 18 July 2021).

[460] UN Peace Women (2000), Security Council Resolution 1325: Introduction; available at: http://www.peacewomen.org/SCR-1325 (accessed on 18 July 2021).

[461] Ibid, UN (2000), UNSC Res. 1325.

focusing on SGBV against women in conflicts.[462] The year 2020 was marked as the 20 anniversary of the adoption of SC resolution 1325 (2000).[463]

It is indeed remarkable that these resolutions have been adopted by the UNSC and the UNGA Are they effective? Cumulatively, these resolutions provide a framework for implementing and monitoring 'women, peace and security agenda', larger agenda of gender equality and discrimination as well as SGBV against women.[464] Initially, the major challenge came from the lack of an accountability mechanisms. These new resolutions, through soft normativity, have in unison tried to mitigate the gap. These resolutions contribute in their own way in slowly reaching towards a systematic framework to address the challenge of SGBV aganist women. The recent resolutions are, however, more focused and cautious about the use of terminology and language.[465] Still, the questions remain as regards the implications and efficacy of these resolutions in bringing ablout changes in the legal and justice mechanism systems of the concerned States (Table 3.3).

(e) Role of Technology in SGBV

With the development of the information and communication technology (ICT), the access to the Internet and mobile technology has greatly increased. Though ICT has positive sides that can be used to reduce SGBV against women. Still, on the other side, because of ICT, the pernicious effect of SGBV on women and girls has spilled over into the digital or online world.[466] It is estimated that some 9 million girls have experienced different forms of cyber violence in Europe. Though men, women and LGBTI people are subjected to online violence, yet it is the women and girls who mostly experience the sexual violence in virtual mode.[467] It is a new challenge even

---

[462] UN (2013), Women, disarmament, non-proliferation and arms control: report of the Secretary-General; UN Doc. A/68/166, 22 July 2013; available at: https://digitallibrary.un.org/record/754967?ln=en (accessed on 18 July 2021).

[463] UN Peacekeeping, *20 Years of Women, Peace and Security*; available at: https://peacekeeping.un.org/en/20-years-of-women-peace-and-security (accessed on 18 July 2021); UN, Security Council Urges Recommitment to Women, Peace, Security Agenda, Unanimously Adopting Resolution 2493 (2019); available at: http://unscr.com/files/2019/02493.pdf (accessed on 18 July 2021).

[464] UN Peacekeeping, "Women, Peace and Security"; available at: https://peacekeeping.un.org/en/women-peace-and-security-to-be-removed (accessed on 18 July 2021).

[465] Tryggestad, Torunn L. (2009), 'Trick or Treat? The UN and Implementation of Security Council Resolution 1325 on Women, Peace, and Security", *Global Governance*, 15 (4): 539–557.

[466] UN Women (2020), "Online and ICT-facilitated violence against women and girls during COVID-19"; available at: https://www.unwomen.org/en/digital-library/publications/2020/04/brief-online-and-ict-facilitated-violence-against-women-and-girls-during-covid-19 (accessed on 18 July 2021).

[467] Hinson L., Mueller J., O'Brien-Milne L., Wandera N. (2018). Technology-facilitated gender-based violence: What is it, and how do we measure it? Washington D.C., International Center for Research on Women; available at: https://www.icrw.org/wp-content/uploads/2018/07/ICRW_TFGBVMarketing_Brief_v8-Web.pdf; Human Rights Council (2018), *Report of the Special Rapporteur on violence against women, its causes and consequences on online violence against women and girls from a human rights perspective*; UN Doc. A/HRC/38/47, 14 June 2018 (advanced edited version); available at: https://www.ohchr.org/EN/HRBodies/HRC/RegularSessions/Session38/Documents/A_HRC_38_47_EN.docx (accessed on 18 July 2021).

Table 3.3 Expression of concern for SGBV against women in the UNSC resolutions

No.	Resolutions	Date of adoption	Theme	Objectives	Regulatory mechanisms
1.	S/2020/1054	30 October 2020; ***Draft***	Women, peace and security	Disproportionate negative impact (especially socio-economic) of the COVID-19 pandemics on women across the world especially in conflict zones, post-conflict situations or humanitarian crises	Advancing gender equality and women's political, social, and economic empowerment
2.	2493	Adopted by the Security Council at its 8649th meeting, on 29 October 2019	Women, peace and security	Implementation of the women, peace and security agenda	Effective institutional arrangements to guarantee their protection and full participation in the peace process
3.	2467	Adopted by the Security Council at its 8514th meeting, on 23 April 2019	Women, peace and security	Demand for the complete cessation with immediate effect by all parties to armed conflict of all acts of sexual violence	Implement specific time-bound commitments to combat sexual violence
4.	2122	Adopted by the Security Council at its 7044th meeting, on 18 October 2013	Women, peace and security	Expressing concern at women's exacerbated vulnerability in armed conflict and post-conflict situations	Implementation of the Arms Trade Treaty can make to reducing violence perpetrated against women and girls in armed conflict and post-conflict situations. Address obstacles in women's access to justice in conflict and post-conflict settings. Women's full and meaningful participation

(continued)

Table 3.3 (continued)

No.	Resolutions	Date of adoption	Theme	Objectives	Regulatory mechanisms
5.	1960	Adopted by the Security Council at its 6453rd meeting, on 16 December 2010	Women, peace and security	Calls upon parties to armed conflict to make and implement specific and time-bound commitments to combat sexual violence. Deeply concerned over the slow progress on the issue of sexual violence	Comply fully with their obligations under applicable international law, including the prohibition on all forms of sexual violence. Complete cessation with immediate effect by all parties to armed conflict of all acts of sexual violence
6.	1888	Adopted by the Security Council at its 6195th meeting, on 30 September 2009	Women peace and security	Reiterating deep concern that, despite its repeated condemnation of violence against women and children including all forms of sexual violence in situations of armed conflict Immediately take appropriate measures to protect civilians, including women and children, from all forms of sexual violence	Stressing the necessity for all States and non-State parties to conflicts to comply fully with their obligations under applicable international law, including the prohibition on all forms of sexual violence Reiterates its demand for the complete cessation by all parties to armed conflict of all acts of sexual violence with immediate effect
7.	1820	Adopted by the Security Council at its 5916th meeting, on 19 June 2008	Women, peace and security	Requests to develop effective mechanisms for providing protection from violence, including in particular sexual violence, to women and girls[468] Deep concern for sexual violence in situations of armed conflict Stresses that sexual violence, when used or commissioned as a tactic of war. Demands the immediate and complete cessation of all acts of sexual violence	Women's participation and full involvement in the prevention and resolution of conflicts Calls upon Member States to comply with their obligations. Stresses the importance of ending impunity

(continued)

[468] UN (1820), Security Council resolution 1888; UN Doc. S/RES/1820 (2008); available at: http://unscr.com/files/2008/01820.pdf (accessed on 18 July 2021).

Table 3.3 (continued)

No.	Resolutions	Date of adoption	Theme	Objectives	Regulatory mechanisms
8.	1325	Adopted by the Security Council at its 4213th meeting, on 31 October 2000	Women, peace and security	Expressing concern particularly for women and children, affected by armed conflict. Calls on all parties to armed conflict to take special measures to protect women and girls from gender-based violence	Reaffirming the important role of women in the prevention and resolution of conflicts and in peacebuilding Implement fully international humanitarian and human rights law Ensure that mine clearance and mine awareness programmes take into account the special needs of women and girls Respect fully international law. End to impunity and to prosecute those responsible for sexual and other violence against women and girls

as the world is grappling with the different challenges of SGBV against women and girls, including its exacerbation by climatic changes,[469] brought about by COVID 10 pandemic during 2020–2022.[470]

The technology-facilitated gender-based violence (GBV)[471] or cyber violence against women and girls[472] or online violence against women is increasing by the day. The World Bank in association with some NGOs like the ICRW,[473] and the UN High Commissioner for Human Rights is addressing the issue as an agenda item of global concern for women's human rights.[474]

The emerging scenario of the virtual world presents a new challenge to the sovereign governments and international institutions to protect fundamental human rights. This is especially so for women who now face new methods, often untraceable, of SGBV. The 2018 report of the *Special Rapporteur on violence against women* (its causes and consequences on online violence against women and girls) observed the new ICT challenge from a human rights perspective:

> Since women's rights are human rights and the prohibition of gender-based violence has been recognized as a principle of international human rights law, women's human rights as developed through comprehensive regional and international conventions, jurisprudence and norms should be protected online, including through the prohibition of gender-based violence in its ICT-facilitated and online forms. Furthermore, States have established positive obligations to ensure that fundamental human rights are protected, respected and fulfilled.[475]

The significant developments concerning checks on the technology-facilitated SGBV have emerged in the shape of the soft law instruments. These instruments help in understanding and recognizing the online gender-based violence against women within the international human rights framework. The issue was first addressed in 2006 (A/61/122/Add.1 and Corr.1) by the UN Secretary-General in his in-depth study

---

[469] Bharat H. Desai and Moumita Mandal (2021), "Role of Climate Change in Exacerbating Sexual and Gender-Based Violence against Women: A New Challenge for International Law", *Environmental Policy and Law*, vol. 51, no. 3, pp. 137–157; available at: https://content.iospress.com/articles/environmental-policy-and-law/epl210055 (accessed on 19 July 2021).

[470] UN (2020), *The Impact of Covid 10 on Women*; available at: https://reliefweb.int/sites/reliefweb.int/files/resources/policy-brief-the-impact-of-covid-19-on-women-en.pdf (last accessed on 15 July 2021).

[471] Hinson, Laura et al. (2017), *Cyber violence: Disrupting the intersection of technology and gender-based violence*, The World Bank Blog, 8 December 2017; available at: https://blogs.worldbank.org/voices/cyber-violence-disrupting-intersection-technology-and-gender-based-violence (accessed on 18 July 2021).

[472] UNESCO, "Cyber Violence against Women and Girls: A World-Wide Wake-Up Call"; available at: https://en.unesco.org/sites/default/files/genderreport2015final.pdf (accessed on 18 July 2021).

[473] Hinson, Laura et al. (2018), n.468.

[474] UN Women (2020), "Online and ICT facilitated violence against women and girls during COVID-19"; available at: https://www.unwomen.org/-/media/headquarters/attachments/sections/library/publications/2020/brief-online-and-ict-facilitated-violence-against-women-and-girls-during-covid-19-en.pdf?la=en&vs=2519; UN OHCHR (2017), *Gender and Technology*, 28 February 2017; available at: https://www.ohchr.org/Documents/Issues/Women/WRGS/GenderDigital/Tearfund.pdf (accessed on 18 July 2021).

[475] Human Rights Council (2018), n.468.

on all forms of violence wherein underlined the need for inquiry on the use of ICT so as to recognize and address the online violence.[476] The Human Rights Council's resolution 20/8 (2012) also called for promotion, protection, and enjoyment of human rights on the Internet. It was emphasized that like offline human rights protection would be applicable for online also. According to the report of the *Special Rapporteur on violence against women*, the relevant international human rights instruments are:

> (a) the right to live free from gender-based violence: the Convention on the Elimination of All Forms of Discrimination against Women, the Declaration on the Elimination of Violence against Women and the Beijing Declaration and Platform for Action; (b) the right to live free from gender-based violence and the right to freedom of expression and access to information: Freedom of expression, enshrined in Article 19 of the Universal Declaration on Human Rights and Article 19 of the International Covenant on Civil and Political Rights; ... Freedom of expression is not, however, an absolute right, given that it cannot be invoked to justify language or other forms of expression designed to incite discrimination, hostility or violence (International Covenant on Civil and Political Rights, Article. 20(2), including online violence against women ... Article 19, paragraph 3 of the Covenant, and respect the principles of necessity and proportionality (see A/HRC/17/27, para. 24 and A/66/290, para. 15) ... 2030 Agenda for Sustainable Development recognizes that the spread of ICT and global interconnectedness has great potential to accelerate human progress, to bridge the digital divide and to develop knowledge societies"; (c) the right to live free from gender-based violence and the right to privacy and data protection: article 12 of the Universal Declaration of Human Rights and article 17 of the International Covenant on Civil and Political Rights.[477]

In 2013, the CSW also called for developing a mechanism to combat ICT driven violence against women.[478] Similarly, the UN GA resolution 68/181 (2013) expressed grave concern for online violence against women human rights defenders and called upon States to take prompt actions against the perpetrators

> 4. Recognizes that violence against women, including domestic violence, can take the form of an isolated act or pattern of abusive behaviour that may occur over a period of time, which as a pattern constitutes violence against women, and can include acts such as cyberbullying and cyberstalking.[479]

The 2015 resolution of the UN Human Rights Council (29/14) in fact identified forms of online GBV such as cyberbullying and cyberstalking within the preview of domestic violence.[480] It considered online grader-based violence is a part of

---

[476] Ibid.

[477] Human Rights Council (2012), *The promotion, protection and enjoyment of human rights on the Internet*, UN-HRC Resolution 20/8 of 5 July 2012; UN Doc. A/HRC/RES/20/8, 16 July 2012; available at: https://digitallibrary.un.org/record/731540 (accessed on 19 July 2021).

[478] UN (2013), *Commission on the Status of Women Report on the fifty-seventh session*, 4–15 March 2013; Economic and Social Council Official Records, 2013 Supp. No. 7; UN Doc. E/2013/27; E/CN.6/2013/11, 2 April 2013; available at: https://undocs.org/E/2013/27 (accessed on 19 July 2021).

[479] UN (2014), General Assembly resolution 68/181; UN Doc. A/RES/68/181 (2014), 30 January 2014; available at: https://undocs.org/en/A/RES/68/181 (accessed on 19 July 2021).

[480] Human Rights Council (2015), *Accelerating efforts to eliminate all forms of violence against women: eliminating domestic violence*; Resolution 29/14 of 2 July 2015; UN Doc.

continuum of violence against women. The primary responsibility would lie on the States for prevention of abuse of the human rights of women and girls through new the new online modes. In 2016, the General Assembly adopted resolution 71/199 on the 'right to privacy in the digital age' that recognized that women are subjected to violation of the right to privacy in the digital age. The resolution explicitly referred to the effect on women and observed:

> Noting also that violations and abuses of the right to privacy in the digital age may affect all individuals, including with particular effects on women, as well as children and those who are vulnerable or marginalized.[481]

In the same vein, the 2017 Human Rights Council's resolution 34/7 focused on violation of right to privacy against women, children and vulnerable group in the digital age.[482]

The GR33 (2015) and 34 (2016) of the CEDAW Committee emphasized on the need for ensuring access to the Internet and other information and communication technology (ICT) to improve access to justice by the women at all level. The GR 33, provided that:

> 35. The Committee recommends that States parties: (a) Emphasize the role that the media and ICT can play in dismantling cultural stereotypes about women in connection with their right to access to justice, paying particular attention to challenging cultural stereotypes concerning gender-based discrimination and violence, including domestic violence, rape and other forms of sexual violence.[483]

In the emerging scenario, the use of ICT is considered essential to overcome different forms of discrimination and stereotypes that have an impact on women's access to justice. It took note of the fact that media, ICT and civil society can play an important role in reinforcing gender stereotypes as well as overcoming them. Hence, it recognized that ICT can play decisive role in dismantling cultural stereotypes in respect of the women's access to justice.

The GR35 (2017) and 36 (2017) again sought to focus on online or ICT-facilitated gender-based violence against women and girls. In the GR 35 the CEDAW Committee made it clear that provisions of the CEDAW would be applicable for the online or ICT driven SGBV against women. As one of the preventive remedies, the CEDAW

A/HRC/RES/29/14, 22 July 2015; available at: https://undocs.org/en/A/HRC/RES/29/14 (accessed on 19 July 2021).

[481] UN (2017), *The right to privacy in the digital age*, General Assembly resolution 71/199 of 19 December 2016; UN Doc. A/RES/71/199 (2016), 25 January 2017; available at: https://undocs.org/en/A/RES/71/199 (accessed on 19 July 2021).

[482] Human Rights Council (2017), *The right to privacy in the digital age*, Resolution 34/7 of 23 March 2017; UN Doc. A/HRC/RES/34/7 (2017), 7 April 2017; available at: https://undocs.org/A/HRC/RES/34/7 (accessed on 2 January 2020).

[483] CEDAW (2015), *General recommendation no. 33 on women's access to justice*, UN Doc. CEDAW/C/GC/33, 3 August 2015; available at: https://digitallibrary.un.org/record/807253. Also see, CEDAW (2016), *General recommendation no. 34 on the rights of rural women;* UN Doc. CEDAW/C/GC/3, 7 March 2016; available at: https://digitallibrary.un.org/record/835897 (accessed on 19 July 2021).

Committee suggested that media need to encourage, adopt and implement effective measures including advertising and ICT to eliminate discrimination against women through harmful and stereotyped portrayal of women or specific group of women (e.g. human rights' defenders).[484]

As already noted earlier, the *Special Rapporteur on violence against women* (its causes and consequences on online violence against women and girls) has specifically mentioned that all the law relating to the discrimination and violence against women offline would be applicable for online protection. It would include the right to live freely from GBV; right to privacy; and freedom of expression and access to information.[485] Furthermore, reading together Goals 5 and 9 of the SDGs 2030 reflect the same concern. One the one hand, the Goal 9.8 stresses on an increased access to ICT and universal and affordable access to the Internet especially to the least developed countries by 2020. It is sought to be balanced in Goal 5.8 that calls for enhancing "the use of enabling technology, in particular information and communications technology, to promote the empowerment of women." That would necessitate prohibition of online and ICT enabled SGBV.[486]

The 2018 report of the Special Rapporteur on violence against women, its causes and consequences on online violence against women and girls from a human rights perspective, specifically mentioned as follows:

> "... online gender-based abuse and violence assaulted the basic principles of equality under international law and freedom of expression, and underline that ensuring an internet free from gender-based violence enhanced women's empowerment. They also highlighted the fact that women victims and survivors needed transparent and fast responses and effective remedies, which could only be achieved if both States and private actors worked together and exercised due diligence to eliminate online violence against women".[487]

Thus, in the wake of the new challenges of the digital age, it would be appropriate to consider applicability of the entire corpus of the international human rights law for providing an effective international legal protection in addressing SGBV against women.

---

[484] CEDAW (2017), *General recommendation no. 35 on gender-based violence against women*, updating general recommendation No. 19; UN Doc. CEDAW/C/GC/35, 14 July 2017; available at: https://www.ohchr.org/EN/HRBodies/CEDAW/Pages/GR35.aspx. Also see, CEDAW, *General recommendation no. 36 on the right of girls and women to education*; UN Doc. CEDAW/C/GC/36, 27 November 2017; available at: https://www.ohchr.org/EN/HRBodies/CEDAW/Pages/Recommendations.aspx (accessed on 19 July 2021).

[485] Human Rights Council (2018), n.468

[486] UNDP, *Transforming our world: the 2030 Agenda for Sustainable Development*, pp. 18 and 21; available at: https://www.un.org/ga/search/view_doc.asp?symbol=A/RES/70/1&Lang=E (accessed on 19 July 2021).

[487] Human Rights Council (2018), n.468, pp. 11–12. Also see OHCHR (2017), "UN experts urge States and companies to address online gender-based abuse but warn against censorship", press release, 8 March 2017.

Conclusion

In view of the above analysis, there does not appear to be any exclusive international legal instrument to govern the challenge of SGBV against women and girls. In view of the developments in the last two decades, there appears beginning of the awareness of gravity and implications of SGBV. Still, it needs to be taken more seriously by the sovereign states and international institutional actors. The existing corpus of international law deals with SGBV only in a scattered and partial way since all the forms of SGBV are not covered.

The facts, role of the actors and outcome of trials in different cases by international criminal courts and tribunals have shown that SGBV has been used as a tactic and weapon of war. In fact, in a maximum number of cases, women were targeted not as a separate gender but as an identity of a particular community as they were treated as 'honour' of the community. Thus, it raises vital questions as regards the identity of the women and treating their bodies literally as a part of the theatre of conflict.

Ironically, a uniform definition of SGBV is still missing within the contemporary discourse in the field of international law. Most of the international legal instruments indirectly deal with issues and aspects of SGBV as a peripheral concern. Hence, it binds only the States parties to the treaty and lack effective compliance mechanisms and judicial forums for redressal SGBV as a scourge and a heinous crime perpetrated against women. All the hybrid and *ad hoc* international criminal courts and tribunals have been tailor-made as a part of post-conflict justice mechanism in each case. It took years for this to crystallize and the processes also take enormous time, energy, cost and have polarising effect in the conflict-ridden societies.

In fact, some states make reservations to some provisions of the treaty (such as 1979 CEDAW) that further reduce effectiveness of the treaty. There are very few customary international law principles that could be applicable to address SGBV against women. Still, it is the soft international law (e.g. resolutions of the SC, the GA and the HRC) that have made considerable contribution in giving shape to normative framework as a protection for women and girls in the wake of SGBV. The soft international law deals with SGBV during both peacetime and conflicts. It has contributed as the subsidiary source of international law in the development of the IHRL, IHL, and ICL. The corpus of resolutions of various organs, programmes, subsidiary bodies, and institutions in the UN system are not binding unless adopted for specific circumstances. Notwithstanding this, they do carry considerable normative value as subsidiary sources of international law.

Though there is no concept of precedent in international law, the case law discussed in this chapter does provide a beacon of hope for guidance in future cases and as an indicator of clarification of various scattered components of international law in addressing the menace of SGBV against women and girls. If we seek to examine the post-conflict justice mechanisms, it shows that except the ICC, there is no permanent forum for trials in international criminal matters. The ICC is a treaty-based court and hence is unable to deal with all the cases in view of issues of jurisdiction as well as the principle of complementarity. There is no uniformity in the HCT system too.

There are variations such as international, hybrid and all are *ad hoc* in nature. These HCTs have not focused on victim-centric approach. Moreover, they lack appropriate mechanisms for the protection of victims and witnesses. Though the ICC and the HCTs have punished some perpetrators, systematic compensation and rehabilitation schemes for the victims are still missing. In view of this, there is an urgent need to work out a concrete specialized international legal instrument either independetly or as a special protocol to the 1949 Geneva Conventions to squarely address the challenge of SGBV so as to provide an effective protection and justice to women and girls.

Chapter 4
Role of the Cultural Factors in SGBV

Introduction

The culture of a particular place or a society reflects the identity of the people who belong to it. It is regarded "as a process and a way of life" ((A/HRC/14/36, para. 5; 22 March 2010). In general, cultural values and practices need to encourage the empowerment of women and protect their fundamental human rights. Ironically, it does not always happen. On the contrary, some cultural norms, practices, customs, traditions and religious values are used directly or indirectly to justify violence against women.[1] In fact violence against women is rooted in patriarchy. The manifestation of patriarchy, in turn, remains rooted in culture. There are different forms of violence against women that emanate from specific cultural values and beliefs.[2] Hence, these cultural norms become the causes of violence against women, including the beliefs such as:

> Some communities believe that a woman's external genitalia have the power to blind anyone attending to her in childbirth; to cause the death of her infant or else physical deformity or madness; or to cause the death of her husband. Female genital mutilation is believed to ensure a girl's virginity. Virginity is a pre-requisite for marriage, which is necessary to maintain a family's honour and to secure the family line.[3]

It is argued that cultural factors behind violence against women "have not been adequately examined, at least in part because of narrow conceptions of what

---

[1] UN (2006), "Ending violence against women from words to action: Study of the Secretary General;" available at: https://www.un.org/womenwatch/daw/public/VAW_Study/VAWstudyE.pdf (accessed on 25 July 2021).

[2] Papp, Aruna (2013), "Conspiracy of Silence: Honour-Based Violence in North America", *Buffalo Journal Of Gender, Law & Social Policy,* 22: 105; available at: https://digitalcommons.law.buffalo.edu/cgi/viewcontent.cgi?article=1018&context=bjglsp (accessed on 25 July 2021).

[3] WHO (2001), *"Female Genital Mutilation: A Teacher's Guide"*; available at: https://apps.who.int/iris/bitstream/handle/10665/66857/WHO_FCH_GWH_01.3_eng.pdf;sequence=1 (accessed on 25 July 2021).

B. H. Desai and M. Mandal, *Sexual and Gender-Based Violence in International Law*,
https://doi.org/10.1007/978-981-19-0894-1_4

constitutes "culture."[4] There are different terms denoting culture-based sexual and gender-based violence (SGBV) such as: 'cultural practices,' 'traditional practices,' 'harmful practices,' 'customary practices,' religious practices,' 'cultural violation of human rights;'[5] etc. For the ease of reference, this study has used all these terms interchangeably.

Role of Culture

Culture shows the unity of human beings of similar nature as well as beliefs or thoughts. It is reflected in the moral, social, aesthetic, spiritual, and technological achievements of human beings. Culture contributes to the subjective identification of any individual, family, and community.[6] It is the amalgamation of all the social habits; traditional modes of belief, rituals, practices; institutions; arts; the way of life of a particular society's people; and so on.[7] Culture is not a static phenomenon.[8] It is a "dynamic historical contested part." It is also regarded as the source of strength as well as oppression to a group of people within a culture.[9]

It brings about social change at various levels and in different forms. It contributes to differentiating a group from another cultural group of people, or an outsider.[10] People of one culture become cautious and sensitive when the question arises as regards the adoption of others' culture or foreign culture. Culture maintains different forms of societal developments in the society, for example, institutional, technological, political, and economic etc. There can be different approaches in responding to the concept of 'culture.' For instance, people of the non-European culture think that modernization and Westernization are two different concepts. There may be different religions, castes, creeds, races, languages, ethnic and regions within a single culture. Culture works as a common connecting thread to maintain correlation among different religions, castes, etc. It shows cultural autonomy within a region or State.[11]

---

[4] UN (2006), n.1.

[5] Zaunbrecher, Katie L., (2011), "When culture hurts: Dispelling the Myth of Cultural Justification for Gender-Based Human Rights Violations," *Houston Journal of International Law*, 33(3): 692; available at: http://www.hjil.org/articles/hjil-33-3-zaunbrecher.pdf (accessed on 25 July 2021).

[6] Singh, Yogendra (1995), "The Significance of Culture in Understanding of Social Change in Contemporary India," *Sociological Bulletin,* 44(1): 1–9; available at: http://ijsw.tiss.edu/collect/sbj/import/vol.44/no.1/1-10.pdf (accessed on 25 July 2021).

[7] Bidney, Davis (1963), "The Two Sources of Culture and Ethics", *The Monist: Ethics and Anthropology,* 47(4): 625–641.

[8] UN OHCHR (2016), "Women's Rights in Africa, p. 54"; available at: https://www.ohchr.org/Documents/Issues/Women/WRGS/WomensRightsinAfrica_singlepages.pdf (accessed on 25 July 2021).

[9] Hodgson, Dorothy L, Ed. (2011), *Gender and Culture at the Limit of Rights*, Philadelphia: University of Pennsylvania Press; available at: https://anthrosource.onlinelibrary.wiley.com/doi/epdf/10.1111/aman.12059_22 (accessed on 25 July 2021).

[10] Singh, Yogendra (1995), n.6.

[11] Ibid.

The diversion of culture and demand for cultural autonomy range from grassroots level to the global level. For example, the tribal community as well as different religious communities demand their cultural autonomy. The diversity among cultures forms cultural integrity for a nation's culture. So, the State plays both subjective and objective roles to protect and preserve the culture of its people. Though there are cultural diversities within a nation, no one expected to interfere in the culture of others while enjoying their cultural rights. 'Culture' is the identity of a particular community within a nation and it also provides an identity of a State at the international level.[12] However, emerging jurisprudence concerning female genital mutilation (FGM) underscores that harmful cultural practices (HCPs) cannot be covered under it. For instance, the African Union Commission has lauded the 17 March 2021 decision by the High Court of the Republic of Kenya that the practice of FGM violates a woman's right to health, human dignity and also undermines international human rights standards.[13]

Both national and international law give importance to the exercise of 'cultural rights.' Since cultural rights form an integral part of fundamental human rights, different international human rights instruments provide for cultural rights as human rights.[14] On 26 March 2009, the Humna Rights Council established (*vide* resolution 10/23) a 'special procedure' entitled "independent expert in the field of cultural rights" with a six point mandate. With her appointment in October 2021, Alexandra Xanthaki, became the third mandate holder (after Farida Shaheed and Karima Bennoune). Her first report (A/HRC/49/54 of 31 January 2022) has sought to provide the 'state of the art' for the 49th session of the Human Rights Council (28 February-01 April 2022). The United Nations Educational, Scientific and Cultural Organization (UNESCO) has also played a crucial role in dealing with cultural rights at international level. Its adoption (at 31st General Conference; 02 November 2001) of the *Universal Declaration on Cultural Diversity* is a landmark in this respect. The concept has been developing under different phrases such as: 'cultural heritage'; 'indigenous cultural rights'; 'cultural rights of minorities'; 'right to culture'.[15]

---

[12] Ibid.

[13] African Union (2021), "African Union Lauds Kenya's Court Ruling Against Female Genital Mutilation"; available at: https://au.int/sites/default/files/pressreleases/40123-pr-fgm_kenyan_case.pdf (accessed on 25 July 2021).

[14] Holder, Cindy (2008), "Culture as an Activity and Human Right: An Important Advance for Indigenous Peoples and International law", *Alternatives: Global Local Political*, Disrupting States: International Discourses of Indigenous Rights and Responsibilities, 33 (1): 7–28; available at: https://journals.sagepub.com/doi/pdf/10.1177/030437540803300102 (accessed on 25 July 2021).

[15] Xanthaki, Alexandra (2021), "Cultural Rights;" available at: https://www.oxfordbibliographies.com/view/document/obo-9780199796953/obo-9780199796953-0123.xml (accessed on 25 July 2021).

Law and Culture

Article 27 of the *International Covenant on Civil and Political Rights* (ICCPR), 1966 provides right to the ethnic, linguistic and religious minorities to enjoy their culture. In the same vein, Article 15 of the 1966 *International Covenant on the Economic Social and Cultural Rights* (ICESCR) lays down that:

> 1.The States Parties to the present Covenant recognize the right of everyone: (a) to take part in cultural life; (b) To enjoy the benefits of scientific progress and its applications; (c) To benefit from the protection of the moral and material interests resulting from any scientific, literary or artistic production of which he is the author, 2. The steps to be taken by the States Parties to the present Covenant to achieve the full realization of this right shall include those necessary for the conservation, the development and the diffusion of science and culture. 3. The States Parties to the present Covenant undertake to respect the freedom indispensable for scientific research and creative activity. 4. The States Parties to the present Covenant recognize the benefits to be derived from the encouragement and development of international contacts and co-operation in the scientific and cultural fields.[16]

Thus, everyone has a right to exercise cultural rights as well as to conserve, develop and defuse culture. In fact, culture could be factored in—as a tool of soft power—to promote international cooperation with other countries. Apart from it, Article 5(e.vi) of the 1965 *International Convention on Racial Discrimination* provides for the "right to equal participation in cultural activities" without distinction of race, colour, national, or ethnic origin.[17] In the same vein, the UNESCO *Principles on International Cultural Cooperation* (adopted at 14th General Conference; 04 November 1966) call for (Article I) respect, preserve the dignity and value of each culture:

1. Each culture has a dignity and value which must be respected and preserved.
2. Every people has the right and the duty to develop its culture.
3. In their rich variety and diversity, and in the reciprocal influences they exert on one another, all cultures form part of the common heritage belonging to all mankind.[18]

It also underscores that people have rights and duties to develop their own culture. The assertation that all cultures are part of the common heritage of all mankind is indeed futuristic. It provides a basis for equal respect for all cultures as reflecting human diversity in different countries, continents and civilizations.

Similarly, the 2001 *Universal Declaration on Cultural Diversity* has considered cultural rights as integral part of the corpus of human rights (Article 5):

---

[16] UN (1967), *International Covenant on Economic Social and Cultural Rights 1966*; available at: https://treaties.un.org/doc/Treaties/1976/01/19760103%2009-57%20PM/Ch_IV_03.pdf (accessed on 25 July 2021).

[17] UN OHCHR (1965), *International Convention on Elimination of Racial Discrimination, 1965*; available at: https://ohchr.org/EN/ProfessionalInterest/Pages/CERD.aspx (accessed on 26 July 2021).

[18] UNESCO (1966), *UNESCO Principle of International Cultural Cooperation;* available at: http://portal.unesco.org/en/ev.php-URL_ID=13147&URL_DO=DO_TOPIC&URL_SECTION=201.html (accessed on 26 July 2021).

> Cultural rights are an integral part of human rights, which are universal, indivisible and interdependent. The flourishing of creative diversity requires the full implementation of cultural rights as defined in Article 27 of the Universal Declaration of Human Rights and in Articles 13 and 15 of the International Covenant on Economic, Social and cultural Rights. All persons should therefore be able to… fully respect their cultural identity; and all persons have the right to participate in the cultural life of their choice and conduct their own cultural practices, subject to respect for human rights and fundamental freedoms.[19]

Among other significant international instruments that explicitly provide high normative value to 'culture' as an expression of human quest for a distinct identity, diversity and a way of life include the following: (i) 1986 *UN Declaration on Right to Development*: that everyone has the right to enjoy their cultural development (Article 1.1)[20]; (ii) 1993 *Vienna Declaration of Programme of Action* provides: "States should, in accordance with international law, take concerted positive steps to ensure respect for all human rights and fundamental freedoms of indigenous people, on the basis of equality and non-discrimination, and recognize the value and diversity of their distinct identities, cultures and social organization" (Article 20)[21]; (iii) 1992 *UN Declaration on Persons Belonging to National Ethnic, Religious and Linguistic Minorities*: responsibility on States to protect cultural identity; the right to enjoy culture; participation in cultural life[22]; (iv) 2007 *UN Declaration on the Rights of Indigenous People*: that indigenous people have the right to maintain and strengthen cultural institutions (Article 5); not to use force to destruct and their culture, deprivation of cultural integrity (Article 8); right to practice cultural traditions and customs that includes ceremonies (Article 11); right to manifest and practise their traditions, customs and ceremonies (Article 12).[23]

Cumulatively, these legally binding as well as soft law instruments do indicate existence of a good corpus of normative principles that place culture and cultural practices on a higher footing in international law and international relations.

[19] UN OHCHR (2001), *Universal Declaration on Cultural Diversity*; available at: https://www.ohchr.org/EN/ProfessionalInterest/Pages/CulturalDiversity.aspx (accessed on 26 July 2021).

[20] UN OHCHR (1986), *Declaration on Right to Development*; available at: https://www.ohchr.org/EN/ProfessionalInterest/Pages/RightToDevelopment.aspx (accessed on 26 July 2021).

[21] UN OHCHR (1993), *Vienna Declaration of Programme of Action*; aadopted by the World Conference on Human Rights in Vienna on 25 June 1993; available at: https://www.ohchr.org/EN/ProfessionalInterest/Pages/Vienna.aspx (accessed on 26 July 2021).

[22] UN OHCHR (1992), *Declaration on Persons Belonging to National Ethnic, Religious and Linguistic Minorities, 1992*; aAdopted by General Assembly resolution 47/135 of 18 December 1992; available at: https://www.ohchr.org/EN/ProfessionalInterest/Pages/Minorities.aspx (accessed on 26 July 2021).

[23] UN (2007), *United Nations Declaration on the Rights of Indigenous People, 2007*; adopted by the UNGA resolution 61/295 of 13 September 2007; available at: https://www.un.org/development/desa/indigenouspeoples/declaration-on-the-rights-of-indigenous-peoples.html (accessed on 10 January 2021).

Gender in Culture

People give shape to their culture as the cultures also give shape to the people who have inherited it. As discussed above, culture or cultural rights are part of the fundamental human rights. Still, the role and exercise of the rights of a particular gender in a society or community is determined by the respective culture.[24] In fact, according to anthropological and historical studies, it is the culture within the cultures that gender identity is preferred rather than individual identity. As observed, for instance, by a writer:

> I am a woman or man; therefore, I am. Human existence without gender identity is inconceivable. One can live without a sense of nationality, without religion, without a job or career, even (although with much more difficulty) without friends; but without a concept of one's gender identity, existence itself is thrown into question.[25]

In this context, the author has used the phrase '*gender culture*' and sought to position 'gender' within the culture.[26] This is especially so since a society sets the parameters, standards, values, and norms as regards how do people of a particular gender behave. Therefore, gender becomes a social construct that is designated as 'gender culture.' It is an effective means of social control over a particular gender such as women. It is a cultural practice that since birth a person has to adopt the norms of 'gender culture.'[27] This explains the context in which cultural norms become an instrumentality for SGBV against women.

Gender roles vary over time within and across culture.[28] This has been a genesis, since time immemorial, for setting the gendered roles of women. The characteristics are more or less the same in every society as seen in earmarking of role of women on the basis of their sex and gender (such as wife, mother, etc.). As a corollary, issues of chastity, obedience, silence also become accepted part of a woman persona and honour of women. Girls are socialized to acquire all the feminine characteristics that are set by the society, e.g. shyness, timidity, restrained nature, being discreet, etc. to protect her chastity and honour. In fact, cultural foundation for the sense of shame for woman comes from the suppression of her sexuality and the knowledge of her inferiority.[29] Thus, it came to be considered as 'normal' in the wake of discussion

---

[24] The European Institute for Gender Equality (2016), "Gender in Culture;" available at: http://eige.europa.eu/rdc/eige-publications/gender-culture (accessed on 10 January 2021).

[25] Ramet, Sabrina Petra (1996) (eds), *Gender Reversals and Gender Cultures: Anthropological and Historical Perspective,* London: Rutledge.

[26] Ibid.

[27] Ibid.

[28] Ibid.

[29] Torjesen, Karen Jo (1996), "Martyrs, Ascetics, and Gnostics: Gender-Crossing in early Christianity. "in Sabrina Petra Ramet, *Gender Reversals and Gender Cultures: Anthropological and Historical Perspective,* London: Rutledge.

on "female martyrdom and gender-crossing" to regard the "naked female body that may be of a female gladiator was a cultural value of shame and inferiority."[30]

The subjugation of women has been often justified in the name of culture. The gender difference is constructed by social or traditional norms. It is one of the cultural tools used to dominate women. It is a cultural norm that masculinity is powerful, aggressive and dominating or controlling. On the contrary, femininity is regarded as dependent, week, submissive, serving, etc. There are many instances wherein women are treated as chattel or commodity[31] and hence freely sought to be traded. In most of the cultures power over things or resources, and people reflects the culture of masculinity. The power relation within the culture shows domination of one gender (especially women) by the other(men). Domination or suppression of women is a way to show or control power. Culture of domination results in the culture of violation. Thus, it is stated that "Cultural violence makes direct and structural violence look, even feel right or at least not wrong."[32] Domination over female body is one of the oldest and widespread forms of power asymmetry in different societies. 'Gender culture' and 'gender relation' shows power asymmetry between men and women from private to public life.[33]

It can be said that dominant culture has always got the support of the people and the States. In most of the cases, the dominant culture is the patriarchal culture. Even law also supports it as it has been proven by the studies of different disciplines, e.g. anthropology, history, sociology, and others.[34] Culture works as main factor behind the son preference in South Asia. Women are deprived of exercising different rights, e.g. economic, reproductive, etc. because of their gender. Hence, because of son preference, sex-selective operations, abortions are embedded in the culture.[35] HCPs such as *Sati,* etc.[36] as well as FGM are supported by a group or community as they justify it as a part of their religious rights or practices. The enormity of the

---

[30] Ibid, it is explained, "A naked female body in the arena could only suggest a passive victim, not an active, powerful protagonist, but the naked male body of the gladiator of Perpetua's vision was a cultural symbol of courage, power, and strength. Inscribed on the female body itself were the cultural values of female shame, women's inferiority made visible. In contrast the male body was an icon of honor and dignity, the visual representation of maleness. The dishonor of the female body was heightened when Perpetua was thrown."

[31] Francis, Diana, (2001), *Culture, Power Asymmetries, and Gender in Conflict Transformation,* Germany: Berghof Handbook for Conflict Transformation.

[32] Ibid.

[33] Ibid.

[34] Goldfarb, Sally, F (2011), "A Clash of Cultures: Women, Domestic Violence and Law in the United States," in Dorothy L Hodgson, *Gender and Culture at the Limit of Rights* (eds.), Philadelphia: University of Pennsylvania Press.

[35] Purewal, Navtej K (2010), *Son Preference Sex Selection, Gender and Culture in South Asia*, Berg, New York: Oxford.

[36] "On 4 September 1987, 18-year-old Roop Kanwar, married only seven months, died on her husband's funeral pyre in Deorala village, about two hours from Jaipur, the capital of Rajasthan. Over 300,000 people attended the *chunari mahotsav,* the function marking the thirteenth day after the sati. Several of those arrested after the sati have been released under political pressure, and

practices and their deleterious effects can be seen from the fact that some 200 million women and girls alive today have been subjected to FGM in 30 countries where it is practiced. UN has estimated 4.1 million women were at risk in 2020[37] and this figure is likely to be 4.2 million in 2022. Even the European[38] countries are not immune to it. These cultural practices continue unabated due to feeling of impunity propelled by flaws in the legislation, policies and institutional inertia.

SGBV against women is seen and accepted in some cultures as a normal phenomenon. As such a culture of silence prevails around it. Therefore, the incidents or stories of the perpetrators are sought to be covered up. In such cases, the cultural notion provides a basis that violence can be committed against women. Alongside this belief, most of the societies do not accept strong women as it does not fit into the cultural norms. In fact, any strong women stand up against violence, they are routinely dubbed as evil characters[39] since timid and feminine nature for a woman has been historically accepted in every culture.

Women's rights or gender equality[40] and patriarchal culture are often seen in contradiction with each other. The popular culture in a society remains in support of patriarchy. Most of the cases, it gets legal support from the governments and often the judiciary though in recent times some winds of change have started blowing in many of the countries. In such a situation, some cultural practices undermine or neglect the basic rights of women even as a human being. It may be family culture; local culture; the culture of a nation[41]; transnational culture[42]; the culture of immigrants; and international culture, e.g. intervention, use of force, imperialism by the capitalist State, conflict, war, etc. Cumulatively, these could contribute to violence against

---

no one has yet been convicted," see, Rajan, Rajeswari Sund (1993), *Real and Imagined Women: Gender, Culture, and Post Colonialism*, New York: Rutledge.

[37] UN (2020), Intensifying global efforts for the elimination of female genital mutilation Report of the Secretary-General; UN Doc.A/75/279 of 30 July 2020; available at: https://undocs.org/en/A/75/279 (accessed on 02 October 2021); Also see UnWomen, *Global Database on Violence against Women;* available at: https://evaw-global-database.unwomen.org/en; UnWomen, *Facts and figures: Ending violence against women;* available at: https://www.unwomen.org/en/what-we-do/ending-violence-against-women/facts-and-figures (accessed on 26 July 2021).

[38] European Institute for Gender Equality (2021), *Estimation of girls at risk of female genital mutilation in the European Union: Denmark, Spain, Luxembourg and Austria;* available at: https://eige.europa.eu/publications/estimation-girls-risk-female-genital-mutilation-european-union-denmark-spain-luxembourg-and-austria#downloads-wrapper (accessed on 26 July 2021).

[39] Frigon, Sylvie, (2006), "Mapping Script and Narratives of Women Who Kill Their Husband in Canada, 1866–1954: Inscribing the Everyday," in Annette Burfoot and Susan Lord, Eds., *Killing Women: The Visual Culture of Gender and Violence,* Canada: Wilfred Laurier University Press.

[40] The opposite of patriarchy is not matriarchy but equality. Here the demand is for the equal rights of women. Hence, gender equality and rights of the women are treated as synonymously.

[41] Levitt, P and S. Engle Merry (2011), "A Clash of Cultures: Women, Domestic Violence and Law in the United States," Dorothy Hodgson, Eds., *Gender and Culture at the Limit of Rights,* Philadelphia: University of Pennsylvania Press.

[42] Ibid.

women.[43] It has been aptly summed up by the UN Development Fund for Women (UNIFEM) that "although violence against women cuts across national, ideological, class, race, and ethnic boundaries, nevertheless, the forms of violence are often culturally determined."[44] It shows how culture remains one of the crucial factors in addressing the challenge of SGBV against women and girls.

Harmful Cultural Practices

Culture is heterogeneous. It incorporates different norms and values. In most of the cases women are treated as a repository of culture. Still, women's contributions and participation in culture gets undermined. Hence, women often lose the chance of getting benefits from the positive aspects of culture; and also suffer by the negative aspects of culture.[45]

In some cases, States and some social groups support both positive and negative aspects of culture. As such the negative or harmful cultural practices (HCP) that are supported by the States can encourage violence against women. Politicization of culture in the name of religion is another challenge in addressing violence against women. The legality and recognition of culture varies according to culture. Thus, cultural practices that support violence against women are shaped accordingly.[46]

As already discussed, the role of a particular gender in a society or community is determined and shaped by culture.[47] In this process, media plays a crucial role in identifying and recognizing the culture of a particular community.[48] At the same time, gender or sexuality of the women get negatively projected through mediums such as newspaper (and magazine) advertisements, hoardings at public places, films and now the social media in the digital age. It shapes people's popular perceptions about women as regards their bodies, sexuality, oppression, vulnerability and subordination etc.[49]

There is a facet of 'legal culture' that "provides the impetus for the use, abuse, or avoidance of the law."[50] It can deny protection as well as a remedy against SGBV. According to the scholars, there are three ways in which it takes effect: "the outer form or legal structure of a community; the inner dimension; or philosophical and

---

43 Ibid.

44 Enna, M. L P and R. Ardos (2003), *Overcoming Violence against Women and Girls: The International Campaign to Eradicate a Worldwide problem*, UK: Rawman and Littlefield Publishers Ltd.

45 UN (2006), n.1.

46 Ibid.

47 European Institute for Gender Equality (2017), "Gender in Culture," pp. 3–4; available at: https://eige.europa.eu/publications/gender-culture (accessed on 28 June 2021).

48 Sanjukta, D. et al. (2012), *Media, Gender, and Popular Culture in India: Tracking Change and Continuity*, New Delhi: Sage.

49 Ibid.

50 Enna, M. L P and R. Ardos (2003), n. 44.

moral principles that animate and support that structure; and the actors within the legal and social system." In view of this, the violence against women gets precedence and justified under the veil of culture or sanctity of social practices. As a result, it is 'legal culture' that legitimizes cultural and social values that support such violence.[51]

On the other hand, political institutions also play a crucial role in the legalization of custom or cultural practices that may be contrary to women's rights. For example, the political institutions in Fiji support the HCP known as *bulubulu.* It entails forgiveness to the sexual violence including 'rape' offenders in a village by acceptance of apology and reconciliation. In fact, such *bulubulu* is accepted by the courts as a reason not to impose a charge or custodial sentence on a convicted rapist. Here the HCP assumes a legitimate form rather than conviction. Faced with opprobrium, the State takes shelter under the garb of local culture for non-compliance[52] as seen in the case of social legitimacy given to *bulubulu* that reinforces sexual violence against women. In a report, the CEDAW Committee called for "prohibiting the reconciliation of cases of rape and sexual assault on the basis of the *bulubulu* custom".[53]

The HCPs include 'harmful traditional practices,' (HTP) or 'harmful practices' (HP).[54] Culture is a macro concept that includes religion, tradition, custom,[55] social norms, and practices.[56] This study has mainly focused on the patriarchal culture that is rooted virtually in every society. Culture-driven SGBV against women is addressed by different terminologies that have already been mentioned. 'Harmful practice' is the most common term used by the OHCHR.[57]

Since, the 1950s, the UN specialized agencies, and human rights bodies have considered the question of 'HTP' that affects women and children. It has been treated

---

[51] Ibid.

[52] UN OHCHR (2018), "Committee on the Elimination of Discrimination against Women assesses the situation of women in Fiji"; available at: https://www.ohchr.org/en/NewsEvents/Pages/DisplayNews.aspx?NewsID=22699&LangID=E. See also, Sally Engle Merry (2006), "Human Rights and Transnational Culture: Regulating Gender Violence Through Global Law", *Osgoode Hall Law Journal*, 44(1): 54 (accessed on 31 July 2021).

[53] UN CEDAW (2002), "Concluding comments of the Committee on the Elimination of Discrimination against Women: Fiji"; CEDAW Committee, Twenty-sixth session, 14 January–1 February 2002; Supplement No. 38 (A/57/38), paragraph 59, p. 5; available at: https://www.un.org/womenwatch/daw/cedaw/cedaw25years/content/english/CONCLUDING_COMMENTS/Fiji/Fiji-CO-1.pdf (accessed on 31 July 2021).

[54] UN (2006), see n.1.

[55] Raday, Frances (2003), "Culture, Religion, and Gender", *International Journal of Constitutional law,* 1(4): 663–715.

[56] UN OHCHR (2014), Eradicating harmful practices against women and girls; available at: https://www.ohchr.org/EN/NewsEvents/Pages/Eradicatingharmfulpracticesagainstwomenandgirls.aspx (accessed on 31 July 2021).

[57] UN Women (2020), "Facts and figures: Ending violence against women"; available at: https://www.unwomen.org/en/what-we-do/ending-violence-against-women/facts-and-figures (accessed on 31 July 2021).

as a cultural issue that relates to 'women and family.'[58] It was the UN General Assembly (UNGA) that initially addressed in the 1950s, the "customs, ancient laws, and practices relating to marriage and family" that were regarded as contrary to the principles set forth in the 1948 UDHR.[59]

The 1954 UNGA resolution (843/IX) on the "Status of women in private law: customs, ancient laws, and practices affecting the human dignity of women" was one of the earliest initiatives taken by the UN to introduce the concept of harmful cultural or traditional practices (HCTP).[60] The resolution explained the rationale that, "in certain areas of the world; women are subjected to customs, ancient laws and practices relating to marriage and the family which inconsistent with the principles of the Charter of the UN and the UDHR 1948." It urged the States to abolish those practices. It specified certain forms of those practices such as "choice of spouse, bride price, the custodial right of children by widow, the right of remarriage of the widow, child marriage, and the betrothal of young girls before puberty."[61]

The UN Economic and Social Council (ECOSOC) called upon the World Health Organization (WHO) in 1958 and 1961 to study "customs subjecting girls to ritual operations." It identified female genital mutilation or cutting (FGM/C) as one of the HCPs. The issue of HCPs started gaining attention fully in the eighties and nineties after adoption of the 1979 Convention on the Elimination of All Forms of Discrimination against Women (CEDAW).[62] CEDAW has explicitly called for abolition of "customs and practices" in a culture that is discriminatory to women.[63] In this respect, the primary focus has been on FGM/C and honour-related crimes that are harmful to the health of women and constitute sexual violence against women. In 1985, a UN working group came out with a study on "traditional practices affecting women's and children's health."[64]

In 1988, the issue was further taken into consideration in the reports of the Special Rapporteur, Mrs. Halima Embarek Warzazi under the theme of HTPs. In 1995, it was addressed in the draft Platform for Action for the Fourth World Conference

---

[58] UN OHCHR (1995), *Fact Sheet 23 Harmful Traditional Practices Affecting the Health of Women and Children*; available at: https://www.ohchr.org/Documents/Publications/FactSheet23en.pdf (accessed on 31 July 2021).

[59] Longman, C and T. Bradley (2015), "Interrogating the Concept of Harmful Cultural Practices", in Chia Longman and Tamsin Bradley, Eds., *Interrogating Harmful Cultural Practices: Gender, Culture and Coercion*, Farnham: Ashgate Publishing.

[60] UN (1954), General Assembly resolution 843 (IX), 17 December 1954; available at: https://www.un.org/en/ga/search/view_doc.asp?symbol=A/RES/843(IX) (accessed on 31 July 2021).

[61] Ibid.

[62] Longman, C and T. Bradley (2015), n. 59.

[63] UN OHCHR (1979), *Convention on the Elimination of All forms of Discrimination against Women*, (1979); available at: https://www.ohchr.org/EN/ProfessionalInterest/Pages/CEDAW.aspx (accessed on 31 July 2021).

[64] Longman, C and T. Bradley (2015), n. 59.

on Women.[65] In 1994, the UN Special Rapporteur, Ms. Radhika Coomaraswamy (appointed by the Commission on Human Rights) examined all the forms of TPs. It was identified that custom and traditions were behind large scale of violence against women.[66] In 1995, the UN OHCHR published the factsheet (23) on HTPs and explained them as follows:

> Traditional cultural practices reflect values and beliefs held by members of a community for periods often spanning generations. Every social grouping in the world has specific traditional cultural practices and beliefs, some of which are beneficial to all members, while others are harmful to a specific group, such as women. These harmful traditional practices include female genital mutilation (FGM); forced feeding of women; early marriage; the various taboos or practices which prevent women from controlling their own fertility; nutritional taboos and traditional birth practices; son preference and its implications for the status of the girl child; female infanticide; early pregnancy; and dowry price. Despite their harmful nature and their violation of international human rights laws, such practices persist because they are not questioned and take on an aura of morality in the eyes of those practicing them.[67]

The issue relating to HTPs against women has now broken the culture of silence. The reasons behind the silence include the fear of losing cultural identity as well as the SGBV against women. The TPs carry the cultural identity of a particular community. Hence the acceptance or imposition of others' culture or TPs may be harmful to the cultural identity of the adopting community. According to the report of the Special Rapporteur (Halima Embaek Waezazi) on TPs affecting the health of women and children, Minister for Women's Affairs of Zimbabwe (Joyce Mujuru), and her staff were entrusted with challenging the practice of "lobola" (literally, bride price), they faced enormous resistance and were accused of "cultural imperialism".[68]

Even the transnational feminist activists, multicultural and postcolonial scholars, journalists, scholars, civil society, have contributed in addressing HT/C practices. Their movement against the subordination of women and considering women rights as human rights has led to the focus on HCPs. It was argued that "critique of colonial feminist and cultural representation of the non-Western other takes place within a global feminist circle, as evidence by a shift of terminology."[69]

It is claimed that the global North undermines the culture of the global South and shows women as a victim of religion, traditional and cultural practices. Some scholars like Uma Narayan, Gayatri Spivak (cited by Longman, C and T. Bradley) claimed that culture is not static rather it is dynamic. It seems all need to raise their

---

65 UN OHCHR (1995), *Fact Sheet 23: Harmful Traditional Practices Affecting the Health of Women and Children*; available at: https://www.ohchr.org/Documents/Publications/FactSheet23en.pdf (accessed on 31 July 2021).

66 UN ECOSOC (1995), *"Preliminary report submitted by the Special Rapporteur on violence against women, its causes and consequences, Ms. Radhika Coomaraswamy, in accordance with Commission on Human Rights resolution 1994/45"*; UN Doc. E/CN.4/1995/42 of 22 November 1994; available at: https://undocs.org/E/CN.4/1995/42 (accessed on 31 July 2021).

67 UN OHCHR (1995), n. 65.

68 UN ECOSOC (1996), "Final report of the Special Rapporteur on traditional practices affecting the health of women and children, Halima Embarek Warzazi"; UN Doc.E/CN.4/Sub.2/1996/6, para 9; available at: https://digitallibrary.un.org/record/236617 (accessed on 310 July 2021).

69 Longman, C and T. Bradley (2015), n. 59.

voices against the global patriarchal culture rather than the culture of any region *per se*. The attention has now shifted from HTP to HCP or HP. Even in the UN documents, the word HCP has replaced HTP as shown in the 2002 report of the UN Special Rapporteur Ms. Radhika Coomaraswamy (causes and consequences of violence against women) expressly used the term "cultural practices" and "harmful practices".[70]

Hence, the main focus needs to be on the global patriarchal culture that primarily undermines women and, in turn, results in violation of women's human rights. The terminologies such as HTP, HCP or HP etc. are used synonymously to underscore practices that are harmful to women and girls. The practices are not a myth or confined in theology or any discipline; rather they present live examples of harmful practises against women all over the world.[71] Apart from it, there are many other forms of HCPs that still remain unidentified and unrecognized.[72] In view of this, it is contended that a harmful cultural or religious practice against women poses a greater threat to the cultural rights and cultural integrity rather than a violation of any of the traditional human rights standards.[73]

Causes of Harmful Practices

It can be surmised that status of women in the society and the patriarchy[74] are the main reasons for the HCP. The cultural norms that have prescribed the role and identity of men and women in society are a significant barrier for the full enjoyment of the rights of women. There are some forms of SGBV against women that are not yet considered as harmful. In Chad, for instance, there are some forms of SGBV against women, especially refugees and IDPs, are not treated as harmful practices. The report of the UNHCR has identified that suppression of women in the family, community or society is one of the reasons behind it.[75]

---

[70] UN Commission on Human Rights (2002), "Report of the Special Rapporteur on violence against women, its causes and consequences, Ms. Radhika Coomaraswamy, submitted in accordance with Commission on Human Rights resolution 2001/49: Cultural practices in the family that are violent towards women"; UN Doc.E/CN.4/2002/83, 31 January 2002; available at: https://www.refworld.org/docid/3d6ce3cc0.html (accessed on 31 July 2021).

[71] Presentation by Prof. Bharat H Desai, Friday Seminar, Centre for International Legal Studies, School of International Studies, Jawaharlal Nehru University, New Delhi (on file with the authors).

[72] UN (2006), n.1; Raday, Frances (2003), n. 55.

[73] Higgins, Tracy E (1996), "Anti-Essentialism, Relativism, and Human Rights", *Harvard Women's Law Journal*, 19:89.

[74] Le Roux, E. and Bartelink, B.E. (2017), *No more 'harmful traditional practices': working effectively with faith leaders. Research report*; available at: https://meal.jliflc.com/wp-content/uploads/2017/11/HTP-report-final-draft.pdf (accessed on 31 July 2021).

[75] UN OHCHCR, *SGBV Strategy 2012–2016: Chad*; available at: https://www.unhcr.org/56b1fd9f9.pdf (accessed on 31 July 2021).

Since birth, women are treated as unequal to men; they are regarded as property and honour of their family and community. The rigid societal structures specify the role of men and women. In most of the cultures, women are forbidden from participating in decision-making even in crucial matters of marriage, childbirth, etc.[76] Lack of economic empowerment creates dependency on a male member of the family. Therefore, culture is used as a defence to justify any crime or violence. This can be seen in cases of honour killing; the practice of *levirate* and *sororat* in Chad (forced marriage with brother-in-law after husbands or sisters death). Some groups of people, e.g. widow, old, disabled women are more vulnerable to SGBV. Disabled women also suffer multiple incidents of victimizations and are at the risk of re-victimization.[77]

Cultural and religious norms, impunity, lack of legal support, and politics encourage the HCPs to continue from generation to generation. Since HCPs are rooted in religious or cultural norms, they are controlled and interpreted by the people having patriarchal mindsets. These practices continue notwithstanding globalization and migration as the people carry their cultural practices wherever they migrate. This has been clearly visible in cases of common practices such as:

> female genital mutilation, forced marriage, son preference, stoning of women, wife inheritance, widowhood rites, sex selective abortions, child marriage, public harassment (euphemistically referred to in some countries as eve teasing), bonded labor, bride price (dowry-related issues), forced impregnation, polygamy, acid attacks… dedication of girls to temples, maltreatment of widows, burning/beheading women thought to be witches, virginity tests, breast ironing, stereotyping, and marital or date rape.[78]

Many of these practices are linked to other forms of violence against women; for instance, the denial of property rights is often linked to the maltreatment of widows, sexual violence to forced marriages, and the receipt of monetary payments for selling women to the traffickers. Some cases of SGBV, such as domestic violence and rape, are often sought to be resolved by the traditional leaders. As a consequence, impunity prevails in most of the cases since the perpetrators could go scot-free as the rape survivor is made to marry the perpetrators and by payment of fine or some money to the SGBV survivor or her family. It also leads to non-reporting of rape cases or other serious forms of sexual violence. Ironically, in both national and international legal systems, the law is used to construct, regulate, and enforce culture in relation to gender. It could take the shape of a treaty, e.g. the CEDAW (international level) or a legislation on personal laws (national level). Thus, there is a sheer legal silence, State enabled impunity and non-interference in private matters by the States.[79]

International human rights treaties as well as most of the national legislations give assurance on the right to equality and cultural freedom as fundamental human rights. However, in many of the cases, national legislations concerning family, marriage,

---

[76] Ibid.

[77] Ibid.

[78] The Advocates (2010), *Types of Harmful Practices*; available at: https://www.stopvaw.org/harmful_practices (accessed on 31 July 2021).

[79] Mehra, Madhu (2007), "Women's Equality and Culture in the Context of Identity Politics", J. *Comp. L.* 2(2):6, 7.

etc., are based on religion and customs. They inherently carry some discriminatory provisions for women and the States justify the laws by taking shelter under the policy of non-interference in private matters (personal laws) on the basis of a reservation in the provision of human rights treaties such as the CEDAW.[80]

HCPs also violate sexual and reproductive life of women.[81] *Ukuthwala* or abduction of girls for marriage is a harmful practice in South Africa that supports child marriage. In such situations, the 6–13-year-old girls are abducted for marriage and at a tender age they become victims of different forms of SGBV, e.g. domestic violence, premature or undesired pregnancy, get exposed to sexually transmitted diseases, HIV/AIDS, etc. In most of the cases, people of poor communities are found mired in these harmful practices.[82]

There are some other practices that are also harmful for the sexual and reproductive health of women, e.g. dry sexual intercourse, *sororate* marriage practices wherein the wife is replaced by her sister; other harmful practices relating to childbirth; dietary taboos during pregnancy and lactation. These HC practices deny the right to sexual and reproductive health care to women and their right to take sexual and reproductive decisions. It, in turn, denies women the right to have control over their own bodies and ensure right to bodily integrity and protection against SGBV. The enormity of HCP gets heightened by the global situation wherein, as per WHO's 2021 estimates, about 1 in 3 (30%) women worldwide have been subjected to sexual violence in their lifetime (see Table 4.1).[83]

Use of Culture as a Tool

There are practical instances wherein 'culture' has been used to defend different forms of violence and crimes against women. It is also known as 'cultural defence.' The tendency of cultural defence has seen mostly in the deep-rooted patriarchal culture, cross-cultural society, among immigrants living in foreign countries. It mainly affects women in general and specifically immigrants, and minorities. Some studies have shown that cultural defence is most successful in case of underlying cultural norms represented by the culture that is different from the native culture. It is a disadvantage for the women.[84] It has been argued that the use of cultural defence

[80] Ibid.

[81] Mubangizi, John Cantius (2015), "An Assessment of the Constitutional, Legislative and Judicial Measures against Harmful Cultural Practices that Violate Sexual and Reproductive Rights of Women in South Africa", Journal *of International Women's Studies*, 16(3), 158–173.

[82] Ibid.

[83] WHO (2021), "Violence against Women", 6 March 2021; available at: https://www.who.int/news-room/fact-sheets/detail/violence-against-women (accessed on 1 August 201).

[84] Ajayi, Victoria (2012), "Violence against Women: The Ethics of Incorporating the Cultural Defense in Legal Narrative", *The Georgetown Journal of Legal Ethics*, 25:401.

Table 4.1 Published Works Showing Different Aspects of Worldwide HCPs

No	Agency/author	Use of terms	Aspects of harmful cultural practices (HCPs)	HCP enablers[85]
1	UNIFEM	Harmful Traditional Practices[86]	Female genital mutilation or cutting (FGM/C), dowry murder for dowry, "honour killing," and early marriage[87]	Family, and the community
2	Zaunbrecher Katie L (2011)	Cultural and traditional practices[88]	Honour killing, genital mutilation, domestic abuse, and rape[89]	Family, community leaders
3	OHCHR, Fact Sheet 23	Traditional cultural practices or harmful traditional practices[90]	Female genital mutilation; forced feeding of women; early marriage; the various taboos or practices which prevent women from controlling their fertility; nutritional taboos and traditional birth practices; son preference; female infanticide; early pregnancy; dowry for marriage.[91] Polygamy	Family, community leaders, religious leaders, and States by supporting the practices

(continued)

[85] UNFPA (2020), "Female genital mutilation (FGM): Frequently asked questions", July 2020; available at: https://www.unfpa.org/resources/female-genital-mutilation-fgm-frequently-asked-questions#practice_origins (accessed on 31 July 2021).

[86] UN Women (2020), "Ending violence against women: Facts and Figures"; available at: https://www.unwomen.org/en/what-we-do/ending-violence-against-women/facts-and-figures#:~:text=%20Facts%20and%20figures%3A%20Ending%20violence%20against%20women,violence%20from%20an%20intimate%20partner%20or...%20More%20 (accessed on 31 July 2021).

[87] Ibid.

[88] Zaunbrecher Katie L (2011), "When Culture Hurts: Dispelling the Myth of Cultural Justification for Gender-based Human Rights Violations", *Houston Journal of International law*, 33(3): 680–716,

[89] Ibid.

[90] UN OHCHR (1995), *Fact Sheet No. 23: Harmful Traditional Practices Affecting the Heath of Women and Children*; available at: https://www.ohchr.org/Documents/Publications/FactSheet23en.pdf; https://www.refworld.org/docid/479477410.html (accessed on 1 August 2021).

[91] Ibid.

Table 4.1 (continued)

No	Agency/author	Use of terms	Aspects of harmful cultural practices (HCPs)	HCP enablers
4	UN News	Harmful traditional practices[92]	Honour killing; child marriage; giving away girls to settle disputes (*Baad*); buying and selling of women for marriage; forced isolation; forcing women for committing self-immolation; denial of the right to education, work and health services; Forced marriages; exchange marriages (*Baadal*); child engagement; high bride price[93]	Religious leaders, elders from the community, (Afghanistan)
5	UN Women	Harmful traditional practices[94]	FGM, Child marriage	Parents, grandparents, the village chief, community (Mali)
6	UNFPA, Beijing + 5, Beijing 1995, ICPD POA, Cairo, 1994, ICPD + 5	Harmful practices, customary and harmful practices, traditional practices harmful to women; harmful and discriminatory attitudes, harmful and unethical practices[95]	FGM, early and child marriage, honour killing, parental sex selection, discrimination and violence against girl child; rape; incest; trafficking; sexual violence and exploitation	Village and religious leaders, community leaders

(continued)

[92] UN (2010), "Harmful Traditional Practices against women Pervasive in Afghanistan", UN News, 9 December 2010; available at: https://news.un.org/en/story/2010/12/361442-harmful-traditional-practices-against-women-pervasive-afghanistan-un (accessed on 10 January 2021).

[93] UNAMA (2010), "Harmful traditional practices and implementation of the law on elimination of violence against women in Afghanistan"; available at: https://unama.unmissions.org/sites/default/files/harmful_traditional_practices_english.pdf (accessed on 1 August 2021).

[94] UN Women (2018), "Ending harmful traditional practices in Mali"; available at: https://untf.unwomen.org/en/news-and-events/stories/2018/02/ending-harmful-traditional-practices-in-mali (accessed on 1 August 2021).

[95] UNFPA, "Issue 5: harmful practices"; available at: https://www.unfpa.org/resources/issue-5-harmful-practices (accessed on 1 August 2021).

Table 4.1 (continued)

No	Agency/author	Use of terms	Aspects of harmful cultural practices (HCPs)	HCP enablers
7	UNICEF	Harmful traditional practices (HTPs)[96]	FGM or cutting, abduction for marriage, early forced and child marriage; etc	Family, community, etc. (Ethiopia)
8	World Bank	Traditional harmful practices[97]	FGM, honour killing, dowry-related violence	Family, community, etc
9	United Nations Economic Commission for Africa	Traditional societal practices, harmful traditional practices, customary practices, sociocultural practices[98]	Polygamy and different forms of gender-based violence	Influential leaders, community leaders, general population (Africa)

(continued)

[96] UNICEF (2019), "National Costed Roadmap to End Child Marriage and FGM/C 2020–2024"; available at: https://www.unicef.org/ethiopia/media/1781/file/National%20Roadmap%20to%20End%20Child%20Marriage%20and%20FGM.pdf (accessed on 1 August 2021).

[97] The World Bank (2009), "Gender-based violence, health and the role of the health sector"; available at: http://web.worldbank.org/archive/website01213/WEB/IMAGES/AAGGBVHE.PDF (accessed on 1 August 2021).

[98] UN Economic Commission for Africa, "Inventory of United Nations Activities to End Violence against Women;" available at: https://evaw-un-inventory.unwomen.org/en/agencies/eca (accessed on 1 August 2021).

Table 4.1 (continued)

No	Agency/author	Use of terms	Aspects of harmful cultural practices (HCPs)	HCP enablers
10	African Union (AU)	Traditional and religious practices; harmful social practices; harmful cultural practices, harmful traditional practices; practices based on tradition and religion; harmful practices; community and family norms[99]	Child marriage; FGM; *telafa* (a practice in Ethiopia where girls are kidnapped, hide, raped, forced impregnation to marry); *ukuthwala*a practice in South Africa to abduct girls for marriage with the consent of the parents. *Trokosi* practices in Ghana, Benin, and Togo sends a young virgin girl to a shrine for the atonement of crime committed by a male member of her family. Co modification of girls and women's sexuality and reproduction. Marital rape and honour killing, dowry	Religious and traditional leaders (Africa, rural area)

(continued)

[99] African Union (2015), "Campaign to the end of child marriage in Africa: The effects of traditional and religious practices of child marriage on Africa's socio-economic development"; available at: https://au.int/sites/default/files/documents/31018-doc-5465_ccmc_africa_report.pdf (accessed on 1 August 2021).

Table 4.1 (continued)

No	Agency/author	Use of terms	Aspects of harmful cultural practices (HCPs)	HCP enablers
11	UN Division for the Advancement of Women: UN Economic Commission for Africa	Harmful traditional practices against women[100]	Early and forced marriage, FMG, massage of the clitoris of the adolescent girls, lips plates, food taboos, force feeding for bride price, breast ironing, bride kidnapping and raping for marriage, Sexual exclusion of wives, domestic violence including sexual, sororate and levirate; dry sexual intercourse; trokosi; widowhood rites; women as war plunder	Family, community, and at the state level (Africa)
12	UNICEF	Harmful traditional practices[101]	Devdasi, Deuki, Devaki or girls offered to temples to provide full service including prostitution; virginity;	Religious leaders, Community leaders and family (Nepal, India; Somalia, Djibouti, Sudan, Egypt, Mali)

(continued)

[100] UN (2009), "Harmful Traditional Practices against Women and Legislation", Expert paper prepared by Dr Morissanda Kouyaté; United Nations Division for the Advancement of Women and United Nations Economic Commission for Africa; available at: https://www.un.org/womenwatch/daw/egm/vaw_legislation_2009/Expert%20Paper%20EGMGPLHP%20_Morissanda%20Kouyate_.pdf (accessed on 1 August 2021).

[101] UN (2006), n.1.

Table 4.1 (continued)

No	Agency/author	Use of terms	Aspects of harmful cultural practices (HCPs)	HCP enablers
13	Michael L P Enna and Raheln Ardos (2003)	Culture-specific practices, culture-specific forms of violence against women, culturally sanctioned forms of violence, against women[102]	Honour killing, acid attack in denying marriage or unwelcome sexual favour, female infanticide, bride burning, female circumcision or surgery, dowry murder	Community, family members (Bangladesh (1996–1998) acid attack reported more than two hundred; honour killing in Pakistan (in 1997 in one province three hundred women); 1999 estimated Gaza two thirds murders were honour killing; Lebanon (thirty-six in honour killing in 1996 and 1998); Yemen (four honour killing in 1997); Egypt (fifty two honour killing in 1997); Dowry Killing in India; female circumcision Sierra Leone, Guinea, Somalia, Ethiopia, Eritrea)
14	Sally Engle Merry	Customary practices, cultural practices, traditional practices[103]	*Bulubulua* traditional village custom uses to take rape cases out of court	Village and community leaders (Fiji)
15	John Cantius Mubangizi	Harmful cultural practices, Cultural and traditional practices	FGM, abduction for marriage (ukuthwala), virginity testing, polygamy, child marriage	Africa

(continued)

[102] Enna, M. L P and R. Ardos (2003), n. 44.

[103] Sally Engle Merry (2006), "Human Rights and Transnational Culture: Regulating Gender Violence Through Global Law", *Osgoode Hall Law Journal*, 54–60.

Table 4.1 (continued)

No	Agency/author	Use of terms	Aspects of harmful cultural practices (HCPs)	HCP enablers
16	Michael Flood	Traditional and cultural practices[104]	Honour killing, dowry death, forced marriage, trafficking, sex-selective abortion, FGM, prostitution early marriage, sexual coercive behaviour as the accepted norm	Community, family, (Somalia, New Zealand, Britain)
17	Chia Longman and Gily Coene	Harmful cultural practices, Cultural Practices, Harmful practices[105]	Forced marriage, honour-based violence, head covering	Family, community (Belgium)
18	Ellen Gruenbaum	Cultural practices, harmful global practices, harmful cultural practices[106]	Female circumcision	Family, community (All over the world)
19	United Nations Division for the Advancement of Women (DAW) in collaboration with UNICE (2006)	Harmful traditional values and practices[107]	Son preference, early marriage and early pregnancy, abduction	Family, community, religious or traditional leaders

(continued)

[104] Flood, Michael, "Harmful Traditional and Cultural Practices Related to Violence Against Women and Successful Strategies to Eliminate Such Practices: Working with Men", pp. 2–3; available at: https://citeseerx.ist.psu.edu/viewdoc/download?doi=10.1.1.581.3370&rep=rep1&type=pdf (accessed on 1 August 2021).

[105] Longman, C and G. Coene (2015), "Harmful Cultural Practices and Minority Women in Europe: From Headscarf Bans to Forced Marriages and Honour Related Violence", in Chia Longman and Tamsin Bradley, Eds., *Interrogating Harmful Cultural Practices: Gender, Culture and Coercion*, Farnham: Ashgate Publishing, pp. 51–61.

[106] Galtung, Johan (2015), "Epilogue: Harm and Well-Being: Cultural Practices and Harmful Global Practices", in Chia Longman and Tamsin Bradley (eds.) *Interrogating Harmful Cultural Practices: Gender, Culture and Coercion*, Farnham: Ashgate Publishing, pp. 193–204.

[107] UN (2006), n. 1.

Table 4.1 (continued)

No	Agency/author	Use of terms	Aspects of harmful cultural practices (HCPs)	HCP enablers
20	Halima Embarek Warzazi, Special Rapporteur, 1996	Traditional practices, harmful traditional practices, harmful practices[108]	FGM, bride price, physical and sexual abuse of girls and women within family, marital rape, removal of the uvula, female excision, early marriage, childbirth and weaning, dietary taboos, removing milk teeth, burning the skin, bleeding the patients, opening the lower part of the abdomen, pausing a prolapsed cervix back into the place holding the foetus in position; scarring, tattooing, piercing the earlobes, gums, lips and nose; prohibition on having sex of menopausal women; taboos relating to menstruation, pregnancy etc.; polygamy, groundless divorce; inheritance of property; and so on	Family, community, religious and traditional leaders, governments, etc. (Pru, America, Netherland, Sudan Guinea, Niger Guinea, Iraq)

(continued)

[108] UN ECOSOC (1996), "Final report of the Special Rapporteur on traditional practices affecting the health of women and children, Mrs. Halima Embarek Warzazi"; UN Doc. E/CN.4/Sub.2/1996/6, 14 June 1996; available at: https://digitallibrary.un.org/record/236617 (accessed on 1 August 2021).

Table 4.1 (continued)

No	Agency/author	Use of terms	Aspects of harmful cultural practices (HCPs)	HCP enablers
21	Bharat H. Desai and Moumita Mandal	Harmful cultural practices or religious practices[109]; elimination of FGM[110]	FGM or *Khatna* or *Khafd/z;* banning menstruating women from entering into the temple	Family, community, religious leaders, etc.
22	Committee of the Covenant of Economic, social and Cultural Rights (General Comment 14)	Harmful traditional cultural practices and norms[111]	All harmful cultural practices that deny enjoying reproductive right and health of women	Both State and individual
23	Beijing Platform for Action, 1995	Harmful and unethical practices; traditional and customary practices; negative cultural attitude and practices[112]	Sex selection, infanticide, etc	Family, community etc

[109] Desai, Bharat H, et al. (2018), "Quest for Women's Right to Bodily Integrity: Reflections on Recent Judicial inroads in India", *Economic and Political Weekly*, 53(51), 29 December 2018; available at: https://www.epw.in/engage/article/quest-womens-right-bodily-integrity-judicial-inroads (accessed on 1 August 2021).

[110] Desai, Bharat H. and Mandal, Moumita (2020), "On Elimination of Female Genital Mutilation: Making International Institutions Work", *Indian Journal of International Law*, vol.61, no.3–4, pp. 195–229.

[111] UN OHCHR (2000), "CESCR General Comment No. 14: The Right to the Highest Attainable Standard of Health (Art. 12)"; adopted on 11 August 2000 at the Twenty-second Session of the Committee on Economic, Social and Cultural Rights (Contained in Document E/C.12/2000/4);
available at: https://www.refworld.org/pdfid/4538838d0.pdf (accessed on 1 August 2021).

[112] UN (1996), "The Report of the Fourth World Conference on Women, 4–15 September 1995, Beijing"; available at: https://www.un.org/womenwatch/daw/beijing/pdf/Beijing%20full%20report%20E.pdf (accessed on 1 August 2021).

to promote violence against women is not only an issue of national law; private international law or conflict of laws; rather an issue of international human rights law. Hence, it has been contended that:

> The so-called 'cultural defense' to human rights violations has been invoked to justify the unabashedly brutal treatment of women through practices like honor killing, genital mutilation, domestic abuse, and rape…Whatever the legitimacy of these practices within the cultures in which they occur, the international community is beginning to recognize that achieving gender equality (and consequently, eradicating the abusive customs) is crucial to maintaining international peace and security.[113]

In this context, cultural defence can be regarded as a denial of international human rights law. The legitimization of cultural defence is a result of a clash between international human rights norms and local cultural practices. If a violation of human rights in any defined culture is invalid, it may be acceptable in another culture. Still, some have sought to claim that the Western nations use international human rights law as an instrument against non-Western States.[114] For instance, an African scholar, Makau Mutua has argued in the work *Universalism of Human Rights* that the "West purported to champion civil and political rights, whereas the Soviet bloc posed as the sole guarantor of economic, social, and cultural rights."[115] This perception emanates from the past history of cultural, military, philosophical, economic domination of Europe over the non-European peoples and their traditions[116] since most of the Asian and African countries were colonized and did not participate in the international human rights law-making processes. Therefore, it has been argued that:

> The basic human rights texts drew heavily from the American Bill of Rights and the French Declaration of the Rights of Man. There is virtually no evidence to suggest that they drew inspiration from Asian, Islamic, Buddhist, Hindu, African, or any other non-European traditions.[117]

Notwithstanding the fact that the modern conception of international human rights has been rooted in the West, yet it has helped in elevating the discourse on the sanctity of human aspirations and lives with finer graces of modern civilization.

Since cultural practices are rooted in the past and come into conflict with modernity, some have questioned the perceived cultural clash in addressing the harmful practices. For example, FGM (female genital mutilation) has been practised by the natives of the different cultures including in the Western societies. It presents a global human rights challenge and could be addressed through education, awareness, intra-cultural dialogue and introspection.

---

[113] Zaunbrecher Katie L (2011), n. 5, pp. 681–682.

[114] Ibid.

[115] Mutua, Makau (2004), "The Complexity of Universalism in Human Right", in Andras Sajo, Ed., *Human Rights with Modesty: The Problem of Universalism*, Leide/Boston: Martinus Nijhoff Publishers.

[116] Ibid.

[117] Ibid.

The discourse on the issue of universalism of human rights has gradually moved to ensuring the enforcement of treaties on the women's rights.[118] Since the 1990s, the human rights paradigm has been invoked in addressing the challenge of violence against women. In the evolutionary process, it has put to test many of the traditional or cultural practices that are seen in conflict with the modern human rights paradigm.[119] Some of the cultural practices have been sought to be justified by the governments on the ground of cultural relativity though they run counter to the tenets of fundamental human rights. It appears the shadow of the patriarchal culture still looms large and hovers over the quest for women's rights.[120]

There are many cases wherein the cultural defence has been successfully applied by the advocates and judges of the national legal systems. In *Rashid v. State* (2013), it was decided by the Supreme Court of Georgia that a father killed his daughter in the name of saving the family honour. In this case, the woman wanted to get divorce from her husband. But the father brutally killed her, as he claimed, the act of the victim action was against the honour of the family.[121] Similarly, the shield of culture was used to justify the 2002 gang rape of a woman ordered by a Pakistani tribal council as punishment for a crime attributed to her brother.[122] The tribal council decided that he violated the honour of the tribe. So, the tribal council ordered for rape of his sister for avenging and restoring the honour of the tribe. Hence, many of the HCPs are reflected in 'honour crimes' against women.

The concept of honour[123] is deep-rooted in many of the communities around the world as the communities prescribe rules or practices that are expected to be strictly followed by its members. It results in women being regarded as 'chattel' or 'heirloom' that leads to menfolk controlling women to protect their so-called honour.[124] In *People v Moua* (1985) a California Superior Court reduced rape charges against a perpetrator who misunderstood his culture. The accused argued that his culture permitted abduction of girls and women for marriage and sexual relationship despite the protest of the girls wherein the victim's protest was construed as a sign of consent. The court, however, accepted the defence in the name of culture and reduced the punishment of the accused person.[125] In *People v Chen*, the accused

---

[118] Zaunbrecher Katie L (2011), n. 5; Ajayi, Victoria (2012), n. 112.

[119] Cully, Pamela (2011), "Gender, History, and Human Rights", in Hodgson, Dorothy L, Ed., *"Gender and Culture at the Limit of Rights"*, University of Pennsylvania Press: Philadelphia.

[120] Edwards, Alice (2012), *Violence against Women under International Human Rights Law,* UK: Cambridge University Press.

[121] *Rashid v. State*, No. S12A1698, 22 January 2013; Supreme Court of Georgia; available at: https://caselaw.findlaw.com/ga-supreme-court/1621305.html (accessed on 08 July 2021).

[122] BBC New (2005), "Pakistan rape-case men rearrested", 18 March 2005; available at: http://news.bbc.co.uk/2/hi/south_asia/4361289.stm (accessed on 08 July 2021).

[123] Ibid.

[124] Hussain, Mazna (2006), "Take My Riches, Give Me Justice: A Contextual Analysis of Pakistan's Honor Crimes Legislation," *Harv. J.L. & Gender*, 29: 223.

[125] Kim, Nancy S. (1997), "The Cultural Defense and the Problem of Cultural Preemption: A Framework for Analysis", 27 *New Mexico Law Review* 101 (1997); available at: https://digitalrepository.unm.edu/nmlr/vol27/iss1/5; Gallin, Alice J. (1994), "The Cultural Defense: Undermining the

killed his wife for having sexual relationship with another man. The court reduced the sentence on the ground that the culture of the accused influenced him to commit the offence.[126]

Similarly, in *Sunita Tiwari vs. Union of India,*[127] the issue of the practice of FGM has been raised before the Supreme Court of India (SCI) in the civil writ petition (No. 286 of 2017) under Article 32 of the Constitution of India. The SCI questioned the practice of FGM or *Khatna,* or *Chafed* or Female Circumcision (FC) and considered it as a violation of the fundamental rights and integrity of the girl.[128] It was submitted that FGM cannot be considered as 'essential religious practice', and can be brought under the 2012 Protection of Children from Sexual Offences Act (POCSO).[129] The Court emphatically underscored that no one has the right to violate the bodily privacy and integrity of women in the name of religion. The petitioner argued that it is a crime under the POCSO Act that protects minor girls from sexual assault. The respondents, in countering the PIL, argued that FGM or *Kahfz* was integral to religious and cultural beliefs and should not be banned. They pleaded that the practice is protected under Articles 25 and 26 of the Constitution of India that deals with the right to practice and propagate religion. However, Justice Chandrachud sternly asked: "Why should the bodily integrity of a woman be subject to some external authority? One's genitals are extremely private affairs."[130]

Making a reference to the UDHR and Child Rights Convention at the case hearing, the SC judges called for a ban on the practice as it is inhuman and violation of Article 21 of the Indian Constitution. It has been argued that the FGM needs to be treated as

---

Policies Against Domestic Violence", 35 *Boston College Law Review* 723 (1994); available at: http://lawdigitalcommons.bc.edu/bclr/vol35/iss3/7; *People v. Moua*, No. 315972 (Fresno Super. Ct. 1985); available at: https://www.casemine.com/judgement/us/5914e339add7b049348f8913 (accessed on 08 August 2021).

126 Wang, Jinghui Vivien, "Cultural Defense as a Shield for Violence", Journal of Gender, Social Policy & the Law (American University), No.2016; available at: https://jgspl.org/cultural-defense-shield-violence/ (accessed on 08 August 2021).

127 *Sunita Tiwari v Union of India*, W.P.(C) No. 000286/2017 Registered on (21-04-2017) [Case status: (Pending Motion Hearing Part Heard Matters) Adjourned (as per record of proceeding)-Ord dt: 24-09-2018], available at: https://indiankanoon.org/doc/181206322/ (accessed on 08 August 2021).

128 The Times of India (2018), "Supreme Court questions practice of female genital mutilation", 9 July 2018, available at: https://timesofindia.indiatimes.com/india/supreme-court-questions-practice-of-female-genital-mutilation/articleshow/64922201.cms (accessed on 08 August 2021).

129 There are three seminal judgements of the Supreme Court of India concerning the Protection of Children from Sexual Offences Act (POCSO) 2012: *Gaurav Jain vs. UoI & Ors.*, 15 November 1989; available at: http://www.hrcr.org/safrica/childrens_rights/India.html#:~:text=Gaurav%20Jain%20v%20Union%20of,pre%2Dstigma%20attached%20on%20them; (accessed on 28 March 2022); *Vishal Jeet vs UoI & Ors.*, 02 May 1990; available at: https://www.ncpcr.gov.in/show_img.php?fid=526; *Sakshi vs UoI & Ors.*, 26 May 2004; available at: https://www.ncpcr.gov.in/show_img.php?fid=527 (accessed on 08 August 2021).

130 Hindustan Times (2018), "Mumbai's Dawoodi Bohra women to SC: Khatna is essential to our faith", 10 July 2018, available at: https://www.hindustantimes.com/mumbai-news/mumbai-s-dawoodi-bohra-women-to-sc-khatna-is-essential-to-our-faith/story-0GuHQMSLbFvoEw6TJm1SPM.html (accessed on 14 August 2021).

an offence under the 1860 Indian Penal Code. The Constitution Bench of the SC is expected to take a call in the near future on FGM's compatibility with fundamental human rights, especially the 'right to bodily integrity' (Article 21) though it has also been defended as an integral part of the freedom of religion (Article 26). FGM results in women and girls being subjected to lifelong physical and psychological impairment.[131] It is now widely accepted that all forms of non-medical FGM, under cultural or religious garb, serve as a primitive tool to curb female sexuality. Therefore, it has been regarded as a serious violation of the rights of children as even minors have a "right of security of person, right to privacy, bodily integrity and the freedom from cruel, inhumane or degrading treatment"[132] as well as subjugates women and their sexuality.[133] Thus, the human rights discourse has progressed to a level wherein culture, tradition, custom, or religious practices cannot be used as a tool that violets the basic rights of women and girls.

Elimination of Harmful Cultural Practices

Though controversies arise as regards the universal application of human rights. In this context, there is no place for cultural defence in international law. It provides for both religious and cultural rights under the international human rights law (IHRL). Still, the cultural interpretation of an IHRL norm is not applicable to support the cultural defence. Universal application of international law cannot be reduced on the ground of the diversity of different cultures, traditions or local practices.[134] The universalism of human rights has been duly underscored and supported by the UNESCO in the 2001 *Universal Declaration on Cultural Diversity*. Article 4 of the Declaration has emphatically declared:

> Human rights as guarantees of cultural diversity: The defence of cultural diversity is an ethnical imperative, inseparable from respect for human dignity. It implies a commitment to human rights and fundamental freedoms, in particular the rights of persons belonging to

---

[131] Hindustan Times (2017), "Female Genital Mutilation debate puts Bohra women on opposite sides", *Hindustan Times*, 29 May 2017, available at: https://www.hindustantimes.com/mumbai-news/female-genital-mutilation-debate-puts-bohra-women-on-opposite-sides/story-jx9r4R6CXFqFMIgsWDBASO.html (accessed on 08 August 2021).

[132] Hindustan Times (2017), "Govt will end female genital mutilation if Bohras don't", *Hindustan Times*, 29 May 2017; available at: https://www.hindustantimes.com/india-news/practise-of-female-genital-mutilation-should-be-banned-in-india-maneka-gandhi/story-kQhNA4rIYOLQTurkN5zAAM.html (accessed on 08 August 2021).

[133] SC refers to five-judge bench plea against female genital mutilation, *Times of India*, 24 September 2018, available at: https://timesofindia.indiatimes.com/india/sc-refers-to-five-judge-bench-plea-against-female-genital-mutilation/articleshow/65936717.cms (accessed on 08 August 2021).

[134] Zaunbrecher Katie L (2011), n. 5.

> minorities and those indigenous peoples. No one may invoke cultural diversity to infringe upon human rights guaranteed by international law, nor to limit their scope.[135]

In view of this, the African Committee on Traditional Practices affecting the health of women and children is one of the first organizations that has acknowledged the role of legislation to eliminate HTPs.[136]

International Human Rights Law

The earlier examples of HCPs included FGM and some specific practices that affected the health of women and children. Since 1960, WHO took up this agenda at the global level. It was followed up by many other international organizations.[137] It has often been argued that there is a conflict between, 'religious or cultural autonomy' and 'gender equality.' The conflict has been addressed in international law and in the various national legal systems in the context of human rights. Hence, the concept of culture has been separated from religion and treated as *secular* in the human rights discourse. The 1948 UDHR and other IHR treaties contain provisions for the right to freedom of religion and conscience as well as the right to enjoyment of one's culture. Still, these principles also include the "women's right to non-discrimination."[138]

According to IHR treaties such as the 1979 CEDAW, requires the States parties to comply with it especially the right to non-discrimination and equality.[139] Ironically, the reservations made to the CEDAW reflect patriarchal attitudes within the concerned States that permit persistence of a 'culture of violence' against women. It speaks volumes about the 'denial mode' pursued by the States parties in CEDAW reservations.[140] It seems CEDAW contains more reservations than any other IHR treaty. It shows resistance in the universal application of the human rights norms that also limits the accountability of the States under various IHR treaties.[141]

In this context, the cultural practices within the States parties remain subject to the limits circumscribed by the treaty-based tenets of human rights. As regards women's rights, cultural practices remain subject to the provision of the CEDAW and other

---

[135] UNESCO (2002), *Universal Declaration on Cultural Diversity 2001*; available at: https://unesdoc.unesco.org/ark:/48223/pf0000127162 (accessed on 08 August 2021).

[136] UN (2009), "Harmful Traditional Practices Against Women And Legislation", Expert paper by Morissanda Kouyate, UN Division for the Advancement of Women, UN Economic Commission for Africa; UN Doc. EGM/GPLHP/2009/EP.07 of 11 May 2009; available at: https://www.un.org/womenwatch/daw/egm/vaw_legislation_2009/Expert%20Paper%20EGMGPLHP%20_Morissanda%20Kouyate_.pdf (accessed on 15 August 2021).

[137] UN (2012), "Harmful Traditional Practices in Three Countries of South Asia: culture, human rights and violence against women; Economic and Social Commission for Asia and the Pacific Gender and Development Discussion Paper Series No. 21"; available at: https://www.unescap.org/resources/harmful-traditional-practices-three-countries-south-asia-culture-human-rights-and-violence (accessed on 15 August 2021).

[138] Raday, Frances (2003), n. 55.

[139] Ibid.

[140] Zaunbrecher Katie L (2011), n. 5.

[141] Mehra, Madhu (2007), n. 79.

relevant IHR instruments. As a result, the 'cultural rights'[142] and the 'religious rights'[143] are often used by the States parties to seek reprieve from the threshold laid down in the IHR norms.

Article 2(f) of the CEDAW requires the State parties to take all appropriate measures and policies to condemn and eliminate all forms of discrimination against women. The appropriate measures would include changes in customs and practices that constitute discrimination against women.[144] Article 5(a) of the CEDAW explicitly call upon the States parties to take all appropriate measures to eliminate customary and other practices that are based on inferiority and superiority between sexes.[145] The obligations of Articles 2(f) and 5(a) of the CEDAW are closely intertwined. Article 2(f) does impose an obligation on the States to intervene in cases of the gender-based discriminatory practices of the religious, cultural, or ethnic groups or communities.[146] Some scholars have argued in their commentary on the CEDAW that most of the States have made reservations to the provisions of Articles 2 and 5. Though Article 5 has a border ambit to eliminate discrimination against women, there is a lack of clarity on its implementation. However, CEDAW as a whole has been criticized for not effectively addressing systematic and structural discrimination against women.[147]

The Committee of the CEDAW, in its GR19, has focused on VAW. It has explained Articles 2(f) and 5 in the general comments and took note that VAW can be committed

---

[142] UN (1966), *International Covenant on Civil and Political Rights*; Article 27 (to enjoy their own culture, to profess and practice their own religion, or to use their own language); available at: https://treaties.un.org/doc/publication/unts/volume%20999/volume-999-i-14668-english.pdf. Also see UN (1948), *Universal Declaration of Human Rights*; Article 22 (right to social security; economic, social and cultural rights); Article 27 (right freely to participate in the cultural life of the community, to enjoy the arts and to share in scientific advancement); available at: https://www.un.org/en/udhrbook/pdf/udhr_booklet_en_web.pdf; UN OHCHR (1966), *Covenant of Economic Social and Cultural Rights 1966*; available at: https://www.ohchr.org/en/professionalinterest/pages/cescr.aspx (accessed on 15 August 2021).

[143] UN (1966), ICCPR Article 18(1) and UN (1948), UDHR, Preamble; available at: https://www.ohchr.org/EN/Issues/FreedomReligion/Pages/Standards.aspx (accessed on 15 August 2021).

[144] UN OHCHR (1979), *Convention of All Forms of Discrimination Against Women 1979*; Article 2(f) states: "States Parties condemn discrimination against women in all its forms, agree to pursue by all appropriate means and without delay a policy of eliminating discrimination against women and, to this end, undertake: (f) To take all appropriate measures, including legislation, to modify or abolish existing laws, regulations, customs and practices which constitute discrimination against women;" available at: https://www.ohchr.org/EN/ProfessionalInterest/Pages/CEDAW.aspx (accessed on 15 August 2021).

[145] UN OHCHR (1979); CEDAW Article 5(a) states: "States Parties shall take all appropriate measures: (a) To modify the social and cultural patterns of conduct of men and women, with a view to achieving the elimination of prejudices and customary and all other practices which are based on the idea of the inferiority or the superiority of either of the sexes or on stereotyped roles for men and women.".

[146] Mrsha, A. F. et al. (2012), "The UN Convention on Elimination of All Forms of Discrimination Against Women: A Commentary", in Marsha A. Freeman, Christine Chinkin, and Beate Rudolf Eds. (2012), *The UN Convention on Elimination of All Forms of Discrimination Against Women: A Commentary*, New York: Oxford University Press.

[147] Ibid.

by the States, organizations, and individuals. The GR19 has considered the States responsible even for the private acts, i.e. SGBV against women. It provides:

> It is emphasized, however, that discrimination under the Convention is not restricted to action by or on behalf of Governments (see articles 2(e), 2(f) and 5). For example, under article 2(e) the Convention calls on States parties to take all appropriate measures to eliminate discrimination against women by any person, organization or enterprise. Under general international law and specific human rights covenants, States may also be responsible for private acts if they fail to act with due diligence to prevent violations of rights or to investigate and punish acts of violence, and for providing compensation.[148]

The HCPs encourage GBV in the name of protection of women as:

> Traditional attitudes by which women are regarded as subordinate to men or as having stereotyped roles perpetuate widespread practices involving violence or coercion, such as family violence and abuse, forced marriage, dowry deaths, acid attacks and female circumcision. Such prejudices and practices may justify gender-based violence as a form of protection or control of women.[149]

GR28 also explains the obligations of the States parties under Article 2 of the CEDAW. Though it provides general legal obligations of the States, sub-paragraphs (a–g) of Article 2 provide for specific obligations of the States. Thus, the States parties need to fulfil the obligations of Article 2(f) within their domestic systems by making relevant laws for the purpose. It forms the essence and any reservation to it can be permissible only after explaining the practical reasons and the promise of withdrawing as soon as possible.[150]

In a significant step in 2014, the Joint GR/GC (revised *vide* CEDAW/C/GC/31/Rev.1–CRC/C/GC/18/Rev.1; 8 May 2019) of the CEDAW Committee (GR31) and CRC (GC18) sought to underscore and explain (CEDAW and CRC) the framework for the elimination of HPs . It states that Articles 2 and 3 of the CEDAW impose an obligation on the States parties to adopt legislation and policies to eliminate discrimination that gives rise to HPs and VAW. According to Article 4(1) of the CRC, the obligations of the States are of immediate nature and the inability cannot be justified by cultural and religious grounds. As such the States parties are obliged to eliminate CPs that are based on sex discrimination and stereotyped roles for men and women. It has made the child marriage illegal under Article 16(2). Under the caption of 'holistic framework for addressing harmful practices', the rationale has been explained thus:

---

[148] UN OHCHR (1992), "General Recommendation No. 19 (1992), paragraph 9"; Committee on the Elimination of Discrimination against Women, available at: https://www.ohchr.org/EN/HRBodies/CEDAW/Pages/Recommendations.aspx (accessed on 15 August 2021).

[149] UN OHCHR (1992), "General Recommendation No. 19, Articles 2(f), 5 and 10(c), paragraph 11.

[150] UN OHCHR (2010), General recommendation No. 28 on the core obligations of States parties under article 2 of the Convention on the Elimination of All Forms of Discrimination against Women, Committee on the Elimination of Discrimination against Women"; UN Doc. CEDAW/C/GC/28, 2010; available at: https://www.ohchr.org/EN/HRBodies/CEDAW/Pages/Recommendations.aspx (accessed on 15 August 2021).

> Both Conventions contain specific references to the elimination of harmful practices. States parties to the Convention on the Elimination of All Forms of Discrimination against Women are obliged to plan and adopt appropriate legislation, policies and measures and ensure that their implementation responds effectively to specific obstacles, barriers and resistance to the elimination of discrimination that give rise to harmful practices and violence against women (Arts. 2 and 3)…Furthermore, the obligation of States parties to pursue such targeted policies is of an immediate nature and States parties cannot justify any delay on any grounds, including cultural and religious grounds. States parties are also obliged to take all appropriate measures, including temporary special measures (Art. 4 (1)).[151]

Article 24(3) of the CRC, provides that States are obliged to take all effective and appropriate measures to abolish appropriate measures to eliminate TPs that are harmful to the health of children. Article 19 of the CRC provides for the right of the child to be protected from all forms of violence including sexual, psychological, and physical violence. Article 37(a) requires the States to prohibit torture, or other cruel, degrading or inhuman treatment. There are four general principles of CRC that ensure elimination of harmful cultural practices: (i) Article 2 on protection from discrimination; (ii) Article 3(1) on ensuring the best interests of the child; (iii) Article 6 on upholding the rights to life, survival, and development; and (iv) Article 12 on the right to be heard.[152] GR14 of CEDAW underscores the need for the elimination of female circumcision and other TPs that are harmful to the health of women. It recommends the States to include information about measures taken to eliminate female circumcision in their reports under Articles 10 and 12 of the CWDAW.[153]

Article 12(1) of the ICESCR[154] provides for the right of enjoyment of physical and mental health. The GC14 of the Committee on the ESCR provides for the normative

---

[151] UN OHCHR (2014), "Joint general recommendation No. 31 of the Committee on the Elimination of Discrimination against Women/General Comment No. 18 of the Committee on the Rights of the Child on harmful practices", paragraph VII; UN Doc. CEDAW/C/GC/31-CRC/C/GC/18, 2014; available at: https://www.ohchr.org/EN/HRBodies/CEDAW/Pages/Recommendations.aspx; https://documents-dds-ny.un.org/doc/UNDOC/GEN/N14/627/78/PDF/N1462778.pdf?OpenElement; https://documents-dds-ny.un.org/doc/UNDOC/GEN/N14/627/78/PDF/N1462778.pdf?OpenElement (accessed on 15 August 2021).

[152] UN OHCHR (1989), Article 32 of the Convention on the Rights of the Child obliges the States parties "to take all effective and appropriate measures with a view to abolishing traditional practices prejudicial to the health of children (Art. 24 (3)). In addition, it provides for the right of the child to be protected from all forms of violence, including physical, sexual or psychological violence (Art. 19) and requires States parties to ensure that no child is subjected to torture or other cruel, inhuman or degrading treatment or punishment (Art. 37 (a)). It applies the four general principles of the Convention to the issue of harmful practices, namely protection from discrimination (Art. 2), ensuring the best interests of the child (Art. 3 (1)), 15 upholding the right to life, survival and development (art. 6) and the right of the child to be heard (Art. 12); available at: https://www.ohchr.org/en/professionalinterest/pages/crc.aspx (accessed on 16 August 2021).

[153] UN OHCHE (1979), "General Recommendation 14 on "Female Circumcision"; available at: https://tbinternet.ohchr.org/Treaties/CEDAW/Shared%20Documents/1_Global/INT_CEDAW_GEC_3729_E.pdf (accessed on 16 August 2021).

[154] UN OHCHR (1966), *International Covenant of Economic, Social and Cultural Rights*, 1966; Article 12, 1 states: "The States Parties to the present Covenant recognize the right of everyone to the enjoyment of the highest attainable standard of physical and mental health;" available at: https://www.ohchr.org/en/professionalinterest/pages/cescr.aspx (accessed on 16 August 2021).

contents of Article 12(1) of the ICESCR. It is underscored that the right to 'health' includes both freedom (include control one's health and body) and entitlement (Right to get a system of equal opportunity for health).[155] The GC has explained the women's right to health under Article 12 by connecting it with different specific issues under the heading of "Specific topics of broad application." It has called for taking an action to "shield" women from the effect of HTCPs and norms that negate them from enjoyment of the full reproductive right.[156]

The growing corpus provisions on elimination of HCPs in IHR instruments (see Table 4.2) underscores the gravity of the situation and the need for concerted concrete international mechanism to uproot such HCPs as a form of SGBV against women.

Resolutions of the UN General Assembly

The General Assembly, as plenary organ of the UN, has played vanguard role in protection and promotion of women's fundamental human rights. It is logical corollary to the UN's foundational purposes and principles that include fundamental freedoms and human rights. In its 1993 Declaration, the Assembly considered all forms of harmful traditional, cultural practices or customary practices are prejudicial to the human rights of women and declared:

> Gender-based violence and all forms of sexual harassment and exploitation, including those resulting from cultural prejudice, are incompatible with the dignity and worth of the human person and which stresses the importance of working towards the eradication of any conflicts which may arise between the rights of women and the harmful effects of certain traditional or customary practices[157].

In this context, the Assembly has called upon the States to "condemn violence against women and should not invoke any custom, tradition or religious consideration to avoid their obligations with respect to its elimination".[158] Hence, HCPs

---

[155] UN OCHHR (2000), "8. The right to health is not to be understood as a right to be healthy. The right to health contains both freedoms and entitlements. The freedoms include the right to control one's health and body, including sexual and reproductive freedom, and the right to be free from interference, such as the right to be free from torture, non-consensual medical treatment and experimentation. By contrast, the entitlements include the right to a system of health protection which provides equality of opportunity for people to enjoy the highest attainable level of health;" see CESCR General Comment No. 14: The Right to the Highest Attainable Standard of Health (Art. 12); adopted at the Twenty-second Session of the Committee on Economic, Social and Cultural Rights on 11 August 2000, UN Doc. E/C.12/2000/4); available at: https://www.refworld.org/pdfid/4538838d0.pdf (accessed on 16 August 2021).

[156] UN OHCHR (2000), *ibid.* It states: "Women and the right to health: 21…It is also important to undertake preventive, promotive and remedial action to shield women from the impact of harmful traditional cultural practices and norms that deny them their full reproductive rights."

[157] UN (1998), "*General Assembly resolution 52/99 on Traditional or customary practices affecting the health of women and girls*"; UN Doc. A/RES/52/99, 1998; available at: https://research.un.org/en/docs/ga/quick/regular/52; https://undocs.org/en/A/RES/52/99 (accessed on 19 August 2021).

[158] UN OHCHR (1993), *Declaration on the Elimination of Violence against Women 1993;* Article 4 of the; General Assembly resolution 48/104; UN Doc. A/RES/48/104, 20 December 1993; available at: https://www.ohchr.org/EN/ProfessionalInterest/Pages/ViolenceAgainstWomen.aspx (accessed on 18 August 2021).

Table 4.2 Comparative Picture of Provisions for HCPs in International Human Right Instruments

No	International mechanisms to end harmful cultural practices	Specific provision/articles	Terminology used to address HCP	Regulatory mechanism
1	UN Convention on the Elimination of All Forms of Discrimination against Women, 1979	Article 2(f)	Customs and practices	Appropriate measures to modify or abolish
		Article 5(a)	Social and cultural patterns of conduct; customary and all other practices	Appropriate measures to modify, eliminate
2	General recommendations of CEDAW	General recommendation No. 14 (1990): Female circumcision	Female circumcision and other harmful traditional practices; traditional practices;	Important action by groups supported by the government; appropriate and effective measures to eradicate; a collection of data; elimination of practices; cooperation especially religious and community leaders, media, etc.; education and tanning; research and funding; adoption of appropriate policies and strategies; UN assistance, a report by the State parties under CEDAW
		General recommendation No. 19 (1992); (Article 2.5 and 5.a): Violence against women	Traditional attitudes, practices involving violence or coercion	States to take positive measures to eliminate all forms of violence against women. States parties to take all appropriate measures to eliminate discrimination against women by any person, organization or enterprise

(continued)

Table 4.2 (continued)

No	International mechanisms to end harmful cultural practices	Specific provision/articles	Terminology used to address HCP	Regulatory mechanism
		General recommendation No. 18 (2010): on the core obligations of States parties under Article 2 of the Convention on the Elimination of All Forms of Discrimination against Women (General Comments 9, 31, and 33)	Customary and all other practices, custom, and practices, women are vulnerable to certain customary law and practices	States' obligation to eliminate by modify and abolish; Courts should draw the attention of appropriate authority[159]
3	The Child Rights Convention, 1989	Article 24(3)	Traditional practices	Effective and appropriate measures to abolish
4	Joint general recommendation/general comment of the CEDAW Committee and the Committee on the Rights of the Child Committee, 2014	GR No.31 of the CEDAW Committee and GR No 18 of the CRC Committee ((revised *vide* CEDAW/C/GC/31/Rev.1–CRC/C/GC/18/Rev.1; 8 May 2019)	Harmful practices	Elimination of harmful practices by law; address HP faced by both girls' boys as gender-based violence. Sanction and criminalize HP by States; adoption of right-based social and cultural norms; empowerment of women and girls; awareness and public dialogue; etc

[159] UN CEDAW (2010), "General Recommendation 18"; UN Doc. CEDAW/C/GC/28 of 16 December 2010, paragraph 33, page 7; available at: https://www.refworld.org/docid/4d467ea72.html (accessed on 18 August 2021). CEDAW Committee has referred to harmful practices in nine of its General Recommendations, including GR No. 3 (1987) on the implementation of article 5 of the Convention, GR No. 14 (1990) on female genital mutilation, GR No. 19 (1992) on violence against women, GR No. 21 (1994) on equality in marriage and family relations, GR No. 24 (1999) on women and health, GR No. 25 (2004) on temporary special measures, GR No. 28 (2010) on the core obligations of States parties under article 2 of the Convention, GR No. 29 (2013) on economic consequences of marriage, family relations and their dissolution as well as GR No. 30 (2013) on women in conflict prevention, conflict and post-conflict situations. In its General Comment No. 8 (2006) on the right of the child to protection from corporal punishment and other cruel or degrading forms of punishment and in GC No. 13 (2011) on the right of the child to freedom from all forms of violence, the CRC Committee provides a non-exhaustive list of harmful practices.

have come on the UNGA's radar screen. It has explicitly sought to address such HCPs in successive resolutions. In fact, various formulations used over a period of time indicates an evolution in thematically addressing HCPs within the larger global challenge of SGBV (see Table 4.3). Notwithstanding the format and 'recomendatory' nature of the UNGA resolutions, it underscores gradual crystallization of the normative threshold. The break-up of three main themes is expalined herein in a tabular form, through three parameters, followed by a normative analysis.

A. **Traditional and customary practices affecting the health of women and girls (1997–2001)**

(i) ***GA resolution 52/99 (1997)***[160]

This resolution sought to make a reference to all the relevant resolutions of the GA, ECOSOC; reports of the Commission on Human Rights; reports of the Special Rapporteur of the Sub-Commission on Prevention of Discrimination and Protection of Minorities on traditional practices affecting the health of women and children.[161] It also took note of all the UN regional seminars on the HTPs,[162] and the Beijing Declaration and the existing IHR instruments that seek to prohibit HTPs.

The resolution emphatically held that certain traditional or customary practices affecting the health of women and girls constitute a definite form of violence against women and girls and a serious violation of their human rights. It expressed concern at the continuing large-scale existence of such practices. Hence, it made a special reference to the practices of FGM as HCP against women and children.[163] It called for adoption of national legislations and policies to prevent HCPs and take appropriate measures against the responsible persons.[164]

The GA resolution 52/99 included the need for economic independence of women, education, and awareness of the people of all sectors of the society about the HCPs.[165]

---

[160] Ibid,.

[161] Ibid, GAR 52/99, preambular paragraph (a), p. 1. It made reference to the following: "(a) General Assembly resolution 843 (IX) of 17 December 1954, Economic and Social Council resolution 1997/24 of 21 July 1997, Commission on Human Rights decision 1997/108 of 22 August 1997,1 and Sub-commission on Prevention of Discrimination and Protection of Minorities resolutions 1983/1 of 23 August 1983,2 1995/20 of 24 August 1995,3 1996/19 of 29 August 19,964 and 1997/8 of 22 August 1997,5 (b) The reports of the Special Rapporteur of the Sub-commission on Prevention of Discrimination and Protection of Minorities on traditional practices affecting the health of women and children and of the Special Rapporteur of the Commission on Human Rights on violence against women, its causes and consequences."

[162] Ibid, preambular paragraph (c), p. 2. It stated: "(c) The reports of the United Nations Regional Seminars on Traditional Practices Affecting the Health of Women and Children, which were held in Burkina Faso in 1991 and Sri Lanka in 1994 and the Plan of Action for the Elimination of Harmful Traditional Practices Affecting the Health of Women and Children."

[163] Ibid, p. 3. It stated: "1. (a) The progress achieved by a number of Governments in their struggle against harmful traditional or customary practices, in particular against female genital mutilation, and encourages the Governments in question to continue and to increase their efforts aimed at the eradication of these practices."

[164] Ibid, paragraph 2 (a), p. 4.

[165] Ibid, paragraph 2 (d), p. 4.

Table 4.3 Showing Comparative Picture of the UNGA resolutions on HCPs as SGBV against Women

No	Themes	Resolutions	Terminology used	Nature of violation	Regulatory mechanisms
1	Intensifying global efforts for the elimination of female genital mutilations	67/146(2012)	FGM is harmful practice[166]	Violence against women	Empowerment of women and girls; awareness and education; condemn all harmful practices by States; punitive measures; end impunity; national action plans and strategies; policies and consultation with communities; an effective legislative framework to eliminate; a collection of data; allocation of resources; participation of women and boys.
2	Crimes Committed in the name of honour (2000–2004)	55/66 (2000)	Crimes against honour	Human rights violation and violence against women; a crime against women	Punishment; cooperation; empowerment of women; adoption, amendment, and implementation of the law; supportive services to the victims; strengthen and facilitate institutional mechanism.

(continued)

[166] UN (2012), the General Assembly resolution 67/146 reaffirmed that "female genital mutilations are a harmful practice that constitutes a serious threat to the health of women and girls, including their psychological, sexual and reproductive health, which can increase their vulnerability to HIV and may have adverse obstetric and prenatal outcomes as well as fatal consequences for the mother and the newborn, and that the abandonment of this harmful practice can be achieved as a result of a comprehensive movement that involves all public and private stakeholders in society, including girls and boys, women and men"; UN Doc. A/RES/67/146 of 20 December 2012; available at: https://research.un.org/en/docs/ga/quick/regular/67; https://undocs.org/en/A/RES/67/146 (accessed on 21 August 2021).

Table 4.3 (continued)

No	Themes	Resolutions	Terminology used	Nature of violation	Regulatory mechanisms
		57/179 (2002)	Crime against honour	As above	Commitment to eliminate by all especially governments; effective participation of women in decision-making; using administrative, legislative and programmatic measures; prompt and thorough investigation; awareness.
		59/165 (2004)	Violence against women and girls including crimes committed in the name of honour	Failure of States' obligation violates and impairs or nullifies the enjoyment of human rights and fundamental freedoms	Address root causes; greater effects and commitment from the part of the governments; engagement of media.
3	Traditional and customary practices affecting the health of women and girls (1997–2001)	52/99, (1997)	Traditional or customary practices; harmful traditional or customary practices[167]	A form of violence against women and girls; serious violation of human rights	Analyse policy and programmers from a gender perspective; national legislation; promote economic independence; education and awareness; men's participation; financial and technical assistance to developing nations.

(continued)

[167] UN (1998), the GA resolution 52/99; UN Doc. A/RES/52/99, 9 February 1998, paragraph 2 (b) stated: "The need for national legislation and/or measures prohibiting harmful traditional or customary practices as well as for their implementation, inter alia, through appropriate measures against those responsible"; available at: https://research.un.org/en/docs/ga/quick/regular/52; https://undocs.org/en/A/RES/52/99 (accessed on 19 August 2021).

Table 4.3 (continued)

No	Themes	Resolutions	Terminology used	Nature of violation	Regulatory mechanisms
		53/117 (1998)	Traditional practices; traditional or customary practices; harmful traditional or customary practices	As above	Commitments from all to eliminate; inclusion about its harmful effect in the education curricula; involves leaders, e.g. religious leaders; consultation with religious and cultural groups etc.; compilation of updated statistics; etc.
		54/133 (1999)	Cultural practices; traditional or customary practices; harmful practices;	Serious violation of human rights	Collection of data; provide services to the victims; promote men's understanding roles; etc.
		56/128 (2001)	Harmful traditional and customary practices; harmful traditional practices;	As above	As above.

It also called for the involvement of public opinion leaders, religious leaders, medical practitioners, educators, women's health and family planning organizations, media, to spread awareness for "promoting a collective and individual awareness of the human rights of women and girls and of how harmful traditional or customary practices violate those rights".[168] The resolution called upon all the States to implement and ratify the existing human rights treaties that deal with the harmful traditional practices, female genital mutilation, and other forms of customary practices.[169]

(ii) ***GA resolution 53/117 (1998)***[170]

This resolution reaffirmed all the development at the UN and the IHR instruments till 1998 relating to VAW as well as HCPs. It also reaffirmed that the continued existence of large-scale HCPs inherently constitutes VAW and a violation of the women's fundamental human rights.[171] It called for efforts and commitments by the governments, international community, and civil societies to eliminate the HCPs.[172] It focused on the inclusion of human rights of women and addresses the issue of HPs in the primary and secondary education curricula.[173] It called for involvement of the leaders, as 1997 resolution, including traditional leaders[174] as well as to explore harmful alternative practices through consultation with religious and cultural groups and their leaders.[175]

(iii) ***GA resolution 54/133 (1999)***[176]

It sought to focus on the same theme as was addressed in the previous two resolutions (53/117 and 52/99). The resolution included the terms such as HPs and CPs separately as well as in conjunction as HCPs.[177] It called upon all the States to collect and circulate basic data regarding the effect of HCPs such as FGM that has harmful effects on the health of women and children.[178] It also called for promotion of understanding, roles, and responsibilities of men to eliminate the HPs [179] as well as need for special focus on immigrant and refugee women and children regarding the FGM practice.[180]

---

[168] Ibid, paragraph 2 (e), p. 4.

[169] Ibid, paragraph 3 (b), p. 4.

[170] UN (1999), General Assembly resolution 53/117; UN Doc.A/RES/53/117, 1999; available at: https://research.un.org/en/docs/ga/quick/regular/53 (accessed on 19 August 2021).

[171] Ibid, preamble, page 2.

[172] Ibid, preamble, page 2.

[173] Ibid, paragraph 3 (e), page 3.

[174] Ibid, paragraph 3 (f), page 3.

[175] Ibid, paragraph 3 (g), page 3.

[176] UN (2000), General Assembly resolution 54/133; UN Doc. A/RES/54/133, 2000; available at: https://research.un.org/en/docs/ga/quick/regular/54 (accessed on 20 August 2021).

[177] Ibid, preamble, page 2.

[178] Ibid, paragraph 3 (c), page 4.

[179] Ibid, paragraph 3 (i), page 4.

[180] Ibid, paragraph 3 (k), page 4.

(iv) *GA resolution 56/128 (2001)*[181]

It covered all the existing soft and hard international law instruments concerning HCPs. While reaffirming the UNGA resolution 54/133, it expressed concern at "continuing large-scale existence of these practices", construed HCPs as a "serious threat to the health of women and girls and may have fatal consequences" especially since these practices also lead to HIV/AIDS and other sexually transmitted diseases.[182] It called upon the States to spread awareness for elimination of HCPs by involving all the organizations that already mentioned in the previous resolutions including "chiefs, teachers, social workers, childcare agencies, relevant non-governmental organizations, the arts, and the media in awareness-raising campaigns".[183]

The above discussion shows that the main focus of the GA resolutions until 2001 was to address the issue of CPs that are harmful to the health of women and children. They give a specific focus to FGM as one of the global human rights concerns. It is the responsibility of the States to take all the measures to punish the perpetrators as well as spreading awareness regarding these HCPs. In the process the UNGA has come up with a series of measures to bring about procedural and structural changes to eliminate the HCPs. These include adoption, ratification and implementation of all the existing soft and hard international law instruments; enactment of national legislation and policies by the states; negotiations regarding adoption of alternative TPs that are good for all; spreading awareness among all members and groups of the community or society; international cooperation among States, international organizations, civil societies, national organizations; and sharing of informational and funding.

B. Crimes Committed against women in the name of honour (2000–2004)

C. *GA resolution 55/66 (2000)*[184]

It has been a high watermark in the practice of the UNGA to construe and equate HCPs as a 'crime against honour'. It underscores seriousness in addressing HCP as a crime of high order against the human persona of women. Hence, by giving a high priority to the HCPs as a serious violation of human rights, the UNGA expects the States to take appropriate steps since:

> crimes against women committed in the name of honour are a human rights issue and that States have an obligation to exercise due diligence to prevent, investigate and punish the perpetrators of such crimes and to provide protection to the victims, and that the failure to do so constitutes a human rights violation.[185]

It has been noticed that "inadequate understanding of the root causes of all violence against women" presents a problem for domestic and international policy-making in addressing SGBV against women. Therefore, for the purposes of elimination of

---

[181] UN (2002), General Assembly resolution 56/128; UN Doc. A/RES/56/128, 2002; available at: https://research.un.org/en/docs/ga/quick/regular/56 (accessed on 20 August 2021).

[182] Ibid, preamble, page 2.

[183] Ibid, paragraph 3 (i), page 4.

[184] UN (2001), General Assembly resolution 55/66; UN Doc. A/RES/55/66 (2001); available at: https://research.un.org/en/docs/ga/quick/regular/55 (accessed on 20 August 2021).

[185] Ibid, preambular paragraph 3, p. 1.

SGBV under the garb of so-called 'honour' will require greater efforts and commitment from the government and the international community, international cooperation among civil society including NGOs, and community organizations. In order to bring about a change in the attitude of the respective societies, "empowerment of women" will constitute an important tool.[186]

The UNGA has called upon the States to prevent and eliminate crime against honour by using "legislative, educational, social and other measures, dissemination of information" as well as involvement of "public opinion leaders, religious leaders, chiefs, and traditional leaders, chief, and the media in awareness-raising campaign."[187] It will also necessitate active role of the law enforcing agencies, e.g. police, judiciary, health personnel to implement laws relating to honour crimes and understanding the causes and consequences of crimes against honour.[188] Apart from this, the States need to "establish, strengthen or facilitate where possible support service" to the victims of honour crimes by providing them "appropriate protection, safe shelter, counselling, legal aid, rehabilitation, and reintegration into society."[189] Cumulatively, it will require robust and sensitive institutional mechanisms to enable the victims of HCPs to report the crimes in a safe and secure environment.[190]

(ii) ***GA resolution 57/179 (2002)***[191]

This resolution called upon the States to fulfil their obligation to exercise due diligence to prevent, investigate and punish the perpetrators and provide protection to the victims of "crimes against women committed in the name of honour".[192] In turn, it has regarded all forms of VAW including honour crimes as a criminal offence. Moreover, such crimes against honour are incompatible with religious and cultural values.[193] Taking a refreshing view, the UNGA called for "empowerment of women and their effective participation in decision-making" processes as "critical tools to prevent and eliminate crimes against women committed in the name of honour".[194] The initiatives that a State can take for "elimination of all other forms of violence against women" can include "adoption of amendments to relevant national laws relating to such crimes; effective implementation of such laws; education; and other measures."[195] It also expressed concern that "women continue to be victims of crimes committed in the name of honour" and such violence takes many different forms, and there are "failures to prosecute and punish perpetrators".[196]

---

[186] Ibid, preambular paragraph 4, p. 2.

[187] Ibid, paragraph 4 (b), p. 3.

[188] Ibid, paragraph 4 (c), p. 3.

[189] Ibid, paragraph 4 (d), p. 3.

[190] Ibid, paragraph 4 (e), p. 3.

[191] UN (2003), General Assembly resolution 57/179; UN Doc. A/RES/57/179 (2003); available at: https://undocs.org/en/A/RES/57/179; http://www.undocs.org/A/RES/57/179 (accessed on 21 August 2021).

[192] Ibid, preambular paragraph 3, p. 1.

[193] Ibid, preambular paragraph 4, p. 2.

[194] Ibid, preambular paragraph 7, p. 2.

[195] Ibid, paragraph 1 (a), p. 2.

[196] Ibid, paragraph 2, p. 3.

(iii) *GA resolution 59/165 (2004)*[197]

In reiterating the previous UNGA resolutions (58/185 and 57/190), this resolution called upon all the States to prevent and eliminate crimes against honour as well as "investigate promptly and thoroughly, prosecute effectively and document cases of crimes against women and girls committed in the name of honour and punish the perpetrators."[198] It called for making efforts to spread awareness among men about their responsibility to "promote gender equality" and "eliminate gender stereotypes."[199] It encouraged media to spread awareness as well as to provide training to the person responsible for enforcing the law to respond positively in cases of complaints relating to honour crimes.[200] It also sought to institutionalize a mechanism to provide appropriate protection, legal aid, and counselling, health care services to respond to the "needs of actual and potential victims" in the society.[201]

C. Elimination of female genital mutilations (2012)[202]

It has affected some 200 million women and girls worldwide. In 2022, some 4.2 million girls are expected to be at risk of undergoing FGM. The UNGA resolution 67/146 (2012) has covered a wide range of international legal instruments for protection of the rights of women and the children. The resolution has recalled the previous UNGA resolutions (such as 53/117 of 9 December 1998 and 56/128 of 19 December 2001) as well as Commission on the Status of Women resolutions (such as 51/2 of 9 March 2007, 1 52/2 of 7 March 2008 and 54/7 of 12 March 2010). Apart from the global conventions on women and children (such as CEDAW and CRC), it reaffirmed a wide range of international declarations, conference statements, programmes of actions and other actions taken by the UN.[203] It has recalled the Protocol to the African Charter on Human and People's Rights of Women in Africa 2003; the decision (1 July 2011) of the African Union for the adoption of GA resolution on banning female genital mutilation.[204] This landmark resolution has construed that "Female genital mutilations are an irreparable, irreversible abuse that impacts negatively on the human rights of women and girls.[205] It has been explicitly held as "a harmful practice that constitutes a serious threat to the health of women and girls, including their psychological, sexual and reproductive health".[206]

---

[197] UN (2004), General Assembly resolution 59/165; UN Doc. A/RES/59/165 of 20 December 2004; available at: https://research.un.org/en/docs/ga/quick/regular/59; https://undocs.org/en/A/RES/59/165 (accessed on 21 August 2021).

[198] Ibid, paragraph 3 (c) p. 3.

[199] Ibid, paragraph 3 (d) p. 3.

[200] Ibid, paragraph 3 (f) and (g), p. 3.

[201] Ibid, paragraph 3 (i), p. 3.

[202] UN (2012), General Assembly resolution 67/146; UN Doc. A/RES/67/146 of 20 December 2012; available at: https://research.un.org/en/docs/ga/quick/regular/67; https://undocs.org/en/A/RES/67/146 (accessed on 21 August 2021).

[203] Ibid, preambular paragraphs 3–6, p. 1–2.

[204] Ibid, preambular paragraphs 4–5, p. 2.

[205] Ibid, preambular paragraph 7, p. 2.

[206] Ibid, preambular paragraph 8, p. 2.

The negative stereotypes towards women constitute the bar to implement the laws relating to the prohibition of sexual discrimination.[207] Funding and gaps in resources remain the problems to implement different programmes that can help in the elimination of FGM. It has regarded empowerment of women as one of the important tools that can eliminate this harmful practice.[208] As a corollary, the resolution called upon the States to eliminate it through a series of concrete steps such as spreading awareness; legislative actions; complementing punitive actions; protection and support to the women subjected to FGM; gender-sensitive education; national policies, action plans, strategies and legislations; cultural sensitiveness; and implementing national and international commitments and obligations relating to women's human rights etc.[209]

Is FGM an Essential Cultural Practice?

As a corollary to the intense debate on the cultural facet of the FGM practice, it has been sought to be countered by the argument that FGM is an 'essential cultural practice' or 'essential religious practice' (e.g. *Sunita Tiwari vs. Union of India, 2017).* What is an essential cultural or religious practice? Does 'violence' constitute an integral part and comes within the ambit of such practices? What are the criteria for adjudging an essential practice? What will be the test of essentiality?[210]

In the context of a major legal challenge to FGM in India, the whole issue has been interpreted in many cases from the colonial era to this present date. The SC of India has tried to give a modernist and rationalist definition of essential religious practice. The essential practice test has been decided by the Indian Supreme Court in various cases.[211] The *Sati* Regulation 1829 stated:

> that all classes of the people be secure in the observance of their religious usages, so long as that system can be adhered to without violation of the paramount dictates of justice and humanity…[212]

---

[207] Ibid., preambular paragraphs 10, p. 2.

[208] Ibid, paragraphs 3–4, pp. 3–4.

[209] Ibid, pp. 3–6.

[210] Desai, Bharat H. and Mandal, Moumita (2020), "On Elimination of Female Genital Mutilation: Making International Institutions Work", *Indian Journal of International Law,* vol.61, no.3–4, pp. 195–229 at p. 213 Also see *Sunita Tiwari v Union of India,* W.P.(C) No. 000286/2017; public interest litigation hearing on 24 September 2018; available at: https://indiankanoon.org/doc/181206322/ (accessed on 21 August 2021).

[211] Sen, Rononjay (2010), *Articles of Faith: Religion, Secularism, and the Indian Supreme Court,* New Delhi: Oxford.

[212] *Sati Regulation XVII, AD 1829 the Bengal Code*; Also see, Kumar Radha (1993), *The History of Doing an Illustrated Account of Movements for Women's Rights and Feminism in India 1800–1990,* New Delhi: Oxford at 10; available at: https://www.indiaofthepast.org/east-india-company/major-events-pre-1950/sati-ban-regulation-december-1829. The Indian Parliament enacted the Commission of Sati (Prevention) Act 1987; available at: https://wcd.nic.in/commission-sati-prevention-act-1987-3-1988-excluding-administration-criminal-justice-regard-offences (accessed on 21 August 2021).

In *Shayara Bano* Case (*Triple talaq* case), the Indian Supreme Court observed that "every sustainable (and enforceable) religious practice must satisfy the overarching constitutional goal of gender equality, gender justice, and dignity." The Court cited different cases to establish the criteria for testing an 'essential' religious practice. It appears that if the fundamentals of the religion do not change after taking away a part of it, that part would remain not essential.[213] In fact a cultural or religious practice does not remain static. As it has seen, the practice of *Sati* was abolished (initially in 1829 and then again in 1987) as it was considered contrary to the societal change and regarded as a violation of the fundamental human rights of women and girls.

Similarly, the preamble to the UN Convention on Consent to Marriage, Minimum Age for Marriage and Registration of Marriage, 1962[214] and the UNGA resolution 843(IX), 17 December 1954[215] reaffirmed and declared abolition of customs, ancient laws and practices relating to marriage that are inconsistent with the principles of the Charter of the UN and the UDHR. The resolution 843(IX) emphatically stated that:

> the elimination of such customs, ancient laws and practices would tend to the recognition of the human dignity of women and contribute to the benefit of the family as an institution.[216]

Thus, FGM is already recognized and declared as a harmful cultural or traditional practice that is in violation of IHRL. Hence, it needs to be abolished as it cannot be considered as an essential cultural or traditional or religious practice.[217] In early 2020, the issue of what constitutes an 'essential religious practices' (including FGM practised by the *Dawoodi Bohra* community) has been referred to a nine-Judge Constitution Bench of the Indian Supreme Court.[218] There are several other jurisdictions where FGM has come to be legally proscribed.

In July 2020, the United Nations Population Fund (UNFPA) sought to explain: Is FGM required by certain religions? It is stated that there is no religion that promotes or

---

[213] *Shayara Bano v. Union of India*, Writ Petition (C) No. 118 (2016), available at: https://main.sci.gov.in/supremecourt/2016/6716/6716_2016_Judgement_22-Aug-2017.pdf (accessed on 21 August 2021).

[214] UN Treaty Collections (1962), *the UN Convention on Consent to Marriage, Minimum Age for Marriage and Registration of Marriage*, (10 December 1962) 521 United Nations, Treaty Series at 231, available at: https://treaties.un.org/doc/Treaties/1964/12/19641223%2002-15%20AM/Ch_XVI_3p.pdf (accessed on 21 August 2021).

[215] UN General Assembly (1954), "Status of women in private law: customs, ancient laws and practices affecting the human dignity of women", U.N. Doc. A/RES/843, (17 December 1954), available at: https://www.refworld.org/docid/3b00f07d20.html (accessed on 21 August 2021).

[216] UN General Assembly (1954), Ibid., preambular paragraph 3.

[217] UN OHCHR (1995), "Fact Sheet No.23, Harmful Traditional Practices Affecting the Health of Women and Children;" available at: https://www.refworld.org/docid/479477410.html (accessed on 21 August 2021).

[218] Supreme Court (2017), *Sunita Tiwari v. Union of India,* Diary No-936 (2017), Case Status/Stage: Pending (Motion Hearing Nine Judges Bench Matters) List On (Date) (18-02-2020)-Ord dt:17-02-2020, available at: https://main.sci.gov.in/jonew/cl/2020-02-06/F_J_1_1_20440.pdf (accessed on 21 August 2021). Also see, Outlook India (2020), "Nine-judge SC bench to frame issues related to discrimination against women in religions", 02 February 2020, available at: https://www.outlookindia.com/newsscroll/ninejudge-sc-bench-to-frame-issues-related-to-discrimination-against-women-in-religions-on-monday/1724403 (accessed on 21 August 2021).

condones FGM, yet, it is practiced by invoking tenets of religions. As it is practised by some religious group of people, it does not mean it is an essential religious practice and all should follow it. The available data shows that it is practised by people belonging to different religions and followers of their own traditions. Thus, FGM and other HPs are cultural rather than religious as no religion could support such HCP.[219] In fact cultural practices cannot be used to condone or permit violence in any form against women, men or LGBTIs community.

The above discussion amply shows that culture or cultural practices do not remain static or are not cast in stone. There is a need for heightened social awareness about the harmful effects of cultural practices, developing positive cultural practices, adoption of laws and policies and institutional mechanisms to bring about changes in the mindset of the people. The authors have called for elimination of FGM,[220] as one the HCPs.

Resolutions of the Human Rights Council

The Human Rights Council (HRC) gave due attention to examining role of culture in the realm of protection and promotion of human rights. As a subsidiary organ of the UNGA, the HRC plays a decisive role in realization of the mandate of the UN Charter. Among a host of initiatives under the Special Procedures, the HRC took initiative to appoint an independent expert *vide* resolution A/HRC/RES/10/23 on 26 March 2009. It laid down the mandate as follows:

(a) To identify best practices in the promotion and protection of cultural rights at the local, national, regional and international levels;

(b) To identify possible obstacles to the promotion and protection of cultural rights, and to submit proposals and/or recommendations to the Council on possible actions in that regard;

(c) To work in cooperation with States in order to foster the adoption of measures at the local, national, regional and international levels aimed at the promotion and protection of cultural rights through concrete proposals enhancing subregional, regional and international cooperation in that regard;

(d) To study the relationship between cultural rights and cultural diversity, in close collaboration with States and other relevant actors, including in particular the United Nations Educational, Scientific and Cultural Organization, with the aim of further promoting cultural rights;

(e) To integrate a gender and disabilities perspective into his and her work;

---

219 UNFPA (2020), *Female Genital Mutilation*; available at: https://www.unfpa.org/resources/female-genital-mutilation-fgm-frequently-asked-questions (accessed on 21 August 2021).

220 Desai, Bharat H. and Mandal, Moumita (2020), "On the Elimination of Female Genital Mutilation: Making International Human Rights Law Work", *Indian Journal of International Law*, vol.61, no.3–4, pp. 195–229.

(f) To work in close coordination, while avoiding unnecessary duplication, with intergovernmental and non-governmental organizations, other special procedures of the Council, the Committee on Economic, Social and Cultural Rights and the United Nations Educational, Scientific and Cultural Organization, as well as with other relevant actors representing the broadest possible range of interests and experiences, within their respective mandates, including by attending and following up on relevant international conferences and events.

During the period of 2009 and 2021, the HRC has adopted 13 resolutions on cultural rights (see Table 4.4) that also saw transformation of the role of the 'independent expert' (A/HRC/RES/10/23 of 26 March 2009) into the 'special rapporteur' (A/HRC/RES/46/9 of 23 March 2021).

Table 4.4 Resolutions of the Human Rights Council on Cultural Rights[221]

HRC Session	Symbol	Title
46th (Feb.–March 2021)	A/HRC/RES/46/9	Mandate of Special Rapporteur in the field of cultural rights
43rd (Feb.–March 2020)	A/HRC/RES/43/9	Promotion of the enjoyment of the cultural rights of everyone and respect for cultural diversity
40th (March 2019)	A/HRC/RES/40/6	Promotion of the enjoyment of the cultural rights of everyone and respect for cultural diversity
37th (March 2018)	A/HRC/RES/37/12	Mandate of the Special Rapporteur in the field of cultural rights
34th (March 2017)	A/HRC/RES/34/2	Promotion of the enjoyment of the cultural rights of everyone and respect for cultural diversity
31st (March 2016)	A/HRC/RES/31/12	Promotion of the enjoyment of the cultural rights of everyone and respect for cultural diversity
28th (March 2015)	A/HRC/RES/28/9	Mandate of the Special Rapporteur in the field of cultural rights
25th (March 2014)	A/HRC/RES/25/19	Promotion of the enjoyment of the cultural rights of everyone and respect for cultural diversity
23rd (June 2013)	A/HRC/RES/23/10	Promotion of the enjoyment of the cultural rights of everyone and respect for cultural diversity
20th (June 2012)	A/HRC/RES/20/11	Promotion of the enjoyment of the cultural rights of everyone and respect for cultural diversity
17th (June 2011)	A/HRC/RES/17/15	Promotion of the enjoyment of the cultural rights of everyone and respect for cultural diversity
14th (June 2010)	A/HRC/RES/14/9	Promotion of the enjoyment of the cultural rights of everyone and respect for cultural diversity
10th (June 2009)	A/HRC/RES/10/23	Independent expert in the field of cultural rights

221 UN OHCHR, *Resolutions of the Human Rights Council*; available at: https://www.ohchr.org/EN/Issues/CulturalRights/Pages/MandateInfo.aspx (accessed on 12 September 2021).

The above role and contribution of the HRC is significant as regards crystallization of the scope and elaboration of series of cultural aspects that constitute and present a challenge of SGBV against women. Hence, the invocation of the SR process concerning exercise of cultural rights is crucial in the articulation and the application of the HRC's actions for the elimination of HCPs as one of the forms of SGBV against women.

Conclusion

Since culture represents the past of a people, it is likely to be used for HCPs that can violate the fundamental human rights of women and girls. In fact, culture need to be taken as a symbol or identity instead of being used as a tool to sanction any kind of VAW. Any practice that falls within the ambit of SGBV is contrary to the modern tenets of IHRL. It can be said that within a particular culture two types of cultures coexist: one culture that is good for all and carries identity of the people, another culture that is also known as 'patriarchal culture' and violates rights of a group of people. This differentiation can also raise a question as regards the culture that supports VAW. Can it be called culture at all? The world is full of diverse cultures, so, it is very difficult to identify HCPs without mass participation of women.

There are many unidentified HCPs that also violate the rights of women and girls. Only education and women's participation in the entire decision-making process can help to eradicate culture-based SGBV against women. The term HCP, however, makes States reluctant to acknowledge the SGBV against women. The use of term HPs may get acceptance of more States. Ironically, in most of the cases, culture is used as a shield to justify 'harmful practices.' The existing corpus of international law is not enough to put an end to this pernicious practice. Thus, there is a need for specific international legal instrument to address SGBV including HCP within its ambit. The extension of the mandate and the appointment (on 30 August 2021), by the President of the UN-HRC, of the SR in the field of cultural rights[222] is a testimony to its active engagement. It calls for progression in crystallization of a specialized legal instrument by the HRC and the UNGA for the elimination of HCPs and HPs against women.

---

[222] UN HCR (2021), "Letter from the President Nazhat S. Khan, Office of the President", 30 August 2021; available at: https://www.ohchr.org/Documents/HRBodies/SP/CallApplications/HRC48/Letter-from-HRC-President-list-SP-candidates-3-vacancies-HRC48.pdf (12 September 2021).

Chapter 5
Role of the International Institutions in Addressing SGBV

Introduction

International Institutions (IIs) have grown by leaps and bounds over the years because of their indespensible role for instituionalized international cooperation in the field of international law. In fact, most of them have taken birth from the 'functional' approach at work in addressing global *problematique*. Notwithstanding the "growing popular backlash against international cooperation",[1] the IIs have provided a vital fulcrum for the global order since their advent in the second half of the nineteenth century.

The IIs create a formal and functional relationship.[2] Hence, they have emerged as important actors for the global governance. In view of growing complexities of international life, IIs have been addressing issues and challenges in a wide range of areas such as human rights, environment, health, commerce, air and space, modern technology etc.[3]

Since the advent of the United Nations (UN) Charter, the member States have grown from original 51 to 193 today. Their quest for institutionalized structures for international cooperation to address global *problematique* has witnessed an unprecedented growth. These State entities need to design and put into place contours for the exercise of 'sovereignty within the law'[4] even as they seek to address different

[1] De Vries, E. Catherine, Hobolt B., Sara and Walter, Stefanie (2021), "Politicizing International Cooperation: The Mass Public, Political Entrepreneurs, and Political Opportunity Structures", *International Organization* 75, Spring 2021, pp. 306–32; available at: https://www.cambridge.org/core/journals/international-organization/article/politicizing-international-cooperation-the-mass-public-political-entrepreneurs-and-political-opportunity-structures/5AC864ED89ACF0DA390C558BECD58FCE (accessed on 23 August 2021).

[2] Duffield, John (2007), "What Are International Institutions?", *International Studies Review* 9: 1–22.

[3] Murthy, C.S.R. (2017), "India and Issues in Global Governance with Reference to Internet Governance", *International Studies* 51: (1–4).

[4] Larson, Arthur, Jenks, C. Wilfred et al. (1965), *Sovereignty within the Law*, Oceana Publications, Stevens & Sons, Dobbs Ferry N.Y., London.

B. H. Desai and M. Mandal, *Sexual and Gender-Based Violence in International Law*,
https://doi.org/10.1007/978-981-19-0894-1_5

issues through regulatory mechanisms. Thus, the emergence of IIs to cater to different areas of global concern has been the need of the hour. As such these IIs lubricate the global wheels of progress and serve as platforms for international cooperation, in a State-centric system, for designing norms, rules, processes, standard-setting and responsibility mechanisms through a marathon regulatory enterprize. In fact, without these IIs, an orderly functioning of the international system would almost be unthinkable as they serve as an instrumentality for orderly handling of the complex global challenges faced by the humankind.

Many of the IIs have been formed under the umbrella of the UN system.[5] There is a corpus of institutions that have come to be christened as international organizations (IOs) upon fulfilment of some specific requirements. So, all the IOs are IIs but all the IIs may not necessarily be IOs. However, for the purposes of this study both the phrases - IIs and IOs - have been used interchangeably.

IIs are actively involved in the "creation, monitoring, and enforcement of international norms and rules that frame, shape, and structure national policy deliberations, formulation, and outcomes and affect individual lives."[6] In the post-cold war period, the formal IIs remain an important focus because of their roles as actors in providing international redistributive or collective goods. They have come to regulate different political, economic and social problems that are traditionally dominated within the States. So, the behaviour and functions of IIs have changed. In fact, they are now influencing the behaviour of the governments and take an active part in the international law-making, institution-building and enforcement processes.[7]

Similarly, it seems, without institutions no social movements can be sustained. There is a need for institutional support for planning the programmes, addressing the issues, and implementing the outcomes. In order to achieve their goals, various social movements take organizational forms and contribute to the law-making process in the field of international law.[8] It has been observed in different studies that there is a need for effective IIs to end sexual and gender-based violence (SGBV) against women.[9] Chaps. 3 and 4 of this study have discussed at length the role of the General Assembly

[5] Desai, Bharat H. (2010), *Multilateral Environmental Agreements: Legal Status of the Secretariat,* New York: Cambridge University Press; Desai, Bharat H. (2014), *International Environmental Governance: Towards UNEPO*, Brill; Desai, Bharat H. (2004), *Institutionalizing International Environmental Law*, Ardsley, New York: Transnational Publishers.

[6] Fomerand, Jacques F. (2017), "The Evolution of International Organizations as Institutional Forms and Historical Processes since 1945: Quis custodiet ipsos custodies?" International Studies Association and Oxford University, available at: https://oxfordre.com/internationalstudies/view/10.1093/acrefore/9780190846626.001.0001/acrefore-9780190846626-e-328 (accessed on 23 August 2021).

[7] Simmons, Beth A. and L. L. Martin (2001), "International Organization and Institutions," in Walter Carlsnaes, Thomas Kisse, Beth Simmons (eds.), *Handbook of International Relations*. Thousand Oaks, CA: Sage.

[8] A doctoral thesis on *Social Movements and International Law: Analyzing Contemporary Reforms* was submitted in August 2020 at Jawaharlal Nehru University by Radhika Jagtap, under the supervision of Prof. Bharat H. Desai, (on file with the author).

[9] UN Women (2016), "Ending violence against women requires that key institutions work together"; available at: https://www.unwomen.org/en/news/stories/2016/12/speech-by-ed-phumzile-mlambo-ngcuka-at-we-unite-conference-india (accessed on 24 August 2021).

(GA) resolutions. It underscores the importance of institutions in addressing the challenge of SGBV as the GA resolution 55/66 stated:

> Emphasizing that the elimination of crimes against women committed in the name of honour requires greater efforts and commitment from Governments and the international community…4. (e) To create, strengthen or facilitate institutional mechanisms so that victims and others can report; 5. Invites the international community, including United Nations bodies, programmes and organizations; 6. Encourages the relevant human rights treaty bodies to continue to address this issue, where appropriate[10]

There are national, regional and international institutions that work at different levels in this concerted processes. IIs have played an important role in the global women's rights movement. They have given a global platform to the women activists, individuals, civil society, etc. to address the women rights issues such as societal status, equality, discrimination, suffrage, employment and violence. In fact, they encourage the women to come at the forefront for different social reform movements.[11] Many of the IIs have worked for the rights of women at national, regional and international levels. In this respect, as already seen, the UN has played a pivotal role as a *prima donna* among the IOs.[12]

Historical Role

Many of the existing IIs working for eliminating SGBV against women are the result of the evolution of organized women's rights movements. Since 1840, the formation of the organizations for the women's rights began with the demand for 'women suffrage.' Different institutions came to be formed gradually to promote the cause for the rights of the women. Among a host of such institutions, the League of Nations and the UN have played a seminal role. During the time of the League, women's groups "were partially successful at ensuring that women would be a greater part of the League of Nations' consideration." Similarly, women also took part in the formation of the UN. It has seen that different women's rights institutions were situation based.[13]

---

[10] UN (2000), "Working towards the elimination of crimes against women committed in the name of honour"; GA Res. 55/66; UN Doc. A/RES/55/66(2000), 4 December 2000, preambular para 8 and paragraphs 4 (e), 5 and 6; available at: https://research.un.org/en/docs/ga/quick/regular/55 (accessed on 25 August 2021).

[11] Joachim, Jutta (2018), "Human Rights, Politics and Sexuality and Gender states", *International Studies*, published online 11 January 2018; Oxford Research Encyclopedias; available at: https://oxfordre.com/internationalstudies/view/10.1093/acrefore/9780190846626.001.0001/acrefore-9780190846626-e-430 (accessed on 25 August 2021).

[12] UN Women (2019), "International Women's Day 2019: Think equal, build smart, innovate for change"; available at: https://www.unwomen.org/en/news/stories/2019/3/statement-ed-phumzile-international-womens-day-2019 (accessed on 25 August 2021).

[13] Stienstra, Deborah (1994), *Women's Movements and International Organizations*, Great Britain: Macmillan Press.

International Council of Women (ICW 1888) was treated as the first formal international organization that advocated for the women's rights. In its first meeting held in 1888, the ICW brought together women from Europe, North America, and India.[14] Similarly, in 1904, the International Woman Suffrage Alliance (IWSA) established. It was subsequently renamed as the International Alliance of Women. Since 1947, it was given general consultative status by the Economic and Social Council (ECOSOC) of the UN.[15] The Socialist International Women (SIW), 1907 was another important organization founded by Clara Zetkin to fight against the effect of war especially on women.[16] The Covenant of the League of Nations (1919) also specifically mentioned about the rights of women in some of the provisions. Article VII of the Covenant provided for the women' right to work for the League at all the levels. Many of the women's organizations started addressing the role and contributions of the women for the development of the organization. Even, women's groups lobbied for the Paris Peace Conference after the end of the World War I.[17] They got access to the 12th meeting of the League of Nations Committee, where they presented "The Women's Charter."[18] Apart from it, the Women's International League for Peace and Freedom (WILPF) was the result of the 1919 International Congress of Women held in Zurich.[19] Though the history of IIs shows contributions of different IIs, the

---

[14] Founded in 1888 in Washington D.C., International Council of Women (ICW) coincided with the establishment of the National Committee of the United States. ICW's founding members included Susan B. Anthony, May Wright Sewall, and Frances Willard. Some 53 women's organizations from 9 countries were represented at the first ICW meeting. It has sought to bring together women's organizations from all the countries. The primary aim of ICW is to promote human rights, equality, peace and women's involvement in all spheres of life. It comprises one council from each country; available at: http://www.icw-cif.com/01/03.php (accessed on 28 August 2021).

[15] International Alliance of Women (IAW), *What is IAW*; IAW is an international NGO comprising 41 member organizations involved in the promotion of women's human rights, of equality and of the empowerment of women. The IAW has general consultative status with the UN Economic and Social Council and is accredited to many of the UN specialized agencies. It also has participatory status with the Council of Europe as well as represented at the Arab League, the African Union and other international organizations; available at: https://www.womenalliance.org/what-is-iaw/ (accessed on 28 August 2021). Also see, Leila J. Rupp and Verta Taylor (1999), "Forging Feminist Identity in an International Movement: A Collective Identity Approach to Twentieth-Century Feminism", *Signs*, Vol. 24, No. 2 (Winter, 1999), pp. 363–386.

[16] The conference of the Socialist International Women took place in Stuttgart, Germany on 17 August 1907. It was attended by fifty-eight participants from Europe, India and Japan. In 1955 the organization was re-founded as the *International Council of Social Democratic Women* and relocated to London, UK. In 1978, its name was changed back to *Socialist International Women*; available at: (accessed on 28 August 2021).

[17] United Nations, *Women and Global Diplomacy: From Peace Movements to the United Nations*; available at: https://libraryresources.unog.ch/womendiplomacy/leagueofnations (accessed on 28 August 2021).

[18] Ibid. It affirmed the *Women's Charter* in which they requested that a woman's nationality be declared independent of her husband, the League ban the trafficking of women and girls, and that women be afforded the same labor rights as men. Many of the women present at the 1919 Paris Peace Conference would later come to be involved with the work of the League of Nations.

[19] Women's International League for Peace and Freedom (WILPF) is an international non-governmental organization (NGO) that comprises national sections in almost every continent. It

formal movement relating to the rights of women and SGBV started only after the establishment of the UN. The next section analyses the role of the existing IIs in addressing the challenge of SGBV against women at the global level.

Contemporary Institutional Practices

There are many IIs that are working at the global level, within the UN and beyond, for the prevention of SGBV and protection of the rights of the women. The IIs have their own set of goals and respective mandates. The developments of international law in areas such as environment protection, human rights, humanitarian law, criminal law has brought into being function specific IIs. For example, there has been rapid growth in the UN human rights bodies (such as the UN Women, Human Rights Council etc.) to address the changing global human rights dynamics including the challenge of SGBV against women.[20] There are different intergovernmental organizations (IGOs), international non-governmental organizations (INGOs) such as the ICRC (Geneva) that have specific focus on SGBV or as a part of their larger mandate as human rights or humanitarian entities. The UN Charter provides the fulcrum in this respect. Still, there have been other IIs active in addressing the SGBV against women.

UN Charter-Based Bodies

The movement for the rights of the women began in earnest with the advent of the UN in 1945. Basic purpose of the UN contained in Article 1 of the Charter underscores respect for human rights and fundamental freedoms for all without distinction of race, sex, etc.[21] Articles 8, 55(c), and 76(c) strengthen it by providing for equal participation of men and women; as well as respect for human rights and fundamental freedoms without distinction of sex.[22] According to Article 7 of the Charter, the UN

---

has an international secretariat in Geneva, and the New York office focuses on the work of the UN; available at: https://www.wilpf.org/our-movement/ (accessed on 28 August 2021).

[20] UN OHCHR, *Brief history of UN Human Rights*; available at: https://www.ohchr.org/EN/AboutUs/Pages/BriefHistory.aspx#:~:text=Brief%20history%20of%20UN%20Human%20Rights%20The%20UN,the%20Centre%20for%20Human%20Rights%20in%20the%201980s (accessed on 29 August 2021).

[21] UN (1945), *Charter of the United Nations*; One of the purposes of the UN laid down in Article 1 (3) states: "To achieve international cooperation in solving international problems of an economic, social, cultural, or humanitarian character, and in promoting and encouraging respect for human rights and for fundamental freedoms for all without distinction as to race, sex, language, or religion"; available at: https://treaties.un.org/doc/Publication/CTC/uncharter.pdf (accessed on 28 August 2021).

[22] UN (1945), ibid. Article 8 and 55(c) state: "The United Nations shall place no restrictions on the eligibility of men and women to participate in any capacity and under conditions of equality in its principal and subsidiary organs". Article 55(c) provides: "universal respect for, and observance of, human rights and fundamental freedoms for all without distinction as to race, sex, language, or religion". Even the UN trusteeship system, though not functional now, in Article 76(c) provided: "to encourage respect for human rights and for fundamental freedoms for all without distinction

has six principal organs: the General Assembly (GA), the Security Council (SC), the Economic and Social Council (ECOSOC), the Trusteeship Council (TC), the International Court of Justice (ICJ) and the Secretariat.[23] The GA, SC and ECOSOC are engaged in addressing violence against women. Both the GA and the SC are working for ending violence against women by adopting emphatic resolutions. In fact, the concern for SGBV has been elevated at the global level in the aftermath of the UNSC resolution 1325 (2000) wherein it called on the "parties in conflict to uphold women's rights and respond to violations, impunity for conflict-related sexual and gender-based violence (SGBV) continues to undermine peace and security".[24] The Secretary-General, as head of the UN Secretariat, also carries out instructions in this respect and gives effect to the decisions of the principal UN organs.

As an IGO, the UN has made an enormous contribution in addressing the challenge of SGBV. Apart from the provisions of the Charter, the UN has contributed[25] with the adoption of the Convention for the Suppression of the Traffic in Person and the Exploitation of the Prostitution of Others 1949.[26] Till 1985, most of the UN works were confined to the areas such as domestic violence; trafficking and sexual exploitation; women in detention; violence against women during armed conflicts. These issues were addressed in the UN decade of women by interlinkage with the 'development, peace and gender equality.' In 1980, the resolution on the violence in the family (at the 1980s World Conference for the UN Decade for Women, Copenhagen), also called for the programme to end violence and protect women and children from physical and mental abuse. In 1985, the World Conference of the UN Decade (Nairobi) started with a forward-looking strategy by calling for enactment of the national legislation on the issue. In 1979, a binding international instrument was adopted, i.e. Convention on the Elimination of All Forms of Discrimination against Women (CEDAW). Unfortunately, the CEDAW did not define violence

---

as to race, sex, language, or religion, and to encourage recognition of the interdependence of the peoples of the world".

[23] UN (2020), *Repertory of Practice of United Nations Organs*; Charter of the UN, Chapter III; Article 7 provides: "1. There are established as the principal organs of the United Nations: a General Assembly, a Security Council, an Economic and Social Council, a Trusteeship Council, an International Court of Justice, and a Secretariat. 2. Such subsidiary organs as may be found necessary may be established in accordance with the present Charter;" available at: https://legal.un.org/repertory/art7.shtml (accessed on 30 August 2021).

[24] UN Women (2017), *Investigating conflict-related sexual and gender-based crimes-lessons from Iraq and Syria*; available at: https://www.unwomen.org/en/news/stories/2017/10/news-event-wps-investigating-conflict-related-sexual-and-gender-based-crimes (accessed on 28 August 2021).

[25] UN Women (2010), "Timeline of policy commitments and international agreements"; available at: https://www.endvawnow.org/en/articles/302-timeline-of-policy-commitments-and-international-agreements-.html (accessed on 30 August 2021).

[26] UN General Assembly (1950), *Convention for the Suppression of the Traffic in Persons and of the Exploitation of the Prostitution* of Others; adopted by the General Assembly resolution 317 (IV) of 2 December 1949 and entered into force on 25 July 1951; available at: OHCHR | Convention for the Suppression of the Traffic in Persons; Refworld | Convention for the Suppression of the Traffic in Persons and of the Exploitation of the Prostitution of Others (accessed on 28 August 2021).

against women.[27] It was the General Assembly that adopted several resolutions in 1985 on domestic violence and other gender issues affecting women and girls.[28] It was followed, in 1989, by the UNGA adoption of the Convention on the Rights of the Child. This Convention addresses some of the issues relating to violence by the parents or caretakers; sexual exploitation; and trafficking.[29]

It was only in 1993 that the UN system fully geared up to address SGBV against women and girls. It brought in active participation of all the relevant UN entities such as the principal organs (e.g. GA, SC, ECOSOC, and the Secretariat); functional commissions; regional commissions; specialized agencies (SA); Special Rapporteurs (SR).[30] In fact, in a mandate directly relevant to the broader challenge of SGBV, the President of the UN-HRC appointed Alexandra Xanthaki (Greece) as the SR in the Field of Cultural Rights on 30 August 2021[31] as a sequel to the HRC's mandate in the resolution (A/HRC/RES/46/9; Table 4.4) of 23 March 2021. The UN has also coordinated the women's rights movements and participation of the governments. The 1993 World Conference on the Human Rights explicitly recognized 'violence against women as human rights violation.' It called for the appointment of the UN Special Rapporteur on the issue of violence against women in the Vienna Declaration and the Programme of Action.[32] The following discussion encapsulates the roles of the relevant IIs.

---

27 UN Women (2010), n.25.

28 UN (1985), General Assembly resolutions 40/36 to 40/38, 29 November 1985; available at: https://www.unodc.org/documents/commissions/CCPCJ/Crime_Resolutions/1980-1989/1985/A-RES-40-36.pdf (accessed on 30 August 2021).

29 UN OHCHR (1989), *Convention on the Rights of the Child*; adopted by the General Assembly resolution 44/25 of 20 November 1989 and entry into force 2 September 1990; available at: https://www.ohchr.org/en/professionalinterest/pages/crc.aspx (accessed on 30 August 2021).

30 UN Women (2020), "*Ending violence against women*"; available at: https://www.unwomen.org/en/what-we-do/ending-violence-against-women (accessed on 30 August 2021).

31 UN HCR (2021), "Letter from the President Nazhat S. Khan, Office of the President", 30 August 2021; available at: https://www.ohchr.org/Documents/HRBodies/SP/CallApplications/HRC48/Letter-from-HRC-President-list-SP-candidates-3-vacancies-HRC48.pdf (12 September 2021); UN HCR (2021), "Mandate of Special Rapporteur in the field of cultural rights"; Doc. A/HRC/RES/46/9 of 23 March 2021; available at: https://www.ohchr.org/EN/HRBodies/HRC/SP/Pages/HRC48.aspx (accessed on 12 September 2021).

32 UN OHCHR (1993), *Vienna Declaration and Programme of Action*; adopted by the World Conference on Human Rights in Vienna on 25 June 1993; OHCHR | Vienna Declaration and Programme of Action (accessed on 30 August 2021).

A. Principal Organs of the United Nations

The General Assembly

The UNGA is the only democratic principal organ of the UN based on sovereign equality and equal representation (one state one vote) for all the member States. They discuss, debate and take decision (resolutions) in consonance with the purposes and principles of the UN Charter revolving around core issues such as development, peace, security, international law, etc. The Third Committee of the GA (Social, Humanitarian, and Cultural) deals with the human rights issues. It discusses the questions relating to the advancement of women, protection of children, refugees, indigenous people etc.[33] The main contributions of the GA include international law-making, or codification,[34] development of international law and institution building.[35] It has adopted treaties or conventions and declarations through its primary instrumentality of resolutions. The Human Rights Council (HRC); the UN trust funds and UN Women are the contribution of the GA in institution building and global governance.[36]

The GA plays a crucial role in conducting meetings and documentation of gender-related agenda items in the sessional meetings. From the 50th session (1995) to the 67th session (2012), the GA adopted numerous resolutions, documents, and reports on the rights of the women and elimination of violence against women and girls.[37] In fact, since 2000, the GA has regularly adopted biannual resolutions and reports on different forms of VAW.[38] It adopted resolution 61/143 (2007) on the "intensification of efforts to eliminate all forms of violence against women" by following upon the "Secretary-General's in-depth study on all forms of violence against women." The GA also addresses VAW under the thematic debate.[39] As provided in Article 11 of the UN Charter, the resolutions of the GA are 'recommendatory' and not legally binding *per se*. There are different opinions on the legal effect of the UNGA resolutions. Hence, it gives latitude to the UN members to decide

---

[33] United Nations, *Protect Human Rights*; available at: https://www.un.org/en/our-work/protect-human-rights; Protect Human Rights | United Nations (accessed on 28 March 2022).

[34] United Nations, *UN Documentation: International Law*; available at: General Assembly & International Law - UN Documentation: International Law - Research Guides at United Nations Dag Hammarskjöld Library (accessed on 05 September 2021).

[35] UN General Assembly, "Functions and powers of the General Assembly"; available at: https://www.un.org/en/ga/about/background.shtml (accessed on 05 September 2021).

[36] United Nations, *Protect Human Rights*, n.33.

[37] UN Women, "Sessional meetings of General Assembly"; available at: https://www.un.org/womenwatch/daw/documents/ga.htm (accessed on 05 September 2021).

[38] UN Women, "Global norms and standards: Ending violence against women"; available at: https://www.unwomen.org/en/what-we-do/ending-violence-against-women/global-norms-and-standards (accessed on 05 September 2021).

[39] UN Women, *Violence against women*: *Work of the General Assembly on violence against women*; available at: https://www.un.org/womenwatch/daw/vaw/v-work-ga.htm (accessed on 05 September 2021).

to give effect to the relevant resolutions.[40] Notwithstanding this, being the plenary organ of the UN, the GA does have considerable authority and legitimacy to lay down consensual decisions (resolutions) that have a large measure of legal effect.[41] The GA has taken another important step towards gender equality and empowerment of women by adopting *Sustainable Development Goals 2030* (SDGs) that contain specific goal of gender equality (5/17 goals).[42] It also underscores elimination of VAW because gender equality is possible only when there is absence of VAW.[43]

The Security Council

It is the most important principal organ of the UN with fifteen members. It works for the maintenance of international peace and security. All the members of the UN are obliged to comply with the decisions of SC.[44] The SC has authority under the Charter to investigate, mediate, dispatch a mission, appoint special envoys, or request the Secretary-General to use his good offices. SC may also direct for a peacekeeping force and has the authority to take any action for imposing sanctions.[45]

In a major milestone, starting with resolution 1325 (2000),[46] the SC began giving serious attention to VAW under the theme of 'women, peace, and security' (see Chap. 3). These resolutions, adopted unanimously, have especially focused on the conflict-related sexual violence against women.[47] The SC resolutions have hammered on the use of SGBV against women as a tactic or a weapon of war. The SC has

[40] Schwebel, Stephen M. (1979), "The Effect of Resolutions of the U.N. General Assembly on Customary International Law" *Proceedings of the Annual Meeting (American Society of International Law)*, 73: 301–309.

[41] Asamoh, Obed Y. (1966), "*The Legal Significance of the Declarations of the General Assembly of the United Nations*"; The Hague: Martinus Nijhoff.

[42] UNDP, *The SDGs in Action*; available at: https://www.undp.org/sustainable-development-goals (accessed on 05 September 2021).

[43] UN (2018), "*Ending Violence against Women*"; available at: https://www.ohchr.org/Documents/Publications/PractitionerToolkit/WA2J_Module3.pdf (accessed on 05 September 2021).

[44] UN, "Security Council"; available at: https://www.un.org/securitycouncil/ (accessed on 05 September 2021).

[45] United Nations, *Protect Human Rights*, n.33.

[46] UN Security Council (2000), Resolution 1325, adopted on 31 October 2000; UN Doc. S/RES/1325 (2000), 31 October 2000; available at: https://undocs.org/S/RES/1325(2000) (accessed on 05 September 2021).

[47] UN Women, "Security Council"; available at: https://www.unwomen.org/en/how-we-work/intergovernmental-support/security-council (accessed on 05 September 2021).

regarded such VAW in warfare as a threat to international peace and security. Moreover, the SC has explicitly used the term 'SGBV' in its resolutions.[48] The resolutions of SC adopted under Chapter VII[49] are binding (action with respect to threats to the peace, breaches of the peace, and acts of aggression). Some scholars have argued that the binding character of resolutions of the SC could be determined by the language used in the resolutions.[50] There has been gradual securitization of SV in conflicts against women and the SGBV exacerbated by climate change[51] (see Table 5.1).

The Economic and Social Council

The UN Economic and Social Council (ECOSOC) is one of the six principal organs of the UN. It is mandated to address economic and social matters. It submits an annual report to the UN's plenary organ, the GA. In fact, 70% of the UN funds are used in addressing decisions and programmes laid down by the ECOSOC. It works through specialized agencies, other functional entities, subsidiary bodies and funding agencies.[52] The different subsidiary bodies of the ECOSOC include functional commissions (e.g. Commission on the Status of Women[53]), regional commissions (e.g. Economic and Social Commission for Asia and Pacific[54]), standing committees (e.g. Committee for Programme and Coordination[55]), expert bodies of governmental experts (e.g. Intergovernmental Working Group of Experts on International Standards of Accounting and Reporting[56]), expert bodies comprising members in their

---

48 Huvé, Sophie (2018), "The Use of UN Sanctions to Address Conflict-Related Sexual Violence", Georgetown University's Institute for Women, Peace and Security; available at: https://giwps.georgetown.edu/wp-content/uploads/2018/03/Use-of-UN-Sanctions-to-Address-Conflict-related-Sexual-Violence.pdf (accessed on 05 September 2021).

49 UN (1945), "Chapter VII: Action with Respect to Threats to the Peace, Breaches of the Peace, and Acts of Aggression"; available at: https://treaties.un.org/doc/Publication/CTC/uncharter.pdf (pp. 9–11); Chapter VII: Action with Respect to Threats to the Peace, Breaches of the Peace, and Acts of Aggression (Articles 39–51) | United Nations (accessed on 05 September 2021).

50 Öberg, Marko Divac (2005), "The Legal Effects of Resolutions of the UN Security Council and General Assembly in the Jurisprudence of the ICJ", *The European Journal of International Law*, 16(5): 879–906, p. 885.

51 Desai, Bharat H. and Mandal, Moumita (2021), "Role of Climate Change in Exacerbating Sexual and gender Based Violence against Women: A New Challenge for International Law", Environmental Policy & Law, vol. 51, no. 3, pp. 137–157; available at: https://content.iospress.com/journals/environmental-policy-and-law/51/3 (accessed on 06 September 2021).

52 UN, "*What does ECOSOC do?*" available at: https://www.un.org/en/ecosoc/meetings/2005/hl2005/ECOSOCinfo%20rev%20et.pdf (accessed on 06 September 2021).

53 UN Women, "Commission on the Status of Women"; available at: https://www.unwomen.org/en/csw (accessed on 06 September 2021).

54 UN ESCAP, *ESCAP 75*; available at: https://www.unescap.org/ (accessed on 06 September 2021).

55 UNGA, "Committee for Programme and Coordination"; available at: https://www.un.org/en/ga/cpc/ (accessed on 06 September 2021).

56 UN, *ECOSOC Subsidiary Bodies*; available at: https://www.un.org/ecosoc/en/content/ecosoc-subsidiary-bodies-0 (accessed on 06 September 2021).

Table 5.1 Key UN Policy Frameworks and Global Agendas for an Integrated Action on Women, Climate Change and Security[57]

Policy framework and key resolutions	Key goals and priorities	Opportunities for integrated action
Women, Peace and Security Agenda: UNSCR 1325 (2000); 1820 (2008); 1888 (2008); 1889 (2009); 1960 (2010); 2106 (2013); 2122 (2013); 2242 (2015); 2467 (2019) and 2493 (2019). In 2020, the Russian draft resolution, S/2020/1054, failed to garner required votes (5 in favour and 10 abstentions; 30 October)	(i) Strengthen women's meaningful participation, protection and rights in all aspects of peacebuilding. (ii) Recognize and respond to the different ways in which women, men, girls and boys contribute to and experience conflict.	(i) Assess climate-related risks and opportunities for women's participation and leadership across all pillars of peacebuilding (ii) Promote women's leadership in natural resource-based conflict prevention and resolution (iii) Increase opportunities for women's economic recovery through climate-resilient sustainable natural resource management in post-conflict countries (iv) Integrate environmental and climate considerations into NAPs for the implementation of UNSCR 1325 (2000).
Sustaining Peace Agenda: General Assembly and Security Council "twin" resolutions A/Res/70/262 and S/Res/2282 (2016)	(i) Prevent the outbreak, escalation, continuation and recurrence of conflict (ii) Emphasize the importance of a comprehensive approach to sustaining peace, particularly through the prevention of conflict and addressing its root causes (iii) Strengthen inclusivity in sustaining peace initiatives (iv) Underscore the importance of women's leadership & participation in conflict prevention, resolution and peacebuilding	(i) Ensure integrated gender, conflict and climate/environmental analysis is systematically conducted to inform peacebuilding programme priorities (ii) Support gender-responsive climate action, i.e. programmes that have co-benefits for women's empowerment and climate adaptation, as a conflict prevention strategy in fragile contexts (iii) Ensure that the gender dimensions of climate-related security risks are addressed in further policy development, including the outcomes of the 2020 Review of the Peacebuilding Architecture.

(continued)

[57] UNEP, UN Women, UNDP and UNDPPA/PBSO (2020), "Gender, Climate & Security: Sustaining inclusive peace on the frontlines of climate change", 2020, Annex 1, p. 46; available at: https://www.undp.org/sites/g/files/zskgke326/files/publications/undp-unep-dppa-unwomen-gpn-cb-bpps-Gender_Climate_and_Security.pdf (accessed on 06 September 2021).

Table 5.1 (continued)

Policy framework and key resolutions	Key goals and priorities	Opportunities for integrated action
Climate Change Agenda: UNFCCC (1992); Kyoto Protocol (1997); Lima Work Programme on Gender (2014); Paris Agreement (2015), report of the Special Rapporteur in the field of Cultural Rights (2020) on climate change and cultural rights; A/HRC/RES/27/24 (2021)	(i) Prevent dangerous human interference with the climate system. (ii) Mitigate climate change through the reduction of harmful activities. (iii) Strengthen States' capacity to adapt to change conditions recognizing the importance of adaptation for peace and development, especially in "developing" countries. (iv) Interlinkage among climate change, SGBV and culture. (v) Participation of women, girls in climate action	(i) Integrate conflict analysis into gender-responsive climate action and policy-making (ii) Harness local knowledge and capacity of primary natural resource users in design of climate adaptation and mitigation strategies (iii) Support women's economic empowerment in conflict-affected contexts through training and resources for climate-resilient sustainable livelihoods (iv) Promote women's leadership in climate action in fragile and conflict-affected contexts.
Agenda for Sustainable Development 2030: 2030 Agenda for Sustainable Development—A/RES/70/1 (2015); United Nations Sustainable Development Cooperation Framework, A/RES/72/279 (2018)	(i) Eradicate poverty (ii) Shift the world onto a sustainable and resilient path (iii) Strengthen universal peace (iv) Leave no one behind, recognizing the specific risks faced by different target populations (v) Achieve 17 Sustainable Development Goals	(i) Ensure integrated gender, conflict and climate/environmental analysis is systematically conducted as part of common country analysis processes (CCAs) (ii) Design integrated projects and programmes addressing gender, climate and security linkages, based on partnerships and complementarity of mandate among UN agencies, funds and programmes.

personal capacity (e.g. the Committee on Economic, Social and Cultural Rights[58]), and other related bodies (e.g. Executive Board of the International Research and Training Institute for the Advancement of Women[59]). There are some *ad hoc* entities (e.g. *Ad Hoc* Open-ended Working Groups); and funds and programmes that send reports to ECOSOC (e.g. UN Development Fund for Women).[60] ECOSOC consults scholars and has numerous affiliated NGOs and business sector representatives with consultative status.[61]

In fact, ECOSOC contributes to ending VAW through its resolutions, documentation and organizing meetings regarding gender-related agenda items.[62] It reviews the work of the Commission of the Status of Women and takes up follow-up actions. It integrates gender equality considerations in its discussions.[63] The resolutions of the ECOSOC are regarded as soft instruments[64] and yet taken seriously by the UN member States.

The Secretariat (UN Secretary-General)

The Secretariat is one of the principal organs of the UN. The Secretary-General (SG) serves as the Chief Executive Officer of the Secretariat that works in different areas.[65] With the launch of his landmark 2006 report, the SG commenced his periodic reports on "all forms of violence against women".[66] It remains the main concerted review in addressing the challenge of SGBV. The SG follows the resolutions of the GA while addressing VAW under different themes.[67] The SG's reports narrate VAW on the basis of information received from the Governments, various entities

---

58 UN OHCHR, "Committee on Economic, Social and Cultural Rights"; available at: https://www.ohchr.org/en/hrbodies/cescr/pages/cescrindex.aspx (accessed on 06 September 2021).

59 UN, *ECOSOC Subsidiary Bodies*; n.57.

60 UN, *Funds and Programs*; available at: https://www.un.org/en/about-us/un-system (accessed on 08 September 2021).

61 UN, *What does ECOSOC do?* n.53.

62 UN Women, "Sessional Meetings of the Economic and Social Council: Gender Related Agenda Items"; available at: https://www.un.org/womenwatch/daw/documents/ecosoc.htm (accessed on 08 September 2021).

63 UN Women, "Intergovernmental Support"; available at: https://www.unwomen.org/en/how-we-work/intergovernmental-support (accessed on 08 September 2021).

64 UNHCR, "International and Regional Legal framework"; available at: https://www.unhcr.org/47cfad542.pdf (accessed on 08 September 2021).

65 UN, "*Secretariat*"; available at: https://www.un.org/en/model-united-nations/secretariat (accessed on 08 September 2021).

66 UN (2006), "*Ending Violence Against Women: From words to action*"; available at: https://www.un.org/womenwatch/daw/vaw/v-sg-study.htm. In 2003, the GA *vide* resolution A/RES/58/185, 22 December 2003 had requested the S-G to prepare an in-depth study on "all forms and manifestations of violence against women"; available at: https://undocs.org/en/A/RES/58/185 (accessed on 08 September 2021).

67 UN Women, "Work of the General Assembly on violence against women"; available at: https://www.un.org/womenwatch/daw/vaw/v-work-ga.htm (accessed on 10 September 2021). The resolutions of GA on VAW are followed by the Secretary-General in his reports under different themes such as: (i) GA resolution on 'Eliminating rape and other forms of sexual violence in all their manifestations, including in conflict and related situations' (A/RES/62/134, of 18 December 2007)

of the UN system and the NGOs. It cites resolutions of the GA, the SC and other works as well as provides concrete suggestions.[68] There have been instances wherein the SG appointed special representatives such as on the sexual violence in conflicts. The 'Human Rights Up Front'[69] is a major interagency initiative of the SG that takes an early and effective action to prevent serious violation of human rights in all countries and humanitarian law. The SG presented a report entitled "conflict-related sexual violence" on 29 March 2022 that provides a comprehensive review of the challenge.[70]

B. Other UN Organs and Bodies

(i) The Human Rights Commission/Council

The Commission on Human Rights (CHR) and the Human Rights Council (HRC) are treated as the Charter-based human rights bodies.[71] During its 50 years long existence (1946–2006), the CHR played a pivotal role in the protection of human rights and freedoms as mandated under the UN Charter. As an intergovernmental body comprising 53 member States, it worked as a subsidiary organ under the supervision of the ECOSOC.[72] Following the GA 60/251 (15 March 2006), all mandates, mechanisms, functions and responsibilities of the CHR, including the Sub-Commission, were assumed by the HRC (as of 19 June 2006). The delegates from the member States and observer States, NGOs used to participate in the regular sessions of CHR in Geneva. It adopted resolutions, decisions, and statements of the chairperson on

---

was followed by the Reports of the Secretary-General on 'Eliminating rape and other forms of sexual violence in all their manifestations, including in conflict and related situations' (A/63/216 of 4 August 2008). There appears an exception as regards absence of the S-Gs report on the GA resolution on 'Intensifying global efforts for the elimination of female genital mutilations' (A/RES/67/146, of 20 December 2012).

[68] UNGA (2008), "*Eliminating rape and other forms of sexual violence in all their manifestations, including in conflict and related situations: Report of the Secretary-General*"; UN Doc. A/63/216, 4 August 2008; available at: https://documents-dds-ny.un.org/doc/UNDOC/GEN/N08/449/78/PDF/N0844978.pdf?OpenElement (accessed on 10 September 2021).

[69] UN Inter-Agency Standing Committee (2015), "Human Rights up Front: An Overview"; available at: https://interagencystandingcommittee.org/system/files/overview_of_human_rights_up_front_july_2015.pdf (accessed on 10 September 2021). The UN Secretary-General's initiative to strengthen prevention of serious problems that cut across the UN's three pillars of peace and security, development and human rights pillars, and most especially problems issues with serious human rights consequences. It is based on mandates from the UN Charter and GA and Security Council resolutions. It applies to the whole UN system and to UN work in all countries and all situations. It introduces three types of change that includes Change to UN engagement with Member States: so as to prevent large-scale human rights violations.

[70] UN (2022), *Report of the Secretary-General: Conclict-related sexual violence*; SC Doc. S/2022/272 of 29 March 2022; available at: https://reliefweb.int/sites/reliefweb.int/files/resources/N2229371.pdf (accessed on 15 April 2022).

[71] UN OHCHR, "Human Rights Bodies"; available at: https://www.ohchr.org/EN/HRBODIES/Pages/HumanRightsBodies.aspx (accessed on 10 September 2021).

[72] UN OHCHR, "Human Rights Council"; available at: https://www.ohchr.org/EN/HRBodies/HRC/Pages/Home.aspx (accessed on 10 September 2021).

the human rights issues. The Sub-Commission assisted CHR on the promotion and protection of human rights. Some working groups, individual experts, representatives and Special Rapporteurs were mandated to report to it on some specific human rights issues.[73] The CHR addressed violence against women by adopting the different resolutions during 1946 to 2006.[74] The Sub-Commission on the Promotion and Protection of Human Rights in association with CHR also played an important role in addressing the same issues.[75]

The advent of the HRC as an intergovernmental body in 2006 heralded a new era for the promotion and protection of human rights around the globe.[76] It was created as a subsidiary organ by the GA *vide* the resolution of 60/251 (15 March 2006).[77] All the mandates, mechanisms, functions, responsibilities, and sub-commission of the CHR (replaced by the HRC Advisory Committee)[78] were taken up by the HRC. These have been treated as part of the HRC from 19 June 2018.

Since 2006, the HRC has considered the reports of the High Commissioner for Human Rights (OHCHR) relating to VAW. It has also adopted resolutions on the elimination of VAW. The Special Rapporteurs (SRs) for VAW have been appointed under the special procedures (SP) or mandates of the HRC. The SRs submit their reports to the Council.[79] The Universal Periodic Review (UPR) and complaint mechanism are the two important functions of the HRC.[80]

---

[73] UN OHCHR, "UN Human Rights Council: Introduction"; available at: https://www.ohchr.org/EN/HRBodies/CHR/Pages/CommissionOnHumanRights.aspx (accessed on 10 September 2021).

[74] UN Women (2006), "Work of the Human Rights Council (2006-present) and the Commission on Human Rights (until 2006)". It states, "Dating from the 1990s to its dissolution in 2006, the Commission on Human Rights addressed the issue of violence against women in resolutions on: 1. The elimination of violence against women; 2. Trafficking in women and girls; 3. Violence against women migrant workers; 4. Integrating the human rights of women in the work of the United Nations; 5. Country-specific situations;" available at: https://www.un.org/womenwatch/daw/vaw/v-hrc.htm#chr (accessed on 10 September 2021).

[75] Ibid, it states, "Sub-Commission on the Promotion and Protection of Human Rights (until 2006) addressed violence against women in resolutions on the following topics: 1. Sexual violence; 2. Systematic rape, sexual slavery and slavery-like practices; 3. Harmful and traditional practices affecting the health of women and the girl-child; 4. Country-specific situations.".

[76] UN OHCHR, "United Nations Human Rights Council"; available at: https://www.ohchr.org/EN/HRBodies/HRC/Pages/Home.aspx (accessed on 10 January 2021).

[77] UN General Assembly (2006), "Resolution 60/251. Human Rights Council"; Doc. A/RES/60/251, 15 March 2006. It stated: "1. Decides to establish the Human Rights Council, based in Geneva, in replacement of the Commission on Human Rights, as a subsidiary organ of the General Assembly; the Assembly shall review the status of the Council within five years;" available at: Refworld | Human Rights Council: resolution/adopted by the General Assembly; A/RES/60/251 - Human Rights Council - UN Documents: Gathering a body of global agreements (un-documents.net) (accessed on 11 September 2021).

[78] UN OHCHR, "United Nations Human Rights Council", n.72.

[79] UN Women (2006), n.74.

[80] UN OHCHR, "United Nations Human Rights Council", n.72.

(ii) Role of the Special Rapporteurs

The appointment of SRs comes within the ambit of SP of the HRC. It was initiated by the predecessor CHR and the HRC has continued with the hallowed tradition. As of 2021, under its special procedures,[81] the HRC has given 44 thematic and country-specific mandates[82] to SRs, working groups and independent experts. There are SRs who have been appointed to report on SGBV against women under different themes either generally or specifically such as: (i) 'violence against women, its causes and consequences;' (ii) 'cultural rights;' (iii) 'trafficking in person, especially women and children;' (iv) 'sale and sexual exploitation of children, including child prostitution, child pornography and other child sexual abuse material;' etc. The mandates and working procedures of the SRs are more or less the same. In order to understand SR's work, this study has sought to examine the working procedure of one SR on the elimination of SGBV against women.

In 1994, the suggestion for the appointment of the UN Special Rapporteur was practically implemented in the appointment of SR on 'violence against women, its causes and consequences.' The issue of the necessity for appointment of the SR has been duly underscored in the UN declarations and resolutions such as the Vienna Declaration of Human Rights 1993; resolution of the UN Commission on Human Rights 1993/46 of 8 March 1993 on the integrating the rights of women into the human rights mechanisms of the United Nations[83]; resolution 1994/45 of the Commission on Human Rights on "Question of integrating the rights of women into the human rights mechanisms of the UN and the elimination of violence against women," adopted on 4 March 1994 to appoint a SR on VAW, including causes and consequences. The resolution provided as follows:

> 4. Calls for the elimination of violence against women in public and private life, of all forms of sexual harassment, exploitation and trafficking in women, the elimination of gender bias in the administration of justice and the eradication of the harmful effects of certain traditional practices or customary practices, cultural prejudice and religious extremism; 6. Decides to appoint, for a three-year period, a special rapporteur on violence against women, including its causes and consequences, who will report to the Commission on an annual basis beginning at its fifty-first session; 7. Invites the Special Rapporteur, in carrying out this mandate, and within the framework of the Universal Declaration of Human Rights and all other international human rights instruments, including the Convention on the Elimination of All Forms of Discrimination against Women and the Declaration on the Elimination of Violence against Women…; 8. Request the Chairman of the Commission, after consultation with the

---

[81] UN OHCHR, *Special Procedures of the Human Rights Council*; available at: https://www.ohchr.org/EN/HRBodies/SP/Pages/Welcomepage.aspx (accessed on 18 September 2021).

[82] UN OHCHR, *Thematic Mandates*; available at: https://spinternet.ohchr.org/ViewAllCountryMandates.aspx?Type=TM&lang=en (accessed on 18 September 2021).

[83] UN OHCHR (1994), The Commission on Human Rights, "Question of integrating the rights of women into the human rights mechanisms of the United Nations and the elimination of violence against women," Res. 1994/45, 4 March 1994, UN Doc. E/CN.4/RES/1994/45; available at: https://www.refworld.org/docid/3b00f47f4.html (accessed 16 September 2021), see also, Commission on Human Rights, "Report of the fiftieth session", 31 January to 11 March 1994, UN Doc. E/CN.4/1994/132, p. 140; available at: https://undocs.org/pdf?symbol=en/E/CN.4/1994/132 (accessed on 10 September 2021).

> other members of the Bureau, to appoint as Special Rapporteur an individual of recognized international standing and experience in addressing the human rights of women.[84]

The mandates of the SR are mentioned in this resolution 1994/45, e.g., seek information; recommend measures, ways and means to eliminate violence against women; and work closely with other bodies. It further stated:

> 7 (a) To seek and receive information from governments, treaty bodies, specialized agencies, other special rapporteurs responsible for various human rights questions, and intergovernmental and non-governmental organizations including women's organizations, and to respond effectively to such information; (b) Recommend of measures, ways, and means at the national, regional, and international levels to eliminate violence against women and its causes and to remedy its consequences; (c) Work closely with other special rapporteurs, special representatives, working groups and independent experts of the Commission on Human Rights and the Sub-Commission on Prevention of Discrimination and Protection of Minorities and with the treaty bodies, taking into account the commission's request that they regularly and systematically include in their reports available information on human rights violations affecting women, and cooperate closely with the Commission on the Status of Women in the discharge of its functions.[85]

In 2003, the mandates were extended by the Commission in its resolution 2003/45 at 59th Session. As stated earlier, the CHR (under ECOSOC) was replaced by the HRC (under GA) in 2006. So, the SRs reports to the Council. The mandates of the SRs are stated in the Council's resolution 16/7 (2011). The Council has laid down that:

> Invites the Special Rapporteur, in carrying out his/her mandate within the framework of the Universal Declaration of Human Rights and all other international human rights instruments, including the Convention on the Elimination of All Forms of Discrimination against Women, the Declaration on the Elimination of Violence against Women and the Beijing Declaration and Platform for Action: (a) To seek and receive information on violence against women, its causes and its consequences, from Governments, treaty bodies, specialized agencies, other special rapporteurs responsible for various human rights questions, and intergovernmental and nongovernmental organizations, including women's organizations, and to respond effectively to such information; (b) To recommend measures, ways and means at the local, national, regional and international levels to eliminate all forms of violence against women and its causes, and to remedy its consequences; (c) To work closely with all special procedures and other human rights mechanisms of the Human Rights Council and with the treaty bodies, taking into account the request of the Council that they regularly and systematically integrate the human rights of women and a gender perspective into their work, and cooperate closely with the Commission on the Status of Women in the discharge of its functions; (d) To continue to adopt a comprehensive and universal approach to the elimination of violence against women, its causes and consequences, including causes of violence against women relating to the civil, cultural, economic, political and social spheres.[86]

---

[84] Ibid.

[85] Ibid.

[86] UN (2011), Human Rights Council, "Mandate of the Special Rapporteur on violence against women, its causes and consequences", Res. 16/7, 24 March 2011, paragraph 3; UN Doc. A/HRC/RES/16/7, 8 April 2011; available at: https://undocs.org/A/HRC/RES/16/7 (accessed on 29 August 2021).

In 2013, the mandates of the SR were again extended by the Council by adopting resolution 23/25(2013).[87] It was further renewed by the Council's resolution 32/19 in 2016.[88] The renewed mandates extended the old mandates and added a fourth mandate to continue to adopt a comprehensive and universal approach to eliminate VAW including its causes and consequences.[89] In the discharge of the above mandates, the SR carries out the functions such as transfer of urgent appeals and communicate the individuals' complaint letters to States. The States are requested to clarify the substance of the alleged allegations as well as ensure the concerns and actions of the government regarding the same. It refers the definition of GBV as mentioned in the UN Declaration on the Elimination of Violence against Women, 1993.[90]

The SR can transmit an urgent appeal to the governments on the basis of reliable information of immediate threat, fear of threat, and violation of right to life and dignity to women. It is to ensure effective and immediate measures taken by the government. The UN entities, e.g. OHCHR, etc. provide the copy of the individual complaint form.[91] It carries address and contact information of the 'Special Rapporteur on the violence against women' and 'Office for the High Commissioner for Human Right'.[92] It also ensures to the petitioner (an individual or an organization) that the information written in the form keep confidential.[93] All the information and communications between the governments and the SRs are kept confidential.[94]

---

[87] UN GA (2014), Human Rights Council, "Accelerating efforts to eliminate all forms of violence against women: preventing and responding to rape and other forms of sexual violence" Res. 23/25, 14 June 2013, UN Doc. A/HRC/RES/23/25, 25 June 2013 provides, "21. Decides to extend the mandate of the Special Rapporteur on violence against women, its causes and consequence, as set out by the Human Rights Council in its resolution 16/7, for a period of three years;" available at: https://documents-dds-ny.un.org/doc/UNDOC/GEN/G13/150/98/PDF/G1315098.pdf?OpenElement (accessed on 10 September 2021).

[88] UN GA (2016), Human Rights Council, "Accelerating efforts to eliminate violence against women: preventing and responding to violence against women and girls, including indigenous women and girls," Res. 32/19, UN Doc. A/HRC/32/L.28/Rev.1, 30 June 2016, states, "17. Decides to extend the mandate of the Special Rapporteur on violence against women, its causes and consequence, as set out by the Human Rights Council in its resolution 23/25 of 14 June 2013, for a period of three years;" also provides, "21. Encourages regular consultations by the Special Rapporteur on violence against women, its causes and consequences, with, inter alia, the Commission on the Status of Women, the World Health Organization, the United Nations Entity for Gender Equality and the Empowerment of Women, the United Nations Population Fund and the Statistics Division of the United Nations on the issue of disaggregated data on violence against women and effective ways of advancing the elimination of violence against women;" available at: https://documents-dds-ny.un.org/doc/UNDOC/LTD/G16/140/31/PDF/G1614031.pdf?OpenElement (accessed on 10 September 2021).

[89] Ibid.

[90] UN OHCHR, "Individual Complaints;" available at: https://www.ohchr.org/EN/Issues/Women/SRWomen/Pages/Complaints.aspx (accessed on 10 January 2021).

[91] Ibid.

[92] Ibid.

[93] Ibid.

[94] Ibid.

SRs undertake country visits that comes under their mandates. The legal basis for this mandate comes from the resolutions of the CHR (CHR, Res. 1994/45, Paragraphs. 7(a), 9 and 10[95]) and the HRC (HRC, Res. 7/24, 2008, Paragraphs 6(a) and 9).[96] The SR carries out the mandate of the country visit either separately or jointly with other SRs, with independent experts and working groups. According to the official reports, the country visit first started in 1995 (country visit by the SR to the Democratic Republic of Korea, Republic of Korea and Japan, July 1995).[97]

The consent of the State is necessary for the SR's country visit. The basic purpose of the country visit is to analyse the human rights situation at the national level. The visit may be either at the invitation by the receiving States to the mandate holders or by "standing invitation." That means States are ready to receive any visit by any thematic mandate holders. According to the reports of the OHCHR, as on 1 January 2015, at least 109 States and one Non-Member Observer State had extended a standing invitation. The mandate holders appointed under the special procedures engage in dialogue with the receiving States at the end of their visit. They discuss their findings and recommendations. At last they submit the reports to the HRC. The reports are known as the "Reports of the Special Rapporteurs."[98] The submission of thematic reports is another mandated act of the SRs. Before 2006, the SRs used to submit their reports to the CHR. After 2006, the SRs submit their reports to the HRC. The reports

---

[95] "7(a) Seek and receive information on violence against women, its causes and consequences from Governments…; 9. Request all Governments to cooperate with and assist the Special Rapporteur in the performance of the tasks and duties mandated and to furnish all information requested; 10. Request the Secretary-General to provide the Special Rapporteur with all necessary assistance, in particular the staff and resources required to perform all mandate factions, especially in carrying out and following up on missions undertaken either separately or jointly with other special rapporteurs and working groups, and adequate assistance for periodic consolations with the Committee on the Elimination of Discrimination against Women and all other treaty bodies," UN OHCHR (1994), n.83.

[96] Human Rights Council (2008), "Elimination of violence against women", Res. 7/24, 28 March 2008, explains, "6. (a) To seek and receive information on violence against women, its causes and its consequences, from Governments; 9. Calls upon all Governments to cooperate with and assist the Special Rapporteur in the performance of his/her mandated tasks and duties, to supply all information requested, including with regard to implementation of the recommendations of the Special Rapporteur, and to give serious consideration to responding favourably to his/her requests for visits and communications;" available at: http://ap.ohchr.org/documents/E/HRC/resolutions/A_HRC_RES_7_24.pdf (accessed on 10 September 2021).

[97] UN ECOSOC (1996), "Report of the Special Rapporteur on violence against women, its causes and consequences, Ms. Radhika Coomaraswamy, in accordance with Commission on Human Rights resolution: Report on the mission to the Democratic People's Republic of Korea, the Republic of Korea and Japan on the issue of military sexual slavery in wartime", Commission on Human Rights Res.1994/45, UN Doc. E/CN.4/1996/53/Add.1, 4 January 1996; available at: https://documents-dds-ny.un.org/doc/UNDOC/GEN/G96/101/23/PDF/G9610123.pdf?OpenElement (accessed on 10 September 2021). See also, UN OHCHR, "Country Visit"; available at: https://www.ohchr.org/EN/Issues/Women/SRWomen/Pages/CountryVisits.aspx (accessed on 11 September 2021).

[98] UN OHCHR, "Special Procedures of the Human Rights Council"; available at: https://www.ohchr.org/EN/HRBodies/SP/Pages/Introduction.aspx (accessed on 11 September 2021).

are available in all the UN official languages. SRs also submit separate reports to the GA and oral reports to the Commission on the Status of Women (CSW).[99]

The appointment of the SR in 1994 was the part of a series of developments that explicitly recognized VAW as a violation of their human rights. The SRs on VAW take note of the work of the women rights movements globally. The SRs have been working to address the issues under their mandates. They also analyse the existing international instruments to eliminate SGBV against women and show the gaps within the remit of their reports.[100] Since 1994 to till date, the SRs have been working to address the issue of SGBV against women either specifically or generally.

(iii) **Special Rapporteur on Violence Against Women**

Since 1994, there have been successive SRs on the violence against women (its causes and consequences) as follows: Reem Alsalem (Jordan; August 2021); Dubravka Simonovic (Croatia; 2015–2021); Ms. Rashida Manjoo (South Africa; 2009–2015); Dr. Yakin Erturk (Turkey; 2003–2009); Ms. Radhika Coomaraswamy (Sri Lanka; 1994–2003).[101] Since the new SR has been appointed at HRCR47 (2021), the next expected appointment will be at HRCR65 in June 2027. The reports of the SRs on VAW, its causes and consequences show different forms of SGBV and the legal development concerning it. In 1994, the SR Radhika Coomaraswamy submitted her report to CHR (4 January 1996). It was prepared on country visits. The SR got invitations from Japan and the Government of the Republic of Korea. Sexual slavery during the WWII by Japan's imperial army was the main theme of the mandate of this SR. This incident of military sexual slavery in wartime is known as 'comfort women.' It comes within the wider framework of VAW. The forms of violence mentioned in the report were rape, sexual slavery; forced labour, etc. The SR analysed the incidents on the basis of existing international law and the position of Japan and Korea. Lastly, the SR gave some recommendations.[102]

On 5 February 1996, the SR submitted another report.[103] The main focus was VAW within the family. She identified and listed some alleged cases on GBV against

---

[99] UN OHCHR (2019), "Report of the Special Rapporteur on violence against women, its causes and consequences: 25 Years Mandate"; available at: https://www.ohchr.org/EN/Issues/Women/SRWomen/Pages/SRWomenIndex.aspx (accessed on 11 September 2021).

[100] UN OHCHR (2009), "United Nations Special Rapporteur on Violence against Women"; available at: https://www2.ohchr.org/english/issues/women/rapporteur/docs/15YearReviewofVAWMandate.pdf (accessed on 11 September 2021).

[101] UN OHCHR (2021), "Current and Former Mandate-Holders for Existing Mandates" (valid as of 1 August 2021); available at: https://www.ohchr.org/EN/HRBodies/SP/Pages/Currentmandateholders.aspx (accessed on 25 September 2021); UN OHCHR (2021), "A framework for legislation on rape: Report of the Special Rapporteur on violence against women, its causes and consequences;" UN Doc. A/HRC/47/26/Add.1, 15 June 2021; available at: https://undocs.org/A/HRC/47/26/Add.1 (accessed on 11 September 2021); UN OHCHR (2021), "Rape as a grave and systematic human rights violation and gender-based violence against women;" available at: https://www.ohchr.org/EN/Issues/Women/SRWomen/Pages/SRVAW.aspx (accessed on 11 September 2021).

[102] UN ECOSOC (1996*)*, n.97.

[103] UN ECOSOC (1996), "Report of the Special Rapporteur on violence against women, its causes and consequences, Ms. Radhika Coomaraswamy, submitted in accordance with Commission on

women. 'Violence in the family' or 'domestic violence' was defined in the report. She used the definition of 'violence against women' and the meaning of 'gender-based violence' that has been explained in the UN Declaration on Violence Against Women and GR19 (1992) of the CEDAW Committee, respectively. The listed forms of VAW were: women battering; marital rape; incest or interfamilial child sexual abuse; forced prostitution; violence against domestic workers; violence against girl child; sex-selective abortion or female feticide and infanticide; traditional practices (used the term traditional or customary practices)[104] affecting health of women and children; female genital mutilation[105]; religious extremism.[106] This report discussed the available remedies under domestic legal system and international legal system. Lastly, the SR gave her recommendations. It carried phrases such as 'State must do,' 'State should,' 'State's duty,' 'UN must allocate resources,' 'adequate resources should,' 'international community should,' etc. These reflect non-binding character of the report. The SR submitted another report on the 'cultural practices in the family against women' (published on 31 January 2002). It elaborately explained different forms of cultural practices against women with some recommendations.[107] There are several other reports this SR submitted to the CHR during the tenure.

After analysing all the reports of the SRs, it is clear that they have used different terminologies under the broader rubric of 'violence against women.' SR Radhika Coomaraswamy mentioned about 'violence against women' and gender-based violence.' On the other hand, SR Rashida Manjoo (31 March 2015) reported upon 'sexual violence including rape', 'gender-based violence including sexual abuse', 'gender-based violence with an emphasis on sexual violence.[108] Similarly, the report of the SR Simonovic (report published on 17 April 2018) used 'violence against

Human Rights resolution 1995/85; Commission on Human Rights," UN Doc. E/CN.4/1996/53, 5 February 1996; available at: https://undocs.org/E/CN.4/1996/53 (accessed on 11 September 2021).

[104] Ibid, "The examples of the practices and acts of violence against women, such as female genital mutilation, female infanticide, prenatal sex selection and dowry-related violence".

[105] Ibid, "the customary practice of female genital mutilation is so serious that it has separately discussed in this report".

[106] Ibid, "the problem of violence in the home resulting from religious extremism has been of serious concern to the Special Rapporteur.".

[107] ECOSOC, Commission on Human Rights, "Report of the Special Rapporteur on violence against women, its causes and consequences, Ms. Radhika Coomaraswamy, submitted in accordance with Commission on Human Rights resolution 2001/49: Cultural practices in the family that are violent towards women", UN Doc. E/CN.4/2002/83, 31 January 2002; available at: http://undocs.org/en/E/CN.4/2002/83 (accessed on 10 September 2021).

[108] GA (2015), Human Rights Council, "Report of the Special Rapporteur on violence against women, its causes and consequences, Rashida Manjoo", UN Doc. A/HRC/29/27/Add.1, 31 March 2015, see, Paragraphs 62, 72, 8; available at: https://documents-dds-ny.un.org/doc/UNDOC/GEN/G15/068/64/PDF/G1506864.pdf?OpenElement (accessed on 10 January 2021).

women', 'sexual violence', 'violence against women including sexual violence',[109] 'gender-based violence against women,'[110] sexual violence including rape,' etc.[111]

Though the SRs have not used or defined the term 'SGBV' in their reports, 'gender-based' and 'sexual violence' is the main problematic issue that has emerged from these reports. SGBV is the predominant one and it has caused more harm than the others. In fact, it has been used to target a particular group. Moreover, it has been used to suppress women in any situation— during peace, conflict and post-conflict. Thus, it remains a challenge faced by women as a human and due to their gender that goes on uninterruptedly all the times.

(iv) **Special Rapporteur in the Field of Cultural Rights**

In 2009, the HRC decided a new special procedure of an "independent expert in the field of cultural rights" for three years. In 2012, it got the status of the SR in the field of cultural rights by the HRC resolution 19/6. The mandate was extended till 2015, then till 2018. There are some objectives of the SR on cultural rights. For example, identify best practices for promotion and protection of cultural rights; possible obstacles of it; integrate gender and disability perspective in SR's work; and so on. The SRs submit their reports to the HRC and the GA.[112] The SRs of cultural rights have been: Karima Bennoune (2015-2021)[113]; Ms. Farida Shaheed (2009–2015). On 23 March 2021 the HRC adopted resolution 46/9 for the appointement of a new SR on cultral rights.[114]

---

[109] GA (2018), Human Rights Council, "Report of the Special Rapporteur on violence against women, its causes and consequences on her mission to Australia," UN Doc. A/HRC/38/47/Add.1, 17 April 2018, see, Paragraph 73; available at: https://digitallibrary.un.org/record/1627464/files/A_HRC_38_47_Add-1-EN.pdf (accessed on 10 September 2021).

[110] Ibid, "Paragraph. 91.c...Expand the definitions of family and domestic violence to cover all forms of gender-based violence against women, including sexual assault, sexual harassment, violence in residential settings and online violence and harassment;".

[111] GA (2016), Human Rights Council, "Report of the Special Rapporteur on violence against women, its causes and consequences on her mission to Georgia," UN Doc. A/HRC/32/42/Add.3, 16 July 2016; available at: https://digitallibrary.un.org/record/842665/files/A_HRC_32_42_Add-3-EN.pdf (accessed on 10 September 2021).

See also, GA (2018), Human Rights Council, "Report of the Special Rapporteur on violence against women, its causes and consequences on online violence against women and girls from a human rights perspective", UN Doc. A/HRC/38/47, 18 June 2018; available at: https://undocs.org/A/HRC/38/47; https://www.ohchr.org/EN/Issues/Women/SRWomen/Pages/AnnualReports.aspx (accessed on 10 September 2021).

[112] OHCHR, "Information on the mandate"; available at: https://www.ohchr.org/EN/Issues/CulturalRights/Pages/MandateInfo.aspx (accessed on 10 September 2021), see also, GA (2012), "Human Rights Council, Special Rapporteur in the field of cultural rights", Res. 19/6, 22 March 2012, UN Doc. A/HRC/RES/19/6, 3 April 2012; available at: https://documents-dds-ny.un.org/doc/RESOLUTION/GEN/G12/127/13/PDF/G1212713.pdf?OpenElement (accessed on 10 September 2021).

[113] OHCHR, "Karima Bennoune, Special Rapporteur in the field of cultural rights"; available at: https://www.ohchr.org/EN/Issues/CulturalRights/Pages/KarimaBennoune.aspx (accessed on 10 January 2021).

[114] OHCHR, "Ms. Farida Shaheed, Special Rapporteur in the field of cultural rights"; available at: https://www.ohchr.org/EN/Issues/CulturalRights/Pages/FaridaShaheed.aspx (accessed on

Ms. Farida Shaheed submitted her report to the HRC.[115] The main focus of the report was equal enjoyment of cultural rights by the both women and men. This report analysed cultural rights as human rights. It also addressed the issue of cultural practices that violets the rights of the women. According to the report, violence against women is often justified by referring to culture, religion, and tradition. In fact, Women form the majority social group that suffers most in the name of culture.[116] Participation of women in cultural rights is needed. Participation also includes right not to participate in "specific traditions, customs and practices" that infringe human rights and dignity of women.[117] It has referred to the Declaration on the Elimination of Violence against Women; reports of the SRs on violence against women, its causes and consequences; the GA resolutions on all forms of violence against women; the UN Declaration of Indigenous People; and so on. It expressed that States are not allowed to invoke any religious, traditional, customary practices that promote or acts as defence for the violence against women.[118] The SR emphasized that direct discrimination against women should be eliminated by challenging discriminatory legal norms. The HRC President appointed a new special rapporteur, Ms Alexandra Xanthaki in October 2021. She gave her first report on 31 January 2022 (A/HRC/49/54) that sought to identify a preliminary list of issues while highlighting the empowering force of cultural rights.[119]

(v) SRs on Trafficking in Person, Especially Women and Children

The CHR decided to appoint SR for trafficking in person, especially women and children *vide* decision of 2004/110 that was, in turn, endorsed in the decision of

---

10 September 2021), see also, UN HRCR 45/9, UN Doc. A/RES/46/9 (1 April 2021); available at: https://daccessods.un.org/tmp/3817887.6042366.html (accessed on 28 March 2022).

[115] GA (2012), "Human Rights Council, Report of the Special Rapporteur in the field of cultural rights", UN Doc. A/HRC/19/L.18, 16 March 2012; available at: https://documents-dds-ny.un.org/doc/RESOLUTION/LTD/G12/121/13/PDF/G1212113.pdf?OpenElement (accessed on 10 September 2021).

[116] Ibid, see also, GA (2012), "Cultural rights Note by the Secretary-General", UN Doc A/67/287, 10 August 2012, expressed, "3:... Nevertheless, many practices and norms that discriminate against women are justified by reference to culture, religion and tradition, leading experts to conclude that "no social group has suffered greater violation of its human rights in the name of culture than women;" available at: https://undocs.org/en/A/67/287 (accessed on 10 September 2021).

[117] Ibid, para. 25.

[118] Ibid, "59: "Other important references include article 4 of the Declaration on the Elimination of Violence against Women prohibiting States from invoking custom, tradition or religious considerations to avoid their obligations... Articles 44 and 46 of the United Nations Declaration on Indigenous Peoples, stipulating that all the rights and freedoms recognized in the Declaration are equally guaranteed to male and female indigenous individuals and that limitation to the exercise of rights shall be non-discriminatory, must also be mentioned." "60. Cultural diversity is not a justification for practices that violate women's human rights.".

[119] UN OHCHR (2022), Report of the Special Rapporteur in the field of cultural rights: Cultural rights: Capturing the state of the art; Human Rights Council Forty-nineth session, 28 February-01 April 2022; UN Doc. A/HRC/49/54 of 31 January 2022; available at: OHCHR | A/HRC/49/54: Cultural rights: an empowering agenda - Report of the Special Rapporteur in the field of cultural rights (accessed on 15 April 2022).

the ECOSOC (2004/228).[120] In 2017, the mandate of the SR was extended for another three years by the resolution 35/5 of the HRC. The mandate of the SR is to focus on the human rights aspects of the victims of trafficking especially women and children as well as to identify the reasons for such trafficking. SRs for this theme are: Ms. Maria Grazia Giammarinaro (Italy; since 2014); Ms. Joy Ngozi (Nigeria; 2008–2014); Ms. Sigma Huda (Bangladesh; 2004–2008).[121]

The reports of the SRs underscore that forced trafficking leads to sexual slavery, sexual exploitation and other forms SGBV against women and children. Victims of transnational trafficking face re-victimization.[122] Trafficked women and children are often subjected to rape, forced prostitution, forced labour, forceful commercial and non-commercial sexual activity, as well as other forms of violation of human rights.[123] The reports have disclosed that forced marriage, kidnapping for marriage and child marriage are different forms of SGBV recognized as forms of human trafficking.[124]

The reports have shown interlinkages among trafficking, forced marriage, and harmful cultural practices. Also, the cultural practices of the different regions around the world do not allow women to take decisions about their marriage. Girls and women are forced into marriage that is regarded as a harmful cultural practice. It pushes women and children into forced trafficking. Forced marriage could lead

[120] ECOSOC (2004), "Decision 2004/228 on Special Rapporteur on trafficking in persons, especially women and children;" available at: https://www.un.org/ecosoc/sites/www.un.org.ecosoc/files/documents/2004/decision-2004-228.pdf (accessed on 10 September 2021).

[121] OHCHR, "Special Rapporteur on trafficking in persons, especially women and children"; available at: https://www.ohchr.org/en/issues/trafficking/pages/traffickingindex.aspx (accessed on 10 January 2021).

[122] ECOSOC, CHR (2004), "Report of the Special Rapporteur on trafficking in persons, especially women and children", UN Doc. E/CN.4/2005/71 22, December 2004, states, "10. Despite its overwhelming human rights dimension, trafficking is often perceived and addressed only as a law and order problem and is primarily located within the crime prevention framework.... Often, victims of trafficking are not protected against violations of the right not to be returned to a country where they would face serious human rights abuses, as established in the Convention against Torture and Other Cruel, Inhuman or Degrading Treatment or Punishment and the Convention relating to the Status of Refugees"; available at: https://documents-dds-ny.un.org/doc/UNDOC/GEN/G04/169/28/PDF/G0416928.pdf?OpenElement (accessed on 10 January 2021).

[123] ECOSOC (2005), "Report of the Special Rapporteur on the human rights aspects of the victims of trafficking in persons, especially women and children, Sigma Huda", UN Doc. E/CN.4/2006/62, 30 November 2005, expressed, "49. Moreover, two important textual points should be noted: the term "sex work" was rejected in the drafting of the Protocol itself, which instead employs the term "prostitution;" and the Protocol's sharp distinction between the "exploitation of prostitution" and "forced labour"; available at: https://documents-dds-ny.un.org/doc/UNDOC/GEN/G05/165/25/PDF/G0516525.pdf?OpenElement (accessed on 10 September 2021).

[124] GA (2007), HRC, "Report of the Special Rapporteur on the human rights aspects of the victims of trafficking in persons, especially women and children, Sigma Huda, Thematic mandate: Forced Marriage In The Context Of Trafficking In Persons, Especially Women And Children", UN Doc. A/HRC/4/23, 24 January 2007; available at: https://documents-dds-ny.un.org/doc/UNDOC/GEN/G07/104/10/PDF/G0710410.pdf?OpenElement; https://www.ohchr.org/EN/Issues/Trafficking/Pages/annual.aspx (accessed on 10 September 2021).

to violence often in extreme form.[125] Honour killing is a pernicious cultural practice wherein men kill their female relatives for suspecting 'immoral behaviour' or marrying outside the community.[126] During the war, trafficking for forced marriage often takes place. Women are recruited, transported, and forced to work as 'wives' of the soldiers. Women and girls who are the victim of forced marriage are subjected to different forms of SGBV during this time.[127]

(vi) SRs on Sale and Sexual Exploitation of Children

The SR on the sale and sexual exploitation of children has been launched in the 1990s. The SR is mandated to analyse the root causes for sale and sexual exploitation of children. Apart from the three mandates (country visit, sending individual complaints, reporting), the SR also conducts awareness and advocates for the protection of the human rights of the children. The SRs for this mandate have been: Ms. Maud de Boer-Buquicchio (Netherlands,; since 2014); Ms. Najat Maalla M'jid (2008–2014); Ms. Juan Miguel Petit (2001–2008); Ms. Ofelia Calsetas Santos (1994–2001); Mr. Vitit Muntarbhorn (1991–1994).[128] The reports of SRs included the issues of child prostitution, child pornography, and child sexual abuse. It has analysed as to how children become victims of sexual abuse and other forms of violence. Illegal adoption, the sale of children, child pornography, and child prostitution result different forms of SGBV against children especially the girls. In October 2021, the HRC adopted resolution 48/L.27 on "Mandate of the Special Rapporteur on the promotion and protection of human rights in the context of climate change". Though it did not expressly address the issues of SGBV, it has mentioned that the consecuences of climate change acuetly effect women. Following this, in a significant development, the 66th Session of the Commission on the Status of Women, 14 to 25 March 2022, gave an "urgent call for commitments and actions towards full and meaningful inclusion of women and girls in climate solutions." [129]

---

[125] UN Women (2014), "Comprehensive approach to end child, early and forced marriage needed;" available at: http://www.unwomen.org/en/news/stories/2014/9/panel-on-ending-child-and-forced-marriage (accessed on 10 September 2021).

[126] GA (2007), n.124, para, 38 and "41…Note that there are links between forced marriages and violence committed against women in the name of "honour". So-called "honour crimes" -an ancient practice sanctioned by culture rather than religion – are rooted in a complex code that allows a man to kill or abuse a female relative or partner for suspected or actual "immoral behavior.".

[127] Ibid, see para. 44.

[128] OHCHR, "Special Rapporteur on the sale and sexual exploitation of children;" available at: https://www.ohchr.org/en/issues/children/pages/childrenindex.aspx (accessed on 10 January 2021).

[129] GA (2016), HRC, "*Report of the Special Rapporteur on the sale of children, child prostitution and child pornography*," UN Doc. A/HRC/34/5522, December 2016; available at: https://digitallibrary.un.org/record/861191/files/A_HRC_34_55-EN.pdf (accessed on 10 January 2021); see also, UN Women (2022), "Women's Leadership in Climate Response and Recovery at the Centre of the UN Commission on the Status of Women"; available at: https://www.unwomen.org/en/news-stories/news/2022/03/womens-leadership-in-climate-response-and-recovery-at-the-centre-of-the-un-commission-on-thestatus-of-women (accessed on 29 March 2022).

Significance of the Reports of the SRs

The relationship between the SRs and the HRC is specified in the mandates. They show the importance and characteristics of the SRs. The reports reflect the effectiveness in promotion and protection of human rights. They also contribute to the development of 'soft' international normativity. The SR as an individual actor performs the role of promoting human rights in the international system[130] and plays a unique role in the international legal system. It is an independent, flexible, and fact-finding instrument. It interprets international instruments based on the factual evidence collected and analysed by the SR.[131] The SRs are conferred with diplomatic immunity and have commensurate visibility to carry out the mandate. The SRs with veritable platter of mandates (see Table 5.2) play a vital role in the mosaic of the UN's architecture for the protection and promotion of human rights especially in addressing the challenge of SGBV against women and girls. The SRs play a vital role through fact finding as well as submitting reports and opinions. The facts and figures of 2021 (UNGA Doc. A/HRC/49/82/Add.1 of 22 March 2022) provided by the HRC with regards to the special procedures underscore their vital contribution to the unique human rights architecture of the UN system.

C. Specialized UN Agencies and Forums

The work on VAW is not confined within the ambit of a particular institution or organ of the UN. Apart from the institutions that have already been discussed above, other entities also contribute to it within the UN system.[132] There are some specialized agencies[133]; funds and programmes of the UN[134]; other organizations and entities[135];

[130] Subedi, Surya P., et al. (2011), "The role of the special rapporteurs of the United Nations Human Rights Council in the development and promotion of international human rights norms," *The International Journal of Human Rights*, 15:2, 155–161.

[131] Piccone, Ted (2011), "The contribution of the UN's special procedures to national level implementation of human rights norms, "The International Journal of Human Rights", 15(2): 206–231.

[132] UN, "Directory of United Nations System Organization" available at: https://www.unsystem.org/directory (accessed on 17 September 2021).

[133] UN, *Specialized Agency*; available at: https://www.unsystem.org/members/specialized-agencies (accessed on 10 September 2021).

[134] "The UN Fund and Programmes: The Funds and Programmes were created by the United Nations to meet needs not envisaged at San Francisco, such as Palestine refugees, development assistance, food aid, or the environment. They are subordinate to the United Nations. They are somewhat more akin to specialized agencies than to "subsidiary organs" such as UN commissions and committees. Moreover, as their activities are more operational and carried out at field level, they have needs dictated by an environment quite different from that of headquarters-centred administrations. The Programmes and Funds apply UN rules and regulations in the realm of administration and personnel. E.g. The United Nations Development Programme (UNDP), Office of the UN High Commissioner for Refugees (UNHCR), United nations Children's Fund (UNICEF), United Nations population Fund (UNFPA), UN Office of Drugs and Crimes (UNODC), UN Women, etc.", see, UN, Directory of United Nations System Organizations, n.147.

[135] "Other Organizations and Entities: UN presents organizations and entities that are not members of the Chief Executives Board for Coordination. It includes organizations and entities that are

Table 5.2 Mandates of the UN Special Rapporteurs on Violence Against Women and Children (in chronological order)

No.	Name	Nationality	Title	Important agendas/thematic title	Year
1.	Dr. Dubravka Simonovic	Croatia	Violence against women, its causes and consequences	Violence against women journalists; online violence against women and girls; a human rights-based approach to integrated services and protection measures on violence against women[136]	2015 till date
	Ms. Rashida Manjoo	South Africa	Violence against women, its causes and consequences	Existing legal standards and practices regarding violence against women in three regional human rights systems and activities being undertaken by civil society regarding the normative gap in international human rights law; state responsibility for eliminating violence against women; gender-related killings of women; gender-motivated killings of women; discrimination and violence against women; reparations to women who have been subjected to violence[137]	2009–2015
	Dr. Yakin Erturk	Turkey	Violence against women, its causes and consequences	Implementation of international norms to end violence against women; intersections of violence against women and HIV/AIDS; due diligence standard as tool to end violence; culture and violence against women; political economy and violence against women; and violence against women and states response[138]	2003–2009
	Ms. Radhika Coomaraswamy	Sri Lanka	Violence against women, its causes and consequences	Human rights of women and gender; violence against women; violence against women during armed conflicts; trafficking in women; women migration; and domestic violence[139]	1994–2003

(continued)

[136] OHCHR, "Annual thematic reports of the Special Rapporteur"; available at: https://www.ohchr.org/EN/Issues/Women/SRWomen/Pages/AnnualReports.aspx (accessed on 11 September 2021). See also, GA (2020), HRC, "Combating violence against women journalists Report of the Special Rapporteur on violence against women, its causes and consequences", UN Doc. A/HRC/44/52, 6 May 2020; available at: https://undocs.org/A/HRC/44/52 (accessed on 19 September 2021).

[137] Ibid.

[138] Ibid.

[139] Ibid.

Table 5.2 (continued)

No.	Name	Nationality	Title	Important agendas/thematic title	Year
2.	Karima Bennoune	Algeria and the United States	Cultural rights	Climate change, culture and cultural rights; cultural rights defenders; the impact of fundamentalism and extremism on the cultural rights of women; the impact of fundamentalism and extremism on the enjoyment of cultural rights; destruction of cultural heritage as a violation of human rights[140]	2015-2021. HRCR46/9 (2021) led to appointment of new SR, Alexandra Xanthaki (Greece) in October 2021.
	Ms. Farida Shaheed	Pakistan	Cultural rights	The enjoyment of cultural rights by women on an equal basis with men; the right of access to and enjoyment of cultural heritage; cultural rights[141]	2009–2015
3.	Ms. Siobhán Mullally[142]	Ireland	On trafficking in person, especially women and children	Report not yet submitted	2020-till date
	Ms. Maria Grazia Giammarinaro	Italy	On trafficking in person, especially women and children	Human rights-based approach to trafficking in persons; trafficking in persons and labour exploitation; trafficking in persons in conflict and post-conflict situations[143]	2014–2020

(continued)

[140] OHCHR, "Annual reports of the Special Rapporteur on cultural rights"; available at: https://www.ohchr.org/EN/Issues/CulturalRights/Pages/AnnualReports.aspx (accessed on 11 September 2021).

[141] Ibid.

[142] OHCHR, "Biography of the Special Rapporteur on trafficking in persons, especially in women and children, Ms Siobhán Mullally"; available at: https://www.ohchr.org/EN/Issues/Trafficking/Pages/SiobhanMullally.aspx (accessed on 11 September 2021).

[143] OHCHR, "Annual reports: Reports to the General Assembly"; available at: https://www.ohchr.org/EN/Issues/Trafficking/Pages/annual.aspx (accessed on 12 September 2021).

Table 5.2 (continued)

No.	Name	Nationality	Title	Important agendas/thematic title	Year
	Ms. Joy Ngozi	Nigeria	On trafficking in person, especially women and children	Fosters all forms of exploitation of persons, especially women and children, effective remedy for trafficked persons; human rights-based approach to combatting trafficking in persons[144]	2008–2014
	Ms. Sigma Huda	Bangladesh	On trafficking in person, especially women and children	Forced marriage in the context of trafficking; demand for commercial sexual exploitation and trafficking; trafficking in persons, especially women and children[145]	2004–2008
4.	Ms. Maud de Boer-Buquicchio	Netherlands	Sale and sexual exploitation of children	Combating and preventing the sale and sexual exploitation of children through the implementation of the SDGs; thematic report on surrogacy; joint study on the vulnerabilities of children to sale, trafficking, and other forms of exploitation in situations of conflict and humanitarian crisis; study on illegal adoptions; sale of children for the purpose of forced labour; tackling the demand for the sexual exploitation of children; information and communication technologies and the sale and sexual exploitation of children[146]	Since 2014

(continued)

[144] Ibid.

[145] Ibid.

[146] OHCHR, "Annual reports to Human Rights Council and General Assembly: Reports to the Human Rights Council/Commission on Human Rights"; available at: https://www.ohchr.org/EN/Issues/Children/Pages/AnnualReports.aspx (accessed on 12 September 2021).

Table 5.2 (continued)

No.	Name	Nationality	Title	Important agendas/thematic title	Year
	Ms. Najat Maalla M'jid	Morocco	Sale and sexual exploitation of children	Sexual exploitation of children in travel and tourism; protection of children from sale and sexual exploitation following humanitarian crisis due to natural disasters; violence against children on child-sensitive complaint mechanisms; child pornography on the internet[147]	2008–2014
	Ms. Juan Miguel Petit	Uruguay	Sale and sexual exploitation of children	Assistance and rehabilitation programmes for child victims of trafficking and sexual commercial exploitation; demand for sexual services deriving from exploitation; child pornography on the internet; prevention of child sexual exploitation; legal consequences of the sale of children, child prostitution and child pornography, and particularly on the criminalization of child victims; HIV/AIDS and sexual exploitation of children[148]	2001–2008
	Ms. Ofelia Calsetas Santos	Philippines	Sale and sexual exploitation of children	The business sector and child exploitation; domestic violence; sale and trafficking of children; the role of the media and education in preventing and contributing to the commercial sexual exploitation of children; national and international initiatives to combat the sale and commercial sexual exploitation of children; commercial sexual exploitation of children and the role of the justice system[149]	1994–2001
	Mr. Vitit Muntarbhorn	Thailand	Sale and sexual exploitation of children	Merging concerns affecting the lives of children; global nature of the sale of children, child prostitution and child pornography[150]	1991–1994

[147] Ibid.

[148] Ibid.

[149] Ibid.

[150] Ibid.

related organizations[151]; research and training institutions[152]; interagency coordination mechanisms[153] that are engaged in addressing the issue of SGBV against women. The following IIs merit attention:

(i) United Nations High Commissioner for Refugees

The United Nations High Commissioner for Refugees (UNHCR) is working to address the issue of SGBV. In the introductory Chap. 1 of this study, it has been expressly mentioned that the definition of SGBV is provided by the UNHCR in its reports and strategies. It mainly focuses on the victims or survivors of SGBV who are affected by displacement and conflicts. It is constantly hammering for the urgency on the issue. For example, in 2011, it organized the Regional Dialogues with Refugee Women as part of the UNHCR's 60th anniversary events. It underscores the importance of the issue and the gravity of impunity associated with SGBV.[154]

Though UNHCR focuses on the refugees, the definition of SGBV given is practically useful for all. It has developed legal and policy directives that can ensure the recognition of SGBV against refugees.[155] It supports and assists States in meeting their international responsibilities in accordance with rule of law as well as ensures access to justice by all. The UNHCR and its partners play an important role at the

---

not listed under the principle directory categories. This list is alphabetically ordered. E.g. Joint UN Programme on HIV/AIDS (UNAIDS), Office of the United Nations High Commissioner for Human Rights (OHCHR), etc.;" see, UN, "Other organizations and entities"; available at: https://www.unsystem.org/more-entities (accessed on 10 January 2021).

[151] "Related organizations: The term "Related Organization" has to be understood as a default expression, describing organizations whose cooperation agreement with the United Nations has many points in common with that of Specialized Agencies, but does not refer to Article 57 and 63 of the United Nations Charter, relevant to Specialized Agencies. Nonetheless, these organizations are part and parcel of the work of CEB. E.g. International Organization for Migration (IOM);" See, *UN*, "Related organizations"; available at: https://www.unsystem.org/members/related-organizations (accessed on 10 January 2021).

[152] "UN research and training institutions: The various research and training institutes were established by the General Assembly (First mentioned in GA Res. 1827 (XVII) of 18 December 1962) to perform independent research and training" see, "UN Institute for Training and Research: History;" available at: https://www.unitar.org/about/unitar/institutes-history (accessed on 19 September 2021).

[153] "Inter-Agency Coordination Mechanism: The Chief Executives Board and its subsidiary mechanisms take into account the many coordination and inter-agency networks already in existence. These groups do not fall under the hierarchical structure but may be classified by their sphere of activity. E.g. the UN SC Working Group on Children and Armed Conflict, Task Force on Children and Armed Conflict, Inter-Agency Standing Committee Task Force on HIV on Humanitarian Situation, and so on;" see, UN, "Inter-Agency Coordination Mechanism;" available at: https://www.un.org/disarmament/disarmsec/coop/ (accessed on 10 September 2021).

[154] Division of International Protection, UNHCR (2013), "Access to Justice for Victims of Sexual and gender-Based violence" available at: https://www.ohchr.org/_layouts/15/WopiFrame.aspx?sourcedoc=/Documents/HRBodies/CEDAW/AccesstoJustice/UNHCR.pdf&action=default&DefaultItemOpen=1 (accessed on 10 September 2021).

[155] UN, "Information Note Division for the Advancement of Women: the United Nations Work on Violence against Women"; available at: http://www.un.org/womenwatch/daw/news/unwvaw.html (accessed on 10 September 2021).

local, regional and global levels, in understanding and helping to address many obstacles faced by the refugees, the internally displaced and the stateless victims of SGBV in accessing justice. It acts as a voice for the victims or survivors of the SGBV to restore their dignity; securing a remedy and ensuring that the perpetrators can be brought to justice delivery mechanisms.[156]

(ii) **UN Women**

In July 2010, the UN GA created the UN Women as a UN entity for the gender-equality and empowerment of women. It was established by the GA resolution 64/289(2010).[157] It came as a part of the UN reform agenda that sought to achieve the UN's goal on gender equality and empowerment of women. It merged four previously established distinct parts of the UN system[158] that were formed to achieve the same goal that the UN Women now has been entrusted with. It works with the governments and the civil society organizations. It assists in designing laws, policies, programmes, and services that are needed to confirm that the standards are effectively implemented for the benefit of the women and girls. It also works to achieve SDGs.[159] It supports the UN member States to achieve gender equality at the global level; works with civil society and the governments to design laws, policies, programmes, and different necessary services for the women and girls. It also works to achieve SDGs for gender equality.[160]

UN Women organizes different programmes in collaboration with other institutions. For example, the European Union, the ILO and the UN Women organized a national Consultative Dialogue on women migrant workers' rights and opportunities as well as ending violence against migrant women on 30 August 2018. During the period of COVID-19, the UN Women has been constantly working in addressing the varied challenges faced globally by women and girls. It provides updated information

[156] Ibid.

[157] GA Res. 64/2892, July 2010, UN Doc. A/RES/64/289, 21 July 2010, states, "49. Decides to establish, by the present resolution, as a composite entity, to be operational by 1 January 2011, the United Nations Entity for Gender Equality and the Empowerment of Women, to be known as UN-Women, by consolidating and transferring to the Entity the existing mandates and functions of the Office of the Special Adviser on Gender Issues and Advancement of Women and the Division for the Advancement of Women of the Secretariat, as well as those of the United Nations Development Fund for Women and the International Research and Training Institute for the Advancement of Women, to function as a secretariat and also to carry out operational activities at the country level;" available at: http://undocs.org/en/A/RES/64/289 (accessed on 10 September 2021).

[158] UN Women, "About UN Women", "UN Women It merges and builds on the important work of four previously distinct parts of the UN system, which focused exclusively on gender equality and women's empowerment: (i) Division for the Advancement of Women (DAW); (ii) International Research and Training Institute for the Advancement of Women (INSTRAW); (iii) Office of the Special Adviser on Gender Issues and Advancement of Women (OSAGI); (iv) United Nations Development Fund for Women (UNIFEM);" available at: http://www.unwomen.org/en/about-us/about-un-women (accessed on 10 September 2021).

[159] Ibid.

[160] Ibid.

and supports the important programmes to fight the 'shadow pandemic of violence against women during COVID-19.'[161]

(iii) UN High Commissioner for Human Rights

The Office of the United Nations High Commissioner for Human Rights (OHCHR) is a leading UN entity mandated to protect and promote human rights for all. It came to be formed through a resolution of the GA in 1993 as a sequel to the Vienna Conference on the Human Rights 1993. It is a part of the UN Secretariat and headquartered in Geneva. The OHCHR as a part of UN human rights programme began working as a small division of the UN Secretariat in New York.[162] The UN's regular budget covers the global funding of the OHCHR at a rate of approximately 40%. The remaining percentage of the funding is covered by voluntary contributions from the UN Member States and other entities such as the ILO.[163] The OHCHR addresses the issue of SGBV against women in its different reports. For example, in 2014, it explained the definition of SGBV and other related issues as SGBV in the context of transnational justice. It submits its reports to the GA, HRC and other UN organs and agencies under its mandate.[164]

D. Other Agencies

The World Health Organization (WHO), the UN Population Fund, the UN Children's Fund (UNICEF) and the UN Development Fund for Women (UNIFEM administers trust fund to eliminate violence against women) have specific policies regarding SGBV against women. The UN Centre for Crime Prevention and Criminal Justice contributes in preparing strategies for confronting domestic violence. The International Labour Organization (ILO) and the World Health Organization (WHO) also address some specific forms of VAW especially the occupational safety and health of the women.[165] The United Nations Population Fund (UNPF) is one of

---

[161] ILO, EU, ILO and UN Women join hands to end violence against women migrant workers in ASEAN/Myanmar; available at: https://www.ilo.org/yangon/press/WCMS_644164/lang--en/index.htm (accessed on 10 January 2021). "Since the outbreak of COVID-19, emerging data and reports from those on the front lines have shown that all types of violence against women and girls, particularly domestic violence, has intensified. This is the Shadow Pandemic growing amidst the COVID-19 crisis and we need a global collective effort to stop it," see, UN (25 December 2020), "The Shadow Pandemic"; available at: https://www.un.org/en/observances/ending-violence-against-women-day (accessed on 12 September 2021).

[162] OHCHR, "A Brief History"; available at: https://www.ohchr.org/EN/AboutUs/Pages/BriefHistory.aspx (accessed on 19 September 2021); see also, "OHCHR, Human Rights Hand Book for Parliamentarians N° 26;" available at: https://www.ohchr.org/Documents/Publications/HandbookParliamentarians.pdf (accessed on 10 September 2021).

[163] OHCHR, "OHCHR's Funding and Budget;" available at: https://www.ohchr.org/EN/AboutUs/Pages/FundingBudget.aspx (accessed on 10 September 2021).

[164] OHCHR (2014), "Sexual and gender-Based Violence in the Context of the Transnational Justice;" available at: https://www.ohchr.org/Documents/Issues/Women/WRGS/OnePagers/Sexual_and_gender-based_violence.pdf (accessed on 10 September 2021).

[165] Ibid, see also, UN, "the United Nations Work on Violence against Women;" available at: http://www.un.org/womenwatch/daw/news/unwvaw.html (accessed on 10 September 2021).

the important agencies that works for the women's empowerment and gender equality at the global level. It also addresses different forms of violence against women.[166] The main focus is on sexual and reproductive health of the women. For example, FGM, HIV/AIDS, childbirth, child marriage, and other harmful practices, etc.[167]

(i) **Independent Experts and Working Groups**

All the human rights treaties have their treaty bodies to receive regular reports from the States parties. These bodies are also known as 'committees' or 'human rights treaty bodies' or 'treaty bodies.'[168] The treaty bodies examine the reports in the presence of the representatives of the States parties. They also receive information informally from the NGOs. All the human rights treaty bodies have the power to make general comments and general recommendations. These recommendations are used to interpret a treaty.[169] These treaty bodies receive an individual inquiry complaint directly from the individual without representing by the States.[170]

For example, the HRC has the power to accept the individual complaints under the Optional Protocol of the Covenant of Civil and Political Rights (ICCPR). This individual complaint mechanism is availed by the individuals whose States have ratified the Optional Protocol to the ICCPR. There are some cases relating to women' rights and violence against women decided by the HRC.[171]

---

[166] UNFPA, "Gender-based violence;" available at: https://www.unfpa.org/gender-based-violence (accessed on 10 September 2021).

[167] UNFPA, "About us;" available at: https://www.unfpa.org/about-us (accessed on 10 September 2021).

[168] "Human Rights Bodies are: There are nine core international human rights treaties. Each of these treaties has established a "treaty body" (Committee) of experts to monitor implementation of the treaty provisions by its States parties. Currently, eight of the human rights treaty bodies (CCPR, CERD, CAT, CEDAW, CRPD, CED, CESCR and CRC) may, under certain conditions, receive and consider individual complaints or communications from individuals," OHCHR, "Human Rights Bodies - Complaints Procedures: Complaining about human rights violations"; available at: https://www.ohchr.org/EN/HRBodies/TBPetitions/Pages/HRTBPetitions.aspx (accessed on 10 September 2021).

[169] Cook, Rebecca J. (1994), "Women's International Human Rights Law: The Way Forward", in Rebecca J. Cook, *Human Rights of Women: National and International Perspectives*, Philadelphia: Pennsylvania University Press.

[170] OHCHR, "Human Rights Bodies - Complaints Procedures: Complaining about human rights violations", n.168.

[171] Cook, Rebecca J. (1994), n.169, pp. 23–24. See also, the cases decided by the Human Rights Committee are: Sandra Lovelace v. Canada, Communication No. R.6/24, U.N. Doc. Supp. No. 40 (A/36/40) at 166 (1981) on the gender discriminatory State law; available at: http://hrlibrary.umn.edu/undocs/session36/6-24.htm (accessed on 10 September 2021); Shirin Aumeeruddy-Cziffra et al. vs. Mauritius (Known as Mauritian Women case); Communication No. R.9/35, U.N. Doc. Supp. No. 40 (A/36/40) at 134 (1981), it was a case on discrimination against women on the basis of sex; available at: http://hrlibrary.umn.edu/undocs/session36/9-35.htm (accessed on 10 September 2021); Broeks vs. Netherlands, Communication No. 172/1984, the Committee found violence against women on the basis of sex; Avellanal vs. Peru, Communication No. 202/1986, discrimination against women on the basis of sex, gender and race relating to property right; Yilmaz-Dogan vs. The Netherlands, Communication No. 1/1984 discrimination against women on the basis of

The Committee on the Elimination of Discrimination against Women (CCEDAW) plays a crucial role in addressing the issue of SGBV. It is a body of twenty-three independent experts around the world that monitors the implementation of the Convention on the Elimination of All Forms of Discrimination against Women, 1979 (CEDAW). According to the Optional Protocol to the CEDAW, it can receive a complaint from the individuals of the States parties to the Protocol. It can initiate inquiries in case there is a situation of grave and systematic violation of women's rights. It formulates general recommendations (GRs) and suggestions.[172] Since 1982, it has made continuous efforts to develop its working methods.

The current method of the CEDAW includes guidelines for making reports by the States parties; considerations of reports by the committee through pre-seasonal working group; constructive dialogue and concluding observation; adoption of strategies to encourage reporting by the States; integration with specialized agencies and bodies of the UN; participation of NGOs in the activities of the Committee; general recommendations; and consult to other human rights treaty bodies.[173] The secretariat of the CEDAW Committee is located in Geneva (Switzerland) both for the treaty and individual complaints.[174] The main contribution of the Committee is its GRs. Though the CEDAW has not covered many important aspects of SGBV against women; still GRs are very useful. For example, VAW is not specifically mentioned in the CEDAW. The GR19 of the Committee has explained that GBV amounts to discrimination against women under the CEDAW.[175]

GRs or GCs are important in understanding the human rights treaty obligations. These are the "indispensable" sources of interpretation of the CEDAW. Though GRs and GCs are useful, yet they are not free from criticisms. Legal validity or normativity can be questioned. For instance, according to Keller and Grover:

---

sex; available at: http://www.un.org/womenwatch/daw/cedaw/protocol/cases.htm (accessed on 10 September 2021).

172 OHCHR, "Committee of the Elimination of All forms of discrimination against Women;" available at: https://www.ohchr.org/EN/HRBodies/CEDAW/Pages/Introduction.aspx (accessed on 10 September 2021). Also see, Membership of the Committee: the Committee on the Elimination of Discrimination against Women; available at: https://www.ohchr.org/EN/HRBodies/CEDAW/Pages/Membership.aspx (accessed on 10 September 2021).

173 Ibid. See also, OHCHR, "Working Methods of the Committee of CEDAW;" available at: https://www.ohchr.org/EN/HRBodies/CEDAW/Pages/WorkingMethods.aspx (accessed on 10 September 2021). See also, Article 21 *of the CEDAW*; available at: https://www.ohchr.org/Documents/ProfessionalInterest/cedaw.pdf (accessed on 10 September 2021).

174 OHCHR, "Secretariat Contact Detain: Committee of the Elimination of All forms of Discrimination against Women (CEDAW)"; available at: https://www.ohchr.org/EN/HRBodies/CEDAW/Pages/Contact.aspx (accessed on 10 September 2021).

175 UNHCR, "Chapter 6: The International and Regional Legal Framework;" available at: http://www.unhcr.org/47cfad542.pdf (accessed on 10 September 2021).

> Reaction to general comments has ranged from regarding them as 'authoritative interpretations' of treaty norm, to 'broad, unsystematic, statements which are not always well founded, and are not deserving of being accorded any particular weight in legal settings.[176]

Sometimes States are critical and deny accepting the statements made in the GRs or GCs. There are also mixed reactions by the national and international courts on GRs. Hence, there is a mixed acceptance of the normativity of the GR by the States parties and the commentators. Therefore, it can be argued that an acceptance of GRs by the States parties brings about soft normativity. If we see the GRs from an international legal perspectives such as 'clear language, sound reasoning, and transparent drafting', they get separate legitimacy both individually and as a body of work.[177]

Legitimacy of the GR does not depend on the acceptance or objections of the States parties. It can be surmised that the GRs are not legally binding on the States parties. The GRs may be treated as soft international law instruments. According to some scholars, GRs come under the preview of "secondary soft law instruments." It means GRs are the "sources of non-binding norms that interpret and add detail to the rights and obligation contained in the respective human rights treaties."[178] The GRs contribute to the international practice of interpretation of the treaties. Some scholars have argued that these could be part of customary international law by virtue of the States practice and *opinio juris*. The GRs are based on the experience gathered from the reports of the States parties and the cases resolved by the HRC and the complaints dealt with by the CEDAW Committee.[179]

The Committee of the Rights of the Child (CRC) is a body of eighteen independent experts for monitoring implementation of the Convention on the Rights of Child (CRC) 1989. It also monitors implementation of two Optional Protocols of the Convention based on 'Protection of children in armed conflicts' and 'Prohibition of sale of children, child prostitution and child pornography.' In 2011, the third Optional Protocol was adopted that provides direct complaint mechanism by the individual children from the States parties.[180] Some provisions of the CRC and CEDAW overlap especially relating to gender-based issues and protection of women and girls. In such a situation, it has seen that both the Committees of the CRC and the CEDAW did joint work in cases such as the Joint GR31 of the CEDAW and GC14 of the CRC. Hence, it can be said that both the conventions are mutually reinforcing and complementary.[181]

---

[176] Keller, H. and L. Grover, (2012), "General Comments of the Human Rights Committee and their legitimacy," in Helen Keller and Geir Ulfstein (eds.), *UN Human Rights Treaty Bodies: Law and Legitimacy*, UK: Cambridge University Press.

[177] Ibid.

[178] Ibid.

[179] Ibid.

[180] OHCHR, "Committee on the Rights of the Child;" available at: https://www.ohchr.org/en/hrbodies/crc/pages/crcindex.aspx (accessed on 10 September 2021).

[181] Goonesekere, S. and R. De Silva-De Alwais (2005), "Women's And Children's Rights In A Human Rights Based Approach To Development," United Nations Children's Fund (UNICEF),

In 1998, the Secretary-General of the UN reported on "Integrating the Gender Perspective into the Work of the UN Human Rights Treaty Bodies." It provided a clear explanation of incorporating gender in the work of the Committee of the CRC. The main focus of the Committee is the protection of the rights of the girl children and the prevention of violence against them. At the same time, the Committee has designated one of its members to follow the work of the Committee of the CEDAW regularly. As a result, the first joint meeting of both the Committees took place in Cairo (Egypt) in 1996. The lifecycle of women and girls show that they face SGBV from the mother's womb to till death. This cycle of violence against women interlinked the work of the two Committees. So, the CRC Committee is working simultaneously and jointly with the CCEDAW. Both are also working separately as a treaty body to address SGBV against women and girls.[182]

The movements against SGBV have drawn global attention because of the UN and its organs. These are working both individually as well as jointly under the umbrella of the UN system. The Secretary-General of the UN addresses the issues with his valuable opinions on the contemporary issues regarding ending SGBV. The recent development shows that the UNSG, Antonio Guterres, is pushing for ending SGBV that he has characterized as a 'blight' on all the societies. On 25 November 2020, on the occasion of 'international day for the elimination of violence against women' the UNSG expressed grave concern that "violence against women and girls is a global emergency requiring urgent action at all levels, in all spaces and by all people."[183] He further observed that:

> Millions of women are being pushed further into poverty by the COVID-19 crisis, and all forms of violence against them are rising. In this context, the global community must continue to build on the momentum we have created to prioritize the voices, experiences and need of women and girls.[184]

The UN Secretary-General's UNiTE to End Violence against Women by 2030 campaign is a multiyear effort that intends to prevent and eliminate SGBV. It calls for the global action to reduce and bridge the funding gaps, ensure essential services for survivors of violence during the COVID-19 crisis, taking preventing measures, and collection of data that necessary services can be provided to the women and girls. The other initiatives and campaigns under the UN system include "Orange the World:

New York; available at: https://www.unicef.org/gender/files/WomensAndChildrensRightsInAHumanRightsBasedApproach.pdf (accessed on 10 September 2021).

[182] Ibid. "While the Committee addresses a variety of issues on a case-by-case basis, the issues most commonly addressed are girls' early marriage age; early/teenage pregnancy; the low status of girls in society; adverse health practices; sexual abuse and exploitation; educational opportunities for girls; and family planning education and services.".

[183] UN (2020), "End gender-based violence, 'once and for all', UN urges on International Day", UN News, 25 November 2020; available at: https://news.un.org/en/story/2020/11/1078492 (accessed on 13 September 2021).

[184] UN (2020), "Build on momentum to end violence against women and girls: Secretary-General", UN News, 25 November 2020; available at: https://news.un.org/en/story/2020/11/1078562 (accessed on 12 September 2021).

Fund, Respond, Prevent, Collect". It began on 25 November, 2020 with 16 days activism against SGBV.[185]

Other International Institutions

The Amnesty International, the Human Rights Watch (HRW), the International Committee of the Red Cross (ICRC), other International Non-Governmental Organizations (INGOs), universities, and, research institutions work as international actors, indicators, defenders and think tanks to address the challenge of SGBV. They have made meaningful contributions in implementing the laws and policies relating to SGBV. They have taken the initiatives to bring forward new voices and perspectives through their research, different programmes, dialogue, and networking. They also take part in the law-making and negotiation processes.[186]

The UN Secretary-General's in-depth study on VAW explains that the involvement of civil society organizations especially women specific organizations are important. They contribute to the enactment of laws; monitoring, review, and reform of legislation; implementation of laws; improving criminal justice mechanism system; providing services; and so on.[187] For example, the NGOs of Luxembourg are involved in combating harmful cultural practices. They provide necessary care and supports to the victims of harmful cultural practices and take necessary acre to empower them.[188]

The International Committee of the Red Cross (established in 1863) works as an independent and neutral humanitarian organization. It has made pioneering contribution in the enactment and development of international humanitarian law (IHL). It works on the basis of voluntary donations and the funds provided by many of the governments.[189] It has contributed in humanizing warfare as well as protecting the people in conflicts. It has specifically addressed the issue of SGBV against women in the conflict zones. ICRC is working in collaboration with other IOs like the UN

[185] UN Women, "UNiTE by 2030 to End Violence against Women campaign;" available at: https://www.unwomen.org/en/what-we-do/ending-violence-against-women/take-action (accessed on 12 September 2021). See also, UN Women, "16 Days of Activism against Gender-Based Violence 2020 UNiTE Campaign Theme: "Orange the World: Fund, Respond, Prevent, Collect!"; available at: https://www.unwomen.org/en/what-we-do/ending-violence-against-women/take-action/16-days-of-activism (accessed on 13 September 2021). See also, UN Women, *In Focus: 16 Days of Activism against Gender-based Violence*; available at: https://www.unwomen.org/en/news/in-focus/end-violence-against-women (accessed on 13 September 2021).

[186] UN Women, "Civil society oversight"; available at: http://www.endvawnow.org/en/articles/1105-civil-society-oversight.html (accessed on 10 September 2021).

[187] UN, "Fighting violence against women;" available at: http://www.un.org/womenwatch/daw/vaw/launch/english/v.a.w-fightE-use.pdf (accessed on 10 September 2021).

[188] OHCHR, "The Committee on the Elimination of Discrimination against Women review the situation of women in Luxemburg;" available at: https://www.ohchr.org/EN/NewsEvents/Pages/DisplayNews.aspx?NewsID=22743&LangID=E (accessed on 10 September 2021).

[189] ICRC, "Our mandate and mission;" available at: https://www.icrc.org/en/who-we-are (accessed on 10 September 2021).

for cohesive and effective response mechanisms in addressing the crimes relating to SGBV.[190] Peter Maurer, President of the ICRC has observed:

> Too often sexual atrocities are accepted as an inevitable by-product of war. This must end. The law is clear: Rape and other forms of sexual violence are a violation; Today we pledge to do better for the survivors of sexual and gender-based violence. We demand an end to sexual atrocities used as a tactic of war; and we demand a change in attitudes that blame survivors, not the perpetrators.[191]

We do not always expressly mention and mostly bypass the contributions of the universities or educational institutions including the scholars.[192] The university-based structures and programmes wherein scholars have made major contributions through cutting-edge scholarly works in addressing SGBV against women. The universities and other educational institutions are engaged in and promote cutting-edge research on the issues concerning SGBV against women. This study is a manifestation of such scholarly audacity in examining the nature, gravity, contributing factors and role of international institutional actors in addressing the challenge of SGBV against women in the field of international law as well as finding solutions to it. The scholars see SGBV against women from different angles including efficacy of the international legal framework. They also identify the causes and consequences of SGBV by linking it with different interdisciplinary areas. The scholars work either individually or in group or by engaging with other intuitions. They impart their ideas and provide suitable solutions to the problems as well as organize seminars, conferences, workshops to generate awareness on the issue.[193]

Judicial Institutions

Transnational justice includes both backward-looking and forward-looking approaches. Backward-looking can be in the form of: punishing the perpetrators, payment or compensation to the victims, returning the property to the owners, revealing the truth. On the other hand, forward-looking approach can comprise establishing peace; recapturing the lost culture or traditions; institution building for the social, economic and political purpose; and other kinds of reforms

---

[190] ICRC, "The primary responsibility for tackling sexual violence rests with the authorities;" available at: https://www.icrc.org/en/document/primary-responsibility-tackling-sexual-violence-rests-authorities-0 (accessed on 10 September 2021), see also, ICRC (2019), "Heads of UN, Red Cross and Red Crescent Movement pledge to step up action on sexual violence in conflict"; available at: https://www.icrc.org/en/document/heads-un-red-crossred-crescent-pledge-step-action-sexual-violence-conflict (accessed on 12 September 2021).

[191] Ibid, see also, ICRC (1919), "Standing together against sexual and gender-based violence Speech by ICRC President"; available at: https://www.icrc.org/en/document/speech-icrc-president-joint-event-sexual-and-gender-based-violence-un-secretary-general (accessed on 12 September 2021).

[192] For example, centre for gender and Violence Research, Bristol University; available at: http://www.bristol.ac.uk/sps/people/group/sps_centres/2983 (accessed on 10 September 2021).

[193] The World Bank (2018), "Research Team at Monash University Awarded for Innovation in Preventing Gender-based violence in Cambodia;" available at: https://www.worldbank.org/en/news/press-release/2018/04/19/research-team-at-monash-university-awarded-for-innovation-in-preventing-gender-based-violence-in-cambodia (accessed on 10 September 2021).

and restructuring of the ruptured post-conflict society.[194] In fact the process and structure of the transnational justice mechanisms is rooted in accountability and redressal for the victims.[195] Thus, it has been observed that:

> Transnational justice refers to the short-term and often temporary judicial and non-judicial mechanisms and processes that address the legacy of human rights abuses and violence during a society's transition away from conflict or authoritative rule.[196]

Survivors or victims are expected to get back their dignity as human beings through the transnational justice processes. They use the existing laws and policies as instruments as well as ensure that the people of a particular country are safe from the abuses carried out by their authorities and others.[197] The initiatives which are adopted by the governments as the 'transnational justice' mechanisms include criminal prosecutions, truth commissions, reparations programmes, and so on.[198] The principles[199] laid down in the UN Secretary-General's 'Guidance Note on the United Nations Approach to Transnational Justice 2010' provide that transnational

---

[194] Ibid.

[195] ICTJ, "What is Transitional Justice?", provides, "Transitional justice refers to the ways countries emerging from periods of conflict and repression address large-scale or systematic human rights violations so numerous and so serious that the normal justice system will not be able to provide an adequate response. Transitional justice is rooted in accountability and redress for victims. It recognizes their dignity as citizens and as human beings. Ignoring massive abuses is an easy way out but it destroys the values on which any decent society can be built. Transitional justice asks the most difficult questions imaginable about law and politics. By putting victims and their dignity first, it signals the way forward for a renewed commitment to make sure ordinary citizens are safe in their own countries – safe from the abuses of their own authorities and effectively protected from violations by others…"; available at: https://www.ictj.org/about/transitional-justice (accessed on 10 September 2021).

[196] Sanam Naraghi Anderlini, Camille Pampell Conaway And Lisa Kays, "Transnational Justice and Reconcilliations"; "Goals of transnational Justice: The goals of transitional justice include: • addressing, and attempting to heal, divisions in society that arise as a result of human rights violations; • bringing closure and healing the wounds of individuals and society, particularly through "truth telling;" • providing justice to victims and accountability for perpetrators; • creating an accurate historical record for society; • restoring the rule of law; • reforming institutions to promote democratisation and human rights; • ensuring that human rights violations are not repeated; and promoting co-existence and sustainable peace;" available at: https://tavaana.org/sites/default/files/49_transitional_justice.pdf (accessed on 10 September 2021).

[197] Ibid.

[198] ICTJ, "What is Transitional Justice?", n.195.

[199] UN, (2010), "Principle 9 of the United Nations Secretary-General's 'Guidance Note on the United Nations Approach to Transnational Justice 2010", provides "Strive to ensure transitional justice processes and mechanisms take account of the root causes of conflict and repressive rule, and address violations of all rights, including economic, social and cultural rights Violations of economic, social, and cultural rights not only exacerbate or spark social or political tensions resulting in conflict or repression, but conflict or repression often precipitate further violations of these rights. Successful strategic approaches to transitional justice necessitate taking account of the root causes of conflict or repressive rule, and must seek to address the related violations of all rights, including economic, social, and cultural rights (e.g., loss or deprivation of property rights). Peace can only prevail if issues such as systematic discrimination, unequal distribution of wealth and social services, and endemic corruption can be addressed in a legitimate and fair manner by trusted

justice process and mechanisms take into account the causes of the conflicts and the process of reparations that are needed. It also focuses on the violation of human rights.[200] Transnational justice comprises both judicial and non-judicial mechanisms, including prosecution initiatives, reparations, and truth-seeking, institutional reform, or a combination thereof. The procedure needs to be according to and in conformity with international legal standard and obligations. There are IOs (e.g. the UN) and other organs of the UN system (e.g. the OHCHR) that provide assistance and guidance on the rule of law regarding transnational justice.[201] Hence, transnational justice is a mechanism and a process for proving justice to the victims of past abuses.[202]

Apart from judicial and non-judicial mechanisms, it could also include initiatives in respect of the right to truth, institutional reforms, national consultations, and reparations.[203] Moreover, approaches such as causes of conflicts, violations of rights of the people during and after the conflicts, human rights can be taken into consideration for incorporation in the transnational justice mechanism systems.[204]

Transnational justice focuses on GBV during and after the conflicts or war. It can provide responses to combating women's marginalization and preventing future violations against women and other communities targeted due to their gender. It can meaningfully address the causes and consequences of violence against women. The past few decades have seen progress in promoting public acknowledgement regarding gender inequality, discrimination, and gender-based violence. It has also been seen that there is a lack of implementation of those public acknowledgements. It is the result of a lack of technical knowledge in implementing measures that can encourage women's participation and adequately address the issue of GBV. It has been seen that women are often excluded from the decision-making processes and resultant peace agreements. This calls for active participation of women in the transnational justice mechanism processes.[205] As women form part of the most of the victims of the SGBV, the gender perspective needs specifically factored into the processes and structures of the transnational justice mechanisms.[206] This could be

---

public institutions;" available at: https://www.un.org/ruleoflaw/files/TJ_Guidance_Note_March_2010FINAL.pdf (accessed on 10 September 2021).

200 UN, "Transitional Justice and Economic, Social and Cultural Rights"; available at: https://www.ohchr.org/Documents/Publications/HR-PUB-13-05.pdf (accessed on 10 September 2021).

201 OHCHR, "Rule of Law Transitional Justice"; available at: https://www.ohchr.org/EN/Issues/RuleOfLaw/Pages/TransitionalJustice.aspx (accessed on 10 September 2021).

202 UN (2010), "Guidance Note of the Secretary-General: United Nations Approach to Transitional Justice", n.199.

203 Ibid.

204 Ibid.

205 ICTJ, "Gender Justice"; available at: https://www.ictj.org/our-work/transitional-justice-issues/gender-justice (accessed on 10 January 2021).

206 Security Council (2003), "Women Suffer Disproportionately During and After War, Security Council Told During Day-Long Debate On Women, Peace And Security," UN Doc. SC/7908 29 October 2003; available at: https://www.un.org/press/en/2003/sc7908.doc.htm (accessed on 10 January 2021).

possible only with an effective participation of women especially local women in reparation, resettlement, rehabilitation, reintegration, peace treaties and post-conflict reconstruction processes.[207]

In a refreshing beginning the international criminal courts and tribunals (ICTs) have also started addressing the issue of SGBV against women in some criminal cases to punish the perpetrators (discussed in Chap. 3 of this book).

Conclusion

Though VAW is as old as the human civilization, the initiatives for combating this on a systematic basis are of recent origin. IIs discussed in this chapter are cumulatively making best efforts, within the limits of their mandate and the resources, in addressing the issue from the grass root level to the international level. There are many institutions that are engaged in addressing the challenge of SGBV against women and different institutions use different terminologies to address different forms of SGBV. Some institutions focus on a particular issue; on the other hand, some are dealing SGBV against women in its entirity.

There are some funding institutions that help in implementing the strategies or policies. Unfortunately, somehow major gaps exist among the institutions. There is a lack of coherence, interlinkages and synergies among the institutions. Every institution is doing its job either individually or jointly. Hence, proper cooperation and coordination among the institutions is the need of the hour. How far these IIs are successful in effectively addressing the issue of SGBV against women? This itself remains a subject of scholarly study that needs to be given a priority due to the gravity of the SGBV as a global scourge.

[207] Fionnuala Ní Aoláin (2009), "Women, Security, and the Patriarchy of Internationalized Transitional Justice", *Human Rights Quarterly*, 31(4):1055–1085.

Chapter 6
The Legal Challenges

Introduction

As discussed in the previous chapters, sexual and gender-based violence (SGBV) against women has become a 'new normal' as part of our daily existence. The situation has reached alarming proportions with the nature and magnitude of SGBV rising graphically in every country and continent on the planet earth. As a shocking reality at the beginning of third decade of the twenty-first century, the United Nations (2020) data shows that (i) "1 in 3 women and girls (estimated 736 million) experience physical or sexual violence in their lifetime, most frequently by an intimate partner" (ii) "71% of all human trafficking victims worldwide are women and girls, and 3 out of 4 of these women and girls are sexually exploited" and (iii) "globally 81,000 women and girls were killed in 2020, around 47,000 of them (58 per cent) died at the hands of an intimate partner or a family member." It underscores the severity of the global challange. The realiztion is gradually downing that SGBV results in significant cost to the States, victims-survivors and communities. During 2021, the Europen Union alone, the early cost of gender-based violence (SBV) and violence against women (VAW) was estimated to be Euro 366 billion and Euro 289 billion (79%), repectively.[1]

The spread and intensity of SGBV in a way also reflects the stage of human 'progress'. In fact, SGBV in conflict zones has been as old as the history of warfare itself. The situation has been compounded by the walls of silence as regards acknowledgement of the very existence of SGBV.[2] In stemming the rising tide of SGBV, there

[1] UN (2020), "International Day for the Elimination of Violence against Women"; available at: https://www.un.org/en/observances/ending-violence-against-women-day (accessed on 16 September 2021). See, European Institute for Gender Equality, "Gender-based violence costs the EU €366 billion a year", 7 July 2021; available at: https://eige.europa.eu/news/gender-based-violence-costs-eu-eu366-billion-year#:~:text=The%20European%20Institute%20for%20Gend er,amounting%20to%20%E2%82%AC289%20billion (accessed on 17 April 2022).

[2] Chapman, Jane Roberts (1990), "Violence against Women as a Violation of Human Rights", *Social Justice, Criminality, Imprisonment & Women's Rights in the 1990s,* 17(2):40; Heineman, Elizabeth

B. H. Desai and M. Mandal, *Sexual and Gender-Based Violence in International Law*,
https://doi.org/10.1007/978-981-19-0894-1_6

are many roadblocks faced by international institutions, States, civil society organizations, scholars, and other concerned actors. Hence, the challenge for elimination of SGBV against women requires a "community-based, multipronged approach, and sustained engagement with multiple stakeholders."[3]

In this context, legal and non-legal challenges are interconnected. These challenges also differ according to the facts and circumstances of the nature of SGBV in a society. For instance, in cases of forced marriages with the perpetrators in post-conflict societies[4]; cases of SGBV go unreported for various reasons including social pressure or social stigmatization both during peace and conflicts[5]; abandonment of the victims[6]; loosing economic, social and cultural rights by the victims[7] and lack of data collection.[8] Cumulatively, they present challenges for the justice delivery mechanisms and the welfare of the survivors. There are some other challenges specifically connected with the attitudes, utterances and actual practices of the States such as reservation to the human rights treaties; non-ratification of the optional protocols; implementation gaps; withdrawal of membership from the human rights bodies[9] and shortage of funding.

Legal Challenges

Law is one of the important tools for societal change. It faces different obstacles such as lack of legal awareness, low probability of apprehension, inconsistency between legislative prohibitions, and cultural norms or practices. However, law alone cannot

---

D (2011), *Sexual Violence in Conflict Zones: From the Ancient World to the Era of Human Rights*, USA: University of Pennsylvania Press.

[3] The World Bank (2019), "Gender-Based Violence: Violence against Women and Girls"; available at: https://www.worldbank.org/en/topic/socialsustainability/brief/violence-against-women-and-girls (accessed on 16 September 2021).

[4] UN (2015), "Fight against Sexual Violence in Conflict Reaches 'New Juncture,' Security Council Told;" available at: https://www.un.org/press/en/2015/sc11862.doc.htm (accessed on 16 September 2021).

[5] India Today, (2016), "Pakistani Women Protest outside the UNHRC Against," *India Today*, 22 September 2016; available at: http://indiatoday.intoday.in/story/pakistani-women-protest-outside-the-unhrc-against/1/770412.html (accessed on 16 September 2021).

[6] Lindsey, Charlotte (2001), ICRC, "Study on the impact of armed conflict on women;" available at: https://www.icrc.org/eng/assets/files/other/icrc_002_0798_women_facing_war.pdf (accessed on 16 September 2021).

[7] UN (2000), "Women, Peace and Security;" available at: https://www.un.org/ruleoflaw/files/womenpeaceandsecurity.pdf (accessed on 16 September 2021).

[8] UN (2005), *Expert Group Meeting* (11–14 April 2005), Organized by the UN Division for the Advancement of Women in Collaboration with the Economic Commission for Europe (ECE) and World Health Organization (WHO), on "Violence against women: a statistical overview, challenges and gaps in data collection and methodology and approaches for overcoming them;" available at: http://www.un.org/womenwatch/daw/egm/vaw-stat-2005/docs/final-report-vaw-stats.pdf (accessed on 16 September 2021).

[9] BBC News (2018), "US quits 'biased' UN human rights council", US & Canada, 20 June 2018; available at: https://www.bbc.com/news/44537372 (accessed on 16 September 2021).

change the mindset of the people to bring about a decisive change in the practices such as child marriages in Bangladesh, sex-selective operations in China, and dowry payment from the side of brides in India.[10] The existing non-legal problems could attain a form wherein they become legal problems. Similarly, the core legal problems or failure of the legal systems encourage in generating problems that include both legal and non-legal problems. For example, gaps within the legislations, slow justice delivery, etc. are unable to provide a proper remedy to the victims even as women and girls face the rising tide of SGBV. Thus, it can be surmised that legal and non-legal challenges are interconnected. In the course of six chapters of this study, an effort has been made to examine the nature and challenge of SGBV, roles of cultural factors and international institutions as well as to propose some solutions to address the challenge. Still, some specific legal challenges could be enlisted as follows:

(i) Lack of Acknowledgement and Awareness

An acknowledgement of the existence of SGBV remains one of the key challenges. Historically, there has been silent about it. There are many forms of SGBV that are unacknowledged or unidentified.[11] In fact, the State and the communities often connive in or overlook the institutionalized forms of violence against women. For example, some cultures *per se* do not consider psychological demeaning behaviour, persistent wife-beating practices, and even sexual harassment in society and the work places as violence against women. Moreover, in some cultures, forced marriage of a widow with the relative of the deceased husband to protect the property of the family has been accepted as a normal practice.

With the rise in education and awareness, growing scrutiny of international human right institutions and socio-religious reformation movements in many countries, specific legislations have been enacted to protect women against violence.[12] Still, in

---

[10] Klugman, Jeni (2017), "Background paper for World Development Report 2017 Gender based violence and the law;" available at: http://pubdocs.worldbank.org/en/232551485539744935/WDR17-BP-Gender-based-violence-and-the-law.pdf (accessed on 16 September 2021).

[11] Chapman, Jane Roberts (1990), n.2.

[12] For example, "In 2011, the Government of Cape Verde passed a new law against gender-based violence; both El Salvador and Mexico have defined femicide as a criminal offence as well as measures to punish it; in 2011, Pakistan and non-governmental advocates, in backing passage of sweeping new legislation to prevent the use of acid attacks on women and to stop harmful customary practices. The Criminal Law Act 2011 for the first time levies prison sentences and fines for acid attacks;" see, UN Women, "Passing and implementing effective laws and policies;" available at: http://www.unwomen.org/en/what-we-do/ending-violence-against-women/passing-strong-laws-and-policies (accessed on 11 September 2021). In 2002, "Bangladesh enacted two specific pieces of legislation to address acid violence: the Acid Crime Control Act (ACCA) and the Acid Control Act (ACA);" see, Avon Global Center for Women and Justice at Cornell Law School and the New York City Bar Association (2011) "Combating Acid Violence in Bangladesh, India and Cambodia;" available at: https://www.ohchr.org/Documents/HRBodies/CEDAW/HarmfulPractices/AvonGlobalCenterforWomenandJustice.pdf (accessed on 16 September 2021). In 2012,

many of the cases, the law enforcement agencies are not aware of the new progressive legislations and due to patriarchal structures and processes, the rights of the women remain on the margins. In many of the situations, the State and the people of a particular community are either ignorant or are afraid to bring about legislative changes to stop harmful cultural practices (HCPs) against women. This is duly facilitated by the gender-biased culture. Hence, in the first place, it necessitates sharing, caring, and recognition of SGBV. This calls for an awareness and sensitization that provide a basis for equality of gender, in all the activities in the public sphere.[13] It will facilitate beginning of the inevitability of change as regards deep rooted inequality and discrimination against women.

In view of this, an awareness or knowledge about the existence of law is very important. Any lack of awareness about the existence of SGBV can create a gap between existing law and its implementation process. The situation becomes precarious when the law seeks to challenge the customary, traditional or cultural practices. In such a situation, the perpetrators commit violence against women with impunity without any fear of punishment. Similarly, on the other side of the spectrum, women cannot raise their voice against SGBV as they need to accept the acts of violence as forming an integral part of the cultural practices. Many women become privy or party to it or for various reasons are co-opted to allow the pernicious practices to continue unabated. For example, in 2014, a study reported that many people in India were not aware of the existing law against intimate partner violence (IPV) against women. Women who were unaware of the existence of law faced more violence from their intimate partners. Thus, it remains a big challenge to give effect to laws regarding SGBV at international law and national levels. Similarly, the female genital mutilation (FGM) has asumed unprecedented levels-in 2022 alone, there are 4.2 million girls around the world who are at risk of undergoing FGM, notwithstanding global outrage against such a serious violation of bodily integrity of women in most of the countries.[14]

Ironically, there are only a few forms of SGBV against women that are considered as criminal offence under international and national criminal laws. SGBV as an independent form is still not designated as a crime *per se* either in national or international legal systems. SGBV against women in conflict zones has been treated as a war crime, crime against humanity or genocide; but it has not been viewed as a distinct and special kind of international crime wherein mostly women and girls are become 'soft' targets especially due to their gender. 'Rape' is given more importance

India adopted *Protection of Children from Sexual Offences Act*; available at: http://www.ncpcr.gov.in/index1.php?lang=1&level=0&linkid=23&lid=593 (accessed on 16 September 2021). *Criminal Amendment Act*, 2018 of India amended different provisions that deals with the changing nature of SGBV against women especially rape, gang rape, etc.; available at: https://mha.gov.in/sites/default/files/CSdivTheCriminalLawAct_14082018_0.pdf (accessed on 16 September 2021).

[13] UNIFEM (2005), "Combating Gender-Based Violence: A Key to Achieving the MDGS"; available at: https://www.unfpa.org/sites/default/files/pub-pdf/combating_gbv_en.pdf (accessed on 16 September 2021).

[14] Klugman, Jeni (2017), n.10.: UN, "Ending Female Genital Mutilation by 2030"; available at: https://www.un.org/en/observances/female-genital-mutilation-day (accessed on 17 April 2022).

though other forms of SGBV that are equally serious but get overlooked. It remains one of the biggest challenges to prohibit SGBV during conflicts and provide justice to the victims-survivors. The vulnerability of the victims not only affects individually but also paralyses an entire group, society, and nation at large. Therefore, it has been aptly opined that SGBV is not inevitable; rather, it is a crime that should be investigated and perpetrators need to be severely punished.[15]

(ii) Ambiguity in Definitions

The first chapter of this study underscores that though women, in general, are the victims of SGBV, some women face double victimization due to their specific situation, e.g. refugee women. One of the key challenges remains ambiguity and lack of precise legal definition of SGBV itself. It is, generally, sought to be explained on the basis of meaning provided by the other disciplines such as sociology, anthropology, etc. The second chapter provides an overview of the challenge of SGBV and seeks to explain as to why SGBV has emerged as a global concern. In view of gravity, global spread, highly detrimental effect especially on women and girls and its exacerbation even due to climatic changes leads us to suggest that SGBV needs to be addressed as a *common concern of humankind*.

Ironically, there is a general tendency to cover the issue of SGBV under the veils of ignorance and silence. It makes the effect pernicious as the dreadful consequences of SGBV remain on the margins in the global discourse and policy-making processes. It is a positive sign that the language of discourse now reflects little seriousness of the issue and takes cognizance of specific forms of violence emanating from specific cultures and traditions. It indicates that SGBV is more than only sexual violence or gender-based violence especially against women.

There is no clear legal definition yet of SGBV. The first chapter of this study has used the explanation of SGBV as defined by the United Nations High Commissioner for Refugees (UNHCR) and the Office of the Commission for Human Rights (OHCHR). The UN Security Council and other concerned international institutions have also used this explanation of SGBV. Notwithstanding a flurry of international legal developments, the contours of SGBV remain elusive in both soft and hard international law instruments.[16] The forms of violence against women have also often

[15] Catherine Boucher, Legal Advisor for the Permanent Mission of Canada to the UN, opening remarks at the panel discussion organized by UN Women (26 October 2017) on "Investigating Conflict Related Sexual and Gender-Based Crimes". Boucher observed: "Over the decades there has been a dramatic shift in the way the world views sexual and gender-based violence. It is not inevitable; it is a crime that must be investigated, prosecuted, and punished"; available at: http://www.unwomen.org/en/news/stories/2017/10/news-event-wps-investigating-conflict-related-sexual-and-gender-based-crimes (accessed on 16 September 2021).

[16] UNHCR, "Sexual and gender-based violence (SGBV) prevention and response"; available at: https://emergency.unhcr.org/entry/60283/sexual-and-gender-based-violence-sgbv-prevention-and-response (accessed on 16 September 2021).

overlapped. Many forms of SGBV comprise a combination of different categories of violence. As such they cannot be strictly assigned to any one category. For instance, FGM falls within the categories of both physical and sexual violence.[17]

The UNHCR and other institutions have used the term 'SGBV' to emphasize the scope and gravity of sexual violence taking place during conflicts and displacement. SGBV is understood to cover all the forms 'sexual violence' (SV), 'gender-based violence' (GBV) and 'violence against women' (VAW) as referred to in various international legal instruments. SGBV *per se* does not remain gender neutral. Hence, women remain the primary victims and sufferers. Moreover, the determination of the existence of different forms of SGBV against women remains a big challenge.[18] It has been aptly construed that SGBV against women "emphasizes the urgency of protection that addresses the criminal character and disruptive consequences of sexual violence for victims or survivors and their families."[19] Primarily, SGBV has been routinely used against women and girls as a tactic or a no-cost weapon in most of the armed conflicts. However, due to its perpetual consequences, it is also used even during peacetime. Hence, the SGBV phrase is used for all the kinds of violence especially against women and girls in peacetime, during conflicts and post-conflict situations.[20]

Another area of legal challenge is that all forms of SGBV against women are not treated as a 'crime' in both international law and national legal systems. International criminal law treats only some forms of SGBV as a 'crime.' The 2014 *Policy Paper* of International Criminal Court (ICC) considered SGBV as a crime. According to the 1998 Rome Statute (Article 7.3), the term 'gender' includes "two sexes, male and female, within the context of society". So the crimes against the 'third gender' do not yet figure under the Rome Statute. The Statute has defined 'gender-based crimes' committed against both male and female that may include even non-sexual attacks because of their gender. 'Sexual crimes' includes the listed crimes under Articles 7(1)(g), 8(2)(b)(xxii), and 8(2)(e)(vi) of the Rome Statute as contained in the 'elements' of crimes (Article 9). In fact, sexual crimes need to include both physical and non-physical, e.g. forced nudity with sexual elements.

In a way, the explanation of 'gender' is based on societal acceptance or socially constructed roles. It could vary from region, community and culture. Thus, gender-based discrimination or gender-based crimes (GBC) depend upon the stereotype roles set by the society for both male and female. 'Sex' is based on biological or psychological character. So, sexual crimes would include sexual elements that are common for all. Sexual and gender-based crimes (SGBC) are based on biological sex

---

[17] UNHCR (2016), "SGBV Prevention and Response"; available at: http://www.unhcr.org/583577ed4.pdf (accessed on 16 September 2021).

[18] Ibid.

[19] UN Women (2013), "Terminology and definitions"; available at: http://www.endvawnow.org/en/articles/1474-terminology-and-definitions.html (accessed on 16 September 2021).

[20] Population Council, "Sexual and Gender-Based Violence;" available at: https://www.popcouncil.org/research/sexual-and-gender-based-violence (accessed on 16 September 2021). See also, Bartels A Susan (2013), "Sexual and gender-based violence," Public Health Action 3(2): 93; available at: https://www.ncbi.nlm.nih.gov/pmc/articles/PMC4463106/ (accessed on 16 September 2021).

as well as the existence of gender norms and inequality in a particular society. Under international criminal law, SGBC are mostly linked to warfare or armed conflicts. However, SGBCs are not yet treated as independent crimes *per se*. They are rather included and construed within the meaning of genocide, crimes against humanity, or war crimes (Rome Statute; Articles 6, 7, 8, respectively). At the same time, all the forms of SGBV during conflicts are also not treated as SGBCs.[21] As a result, SGBV violence includes all forms of violence—sexual and gender in nature—committed during peacetime and conflicts. Since all forms of SGBV are not regarded as a crime and they may not fall within the independent elements of offence or crimes under the rubric of 'SGBV', it presents a serious definitional challenge for international criminal law.

Apart from it, international institutions like the UNHCR as well as people working in the fields of sociology, public health, etc.[22] prefer to use the term 'survivors' rather than 'victims' of SGBV. It is contended that the term 'victim' is used in the legal field to denote the people who were subjected to violence during war or conflicts. The term 'survivor' has been preferred more because it implies resilience too.[23] Hence, a vital question arises: Who are the victims? Does it also include dependents or family members who also suffer physically and mentally? Thus, the definition of survivors or victims is a grey area that needs to be bridged properly in the international legal instruments as well as national legal systems.

(iii) Gaps in International Law

The third chapter of the study has identified that there is no specific international legal instrument on SGBV. The issue still remains on the margins and all forms of SGBV are not yet included. Similarly, the lack of coherence and vagueness remain constraints in the existing international law framework on SGBV. The debate relating to normativity of public international law is not new. However, in the first quarter of the twenty-first century, the soft international law tools have emerged as an important hallmark especially in the area of SGBV as an emerging global common concern of humankind.

Interestingly, the thin dividing line between hard and soft international law instruments is gradually getting blurred and yet they are being taken seriously. This came to the fore in the explicit reference to the UN Security council resolution 1325 (2000) by the Chairperson of the Norwegian Nobel Committee in the award ceremony of the 2018 Nobel Peace Prize (Nadia Muard and Denis Mukhwege). It appears, to begin

[21] International Criminal Court (2014), "Policy Paper on Sexual and Gender-Based Crimes;" available at: https://www.icc-cpi.int/iccdocs/otp/OTP-Policy-Paper-on-Sexual-and-Gender-Based-Crimes--June-2014.pdf (accessed on 16 September 2021).

[22] Buard, V. Et al. (2013), "Characteristics, medical management and outcomes of survivors of sexual gender-based violence, Nairobi, Kenya," Public Health Action, 3(2): 109–112; available at: https://www.ncbi.nlm.nih.gov/pmc/articles/PMC4463105/ (accessed on 16 September 2021).

[23] UNHCR (2016), n.17.

with, the so-called soft international law is filling the gaps in the existing treaty and customary international law. It would provide a stepping stone for crystallization of a *lex specialis* required for the effective prohibition and elimination of SGBV.

The normative gaps in international law relating to SGBV against women, have been sought to addressed in recent years, among others, by the UN Special Rapporteurs (SRs); international law scholars, international institutions (IIs) and human rights defenders. The UNSR (Rashida Manjoo) argued that there are normative gaps in international law because there is no specific legally binding instrument - *lex specialis* - on SGBV against women. Moreover, the provisions of the non-binding international legal instruments are not part of customary international law that would provide a basis for application to the States irrespective of being a party to the treaty.[24] One of the legally binding international instruments, the Convention on the Elimination of All Forms of Discrimination against Women (CEDAW), seeks to deal with the women's rights and yet it does not specifically address SGBV against women. In fact, the general recommendation (GR) 19 of the Committee of the CEDAW, has underscored the link between SGBV and the CEDAW. The GRs are non-binding international law instruments. So, these normative gaps do provide justification for the adoption of the new binding international legal instrument, as *lex specialis,* to addess the challenge of SGBV against women.[25]

(iv) Taming the Cultural Factors

The fourth chapter has specifically focused on the role of the cultural factors in enabling and exacerbating SGBV against women. It shows that culture may not always be good for the people of a particular region. In fact, harmful cultural practices (HCPs) result in gross violation of the fundamental human rights of the women and girls. A 'patriarchal' and outdated cultural norms that nurture SGBV as well as encourage violence against women need to be tamed, changed and eliminated. For instance, the discourse on FGM now revolves around its elimination since it

[24] International Women Rights Action Watch Asia Pacific, in its discussion paper stated, "Asia Specific, Gender-Based Violence Against Women And International Human Rights Law: Options For Strengthening The International Framework Discussion Paper," has explained that, "[t]he lack of a legally binding instrument on violence against women precludes the articulation of the issue as a human rights violation in and of itself, comprehensively addressing all forms of violence against women and clearly stating the obligations of States to act with due diligence to eliminate violence against women. The current norms and standards within the United Nations system emanate from soft law developments and are of persuasive value, but are not legally binding. The normative gap under international human rights law raises crucial questions about the State responsibility to act with due diligence and the responsibility of the State as the ultimate duty bearer to protect women and girls from violence, its causes and consequences;" see, OHCHR, "IWRAW: Asia Pacific Discussion Paper Option International Mechanism;" available at: https://www.ohchr.org/Documents/Issues/Women/SR/Framework/2.IWRAW-AsiaPacificDiscussionPaperOptionInternationalMechnisms.pdf (accessed on 16 September 2021).

[25] Ibid.

causes 'irreparable and irreplaceable' harm to female bodily integrity. Similarly, many unidentified HCPs transgress and violate the rights of the women and girls. In order to address and eradicate such HCPs, education and women's participation in the entire decision-making process are required.

In this context, it appears, reporting of the cases relating to SGBV is very important to make the perpetrators accountable so as to provide justice to the victims-survivors. In most of the cases of SGBV, there is an element of stigma. It results in 'bricks of shame' and 'walls of silence' that in practice contribute to the maintenance of the 'culture of impunity' for the perpetrators. Any absence of fear of prosecution and punishment can only allow the perpetrators (evil) to be more aggressive in causing wanton harm to the victims of SGBV and upset the societal fabric. It results in negation of the principle of victory of 'good' over 'evil' that has been, since time immemorial, rooted in allmost all civilizations, cultures and religions. It requires timely reporting of the cases to trigger the process for availing help from police, social workers, lawyers, doctors and other counsellors.[26]

The victims of SGBV, especially those who are living with health-related problems, e.g. women having HIV/AIDS after mass rapes continue to face societal stigmatization. They are discriminated; socially boycotted; forced to live in shame, fear, and anger. In extreme situations of some cultures, the survivors or victims are treated as an evil spirit and, in turn, no one comes forward to help them. They are targeted physically, abused emotionally, and sometimes murdered by the family or the community in the name of honour. This inevitably leads to 'silence' of the victims, non-reporting of the cases and hence provides virtual impunity to the perpetrators who may actually be from the same community or from the rival groups.[27]

Thus, impunity and roll out of the 'red carpet' syndrome for the perpetrators remains the biggest challenge in effectively addressing SGBV against women. The existing societal environment, lack of victim support system and absence of justice delivery mechanisms for SGBV inevitably provides impunity for the perpetrators and renders the victims-survivors helpless.[28] It becomes more ominous especially if the perpetrators hold high positions in the government or the military.[29] As a result, it presents an insurmountable challenge in most of the post-conflict justice mechanisms to punish the perpetrators. It can lead to atrocious situations that add insult to injury wherein the victims are forced into marriages with the perpetrators or any family members of the perpetrator and even forced abortions, etc.

As in most of the cases, 'culture' is used as a tool to defend the SGBV They are covering up violence against women under the belief of 'essential cultural practices,' or 'integral part of cultural or religious practices.'[30] Unfortunately, it is never

---

[26] Jeni Klugman (2017), n.10.

[27] UNIFEM (2005), n.13.

[28] Manjoo, R and C. McRaith, (2011), "Gender-Based Violence and Justice in Conflict and Post Conflict Areas," *Cornell International Law Journal,* 44: 11–31; Available at: https://ww3.lawschool.cornell.edu/research/ILJ/upload/Manjoo-McRaith-final.pdf (accessed on 16 September 2021).

[29] Ibid.

[30] For further details see, *Sunita Tiwari v. Union of India* (2008), "A counter affidavit has been filed resisting the stand of the petitioner on a number of grounds… the said practice an integral part of

entirely clear as to: What could be the essential cultural or religious practices? Similarly, some other questions pertain to the nature and characteristics of essential practices: Who has the authority to determine them etc. These crucial legal challenges need to be resolved to make a dent of the lethal effect of SGBV against women.

(v) Need for Cooperation Among Institutions

The chapter five has placed under the scanner importance and role of the institutions in addressing the challenge of SGBV from the grassroots level to the international level. Many of the institutions are engaged in ending SGBV against women. Yet there are gaping holes in the roles performed by the institutions and between institutions as well as overlapping or conflicting jurisdictions among the institutions as regards their work and the mandates. They often end up working at cross purposes due to lack of coordination and synergies among them. These IIs have made use of different terminologies to address SGBV such as 'violence against women,' 'gender-based violence,' 'and sexual violence,' SGBV etc. It shows the need for resolving the quagmire of interagency[31] engagement of different international institutions. It raises the question: How far these IIs are successful in addressing the issue of SGBV against women? The multiplicity of organs, institutional ego, turf wars, wastage of resources, etc. cumulatively end up in dampening the interests of the States in addressing the simmering global crisis of SGBV against women. As a result, it will have a fatigue effect on the sovereign States. Thus, there is a need for a global programme of action, a *lex specialis* international legal instrument to address SGBV as a heinous crime and a scourge against women and an overreaching umbrella organization for addressing SGBV that can effectively coordinate the work of different institutions so as to ensure timely results.

(vi) Complexities of Justice Delivery Mechanisms

It has seen in various cases, especially in the post-conflict justice mechanisms, that the procedure is lengthy, complex and expensive. It takes a long time and procedural steps to punish the perpetrators. Irrespective of the colour imparted, these mass crimes carry the special flavour of 'hitting where it hurts the most' including SGBV against women and girls, environment and heritage (cultural and natural) sites. It can comprise people of their own nationalities and others. A perusal of most of the

---

the religion... the matter should be referred to a larger Bench for an authoritative pronouncement because the practice is an essential and integral practice of the religious sect;" available at: https://indiankanoon.org/doc/181206322/ (accessed on 16 September 2021).

[31] UNICEF (2020), *Gender-Based Violence: UNICEF Leadership in Inter-Agency Initiatives*, available at: Gender-based violence in emergencies | UNICEF (accessed on 21 September 2021).

conflicts in recent decades show that the marauding hordes who engage in brutalities, carry them out with an acute sense of complexities of the post-conflict justice delivery systems. That is why many of the notorious perpetrators such as Idi Amin (Uganda), Pol Pot (Cambodia) went scot-free. Even after his overthrow in a military coup, Al-Bashir (Sudan) is still out of the reach of the prosecutors of the ICC. Similarly, justice still eludes the hundreds of thousands of women victim-survivors of mass rapes during the 1971 Bangladesh liberation war.[32] In fact, it took 38 long years even to start the trial procedure, without bringing to book the main perpetrators of the Pakistani Army, by the International Crimes Tribunal (Bangladesh) in 2009.[33] There are many other cases, wherein the formal justice delivery mechanism to punish the perpetrators has not yet been adopted, e.g. the Korean 'comfort women' issue. As a result, victims-survivors suffer the most. In fact, apart from justice, there is no mechanism whatsoever to provide succour, relief, and counselling to heals the wounds of the traumatized women.

It remains one of the biggest tragedies of this Digital Age and Space Age that SGBV has assumed global proportions, women and girls remain one of the 'soft' targets (apart from environment and heritage sites), it is spoken in hushed tones, international institutions prefer to be cautious and even scholars sparsely choose to write on these heinous crimes. Apart from it, no global mechanism whatsoever exists that enables the affected families and societies to use the self-help deterrent to de-stigmatize mass rapes in conflicts. The complexity gets worsened due to pervasive attitudes about the bodily integrity of women, as well as outdated notions of 'defilement' and 'impurity.' Similarly, the lives and security of the victims, witnesses, and the human rights defenders are threatened.[34] Some of the worrisome cases include attacks on the humanitarian workers in Mali[35]; in 2019, Nasrin Sotoudeh (Iranian lawyer) was sentenced to imprisonment for protesting against headscarf[36]; Afzal Kohistani (human rights activist) was shot dead in Abbottabad (Pakistan) for seeking justice in the 2019 'honour killing'.[37]

---

[32] Adrija, Roychowdhury (2016), "Birth of Bangladesh: When raped women and war babies paid the price of a new nation," *Indian Express*, 19 December 2016; available at: http://indianexpress.com/article/research/birth-of-bangladesh-when-raped-women-and-war-babies-paid-the-price-of-a-new-nation-victory-day-4430420/ (accessed on 16 September 2021).

[33] International Crimes Tribunal-1, Bangladesh; available at: http://www.ict-bd.org/ict1/ (accessed on 16 September 2021); BBC News (2016), "Bangladesh war crimes trial: Key accused", 4 September 2016; available at: http://www.bbc.com/news/world-asia-20970123 (accessed on 16 September 2021).

[34] Ibid.

[35] Ibid.

[36] BBC News (2019), "Nasrin Sotoudeh: Iran lawyer who defended headscarf protesters jailed," 11 March 2019; available at: https://www.bbc.com/news/world-middle-east-47531312 (accessed on 16 September 2021).

[37] BBC News (2019), "Afzal Kohistani: Calls for justice after 'honour killing' activist's murder," 8 March 2019; available at: https://www.bbc.com/news/world-asia-47497096 (accessed on 16 September 2021). for further details see, International Crimes Tribunal, Bangladesh; available at: https://www.ict-bd.org/ (accessed on 16 September 2021).

(vii) Quest for Victim-Survivor Centric Approaches

As seen in most of the cases, victims-survivors are the primary eyewitnesses. Human memory can fade away with the passage of time or death of victims or other witnesses. In fact, undue delay also denies justice and often complicates the quest for justice. The perpetrators also destroy evidence. For instance, there are very few 'comfort women' who are alive though it remains a bone of contention mainly between Korea and Japan. Most of the 'comfort women' did not get justice during their lifetime. On the other side, it is difficult to prove the victimhood of the women and girls in the conflict zones. The situation of a conflict-affected society is always unstable, full of turmoil and most of the structures of justice delivery system collapse during prolonged conflicts. Hence, the collection of evidence is not possible and victims and the witnesses are unable to identify the perpetrators. Similarly, due to systematic and mass rapes under orders, most of the victims-survivors suffer from various diseases such as sexually transmitted disease, HIV/AIDS, different physical and psychological trauma etc. They are denied reproductive life and right to health itself.[38] As a result, in most of the cases, women victims-survivors are unable to cooperate and participate in the peacebuilding processes. Therefore, at the minimum level, a victim-centric approach needs to be the cornerstone of any robust post-conflict justice mechanism.

Other Important Challenges

The victims-survivors of SGBV are often denied their right to property. In most of the cases, victims are deprived of their economic, social, cultural, and political rights. They are forced to live in extreme poverty without having recourse to even basic human rights.[39] These situations push them into extreme poverty, human trafficking or other exploitative works.[40] It also leads to rise in heinous crimes such as cross-border trafficking, illegal human trade, smuggling and narcotics trade.[41] Since 2009, in the post-conflict Sri Lankan society, 80% of the women are either widow, unmarried, divorced or living separately from their husbands. In fact, 70% of women head the households, and large numbers of women are still jobless. Women in rural areas of Sri Lanka are facing problems to earn their livelihood.[42] As a consequence,

---

[38] UN (2000), "Women, Peace and Security;" available at: https://www.un.org/ruleoflaw/files/womenpeaceandsecurity.pdf (accessed on 16 September 2021).

[39] Ibid.

[40] Cameron, Hazel (2016), *The New Raw Resources Passing Through the Shadows, Human Trafficking: The Complexities of Exploitation*, in Malloch, M and P. Rigby (Ed.), UK: Edinburgh University Press.

[41] Ibid.

[42] Guneratne, Camena (2016), "Civil Society Activism in a Challenging Political Landscape of Sri Lanka: Some Issues," Lecture delivered on 29 January 2016 at the Centre for International Legal studies, School of International studies, Jawaharlal Nehru University: New Delhi.

women, especially widow and single mothers, are trafficked to other countries. Even children and women are subjected to sex trafficking in brothels within their own country.[43]

It has been seen that in many of the cases, terrorist groups use the helpless situation of the victims-survivors. They use and force women victims-survivors as a cover to further spread terror. For example, in Iraq, women have been subjected to violence as result of the armed conflict as well as terrorism.[44] Identity crisis is one of the complex challenges in the post-war societies that the women and children born out of rape mostly face[45] as these children are treated as mixed blood or mixed race.[46] They are deprived of their rights, identity, and future. Thus, the post-conflict societies face a lot of complex situations. Hence, it is highly probable to have re-occurrence of conflicts or war. The Democratic Republic of Congo is a classic example of being entrapped in the quagmire of perennial conflict. The recent stories of conflict-ridden countries such as Congo, Iraq, Sudan, Syria and Yemen graphically underscore this brutal reality.

(i) Participation of Women in Peace Treaties

In most of the cases, women victims-survivors do not get an opportunity to share their experiences of SGBV in absence of post-conflict justice delivery mechanisms. In most of the cases, if such a mechanism somehow takes shape, these women have to depend upon their family members for their testimonies wherein they are forced state what their family members want, or they hide the real facts for the sake of family honour or security of their family. Women are not encouraged to speak about their victimhood because of the fears of social oppression, ostracization and stigmatization. The situation becomes worse when women have undergone systematic and large-scale sexual violence and mass rapes. In such circumstances, women do not dare to share their sufferings. For instance, it has remained a graphic reality even after 50 years of genocide and mass rapes (estimated between 200,000 to 400,000) in the Bangladesh liberation war (1971) wherein retreating Pakistani troops were let loose on the populace amidst prepartion by their higher command to sign the instrument of surrender before the top command of the Indian army. In most of the cases, women victims-survivors do not report about the heinous sexual crimes committed

---

[43] ICAN (2013), International Civil Society Action Network, "Elusive Peace, Pervasive Violence: Sri Lankan Women's Struggle for Security and Justice;" available at: http://tamilwritersguild.com/Elusive_Peace_Pervasive_Violence_Sri_Lan.pdf (accessed on 21 September 2021).

[44] SC (2015), "Conflict-related sexual violence Report of the Secretary-General," UN Doc. S/2015/203, 23 March 2015 available at: http://www.securitycouncilreport.org/atf/cf/%7B65BFCF9B-6D27-4E9C-8CD3-CF6E4FF96FF9%7D/s_2015_203.pdf (accessed on 11 September 2021).

[45] Leatherman, Janie, (2007), "Sexual Violence and Armed Conflict: Complex Dynamics of Re-Victimization," *International Journal of Peace Studies*, 12(1): 53–71.

[46] Ibid.

against them as they are afraid of social exclusion, reputation of their family, and the future of their children. As a result, victim-survivors are unable to get any legal redress *per se*, reparations and justice. This is especially so since:

> Women are affected in many ways during war, but there has been particular attention given to sex-based crimes…In practice, however, gender-based crimes are underrepresented in international tribunals and in national courts. This is, in part, because few women are in leadership positions within these institutions and are rarely consulted during the design of tribunals…Even when women are willing to come forward, they are often faced with having to relive their worst experiences without having the opportunity to fully tell their stories.[47]

The international community and the civil society groups have suggested for the adoption of a women's or gender perspective in the transactional justice mechanisms and the peace treaties. This calls for focusing on the experience of women and girls as human beings and not as a member of any particular race or group. The transnational justice mechanism (TJM) have different elements including restorative that make women feel comfortable to freely share their experiences. It would facilitate an environment of hope for women victim-survivors in getting justice, recover from the trauma and live with positivity. Thus, it has been emphatically contended that:

> In this regard, transitional Justice includes restorative and retributive aspects. By restoring, the tendency is making the oppressed person feeling better; healing the pain of victim through apologies and restitution, moving from trauma to positive and hope. In the other hand, it is bearing the retributive aspect by which recognition is taken of what has been done and appropriate punishment applied. In all process we will underline the role of women in each component of transitional justice.[48]

The TJM addresses the causes and consequences of violence against women. As a result, considerable progress has been seen in the recent decades in promoting public acknowledgement of gender inequality, discrimination, and gender-based violence. In most of the conflict-ridden societies, there is a lack of appropriate mechanism for such public acknowledgement for the women victim-survivors. It has been found that there is insufficient technical knowledge in adopting the measures for encouraging women's participation in the peace processes and crafting of the peace agreements. It may complicate and exacerbate the challenge of SGBV and would lead to situations wherein:

> In periods of conflict or authoritarianism, women often become targets of human rights violations because of their gender and the marginalization they suffer in many societies. They may suffer physical and sexual violence — as well as other violations that affect them in unique ways, such as enforced disappearance of their loved ones, displacement, or socioeconomic discrimination. Transitional justice responses to gender-based violations during conflict and

---

[47] Sanam, N. A. et al., "Transnational Justice and Reconciliations"; available at: https://tavaana.org/sites/default/files/49_transitional_justice.pdf (accessed on 11 September 2021).

[48] Liberata Gahongayire (2016), "Essay on the role of women in transitional justice in post conflict societies"; *International Journal of Innovation and Applied Studies*, 16 (2): 304–308; available at: http://www.cnlg.gov.rw/fileadmin/templates/Publications/IJIAS-16-058-05__1_.pdf (accessed on 11 September 2021).

> authoritarian rule are essential for ensuring justice for victims, combating women's marginalization, and preventing future violations against women and other communities targeted for their gender....[49]

Hence, the direct participation of women in post-conflict peace processes needs to be encouraged and duly facilitated.[50] As a logical corollary, any peacebuilding process would be successful when there is direct engagement of women in reparation, resettlement, rehabilitation, reintegration, and post-conflict reconstruction process.[51] The absence of meaningful security for women affects the interest and participation of the women in the accountability processes and justice delivery mechanisms during peace, conflicts and post-conflict situations.[52]

In a refreshing change, in some cases, the women are coming into the public sphere in the making of the justice delivery mechanisms. In 2014, women survivors of the thirty-six-years-long internal armed conflicts in Guatemala and Colombia started sharing their stories and experiences. They demanded for the transnational justice in a workshop that was organized by the women' human rights organizations. The organizers felt that the victims could get recognition through the justice delivery mechanism. It could, in turn, promote peace, reconciliation, accountability, and democratic stability in the society. In the interactive sessions, women sought justice for the violence they faced during the prolonged armed conflicts. The sharing of experiences by the women leaders led to exchange of ideas regarding best practices and commitments to share their victimhood.[53]

There are some cases wherein women as peace-builders have strengthened the TJM and encouraged participation of the victims-survivors. For example, in Rwanda, women took responsibilities to grapple with the difficulties including SGBV they faced after the conflict including in the restructuring of the government as well as promotion of women and children's rights and participation of women in the economic development. In turn, the women participants assisted the genocide survivors, offered counselling to the victims and widows to overcome the trauma,

---

49 ICTJ, "Gender Justice"; available at: https://www.ictj.org/our-work/transitional-justice-issues/gender-justice (accessed on 11 September 2021).

50 Security Council states, "...the Council called on all actors involved in peace negotiations, peacekeeping and peace-building to adopt a gender perspective that included the special needs of women and girls during repatriation and resettlement, rehabilitation, reintegration and post-conflict reconstruction;" see, SC (2003), "Women Suffer Disproportionately During And After War, Security Council Told During Day-Long Debate on Women, Peace and Security: Briefed by Peacekeeping Under-Secretary-General, Senior Gender Adviser for UN Mission in Democratic Republic of Congo", 4852nd Meeting, Press Released, SC/7908, 29 October 2003 available at: https://www.un.org/press/en/2003/sc7908.doc.htm (accessed on11 September 2021).

51 FionnualaNíAoláin (2009), "Women, Security, and the Patriarchy of Internationalized Transitional Justice," *Human Rights Quarterly*, 31(4): 1055–1085.

52 Chapman, Jane Roberts (1990), n.2.

53 Guatemala Human Rights Commission (2015), workshop on "The Role of Women in Transnational Justice Processes in Guatemala and Colombia" organized by the GHRC and MARDE, February 2015, available at: https://www.ghrc-usa.org/our-work/themes/truth-justice-and-historic-memory/the-role-of-women-in-transitional-justice-processes-in-guatemala-and-colombia/ (accessed on 11 September 2021).

negotiated and lobbied on behalf of the victims' rights and enabled women to share their experiences regarding sexual violence during conflicts.[54] As a result, women victims and witnesses got the courage to share their experiences before the International Criminal Tribunal for Rwanda.[55]

Similarly, in Nepal, many of the women assisted the victims-survivors in getting compensation from the government for the destruction of their property; violence against people during the period of the decade-long Maoist insurgency.[56] They came to the aid of the victims' families in lodging complaints about the missing members as well as gave training to the survivors, civil society, journalists and the representative of the local administration bodies in understanding the relief process, getting compensation, and so on.[57] Since women suffer disproportionately during most of the conflicts, their role and participation is a prerequisite for fairness of the post-conflict justice mechanisms. In view of many simmering conflicts still raging around the world, it remains a big challenge to work out the legal structures and processes for the direct participation of the women and girls in the peacebuilding processes, peace agreements and justice delivery mechanisms.

(ii) Economic Implications

SGBV against women is a scourge and an extreme form of human rights violation. It causes a huge economic loss for the women, families, communities, and the States. At the 57th session (2013) of the Commission on the Status of Women, it

[54] Rirhandu Mageza-Barthel (2011), "Asserting Their Presence! Women's Quest for Transitional Justice in Post-Genocide Rwanda", in Susanne Buckley-Zistel (ed.), *Gender in Transitional Justice,* UK: Palgrave Macmillan.

[55] Mirjam van Reisen and Daniel R Mekonnen (2013), "Exploring New Spaces for Women in Transitional Justice in Eritrea and Zimbabwe", Tilburg University; available at: https://www.researchgate.net/publication/254777011_Exploring_new_spaces_for_women_in_transitional_justice_in_Eritrea_and_Zimbabwe (accessed on 11 September 2021); also see, UN Women, "Strengthening Women's Access to Justice;" available at: http://www.unwomen.org/en/news/in-focus/strengthening-womens-access-to-justice (accessed on 11 September 2021).

[56] UN Women (2011), "Women as Peace builders: Strengthening women's leadership in post-conflict Nepal," 10 January 2011; available at: https://asiapacific.unwomen.org/en/news-and-events/stories/2011/1/women-as-peacebuilders-strengthening-womens-leadership-in-post-conflict-nepal (accessed on 11 September 2021).

[57] Ibid; see also, in 2013, Sama Shrestha, UN Women Nepal at the launch of the ICTJ's Report on "Addressing the Rights and Needs of Nepal's Wives of the Disappeared", remarked, "Sabitri conducted her own training programme for survivors, representatives of local administration bodies, civil society and journalists. When asked what about the training inspired her to come out of her shell, Sabitri said, I learnt for the first time that there are mechanisms that center around victims and now with information on these processes I know what I should let other victims know;" see, UN Women (2013), "Remarks by Sama Shrestha, UN Women Nepal at the launch of the ICTJ's Report on Addressing the Rights and Needs of Nepal's Wives of the Disappeared;" available at: http://asiapacific.unwomen.org/en/news-and-events/stories/2013/8/remarks-by-sama-shrestha-un-women-nepal-ictj (accessed on 11 September 2021).

was accepted that "violence against women results in social and economic harm." In a shocking revelation, it was shown that "the cost of violence could amount to approximately two per cent of the global gross domestic product (GDP), i.e. equivalent to 1.5 trillion".[58] This is the cost paid by the societies and the States through spending money for the health system, counselling, welfare support, justice system, and other related services. Moreover, the States pay the indirect cost for the loss of wages, employment, productivity etc. On the other hand, SGBV against women has a negative impact on women's participation in education, employment, and social life. It also undermines the goals of poverty reduction and other sustainable development goals (SDGs 2030). Thus, it requires a sizeable amount of money and resources for the social service, justice mechanism system, health care services, peacebuilding, and resettlement processes.[59]

In a futuristic way, SGBV remains the biggest barrier in achieving the agenda of the SDG 2030. It presents a challenge in the achievement of gender equality and the empowerment of women and girls.[60] It will also require huge cost to provide essential services for the survivors of SGBV, e.g. access to medical care, psychological support, economic reintegration, income generating activities, vocational and literacy training, legal assistance to fight against impunity for the perpetrators, awareness campaign, etc. Cumulatively, the economic cost of SGBV needs to be realized, accepted and factored into the post-conflict societies so as to enable the victims-survivors to live with peace, justice and dignity.[61]

(iii) Delegitimization of SGBV

As already discussed, in spite of existence of the corpus of international instruments and international institutions in the field, the sheer spread and magnitude of SGBV presents a grim scenario. Women still constitute a 'soft belly' of international humanitarian law. They have remained the main targets during peace, conflicts and post-conflict situations. SGBV, especially sexual violence, is still being used as an important 'tactic' and a 'weapon of war' with use of women bodies as a 'turf' in most

---

[58] UN Women (2016), "The Economic Costs of Violence against Women;" available at: http://www.unwomen.org/en/news/stories/2016/9/speech-by-lakshmi-puri-on-economic-costs-of-violence-against-women (accessed on 11 September 2021).

[59] Ibid.

[60] Ibid., the UN Assistant Secretary-General and Duty Executive Director of the UN Women, Lakshmi Puri, at the high-level discussion on the "Economic Cost of the Violence against Women it is stated UN Women on 21 September 2016, remarked, "The Economic Costs of Violence against Women," states, "Research indicates that the cost of violence against women could amount to around 2 per cent of the global gross domestic product (GDP). This is equivalent to 1.5 trillion, approximately, the size of the economy of Canada."

[61] US AID (2017), "Sexual and Gender-Based Violence Fact Sheet;" available at: https://www.usaid.gov/democratic-republic-congo/fact-sheets/usaiddrc-fact-sheet-sexual-and-gender-based-violence (accessed on 11 September 2021).

of the conflicts even though it remains unacknowledged and unaddressed by all the warring factions. Its effect is not only destructive but also remains perpetual. SGBV against women occurs because of its multidimensional effects surrounded by walls of shame and fears of honour. Woman's body virtually becomes a battlefield since it is a soft and low-cost target yet leaves lasting wounds as it hurts the most to the targeted communities. It is resorted to, especially rape under orders, by both the winning and vanquished sides. Ironically, it is the survivors of the SGBV that become virtual 'cannon fodder' to satiate inflated egos of the warring factions. They end up being socially stigmatized and forced to be suffer the shame as they are deemed to have lost their chastity for no fault of theirs. The challenge emanating from this heinous practice in conflict zones around the world has been duly underscored in the wake-up call of the 2018 Nobel Peace Prize (to Nadia Murad and Denis Mukewege). In invoking SGBV—especially 'rape'—as a 'tactic' or a 'weapon' of war by the warring factions, they seek to legitimize violence and justify it as insignificant 'collateral damage'.

The persistence, worldwide spread, sheer lethality and the cost of SGBV raise larger issues of not only containment and elimination but also as regards means and methods to blunt its edges so as to render it an ineffective weapon of warfare. This is especially so since patriarchal norms have regarded women as the weakest member of a group and their bodies considered as valuable assets that need to be protected. This provides the value, trigger and lethal edge to the use of SGBV as a weapon during peace and conflicts. Hence, it leads us to posit a vital question: Can we delegitimize SGBV or defang it? How best to reduce the lethal effect of SGBV on the women victims-survivors? What structures, processes and changes in the mindsets would be warranted to deter the perpetrators of SGBV?

The quest and effectiveness of such *de-legitimization* will need to comprise a concerted process and require concrete steps by all the stakeholders in peace, conflict and post-conflict situations. The primary aim would need to be to avert women being targeted through revenge or gender-based collective punishments. This can be carried by both victorious and vanquished sides in armed conflicts. Thus, in order to de-fang the lethality arising from the revengeful actions , it calls for a strong and effective set of international instruments; effective protective umbrella for women survivors in the conflict zones. The process and content of concerted plan of action for de-stigmatization of SGBV would require, among others, its treatment as a separate and independent heinous crime (instead of being part of genocide, war crime and crime against humanity as in the Rome Statute); end of impunity and the social boycott of the perpetrators.[62] Thus an important remedy will lie in stigmatizing the perpetrators instead of the survivors as well as drawing the 'red lines' instead of spreading the red carpets for the perpetrators. In view of the limits of time, space and focus of the present study, the idea of 'delegitimization of SGBV' is expected to be mapped, analysed and ideated in detail separately—in a sequel study.

---

[62] In 2018, Denis Mukwege stated in his Nobel lecture, "States must stop welcoming them by rolling out the red carpet, and instead draw a red line against the use of rape as a weapon of war. This red line would consist of imposing economic and political sanctions on these leaders and taking them to court;" see, Denis Mukwege-Nobel lecture (2018); available at: https://www.nobelprize.org/prizes/peace/2018/mukwege/55721-denis-mukwege-nobel-lecture-2/ (accessed on 16 September 2021).

Conclusion

The above listed cumulative legal challenges remain the main obstacles for the establishment of international peace, security, and peacebuilding processes. There are many other challenges that national, regional, and international institutions are facing to provide justice to the victims-survivors. As sunlight remains the best disinfectant, it is equally important that all concerned including women victims-survivors in the conflict-ridden societies speak up loudly and boldly about SGBV by jettisoning the stigma, fear and shame. SGBV against women now needs to be considered as a heinous crime that globally afflicts the womenkind and treated as a *common concern of humankind* for crafting of a *lex specialis* international legal instrument. The challenge of SGBV needs to be duly addressed by the scholars of international law as well as international institutions working in the fields of international human rights, international humanitarian works and international criminal justice system. The system of international law needs to rise to the occasion so as to provide an effective and timely response for the elimination of SGBV especially against women. Through this work, an earnest effort has been made to sow some ideational seeds in the scholarly realm as a modest contribution to bring about the beginning of the end of global scourge of SGBV against women in the coming decades. Its process, content, pathway and outcome lies in the womb of the future. Only time will provide the answer.

Chapter 7
Conclusions

In the recent decades, sexual and gender-based violence (SGBV) has emerged as a serious cause of global common concern for all. SGBV can be considered as one of the most pervasive international human rights violations in the world. In 2021, the report of the United Nations (UN) *Special Rapporteur on violence against women* has considered SGBV as a grave, systematic and widespread human rights violation.[1] Ironically, the UN data in February 2022 also showed that: (i) "1 in 3 women and girls (736 million) experience physical and sexual violence in their lifetime", (ii) "71% of all human trafficking victims worldwide are women and girls, and 3 out of 4 of these women and girls are sexually exploited" and (iii) "globally 81,000 women and girls were killed in 2020, around 47,000 of them (58 per cent) died at the hands of an intimate partner or a family member".[2]

Historically, studies show that use of sexual violence as a weapon or tactic in conflict zones is as old as the history of warfare. However, there have been walls

[1] UN (2021), "Rape as a grave, systematic and widespread human rights violation, a crime and a manifestation of gender-based violence against women and girls, and its prevention Report of the Special Rapporteur on violence against women, its causes and consequences, Dubravka Šimonović", UN Doc. A/HRC/47/26, 19 April 2021; available at: https://undocs.org/A/HRC/47/26 (accessed on 26 September 2021); UN (2021), "A framework for legislation on rape (model rape law) Report of the Special Rapporteur on violence against women, its causes and consequences," UN Doc. A/HRC/47/26/Add.1, 15 June 2021; available at: https://undocs.org/A/HRC/47/26/Add.1 (accessed on 26 September 2021).

[2] UN Women (2022), "Facts and figures: Ending violence against women"; available at: https://www.unwomen.org/en/what-we-do/ending-violence-against-women/facts-and-figures#notes (accessed on 18 April 2022); UN (2020), "International Day for the Elimination of Violence against Women"; available at: https://www.un.org/en/events/endviolenceday/index.shtml (accessed on 17 April 2022).

The original version of this chapter was revised: The incorrect texts have been updated. The correction to this chapter is available at https://doi.org/10.1007/978-981-19-0894-1_8

B. H. Desai and M. Mandal, *Sexual and Gender-Based Violence in International Law*,
https://doi.org/10.1007/978-981-19-0894-1_7

of silence as regards acknowledgement of the existence of SGBV.[3] There are many other roadblocks that international institutions, States, civil society organizations, scholars, and people, in general, are constantly facing. Hence, elimination of SGBV against women requires a "community-based, multipronged approach, and sustained engagement with multiple stakeholders".[4]

SGBV has now assumed an institutionalized form of violence against women (VAW). The 2018 Nobel Peace Prize graphically showed that rape, as a form of SGBV, has been used worldwide over the years as a 'weapon of war'. The warring factions take recourse to rape as the cheapest weapon that has deadly and long-term consequences for the populace wherein warring factions tear up societies with lethal effect. The available data for the 2020-2022 COVID-19 pandemic shows that SGBV, especially domestic violence, has only intensified. In this context the UN Women has been used the term 'shadow pandemic' to address the seriousness of the issues. It has called upon UNiTE to come together to end SGBV. In the same vein, a 2019 World Bank brief has chillingly reminded about the gender-based violence against women and girls has become a "global pandemic".[5]

Similarly, an account provided by the UN High Commissioner for Human Rights admits that it has become "more dangerous to be a woman than a soldier in armed conflict".[6] It has assumed a grim reality with greater recourse to mass rapes in most of the global armed conflicts. Some come to the light, others do not even get acknowledged. Hence, accountability rarely becomes a subject of discussion in the post-conflict justice delivery mechanisms. As argued by Rashida Manjoo and Calleigh McRaith, the warring factions justify it as an insignificant and 'collateral damage'.[7]

In view of this, SGBV presents a daunting global ideational challenge for the scholars. Since the women's bodies become the battleground in the theatres of

---

[3] Chapman, Jane Roberts (1990), "Violence against Women as a Violation of Human Rights", *Social Justice, Criminality, Imprisonment and Women's Rights in the 1990s,* 17 (2):40; see also, Heineman, Elizabeth D (2011), *Sexual Violence in Conflict Zones:* From the Ancient World to the Era of Human Rights, USA: University of Pennsylvania Press.

[4] The World Bank (2008), "Gender-based violence: violence against women and girls;" available at: https://www.worldbank.org/en/topic/socialdevelopment/brief/violence-against-women-and-girls (accessed on 11 September 2021). See also, The World Bank (2019), "Gender-based violence: violence against women and girls, September 25, 2019;" available at: https://www.worldbank.org/en/topic/socialsustainability/brief/violence-against-women-and-girls (accessed on 25 September 2021).

[5] UN Women, "The Shadow Pandemic;" available at: https://www.un.org/en/observances/ending-violence-against-women-day (accessed on 26 September 2021); see, World Bank (2019), "Gender-Based Violence (Violence Against Women and Girls)"; available at: https://www.worldbank.org/en/topic/socialsustainability/brief/violence-against-women-and-girls?cid=EXT_WBSocialShare_EXT (accessed on 25 September 2021).

[6] UNOCHR, *Rape:* "Weapon of War;" available at: https://www.ohchr.org/en/newsevents/pages/rapeweaponwar.aspx. (accessed on 25 September 2021). Also UN(2008), Security Council resolution 1820 of 19 June 2008; available at: https://www.un.org/ruleoflaw/files/women_peace_security_resolution1820.pdf (accessed on 25 September 2021).

[7] Manjoo and McRaith (2011), "Gender-Based Violence and Justice in Conflict and Post-Conflict Areas," *Cornell International Law Journal*, 44: 11–31.

warfare,[8] it is the honour of the women's bodies that need to be respected through a concerted process. Any harm to the women's body is considered as harm to the families and the community. This provides lethal sharpness to rape as a tactical weapon since it hits where it hurts the most. By hurting the said honour, as contended by Judith Gardam and Hilary Charlesworth, the perpetrators seek to leave lasting wounds through the use of sexual violence as a weapon of war.[9] In post-conflict societies, this results in a grim situation wherein the defeated communities mostly shun women subjected to sexual violence and the children born out of mass rapes.[10]

We have numerous examples such as the use of mass rape during the 1971 Bangladesh liberation war perpetrated by the retreating Pakistani forces even while preparing for surrender to the Indian army. Mass rapes were resorted to, ostensibly under orders, to inflict lasting wounds (estimated between 200, 000 to 400, 000) on the Bangladeshi women.[11] The anguish on use of SGBV against women in conflicts came to be vividly reflected in the citation of the 2018 Nobel Peace Prize awarded to Nadia Murad and Denis Mukwege "for their efforts to end the use of sexual violence as a weapon of war and armed conflict".[12] It underscores the graphic reality of the nature of the grave crisis that confronts the world today. There is an enormous cost of SGBV. During 2021, in European Union alone, the yearly cost of GBV and VAW was estimated to be Euro 366 billion and Euro 289 billion, respectively.

SGBV is also rooted in cultural factors. These comprise challenges that include female genital mutilation (FGM). It is sought to be justified as being 'essential' practices. In view of this, there is a growing global concern for the elimination of FGM. In 2022 alone, it is estimated, some 4.2 million women are at risk of undergoing FGM. As a 2020 landmark study shows, many of such harmful cultural practices (HCPs) present biggest international human rights law challenges in the elimination of FGM.[13]

---

[8] UN, "Armed Conflict and Women—10 Years of Security Council Resolution 1325", by Rachel Mayanja, Special Adviser to the United Nations Secretary-General on Gender Issues and Advancement of Women in *UN Chronicle*; available at: https://www.un.org/en/chronicle/article/armed-conflict-and-women-10-years-security-council-resolution-1325 (accessed on 25 September 2021).

[9] Gardam, Judith and H. Charlesworth (2000), "Protection of Women in Armed Conflict," *Human Rights Quarterly*, 22 (1): 148–166.

[10] Rehn, Elisabeth and Sirleaf, Ellen Johnson (2002), "Women, War and Peace: The Independent Experts' Assessment on the Impact of Armed Conflict on Women and Women's Role in Peace-building", United Nations Development Fund for Women, New York; available at: https://www.unfpa.org/sites/default/files/pub-pdf/3F71081FF391653DC1256C69003170E9-unicef-WomenWarPeace.pdf (accessed on 25 September 2021).

[11] BB (2016), "Bangladesh war crimes trial: Key accused", BBC News, 4 September 2016; available at: https://www.bbc.com/news/world-asia-20970123 (accessed on 25 September 2021).

[12] Nobel Foundation (2018), "The Nobel Peace Prize 2018"; available at: https://www.nobelprize.org/prizes/peace/2018/summary/ (accessed on 25 September 2021).

[13] European Institute for Gender Equality, "Gender-based violence costs the EU €366 billion a year", 7 July 2021; available at: https://eige.europa.eu/news/gender-based-violence-costs-eu-eu366-billionyear#:~:text=The%20European%20Institute%20for%20Gender,do%20not%20have%20a%20price (accessed on 18 April 2022). See also, UN Women (2022), n. 2. See, UN, "Ending Female

Making International Law & Institutions Work

It has been seen that both legal and non-legal challenges are interconnected. They do differ according to the facts and circumstances in conflict-ridden societies such as: forced marriages with the perpetrators in post-conflict societies[14]; cases of SGBV go unreported because of social pressure or social stigmatization both during peace and conflicts[15]; abandonment of the victims[16]; losing economic, social, and cultural rights by the victims[17] and lack of data collection.[18] Cumulatively, these challenges present obstacles for the justice delivery mechanisms and the welfare of the victims. Apart from it, attitudes and actual conduct of the States also play crucial role and can create obstacles such as reservations to the human rights treaties; non-ratification of the optional protocols; implementation gaps, funding and in some cases even withdrawal of membership from the human rights bodies.[19]

There are limits to the function of law in a society as it faces obstacles such as lack of legal awareness, low probability of apprehension, inconsistency between legislative prohibitions, and cultural practices. In fact, law alone cannot change the mindset of the people to bring about a desired change in pernicious practices such as child marriages in Bangladesh, sex-selective operations in China, and dowry related deaths of women in India.[20] The existing non-legal problems could attain a form wherein they become legal problems. Similarly, the core legal problems or failure of the legal systems lead to emergence of some gaps within the legislation, a slow

---

Genital Mutilation by 2030"; available at: https://www.un.org/en/observances/female-genital-mutilation-day (accessed on 18 April 2022). Desai Bharat H and Mandal, Moumita (2020), "On the Elimination of Female Genital Mutilation: Making International Human Rights Law Work", *Indian Journal of International Law,* 60:195–229.

[14] UN (2015), "Fight against Sexual Violence in Conflict Reaches 'New Juncture," Security Council told, 7428th Meeting of SC, UN Doc. SC/11862, 15 April 2015 available at: https://www.un.org/press/en/2015/sc11862.doc.htm (accessed on 25 September 2021).

[15] India Today, (2016), "Pakistani Women Protest Outside the UNHRC Against," *India Today*, 22 September 2016; available at: https://indiatoday.intoday.in/story/pakistani-women-protest-outside-the-unhrc-against/1/770412.html(accessed on 11 September 2021).

[16] Lindsey, Charlotte (2001), ICRC, "Study on the impact of armed conflict on women;" available at: https://www.icrc.org/eng/assets/files/other/icrc_002_0798_women_facing_war.pdf (accessed on 11 September 2021).

[17] UN (2002), "Women, Peace and Security;" available at: https://www.un.org/ruleoflaw/files/womenpeaceandsecurity.pdf (accessed on 11 September 2021).

[18] UN (2005), "Expert Group Meeting (11–14 April 2005)," Organized by the UN Division for the Advancement of Women in Collaboration with the Economic Commission for Europe (ECE) and World Health Organization (WHO), on "Violence against women: a statistical overview, challenges and gaps in data collection and methodology and approaches for overcoming them;" available at: https://www.un.org/womenwatch/daw/egm/vaw-stat-2005/docs/final-report-vaw-stats.pdf (accessed on 11 September 2021).

[19] BBC (2018), "US quits 'biased' UN human rights council", US & Canada, *BBC News*, 20 June 2018; available at: https://www.bbc.com/news/44537372 (accessed on 25 September 2021).

[20] Klugman, Jeni (2017), "Background paper for World Development Report 2017 Gender based violence and the law;" available at: https://pubdocs.worldbank.org/en/232551485539744935/WDR17-BP-Gender-based-violence-and-the-law.pdf (accessed on 25 September 2021).

justice mechanism system, etc. that are unable to provide a proper remedy to the victims. As a result, there is exacerbation[21] of SGBV against women and girls. In this way, legal and non-legal challenges are interconnected. The study, through the in-depth study in the previous six chapters, has made an earnest effort to examine the nature and content of the challenge of SGBV as well as explore possible solutions.

At this crucial juncture, international law as a global regulatory instrumentality needs to provide an effective protective shield to all the people who face the risk of SGBV. The usage of terms such as 'sexual violence,' 'gender-based violence,' 'SGBV' have not remained gender-specific. They are now gender-neutral since the victims-survivors may be from any group of gender. As women form an overwhelming majority of the victim-survivors, this study has focused on the challenge of SGBV against women. This study has used all the terminologies synonymously to address all forms of SGBV against women. The women subjected to SGBV need to be brought under the protective umbrella of international law since it has now emerged as one of the major global *common concerns of humankind.*

The global challenge of SGBV, as a scourge faced by women, also poses a serious threat to international peace and security. If the problem persists as the current trends indicate, it will imperil the peace, harmony, tranquillity, and progress of human civilization as it can be seen in many of the armed conflicts raging across the world. It worrisome that warring groups (government troops; insurgents and belligerents such as LTTE and Maoist rebels and even terror outfits such as Taliban and Boko Haram) have freely invoked mass rapes in conflict zones as the cheapest and easily available weapon of war with lethal consequences on the targeted groups of women and girls. In some instances, even the UN peacekeepers have also been cloud for being involved in SGBV in the areas entrusted to them under the UNSC mandate. It shows protectors can also become predators. The occurrence of SGBV against women even in the UNSC mandated peacekeeping operations is a cause of great concern since they happen notwithstanding the foundational principles of protection of women and girls in the UNSC 'women, peace and security' (WPS) resolution 1325 (2000). It has been further emphasized in UNSC resolutions 1820 (2008), 1888 (2009), 1960 (2010), 2106 (2013), 2467 (2019) and 2493 (2019). Therefore, the challenge calls for a wide range of concerted international legal and instittutional measures to stem the tide of SGBV as a heinous crime. It needs to be squarely eliminated as its effect is not only destructive but also traumatic and perpetual.

As already discussed in previous chapters, women and girls are subjected to SGBV during peace, conflicts and post-conflict situations. It has been observed that the causes remain the same in all such cases; only some situation-specific factors surface during the conflicts. Similarly, it has been widely seen that some cultural practices condone SGBV though these practices are inherently harmful, cause irreparable

[21] Desai, Bharat H and Mandal, Moumita (2021), "Role of Climate Change in Exacerbation of Sexual and Gender-Based Violence: A New Challenge for International Law", *Environmental Policy and Law*, vo.51, no.3, 137–157; available at: https://www.un.org/sexualviolenceinconfl ict/wp-content/uploads/2021/10/report/role-of-climate-change-in-exacerbatingsexual-and-gender-based-violence-against-women-a-new-challenge-for-international-law/epl_2021_51-3_epl-51-3-epl210055_epl-51-epl210055.pdf; (accessed on 29 March 2022).

violation of the human rights of women. Through institutionalized 'harmful cultural practices,' (HCPs) the perpetrators invoke culture, tradition and religion as a shield to protect themselves. Hence, it raises crucial questions as regards usage of 'culture' as an identity of any particular family, group, and nation. Can culture justify or encourage harmful practices that provide a basis for SGBV against women? Such HCPs are inherently a violation of the human rights of women, especially the right to health, bodily integrity, and fundamental freedoms. Thus, HCPs constitute a global common concern as they do not remain specific to a particular region, religion or group. They need to be addressed through *lex specialise* internatioal legal instruments and concrete actions of the relevant international institutions such as UN Women, WHO and UNICEF as well as treaty-based mechanisms such as committees of the 1979 CEDAW (UNGA resolution 34/180 of 18 December 1979) and 1989 CRC (UNGA resolution 44/25 of 20 November 1989).

Women are often treated as a separate group of gender or sex because of their biological difference and cultural or social identity. To nip such gender-driven discrimination and violence, it has become a paramount need for women and girls to be considered as full individual human beings. The prism of a separate gender or sex pushes women and girls into an inferior position. It leads to deleterious consequences of dependency, weakness, lack of decision-making power and non-participation. It shows that power imbalance exists between two groups of human beings who are also carrying on two different identities wherein women and girls perennially remain on the margins. It has been seen that the patriarchal culture seeks to control women at different stages of their lives. They use the social and cultural identity of women as a tool or tactic to suppress them. It is this that forms a basis as well as serves as a means and method of institutionalized violence against women and girls. It is this deeply embedded stereotype and norms that have to be dismantled through designing of a futuristic international legal instrument to specifically stamp out SGBV against women. As a corollary, international institutions need to rise to the occasion and put into place an integrated and cohesive response mechanisms to bring about concrete changes in attitudes and dignified treatment of women both as a humanbeing and as a female gender.

The naturally endowed inherent strength, sexuality and reproductive capacity has made women the strongest human being. They contribute to nature's system or natural law by bringing in the future generation. It is an unparalleled entrustment and gift of nature that places women as the creator of human civilization almost at par with nature. In this context, the evil of SGBV has no place or justification under any circumstance.

The genesis of the challenge of SGBV arise from the fact that women largely remain unaware of their strength due to their societal nurturing that imposes socially and culturally scripted roles, identity and existence. It forces them to think as a different 'sex' or 'gender' and not primarily as a full human being. In fact, worldwide, the girls since their birth are compelled to follow different societal and cultural norms that are set by the patriarchal systems. It is these patriarchal norms that have circumscribed their roles premised upon women's sexuality and reproductive system.

Apart from it, different strategies have been used to control women and girls through emotive issues such as family honour and reputation as well as even forcible suppression through violence. These strategies cumulatively used by the patriarchy in many of the societies enables them to exercise control over the lives and bodies of women virtually as *chattel* as borne out by horrific cases of growing violence against women and girls. This study has primarily sought to focus on the patriarchal culture that forms the basis and facilitates all kinds of SGBV violence against women. The perpetrators include not only men but also women who become collaborators in discrimination, atrocities and violence against other women. In most of such cases, women are coopted to support the patriarchy and become co-perpetrators of SGBV. It has been observed that women and girls are specifically targeted by the patriarchy during peace, conflicts and post-conflict situations.

Though there is no specific legal definition *per se* of SGBV. Still, SGBV has been described by entities such as the United Nations High Commissioner for Refugees (UNHCR) as including all forms of violence against women (VAW), sexual violence (SV), and gender-based violence (GBV). Though sexual violence is mostly used as a tactic or weapon of war, other forms of violence perpetrated against women and girls may not be sexual *per se*. So, SGBV is more than only sexual or gender-based violence. However, sexual violence gets prioritized because it is mostly used as a weapon of war or tactic against women in all situations.

In view of the above, the study has examined and analysed the causes, consequences, cultural factors, institutions, and the legal issues regarding the simmering challenge of SGBV as one of the global common concerns. Ironically, there is no *lex specialise* international law instrument that deals exclusively with the challenge of SGBV. The relevant legal instruments in the fields of international human rights law (IHRL), international humanitarian law (IHL), international criminal law (ICL) and some of the law-making processes of the UN—especially resolutions of the General Assembly and the Security Council—do not adequately deal with SGBV widely regarded (in the UN system) as a scourge and a heinous crime. In general, the existing international law instruments use the charity-based terms such as 'honour,' 'vulnerable,' 'protection' for the women victims-survivors. For historical reasons including peace processes devoid of women participants as well as role of predominantly male negotiators and drafters, the international legal instruments appear feeble as they lack sensitivity, seriousness and deterrence value in effectively addressing the global menace of SGBV. That reduces the effectiveness of the international instruments since women need to be treated as fully capable human beings capable of possessing and exercising roles and equal rights. It is an inherent right of women not to be subjected to any form of SGBV. Ironically, the right-based approaches (as compared to charity-based) have not yet come up on the global agenda.

In view of the above scenario, there is a need for *lex specialis* international legal (treaty) instrument comprising all aspects of the challenge of SGBV faced by women. It would be possible only with the active participation of both men and women as underscored in many of the resolutions of the General Assembly (see Chapters 3 and 4). Such *lex specialis* international legal instrument will not invoke terms based on pity, mercy, chastity, subject of honor and charity-based approaches. Any such specific international instrument (soft law or a treaty) will need to construe all forms of SGBV as an international crime. It is high time to enlist SGBV as a separate and independent crime under the Rome Statute (beyond Articles 6, 7 and 8). One of the critical challenges for the justice delivery mechanisms pertains to acceptance of only a few forms of SGBV as a *crime* against women. The situation is the same in national as well as international legal systems. In the international legal system, some forms of SGBV that figure in the international criminal law are treated as a crime. Both ICL and IHL prohibit and talk about some forms of SGBV, especially during conflicts. There has to be a realization that SGBV is not inevitable. Hence, it is a crime that should be investigated, prosecuted and punishment need to be meted out to the perpetrators.[22]

As a corollary to the above, there is a need for explicit mechanism in an appropriate legal instruments, including the 1949 Geneva Conventions, to prohibit any recourse to the use of SGBV as a tactic or weapon of warfare. Thus, it needs to be elevated as *jus cogens*—one of the peremptory (fundamental) principles of international law. There is a need for a compulsory and speedy justice mechanism to eliminate the lingering shadow of impunity for the perpetrators. The process and the structure for protection of victims and witnesses, will ensure minimum chances of secondary victimization. It was contended by the 2018 Nobel Peace Prize awardee Nadia Murad that "all the victims deserve a safe haven until justice is done for them".[23] There is also a need for proper compensation and rehabilitation scheme for the victims as well as their dependents, especially children born as a consequence of rapes that mostly take place under orders of the military commanders. The State should not deny its responsibility towards victims of SGBV. Moreover, there needs to be stigmatization of the perpetrators of SGBV rather than the victim-survivors. It requires fundamental changes in the attitudes, mindsets, processes and existing structures to provide protective shield to ensure women are not to be subjected to SGBV as well as triggering of prompt and effective justice delivery if SGBV does take place.

[22] Catherine Boucher, Legal Advisor for the Permanent Mission of Canada to the UN, opening remarks at the panel discussion organized by UN Women (26 October 2017) on "Investigating Conflict Related Sexual and Gender-Based Crimes". Boucher observed: "Over the decades there has been a dramatic shift in the way the world views sexual and gender-based violence. It is not inevitable; it is a crime that must be investigated, prosecuted, and punished"; available at: https://www.unwomen.org/en/news/stories/2017/10/news-event-wps-investigating-conflict-related-sexual-and-gender-based-crimes (accessed on 16 September 2021).

[23] The Hindu (2018), "World must protect victims of wartime sexual violence," *The Hindu*, 11 December 2018; available at: https://www.thehindu.com/news/international/world-must-protect-victims-of-wartime-sexual-violence/article25712392.ece (accessed on 11 September 2021).

Ideating for the Future

The complex web of SGBV comprises many issues, mindsets, structures, contributing factors, and roles of different actors. Hence, this work has sought to examine some international law aspects relating to SGBV with a specific focus on role of the cultural factors in SGBV against women and role of the international institutions in effectively addressing the menace. In view of this, a modest effort has been made to address a host of issues that include the role of international criminal courts and tribunals (ICC&Ts), application of *jus cogens* norms, a detailed discussion of all forms of SGBV and role of the States, participation of women in peace treaties, awareness in ending SGBV, critical analysis of all the harmful cultural practices, and so on. As a corollary, it will be in the fitness of things to crystallize the following specific ideas and suggestions to address the challenge of SGBV squarely in the coming years:

***(i) Need for a Special Convention on SGBV and the Second Optional Protocol to the CEDAW on SGBV*:**

As there is no such specific law *lex specialis* that directly deals with all the forms of SGBV, the existing international human rights law including CEDAW deals with the issue either as discrimination or violation of the human rights of women in general. Only the soft international law is available to deal with the issue (discussed in Chapter 3) of this book. So, there is a need to adopt a separate international convention and the Second Optional Protocol to the CEDAW.

***(ii) Need for a Special Protocol on Sexual and Gender-Based Violence against Women in Armed Conflicts*:** There is a need for the adoption of a special protocol under the 1949 Geneva Conventions to specifically address SGBV. The existing Geneva Conventions and the two Additional Protocols are not adequate enough to deal with all forms of SGBV that women suffer during the armed conflicts. SGBV in general and sexual violence (SV) in particular is a graphic reality of the modern day warfare now needs greater focus because it has been specifically used as a tactic and a weapon of war. There are several forms of gender-based violence (GBV) that are as serious as sexual violence. These includes GBVs such as forced marriage, conversion, sterilization or abortion, abduction, murder etc. The proposed special protocol to the Geneva Conventions would address all the facets of SGBV. It can comprise use of appropriate terminology to denote SGBV as one of the grave crimes against women both as a human and due to their female gender. It can provide the survivor (victim)-centric justice delivery mechanism with zero impunity to the perpetrators, rehabilitation and reconciliation mechanism as well as direct participation of the women in the peace processes.

***(iii) Need for an Umbrella UN Entity to Coordinate and Supervise the System-wide Efforts to address Challenges of SGBV against Women*.** There is a need for an umbrella entity under the UN system that would coordinate with all the relevant international institutions engaged in addressing the challenge of SGBV. Such an entity could provide clear guidelines, processes and pathways for all the IIs. It can comprise the strategy and programmes that IIs will uniformly adopt to grapple with the challenges of SGBV; the exact terminology they will use for their work and the international legal instruments that need to implemented. Such an umbrella UN entity could be created by bringing together all relevant UN programmes so as to provide them a coherent mandate and funding to channelize their work to effectively address the challenge of SGBV.

(iv) Global Fund to cater to Concerted Efforts for Rescue, Relief, Rehabilitation of the Victims of Sexual Violence and Institution Building: It is high time to organize a global funding mechanism to provide required funding for the campaign to end SGBV. The aim and agenda of the funding mechanism need to be survivor (victim)-centric. It will especially concentrate on rescue, relief, rehabilitation, and resettlement of the victims-survivors. It can be accompanied by an oversight mechanism to act as a watchdog for efficient use of funding.

(v) Need for a Special Provision in the Rome Statute as well as Statutes of other ad hoc International Criminal Tribunals for Prosecution and Punishment of SGBV against Women**:** The 1998 Rome Statute and Statutes of the other ICTs necessitate an explicit provision under the the heading of SGBV. SGBV needs to be treated as a separate crime and not as a part of one of the elements of crimes against humanity or war crimes or genocide (Rome Statute; articles 6, 7 and 8). It needs to employ specific terminology that will comprise all forms of SGBV. It is a challenge for international law that needs to be duly addressed in a timely manner.[24]

(vi) Need for the Appointment of a Special Rapporteur[25] on the elimination of female genital mutilation (FGM) as one of the (harmful cultural practices) specific forms of SGBV. The SR can be given a specific mandate through an appropriate resolution of the UN Human Rights Council. This has assumed urgency in view of worrisome consistent trend in 4.2 million women and girls at risk of being subjected to FGM in 2022 alone. The UN General Assembly resolutions have now construed FGM as causing 'irreparable and irreplaceable' harm to the female genitalia and violation of the women's right to bodily integrity. The SR can entrusted with responsibility to put into place a process for the elimination of FGM by the year 2030.

De-legitimization of SGBV

SGBV against women during peace, conflicts and post-conflict situations need to be de-legitimized. It is a process that should be taken as a technique to de-stigmatize and treat women as human beings are subjected to a serious form of bodily harm for non-medical purposes that can be cured with due support mechanism of their families

[24] Desai, Bharat H and Mandal, Moumita (2021), n. 21.

[25] Desai, Bharat H and Mandal, Moumita (2020), "On the Elimination of Female Genital Mutilation: Making International Human Rights Law Work", *Indian Journal of International Law,* 60 (3–4):195–229.

and the community. Women survivors/victims of SGBV need to get all the support in order to quickly heal their grievous mental and bodily wounds. Apart from it, it needs to be ensured that the perpetrators will not get any red carpet treatment or impunity, as well as are ostracized and stigmatized by all. It can be part of a process to bring them to book and hold them responsible. Cumulatively, it can provide some form of a deterrence against use of sexual violence as a weapon against women and girls during peace, conflicts and post-conflict situations to avert women being targeted as a form of revenge or gender-based collective punishment.

The process and mechanism for de-legitimizing SGBV will work to defang and de-stigmatize it or at least reduce its vicious effect on the women victims-survivors. This is especially so in view of ineffectiveness of the existing international law architecture to stamp out the scourge of SGBV.

The authors' further work on the subject would seek to focus on this simmering question to provide a roadmap for the future. It would engage in an in-depth study on three key questions:

(i) **Use of sexual violence as a tool against women in conflict zones**

Both men and women in the family and community carry the indoctrinated view that women's sexuality is a matter of their 'honour'. Thus, any harm to women's sexuality is attributed as trauma and shame for society as it is suffered in silence. Hence, the then UN Deputy Secretary-General, Asha-Rose Migiro underscored the need for "whispering must end; there must be an outcry".[26] It has been regarded as a collective failure not to be able to save women's honour from the enemy. However, instead of providing succour, support, and counselling, the societies mostly end up punishing or abandoning the women victims-survivors. This vindicates the very purpose of the perpetrators to inflict wounds on the society through SV against women since they hit where it hurts the most. As a result, it is the women's bodies that become the cannon fodder and a battle-field in the nefarious game of vengeance. The enemy uses SV as a weapon as they know that the patriarchal attitude itself will ostracize the women victims-survivors. It leads to a bizarre situation wherein instead of finding ways and means to punish the perpetrators, the societies end up punishing the women victims-survivors. This happens due to the fact that the perpetrators of sexual violence know that the concerned community is too rigid, insecure and possessive about women's sexuality. Since societies treat women as their honour, it is by hurting the said honour, the perpetrators resort to SGBV as a deadly weapon to inflict lasting wounds on the targeted population. Thus, the targeted groups of women suffer on all the sides since their female gender becomes literally a curse for them. It is this pernicious malady that needs to be de-mystified so as to be de-fanged, de-stigmatized and de-legitimized.

There have been numerous examples wherein the armed forces have used the weapon of mass rapes against women. The history of the World Wars I

---

[26] UN (2009), "Deputy Secretary-General Statement: The Time to End Violence against Women and Girls Is Now;" UN Doc. DSG/SM/440-WOM/1711, 23 February 2009; available at: https://www.un.org/press/en/2009/dsgsm440.doc.htm (accessed on 25 September 2021).

and II does not explicitly mention the commission of 'rape' or any other forms of sexual violence except recorded practices such as 'comfort' stations set up for the Japanese troops. It still remains a major obstacle in Japan–South Korea relations.[27] The horror stories of widespread sexual violence and mass rapes resorted to in recent conflicts and estimated figures of affected women are self-explanatory: former Yugoslavia (1992–95; 60,000); Rwanda (1994; 100,000–250,000); civil war in Liberia (1989–2003; 40,000); civil war in Sierra Leone (1991–2002; 60,000) and the Democratic Republic of Congo (since 1998; 200,000).[28]

The latest, 29 March 2022 report (S/2022/272) of the UN Secretary-General, Antonio Guterres, on 'conflict-related sexual violence' (CRSV; to be read in conjunction with 12 previous reports) provides stunning cumulative account by enlisting 49 parties comprising both States and non-State actors including UNSC designated terror groups. The report describes these warring parties as "credibly suspected of committing or being responsible for patterns of rape or other forms of sexual violence in situations of armed conflict on the agenda of the Security Council".[29] It provides vivid accounts of enlisted conflict-ridden countries such as Afghanistan, Central African Republic, Colombia, Democratic Republic of the Congo, Iraq, Libya, Mali, Myanmar, Somalia, South Sudan, The Sudan, Syrian Arab Republic and Yemen (and other situations of concern in Ethiopia and Nigeria) where women and girls face systematic CRSV. These sordid accounts show as to how women and girls (and in some cases even men and boys) are especially being subjected to rape, sexual slavery, forced prostitution, forced pregnancy, forced abortion, enforced sterilization, forced marriage, and other forms of sexual violence. Women and girls have also faced a high level of sexual violence in Nepal and Sri Lanka during their respective decade long internal armed conflicts. In 2017, sexual violence committed by Myanmar troops against the Rohingya women and girls has again underscored brutal genocidal intent to destroy the ethnic minority through predominant attacks on bodies of women and girls as soft targets.[30] This came to be confirmed in provisional measures[31] pronounced on 23 January 2020 by the

---

[27] UN (2016), "Voices of survivors must be heard, UN News, 11 March 2016;" available at: https://news.un.org/en/story/2016/03/524192-voices-survivors-must-be-heard-un-chief-says-after-meeting-comfort-women-victim (accessed on 25 September 2021).

[28] UN (2014), "Sexual Violence: a Tool of War;" available at: https://www.un.org/es/preventgenocide/rwanda/assets/pdf/Backgrounder%20Sexual%20Violence%202014.pdf (accessed on 25 September 2021).

[29] UN (2022); "Conflict Related Sexual Violence: Report of the United Nations Secretary-General"; UN Doc. S/2022/287 of 29 March 2022; https://reliefweb.int/report/world/conflict-related-sexual-violence-report-secretary-general-s2022272-enarruzh (accessed on 17 April 2022).

[30] Human Rights Watch (2017), "Sexual Violence against Rohingya Women and Girls in Burma"; available at: https://www.hrw.org/report/2017/11/16/all-my-body-was-pain/sexual-violence-against-rohingya-women-and-girls-burma (accessed on 25 September 2021).

[31] International Court of Justice (2020), *Application of the Convention on the Prevention and Punishment of the Crime of Genocide* (*The Gambia V. Myanmar*); Request for the Indication of Provisional

ICJ in a case brought by Gambia (on behalf of the Organization of Islamic Countries) against Myanmar.

In this unprecedented case, the ICJ ordered that Myanmar shall "take all measures within its power to prevent the commission of all acts…in relation to the members of the Rohingya group in its territory".[32] The ICJ order covered a list of acts "in accordance with its (Myanmar) obligations" listed in Article II of the Convention on the Prevention and Punishment of the Crime of Genocide (1948), such as killing members of the group, causing serious bodily or mental harm, deliberately inflicting on the group conditions of life calculated to bring about its physical destruction in whole or in part and imposing measures intended to prevent births within the group.

These spine-chilling accounts of systematic use of sexual violence show that women's body still are being used as a battleground even in the third decade of the twenty-first century, and that it is linked with their honour and shame. Here women's body and sexuality work as a medium to reflect upon the cultural glory of men, family, and the community. Ironically, these practices provide vivid examples in not treating women even as an individual human beings who are forced to suffer SGBV as a brutal forms of heinous bodily harms. In most cases, women feel shame imposed upon them by the societal norms regarding SGBV against women, as most debilitating. It is a reflection of the peacetime treatment of the woman's body as an agent that symbolizes the emotions and pains of an individual, community, and the State.

The *Prosecutor versus Jean-Paul Akayesu* (ICTR, 1998)[33] became the first case to punish the perpetrators for wartime rape as a crime against humanity. It underscored that SGBV against women was used as a weapon to defeat the opponent group as well as to show that the male members of the community were unable to protect their women. It became a matter of shame for the community, disgrace for the family and a battleground to defeat the entire ethnic group. For instance, in a landmark 2017 judgement in the *Chief Prosecutor versus Md. Moslem Prodhan, and Syed Md. Hussain alias Hossain*, the International Criminal Court (Dhaka, Bangladesh)[34] observed:

Measures, Order of 23 January 2020; available at: https://www.icj-cij.org/public/files/case-related/178/178-20200123-ORD-01-00-EN.pdf (accessed on 25 September 2021).

[32] Desai, Bharat H (2020), "ICJ Order on Rohingya upholds majesty of law", The Tribune, 29 January 2020; available at: https://www.tribuneindia.com/news/comment/icj-order-on-rohingya-upholds-majesty-of-law-32735 (accessed on 25 September 2021).

[33] United Nations, ICTR (2001), *The Prosecutor v. Jean-Paul Akayesu* (ICTR-96–4); Appeal Court Judgement of 01 June 2001; available at: https://unictr.irmct.org/en/cases/ictr-96-4; https://unictr.irmct.org/sites/unictr.org/files/case-documents/ictr-96-4/trial-cjudgements/en/980902.pdf; https://unictr.irmct.org/sites/unictr.org/files/case-documents/ictr-96-4/appeals-chamber-judgements/en/010601.pdf (accessed on 25 September 2021).

[34] International Crimes Tribunal (2016), *Chief Prosecutor versus Md. Moslem Prodhan, and Syed Md. Hussain alias Hossain* (ICT-BD [ICT-1] Case No.01/2016, ICT 19 April 2017; ICT-BD [ICT-1] Case No.01 OF 2016; available at: https://www.ict-bd.org/ict1/Judgment%202016/ICT-BD%201%202017.pdf (accessed on 25 September 2021).

> The research on wartime rape shows that in war time, the soldiers assumed the use of rape as an effective weapon of launching attack not simply against an individual, but against social and gender stigmas aiming for the advancement of societal break-down. When rape is used as weapon instead a bullet, the weapon continues to exert its effect beyond the primary victim and it eventually outrages the civility. In the case in hand, pattern and extent of the attack suggest that using the act of rape upon Hindu women as a weapon the perpetrators intended to break-down their community which signifies their 'special intent'. Sexual violence committed in conjunction with the attack was an integral part of the process of destruction, specifically targeting Hindu women and contributing to the destruction of the Hindu religious group.[35]

Thus, it shows that sexual violence against women in general and wartime rapes in particular often take place 'under orders' as a tool or a tactic to inflict collective forms of punishment on women as 'soft' and least cost target in a particular groups of populations. The rape used against such soft targets hurts targeted communities the most and the perpetrators feel a sense of impunity as they mostly go scot-free. It holds the crux of the menace of SGBV that needs to be first cracked. It will provide a basis to de-fang, de-stigmatize and de-legitimize use of SGBV against women.

(ii) **Is International Humanitarian Law adequate to address the SGBV challenge?**

There are only a few provisions in the existing IHL (the Four Geneva Conventions, 1949 and two Additional Protocols 1977) that deal with women subjected to rape and sexual violence during armed conflicts. These instruments include terms such as 'honour' and 'modesty'. For instance, Article 27 of the Fourth Geneva Convention (1949) provides: "Women shall be protected against any attack on their honour, in particular against rape, enforced prostitution, or any form of indecent assault".[36] It implicitly legitimizes the women's body merely as an object. Most of the provisions are applicable only for the protection of the civilian women. Some scholars have criticized the use of the specific phrase 'honour of women should be protected.' The word women's honour attributes certain characteristics that are sexual in nature (primitive and mediaeval) and gender-specific. It includes terms such as modesty, chastity and virginity. It is this that provides a lethal weapon for the perpetrators to inflict wounds ostensibly on the targeted communities. But it is the women who become 'cannon-fodder' in the nefarious game of egos and vengeance among the warring factions in the conflict zones.

In most of the international legal instruments, the terminology used is for 'protection' rather than 'prohibition' *per se*. Thus, such charity-based approach, instead of rights-based approach, perpetuates and gives a fillip to the prevailing menace of SGBV. In fact, Gardam and Charlesworth, have

---

[35] Ibid, p. 160, para 380–381.

[36] *Geneva Convention Relative to the Protection of Civilian Persons in Time of War of 12 August 1949*; available at: https://www.un.org/en/genocideprevention/documents/atrocity-crimes/Doc.33_GC-IV-EN.pdf (accessed on 25 September 2021).

construed the concept of 'honour' as a gender-biased term.[37] It is this notion that forms the basis for using SGBV against women as soft targets, and a tactical weapon of war in most of the armed conflicts. IHL appears to be too feeble to address and promote the right-based approach, fails to cover all forms of SGBV against women and still does not recognize use of SGBV as a weapon of war. This calls for working on a 'special protocol' to the Geneva Conventions to explicitly proscribe SGBV and holds all concerned accountable.

(iii) How to de-legitimize SGBV as a 'weapon of war'?

The widespread use of sexual violence as a 'weapon of war' proves an unprecedented threat especially to women in the conflict zones. SGBV is cheap, easily available with impunity or without restriction, and proves highly destructive. It works instantly with fatal effects on the targeted populace especially women and girls. The entire notion of SGBV against women in conflict zones as a 'weapon of war' is sought to be covered, as described above, under the rubrics such as 'honour', 'assistance' and 'protection' as well as it appears ineffective in protecting the victims of the SGBV in conflict zones. Hence, it is not surprising that the UNSC resolution 2467 (2019), emphatically decided to:

> Reiterates its demand for the complete cessation with immediate effect by all parties to armed conflict of all acts of sexual violence and its call for these parties to make and implement specific time-bound commitments to combat sexual violence, which should include, inter alia, issuance of clear orders through chains of command and development of codes of conduct prohibiting sexual violence and establishment of related enforcement procedures to ensure accountability for breaching these orders, commitments by individual commanders, investigation of all credible allegations including on the basis of information reported by relevant UN entities and accountability for those responsible, unimpeded access for monitoring and provision of services and humanitarian assistance in areas under their control.[38]

Notwithstanding this, the workability of the UNSC resolution remains limited as it is not an 'enforcement' resolution under Chapter 7, and hence, the warring groups will not take it seriously. This calls for further rigorous ideational work to enunciate effective means and methods of remedial legal architecture to prohibit, de-fang and de-legitimize use of SGBV as a 'weapon of war' against women and girls.

It is truism to state that the patriarchal norms in different societies have construed women as weak human beings and their bodies are treated merely as valuable assets (chattel) and hence they become a 'soft' battlefront laced with impunity for the perpetrators.

Therefore, de-legitimization will need to be a structured process and require concerted steps by all the stakeholders in peace, conflict and post-conflict situations

---

[37] Gardam, Judith and Charlesworth (2000), "Protection of Women in Armed Conflict," *Human Rights Quarterly*, 22 (1): 148–166.

[38] UNSC (2019), "Resolution 2467 (2019)", adopted by the UNSC at its 8514th meeting", on 23 April 2019; UN Doc. S/RES/2467 (2019), 23 April 2019, page 4, paragraph 1; available at: https://undocs.org/en/S/RES/2467(2019) (accessed on 19 September 2021).

to avert women being targeted through revenge or gender-based collective punishments. As a corollary, it will necessitate a strong and effective set up of international instruments; effective protective umbrella for women in the conflict zones; innovative legal and societal approaches to de-stigmatize SV.

As a corollary, the following questions would need to be grappled with: Can SGBV be treated as an abhorrent crime at least equivalent (if not higher) to murder or grievous bodily violence? Can we expand the ambit of Article 6 (Genocide) of the Statute of International Criminal Court (ICC) to explicitly cover sexual violence as is the case with Article 7 (Crimes against Humanity) and Article 8 (War Crimes)? Does the Rome Statute require an amendment by insertion of a separate new article on SGBV? How do we put an end to the impunity for the perpetrators? These simmering questions necessitate effective legal remedies that include stigmatizing the perpetrators *per se* (instead of the survivors) as well as drawing the 'red lines' instead of spreading 'red carpets' for the perpetrators.

In view of the simmering global challenges concerning the use of sexual violence against women especially as a weapon of war in the armed conflicts, we need to work out concerted legal approaches. It calls for imparting full respect to the women victims-survivors as full human beings who also go through horrors of sexual violence due to their female gender. At the minimum, the survivors of SGBV also need to be treated like other survivors who are subjected to grievous bodily harm that explicitly comes within the ambit of 'crimes against humanity' (Article 7(g) of the 1998 ICC Statute) and 'war crimes' [Article 8(b) (xxii) and (e) (vi) of the 1998 ICC Statute].

SGBV could be de-fanged, de-inevitablized and de-stigmatized by providing a healthy environment, succour, and emphatic acceptance by the communities of the targeted women survivors and their dependents. The comprehensive approach in addressing the menace of SGBV as a 'weapon of war' would need to comprise innovative approaches, processes and structures as well as means and methods that lead to its effective de-legitimization so as to blunt the edges of this heinous weapon of war and its eventual complete elimination. There should be naming and shaming as well as drawing of 'red lines' and deterrent punishment for the perpetrators without exceptions. It can be duly enshrined—with women participation—in every peace treaty and every post-conflict justice mechanism.

Inevitability of Elimination of SGBV

It appears that the final salvation for women afflicted by SGBV in peace, conflicts and post-conflict situations, calls for decisive end to all forms of SGBV by comprehensive mechanisms for 3Ds—de-fanging, de-inevitablizing and de-legitimizing—the use of SGBV in all situations indulging as a tactic and a 'weapon of war'. It needs to ensure equal rights to women as individual human beings during peace and conflicts as well as in the working of post-conflict justice mechanisms. It can be given effect to different approaches and international instruments (IIs) including (i) specially designed legally binding protocol on SGBV under the 1949 Geneva

Conventions (ii) insertion of a separate crime of SGBV under the Rome Statute and (iii) designing of a *lex specialis* international legal instrument (comprising, among others, a comprehensive definition of SGBV; causes and consequences; patterns and practices of SGBV; prohibitory clauses on use of rape and SV as tactics or weapons of war; exemplary punishments for reprisals, collective punishments, sexual slavery, forcible impregnation and nudity etc.; harmful cultural practices; elements of crimes, accountability mechanisms and referrals to the ICC and special criminal tribunals for accountability of perpetrators of SGBV including government officials, non-state actors and terror outfits. It presents a big scholarly challenge to work out the contours and contents of such *3Ds* and the *3IIs*, as suggested and elaborated above. Moreover, the entire UN system, through concerted processes led by the political organs of the UNGA or the UNSC, need to work in unison to give effect to the ultimate goal of 'de-legitimization' of SGBV so as to eventually eliminate this scourge in the coming decades of the twenty-first century. It presents an ideational challenge for international law scholars to work out the process, content, structure, and desired objectives of such *3Ds* and *3IIs* that could cumulatively provide concrete mechanisms that go beyond the rituals of annuals reports, resolutions and debates under the WPS theme in the UNSC. If the time, circumstances, energy requirements and the working environment permit, the author would surely seek to modestly contribute in working out the suggested *3Ds* and *3IIs* in this cutting-edge scholarly challenge of SGBV, as a sequel to this work. The elimination of the scourge of SGBV against women is inevitable. Still, even as this work makes an honest human effort to sow some seeds in the scholarly realm, the time needs to ordain it.

Correction to: Conclusions

Correction to:
Chapter 7 in: B. H. Desai and M. Mandal, *Sexual and Gender-Based Violence in International Law*, https://doi.org/10.1007/978-981-19-0894-1_7

The original version of the book was inadvertently published with incorrect information in Chapter 7, which have now been corrected and updated as follows:

> "SGBV could be de-fanged, de-ostracized and de-stigmatized by providing a" has been changed to "SGBV could be de-fanged, de-inevitablized and de-stigmatized by providing a".
>
> "comprehensive mechanisms for 3Ds—de-fanging, de-ostracizing and de-legitimizing—the" has been changed to "comprehensive mechanisms for 3Ds—de-fanging, de-inevitablizing and de-legitimizing—the".
>
> "of a lex specialis of na international legal isntrument (comprising, among others, a" has been changed to "of a *lex specialis* international legal instrument (comprising, among others, a".

The book and the chapter have been updated with the changes.

The updated version of this chapter can be found at
https://doi.org/10.1007/978-981-19-0894-1_7

B. H. Desai and M. Mandal, *Sexual and Gender-Based Violence in International Law*,
https://doi.org/10.1007/978-981-19-0894-1_8

MIX
Papier aus verantwortungsvollen Quellen
Paper from responsible sources
FSC® C105338
www.fsc.org

If you have any concerns about our products,
you can contact us on
ProductSafety@springernature.com

In case Publisher is established outside the EU,
the EU authorized representative is:
Springer Nature Customer Service Center GmbH
Europaplatz 3, 69115 Heidelberg, Germany

Printed by Libri Plureos GmbH
in Hamburg, Germany